Toussaint Louverture

Also by Philippe Girard

Clinton in Haiti: The 1994 US Invasion of Haiti

Haiti: The Tumultuous History, from Pearl of the Caribbean to Broken Nation

The Slaves Who Defeated Napoléon: Toussaint Louverture and the Haitian War of Independence, 1801–1804

Editor, *The Memoir of Toussaint Louverture*

TOUSSAINT

A REVOLUTIONARY LIFE

LOUVERTURE

Philippe Girard

BASIC BOOKS
New York

Frontispiece: Toussaint Louverture as a French general. The engraving was possibly modeled after a contemporary portrait. Reprinted from François Séraphin Delpech, *Iconographie des contemporains depuis 1789 jusqu'à 1829*, vol. 2 (Paris: Delpech, 1832).

Designed by Amy Quinn

Library of Congress Cataloging-in-Publication Data

Names: Girard, Philippe R., author.
Title: Toussaint Louverture : a revolutionary life / Philippe Girard.
Description: First edition. | New York : Basic Books, [2016] | Includes
   bibliographical references and index.
Identifiers: LCCN 2016018088 (print) | LCCN 2016018559 (e-book) | ISBN
   9780465094134 (hardcover) | ISBN 9780465094141 (e-book)
Subjects: LCSH: Toussaint Louverture, 1743–1803. |
   Haiti—History—Revolution, 1791–1804—Biography. |
   Revolutionaries—Haiti—Biography. | Generals—Haiti—Biography.
Classification: LCC F1923.T69 G57 2016 (print) | LCC F1923.T69 (e-book) |
DDC
   972.94/03092 [B] —dc23
LC record available at https://lccn.loc.gov/2016018088

10 9 8 7 6 5 4 3 2 1

À Cécile, Hélène, Flore, Rémy, et tous
les esclaves de la plantation Bréda

Toussaint Louverture

CONTENTS

Atlantic Ocean

Jean-Rabel   Port-de-Paix   Le Borgne
St. Louis
Môle St. Nicolas   Cap-Français
Gros-Morne   Fort-Dauphin
Bombarde   Plaisance
Ennery   Ouanaminthe
Dondon
Gonaïves

**SAINT-DOMINGUE
(HAITI)**

Hinche

St. Marc   **Santo Domingo**

Pte-Rivière

Verrettes
Mirebalais

Jérémie   Arcahaye
Port-au-Prince
Léogane   **Saint-Domingue**
Petit-Goâve

Tiburon   St. Louis
Cayes   Jacmel
Port-Salut

Caribbean Sea

0   10   20   30   40 km

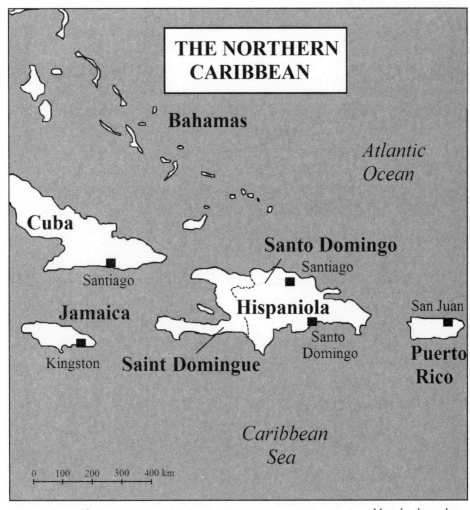

THE NORTHERN CARIBBEAN

Bahamas

Atlantic Ocean

Cuba

Santiago

Santo Domingo

Santiago

Hispaniola

San Juan

Jamaica

Saint Domingue

Santo Domingo

Puerto Rico

Kingston

Caribbean Sea

0   100   200   300   400 km

Maps by the author.

INTRODUCTION

IN SEPTEMBER 1802, in a dank cell of a fort in eastern France, an elderly officer began to dictate an account of his career to a secretary. He had much to say. His life had taken him from bondage on a sugar plantation to the governorship of France's richest colony, Saint-Domingue. For almost five decades he had labored as a slave and a muleteer before launching a revolution in 1791 that became the only successful slave revolt in world history. He had fought off invasions by Spain and Britain in 1793–1798. He had conquered the neighboring colony of Santo Domingo in 1801. In the process, he had become one of the richest men in the Americas.

"Every body has heard of Toussaint, the famous Negro general," noted one of his first biographers, the British abolitionist James Stephen, in 1803. So great was public interest in his life that Stephen's book went through four printings in a year. By that date, other biographies had been published in France, the United States, Germany, Italy, Denmark, and Sweden. To his admirers, Toussaint Louverture was the George Washington of his race, the black Napoléon, the new Spartacus, or even the Messiah. Black men and women sang songs about his revolution from Venezuela to Brazil; William Wordsworth wrote verses in his honor in Britain; and in Germany, Friedrich Hegel developed his master-slave dialectic based on the lessons of the Haitian slave revolt. The British *Annual Register* named him 1802's most significant world figure.[1]

But Napoléon, the first consul of France, so feared Louverture's growing power that in 1801 he had sent an expedition to overthrow, arrest, and deport him. Before 1802 was over, the powerful governor of Saint-Domingue was a prisoner in the Fort de Joux in eastern France. Louverture had summoned a secretary to his cell in the hope that Napoléon would free him if only he read a full account of his career.

Louverture labored over the text for days. He proofread and amended the secretary's first draft, annotated and edited a second, then added a conclusion to a third. Finally, he wrote a fourth and final version entirely in his own hand. This was a monumental effort for a man who had grown up illiterate. The result was a rendering of the Haitian Revolution from the vantage point of its central figure, but it left many questions unanswered. Louverture made heartfelt references to his family members, but he largely glossed over his personal life; he defended his views on race and forced labor, but he occasionally misrepresented his record on both in order to ingratiate himself to the French consul. The memoir is as beguiling as it is frustrating. "I was a Slave, I dare to announce it," he wrote. This passing comment was Louverture's only reference to his prerevolutionary life, the only acknowledgment that he had once been enslaved. Though today he is remembered as the leader of a slave rebellion, that is not how he wanted to be defined. He had also been a freedman, a father, and a planter; most of all, as he repeated throughout the memoir, he was an officer and an official of the French republic who had transcended class and race to take his place among the great statesmen of the revolutionary era.[2]

The challenges that the biographer of Louverture faces are many. Secretive, guarded, and occasionally deceitful, he preferred to keep his innermost fears and dreams to himself. He had many foes and no true friends. His relatives knew him better than anyone else, but aside from the partial recollections of two of his sons and one of his nieces, they have left us few accounts of his private life. For these reasons, there have been few scholarly biographies of Louverture. In English, the most recent biography based on extensive primary research was C. L. R. James's *The Black Jacobins*, first published in 1938.

We are not even sure what Louverture looked like. Written sources indicate that the man who defied Napoléon was just five-foot-two and frail of stature. Contemporary white authors deemed him ugly by their standards of beauty—but we cannot judge for ourselves, because he refused to have a portrait made. As a result, the portraits of him that did appear were often drawn by people who had not met him in person; they simply projected onto a canvas their vision of what a black general should look like. His enemies made him apelike to discredit him; nineteenth-century abolitionists lightened the color of his skin to make him seem less threatening to European audiences; contemporary Haitian artists depict him in the heroic pose of a triumphant general. The image on the jacket and the frontispiece of this book date from Louverture's time and are consistent with written depictions by his contemporaries, making them some of the best, if imperfect, illustrations available.

And yet it is possible to understand Louverture, and it is possible for the very reason that we want to read about him in the first place. Writing about slaves is usually difficult, because history is written by the winners, so planters dominate the archival record. But in Haiti, uniquely, *it was the slaves who won*. Louverture alone left behind thousands of letters, reports, and other documents. Many of his fellow revolutionaries did the same.

These sources have been read in many different ways. Because Louverture is the bridge between the slave-holding French colony of Saint-Domingue, where he was born and raised, and the independent black republic of Haiti, which grew out of the slave revolt he helped initiate, scholars have focused on his views on slave labor, on his relationship to colonialism, and on his African heritage. For many years, their verdict was clear-cut: Louverture was the idealistic herald of slave emancipation, the forefather of an independent Haiti, and a black nationalist. Then new archival finds in the past forty years revealed that Louverture once owned and exploited slaves, leading some modern historians to describe him instead as a selfish would-be planter who never completely forsook France and white society.

Neither view is accurate. And the more we learn of Louverture, the harder it is to pin him down. He was of African descent but embraced the cultural model of his French masters; he launched a slave revolt but sharply restricted the rights of freedmen after he seized power; he charted an autonomist path for Saint-Domingue but insisted until his dying breath that he was a loyal servant of France.

So how are we supposed to make sense of him? How it is possible to write about him at all? By accepting that he was all of these things at once. He came from a colony shaped by French, African, and American influences, and he lived through a revolutionary era so tumultuous that he often had no choice but to accommodate his enemies' agendas. By obligation and by personal taste, he operated in multiple worlds simultaneously. His parents, who were among the million Africans brought to Saint-Domingue between 1697 and 1793, raised him in their native language, Fon, and probably introduced him to their native religion, Vodou. Born in the French Caribbean, Louverture also grew up in the Afro-French language Kreyòl, on plantations producing sugar, coffee, and cotton for the European market, and observing a racial imbalance that saw a tiny minority of whites control a vast population of blacks and people of mixed race. Then there was France, the distant metropole that had imposed colonial rule in Saint-Domingue and imported the Catholic religion, the French language, and eventually the revolutionary ideals that would inspire the Haitian Revolution itself.

Louverture navigated all three of these worlds, switching from one to another as needed. He was a slave rebel and a conservative planter, a caring father and a cold-blooded general, a passionate idealist and a scheming politician. Above all, he was a pragmatist. In his early life he proved willing to accept slavery because it was the prevailing form of labor in the Caribbean; during the Revolution he came to regard universal emancipation as the only system acceptable to his supporters; and when he confronted the problem of how best to actually govern the colony, he backtracked and reintroduced compulsory labor rules, which, in his view, were the only way to avoid the economic ruin of the colony.

If we examine Louverture solely through the prism of our current preoccupations with race, slavery, and imperialism, we risk missing the issues that mattered to *him*, starting with his personal ambition. His political views were often scattershot, but his craving for social status was a constant. Educating himself, seeing to his children's future, making money, gaining and retaining power, and achieving recognition as a great man: he never wavered from the pursuit of these ends. He was a social climber and a self-made man, which in no way diminishes his accomplishments. In fact, it humanizes a figure who can seem unapproachable otherwise. From the slave quarters to the governor's mansion, his life journey was a remarkable story of a black man of humble origins fighting his way to the top of a white-dominated world.

Louverture was almost fifty when the Haitian Revolution broke out, so for most of his life he lived in a society where it was legal not only to own and whip a slave, but also, with a judge's order, to torture, mutilate, and burn him or her alive. He owned nothing, not his own body, or his children. Opportunities for manumission were rare, and a free person of color could only hope for secondary status under the law. Saint-Domingue was controlled by a European power. The few armed people of color in the colony were employed as slave-catchers. Slavery, racism, inequality, and imperialism seemed unchallengeable facts of life.

Yet Louverture presided over a revolution—the most radical of the late eighteenth century—that turned on their head the entrenched beliefs, practices, and habits of his society. No European power had abolished slavery in an American colony; Louverture's revolution forced France to emancipate all its slaves in all its colonies. His white contemporaries took it for granted that a single white man could subdue a hundred Africans with the snap of the whip; he built an army of freedmen strong enough to threaten British Jamaica, Spanish Cuba, and the southern United States. Slaves had been listed alongside cattle on plantation records; he and other black males became bona fide citizens of France, generals in the French Army, and deputies in the French parliament. France had ruled Saint-Domingue through its appointed governors; he secured that title for himself and drafted a constitution to support his claim. At the apex of his career in 1801, Louverture was an international statesman who corresponded and signed treaties with the governments of Britain, Spain, the United States, and France. The slave-owning Thomas Jefferson feared his power while negotiating for a share of the trade of Saint-Domingue, the United States' second-largest trading partner.

The tragedy of Louverture's life was that, despite orchestrating one of the most important revolutions in the history of mankind, he never got the recognition he felt he deserved. "I am black but I have the soul of a white man," he once told a French colonial official. Yet "because I am black and ignorant," he noted bitterly in his memoir, "I must not count as one of the soldiers of the Republic." Napoléon did not even bother to read the memoir. By refusing to accept "this negro" as an equal, the French emperor reduced him. He made Louverture into what he is remembered as today—a former slave who would always be defined by his African ancestry—when in fact his servile past was just one of the many facets of Louverture's revolutionary life.[3]

ONE

ARISTOCRAT

c. 1740

IN THE EARLY DECADES of the nineteenth century, Toussaint Louverture's son Isaac set out to gather all the information he could find about his African ancestors. He uncovered a tragic story that began in privilege and ended in bondage. Toussaint Louverture's grandfather Gaou Guinou was a "powerful African king" of the so-called "Slave Coast" of West Africa, but Gaou Guinou's son Hippolyte (Louverture's father) was captured and sold alongside his wife—"according to the barbarous custom of the Africans"—and became a slave in Saint-Domingue.[1]

These family traditions must be handled with caution because they were recorded nearly a century after the fact. They are also tainted by Isaac's competing urges to aggrandize his ancestors ("powerful African king") and reject his African heritage ("barbarous custom"). But the story, which Isaac must have originally heard from his father, is our guide as we follow Louverture's parents from their youth to the distant and mysterious island to which the

In the early 1700s, the portion of the Slave C to present-day Benin was home to several minista mon foundation myths and the Fon language. The c. was "the greatest trading place on the coast," accordin kingdom of Allada stood farther inland, and the great warrior kingdom of Dahomey farther inland still.[2]

Family traditions held that Louverture's grandfather Gaou Guinou was the king of Allada and that his father, Hippolyte, a prince of royal blood, was married to the "daughter of Affiba, king of the Ajas," another people from the Slave Coast. But Allada royal dynasties mention no king named Gaou Guinou, so Louverture's descendants most likely made up their royal parentage to lessen the stigma of their slave ancestry. Gaou Guinou's first name in fact suggests that he was merely a *gan* (a prominent official of the Allada kingdom), and therefore that his son Hippolyte—as well as, ultimately, Toussaint Louverture—was not a prince, but an aristocrat.[3]

Gentilhomme du Royaume d'Aardra

istocrat from the Allada kingdom. Reprinted from J. Grasset de Saint-Sauveur, *lopédie des Voyages* (Paris: Derot, 1796), 131.

In any case, enslavement was destined to upend the privileged life of Louverture's father. Slavery was a fact of life in Allada, where it had existed locally since time immemorial (given his social prominence, Hippolyte likely owned slaves himself). West African slaves had also been exported to the Muslim world for a thousand years, and a third market, the Americas, had grown exponentially since 1492. Spanish conquistadors in the Caribbean had originally subjected native Amerindians to a type of serfdom they called *repartimiento*, and French colonizers had imported white indentured servants. But the punishing death rate of the Caribbean had made both systems uneconomic, and African slave labor reigned supreme by the 1700s. Though costly to purchase, African slaves tended to survive longer than other laborers because they had some natural immunity to the diseases of European and African origins that had made the New World so deadly to Amerindian and European workers.[4]

By the time the Atlantic slave trade ended in the 1800s, 12 million human beings had been transported from Africa to the Americas. Only a small minority went to what had by then become the United States (about 6 percent). Most went to Brazil (40 percent) and the Caribbean (50 percent), including Saint-Domingue (Haiti), which alone imported more slaves than the United States. Slave traders originally preyed on the northwestern coast of Africa, but by Hippolyte's time they had shifted their focus south to the Slave Coast. From 1,200 a year in the 1640s, exports from the region of Allada shot up to 10,000 a year in the 1690s and to more than 15,000 a year in the 1700s and 1710s.

This increase was made possible by the unstable political context along the Slave Coast, and ultimately by the willingness of local officials like Hippolyte's father to sell their enemies to European traders. At once predator and prey, the Alladas fought the vassal state of Whydah to the south and then the expanding kingdoms of Akwamu, Dahomey, and Oyo to the west, north, and east. The wars reached their tragic climax in 1724–1726 when King Agaja of Dahomey conquered Allada. The Dahomey king's pacification of Allada and its successor states, and then his further expansion to Whydah and the coast, lasted until 1740, at which point Agaja died and his people became embroiled in a succession war of their own. These troubled times provided plenty of opportunities to raid and kidnap and sell. From the 1720s to the 1740s, Dahomey alone exported 6,000 slaves a year, most of them captured in and around the old Allada kingdom.

Louverture's father, Hippolyte, "made prisoner and sold" when "his great tribe was incorporated into the kingdom of Dahomey," was among the casualties of Dahomean imperialism. So was his first wife. Their children were apparently deported alongside their parents as well.[5]

Slaves who had been purchased or captured in the interior of Allada were usually taken to the slave emporium of Glehue near the coast, where they awaited their fate in a dreadful stockade. This must have been a traumatic experience for Hippolyte, who could legitimately fear the worst for himself and his family. Slaves who attracted no buyers could be killed outright. His only hope was to be ransomed by relatives or sold locally so that he could at least remain in his homeland.

Both of those options eluded him, however, and in or around 1740, Hippolyte and his family were sold to French slave traders. A family tradition specifies that it was an Arab merchant who arranged the sale, which is possible, as some Arab merchants were active in Glehue. The main currency in western Africa was the cowry, a type of seashell from the Maldives; Hippolyte's life was worth three hundred pounds of those.[6]

Because Glehue is located three miles inland, Hippolyte and his family were then taken across a lagoon to a sandbar, where they were stripped of their clothes, branded, and handed over to their European buyers. Louverture's father, whose tattoos and scarifications were a sign of pride, because they indicated his rank as an Allada aristocrat, now bore a shameful mark of his servile status on his burning skin. So did his wife and crying children. They were led onto a shallop, which battled the frightful surf all the way to a European ship waiting offshore. In time, this ship would ferry the hapless family to some unknown destination.

It probably took several months for the ship to fill up with enough captives to make the trip. Meanwhile, the white sailors, who had no immunity against African fevers, would have fretted about the delays. But the delays gave Hippolyte some time to familiarize himself with the floating prison that had become his home. Women and children were probably few on his ship, because two-thirds of all the slaves bought by French slavers were adult men, and probably more so in a war zone like the Slave Coast.[7]

French slaving records rarely mention the names of individual slaves, so we cannot know definitively on which ship Hippolyte and his family embarked. But the ship was probably outfitted in Nantes, which was the main slave-trading port in France, or Le Havre, where the French planters who eventually bought Louverture's father had a business partner. The ship that best fits the timeline is the *Hermione*, a slave trader that visited the Slave Coast in the fall of 1739 and left the island of Principe, just off the African continent, on May 7, 1740, with a cargo of 260 souls.

Two generations before the Haitian Revolution, resistance was already the order of the day. No fewer than 37 crewmen were on the *Hermione* to guard against a slave revolt (a distinct possibility, since revolts broke out on 150 of the 3,300 slaving expeditions launched from France). Despite such tight security, two men and three women managed to throw themselves overboard and drown, regaining in death a degree of control over their own fate that they had lost as living beings. Altogether, the Atlantic claimed the lives of 26 of the slaves and 7 of the crewmen on board the *Hermione*. As an adult, Louverture was deathly afraid of sea travel, and it is not hard to see why: he must have heard many a horrifying tale of the Middle Passage from his father while growing up.[8]

When sailing, men spent most of their time packed and locked below decks while women stayed in the main quarters, where they were expected to entertain the crew in any way the crewmen deemed fit. Hippolyte may have found himself just a few feet away from his wife, close enough to hear what was happening, yet bound and impotent to do anything about it.

It took two months and two thousand leagues over the sea before the *Hermione* finally reached the small islands of the Lesser Antilles in the southern Caribbean, veered to the northwest, and proceeded on a broad reach with the trade winds behind her until the island of Hispaniola (Haiti and the Dominican Republic today) rose above the horizon. Louverture's father was bound for France's largest and richest Caribbean colony, Saint-Domingue, which alone consumed 80 percent of the slaves sold in France's American empire.

Officially ceded by Spain in 1697, Saint-Domingue was a young colony compared with Santo Domingo (conquered by Spain in 1493), Cuba (Spain, 1511), Guadeloupe and Martinique (France, 1635), and Jamaica (Britain, 1659). A haven for stateless hunters and pirates in the early decades of French rule, the colony was still rough around the edges in the 1740s. But this late bloomer, blessed with fertile soil, abundant rain and sun, and the entrepreneurial spirit of its inhabitants, was destined to surpass all other Caribbean colonies, French and otherwise.

Saint-Domingue's economic rise was accompanied by a dramatic increase in slave imports, which eventually totaled over 900,000. By comparison, the United States imported fewer than 500,000. But the death rate in Saint-Domingue was so high, even for African natives with some degree of immunity to tropical diseases, that the slave population only rose gradually, from 9,000 in 1700 to 47,000 in 1720, 148,000 in 1751, and 465,000 in 1789, by which point there were already 694,000 slaves in the United States, even though Saint-Domingue had imported far more slaves.[9]

Had Hippolyte landed in South Carolina instead of Saint-Domingue, Toussaint Louverture would have lived through the American Revolution instead of the Haitian Revolution, and history might have unfolded differently. But the *Hermione* was bound for Saint-Domingue, which she finally reached after seventy-five days of sailing. The ship surgeon was concerned that thirty slaves were in immediate danger of dying and urged the captain to stop in the first major port of Saint-Domingue. It was the city of Cap, which the *Hermione* reached on August 21, 1740.

For Louverture's father and his family, the Middle Passage ended the day their ship sailed into the Bay of Cap on the northern coast of Saint-Domingue. The town was wedged between a row of steep hills and the bay, which was dotted with warships and merchantmen. It was a recent French settlement that had only become the capital of the colony in 1711. Half of Cap had burned in a fire in 1735—one of many conflagrations it would endure in Louverture's time—but it had been rebuilt in stone and was fast becoming a sizable town. The plain of Cap, dominated by sugar plantations, loomed farther to the south.

The anchor dropped. As was the norm, slaves would have been prepped for sale, fed, and oiled while they wondered what would become of them. Equally bewildering was the Jesuit priest who guided the slaves into performing the sign of the cross before baptizing them under a deluge of Latin and French phrases. A doctor certified that the ship did not carry epidemic diseases, and eager purchasers then rushed onboard to get first pick, all the while complaining about the rising price of Allada slaves. "Almost all sugar makers want slaves from this nation," wrote an overseer of the plantation where Louverture grew up, so "they cost a lot." Natives of Allada were particularly sought after by French planters, who viewed them as "hard-working" and "intelligent" people who were "better suited to sugar work" than other West Africans, but one should be wary of using ethnic stereotypes to understand Louverture, especially since he never defined himself as an Allada as an adult.[10]

Hippolyte could understand nothing of the rapid-fire French of the negotiators, but he must have sensed that something was taking place that was a matter of life and death. Some slaves changed hands, while others, too sickly to be sold, were sent ashore to holding pens that even apologists of slavery found "heartbreaking."[11]

Tragically, Hippolyte's wife and children were taken away from him after they reached Saint-Domingue. A French colonist bought them and took them to the region of Cayes in the southern province, where Hippolyte's wife was baptized and given the Christian name of Catherine. Separated from her husband by two hundred miles, she never adjusted to her new life and the demise of her marriage. According to a family tradition, "a mortal sorrow took over her soul" and she died. She was not forgotten: decades later, Louverture still remembered how the Atlantic slave trade had "torn the son from his mother, the brother from his sister, and the father from his son." There was little to do but mourn until the wars of the Haitian Revolution finally gave Toussaint Louverture a chance to visit southern Saint-Domingue and reunite with his estranged half-sister.[12]

Hippolyte's journey ended much closer to port: he was taken to the Bréda plantation just outside Cap, which was named after its founder, Pantaléon de Bréda. Bréda was a native of southwestern France, as were many of his employees, which likely explains why Louverture spoke French with a pronounced southern accent (Louverture was otherwise not very impressed by French southerners, whom he viewed as braggarts with a tendency to make toothless threats). Bréda, a fourth son who did not stand to inherit significant property in France, had enrolled in the navy in the late seventeenth century. Once in Saint-Domingue, he had married a local heiress, Elizabeth Bodin. Their marriage, unequal parts love and economic interest, was typical of their milieu: the well-born Bréda gained access to a network of in-laws, while the financial success of the Bodins was validated by a prestigious marriage to a French noble.[13]

Bréda had picked a perfect time to come to Saint-Domingue. The colony was still largely unsettled in the early 1700s, so French authorities granted homesteads for free to anyone who promised to develop the land. France had instituted pesky trade restrictions, but they were largely ineffective owing to near-constant wars with Britain and widespread smuggling. The economy was booming. Cattle, tobacco, and indigo had successively dominated, but sugar was now king. The number of sugar estates jumped from 138 in 1713 to 339 in 1730 and 450 in 1739. Within a generation, Saint-Domingue became the world's largest exporter of sugar.[14]

At a time when land and slaves were still affordable, a newcomer could make a fortune in his lifetime, especially if, like Pantaléon de Bréda, he got a head start by marrying well. Bréda was a rich man when he died in 1738. The assets of his widow, Elizabeth Bodin-Bréda, who

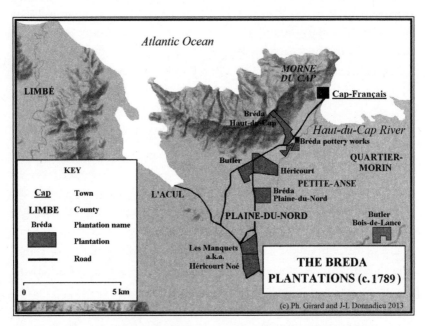

The Bréda plantations. Drawn by Philippe Girard and Jean-Louis Donnadieu.

managed the family fortune by the time Louverture's father landed in Cap, were estimated at the impressive sum of 1.7 million colonial livres in 1750, and 2.3 million in 1754, by which point the Bréda family plantations were scattered all over the plain of Cap. It was on one of those plantations, the Bréda estate in Haut-du-Cap, that Louverture's father lived out the rest of his life.[15]

Transitioning to a Caribbean environment—a process known as "seasoning" in the planter lingo—was hard for African-born slaves. They had to adapt to a new trade, new food, and new people speaking French, unfamiliar tongues from other regions of Africa, and the local Kreyòl pidgin. Ethnic identities, already in flux on the coast of Africa as a result of the disruptions caused by the slave trade, were reshuffled once more. Even one's gods and name were up for renegotiation: like his estranged wife, Catherine, Louverture's father was baptized; it was at his baptism that he received the Christian name of Hippolyte. His original African name has been lost to us.

Unable to adapt, some freshly imported slaves would "let themselves die rather than work," a plantation overseer later reported. To lessen the risk of suicide and facilitate the transition to plantation life, the Brédas usually placed new imports under the tutelage of an older slave from the same ethnic group. They fed them a richer diet than the rest of their slaves and gave them less demanding tasks, such as weeding the cane fields, until they were able to perform more arduous labor.[16]

According to a family tradition, Hippolyte was soon granted his freedom along with the use of five slaves because he was a king's son, but such privileged treatment is implausible on a for-profit plantation. More likely, he benefited from a large support network because he was of aristocratic background and because there were so many other Alladas in the area. Alladas were the single largest ethnic group in Saint-Domingue in the 1740s. Even in later decades, when they were eclipsed by the growing number of imports from the Congo, people of Allada descent retained a special aura in Saint-Domingue. However low Hippolyte had fallen, there were many slaves in Saint-Domingue who ranked even lower than he did.[17]

After he was separated from his first wife, Hippolyte remarried a fellow slave named Pauline: Louverture's mother. Nothing is known of her background except that, like Hippolyte's first wife, she was a native of the Slave Coast and a member of the Aja ethnic group. She was "beautiful and virtuous," according to Louverture's son, who never knew her personally, and so must have gotten his information from his father. Beginning their lives anew, the couple started a family together. They gave their firstborn child a Christian name: Toussaint.[18]

TWO

CHILD
c. 1743–1754

PARISHIONERS GATHERED at the Catholic church in Cap on November 1, 1743, to celebrate All Saints' Day. The Mass unfolded uneventfully until, in the midst of Holy Communion, a kerfuffle broke out in the front pews. As members of the colonial elite lined up to receive the Eucharist, a senior court clerk and the assistant district attorney jostled for position. Elbows flailed and tempers frayed, but neither man was willing to concede that the other stood one step higher on the social ladder and should take Communion before him. Their silly dispute may seem trivial to us, but the matter was considered so important in the highly stratified society of Saint-Domingue that the colonial court of appeals in Cap dedicated its entire session to it the following day (the clerk won).[1]

Meanwhile, just a few miles away on the Bréda plantation of Haut-du-Cap, a woman was giving birth to her infant son. Young, black, and enslaved, he was a nobody by the standards of the colony. Yet fifty-eight years later he would become governor of Saint-Domingue and outrank all the elite whites who had towered above him at the moment of his birth.

Retracing the childhood of a slave is an arduous task. In the documentary record, slaves are little more than entries on accounting ledgers—and these are missing prior to 1785 for the Bréda plantation. Haitian oral traditions help fill in some blanks, but by nature they are unreliable; so are the recollections of Louverture's offspring and later accounts written by French authors who did not know him during his youth.[2]

As a result, the exact circumstances of Louverture's birth remain a mystery. His full name is usually rendered as "François Dominique Toussaint Louverture," though early documents only list him as "Toussaint from Bréda," after the plantation on which he was born. The year of his birth is traditionally listed as 1743, which is plausible, but no baptismal record has been found, and the earliest archival sources list alternate dates, ranging from 1737 to 1756. His birthday fell on May 20, according to oral traditions, but his first name, which means "All Saints' Day" in French, strongly suggests that he was actually born on November 1.[3]

Louverture's origins are also obscure because he wished to keep them so. After learning to read and write as an adult, he could have recorded his early life for posterity, yet he chose not to. In the lengthy personal memoir that he wrote shortly before his death, he only mentioned in passing that "I was a Slave." Did he not want his French colleagues to think of him as a son of Africa? Did he want to hide from the black population that his experience of slavery had been far from typical? We do not know. Instead, we must turn to surviving plantation and church records to re-create his youth.[4]

Louverture entered our world on the Bréda plantation of Haut-du-Cap in the outskirts of Cap-Français. According to Haitian traditions, the midwife foresaw his destiny and raised him skyward, incanting, "Boy, whites will kneel before you." As was the custom of Allada midwives, she then cauterized his umbilical cord with a glowing ember.[5]

Some slaves killed their infants to spare them a life of misery and allow them to rejoin their ancestors in Africa, which the Vodou religion associates with Heaven. Louverture's parents, who brought one child after another into the world, clearly had different plans. However unwelcome the chain of events that had brought them to Saint-Domingue, the colony was their new home. Louverture inherited their attitude: instead of lamenting his misfortune, he chose to adapt.

Louverture was the first of Pauline and Hippolyte's children. More followed as years passed, five of whom survived early childhood. After Toussaint came Marie-Jeanne, then Paul, Pierre, and Jean. Toussaint Louverture was particularly close to his brother Paul, whom he later promoted to general, albeit in the protective and overbearing manner of an older brother. His youngest sibling, nicknamed Gaou because he looked just like his African grandfather, was born in 1774, by which point Louverture was about thirty, so Louverture's mother must have been very young when she had him.[6]

The young Louverture originally had "a taste for the history as well as the language of his forefathers," which he spoke with ease. His first words must have been words from the Fon language of his parents, such as *tō* (father) and *nō* (mother). Fon has a poetic way of using two root words to create a third, combining *su* (moon) and *vi* (child), for example, to create the word *suvi* (star): a child of the moon. Perhaps this is where Louverture got his knack for colorful metaphors, which remained a feature of his oratorical style throughout his life. Nevertheless, he quickly dropped Fon in favor of Kreyòl (also known as Haitian Creole), a mix of French and African languages that was more highly esteemed in Saint-Domingue. A slave using Kreyòl was viewed as someone who had weaned himself from his African roots and acculturated to the New World. In his later years, Louverture decided that even Kreyòl was beneath him, and he strove to learn standard French so as to gain access to the highest spheres of European society. He retained Fon until the end of his life, but he only used it when it was politically convenient to prove his credentials to the black population.[7]

Louverture learned to walk outside one of the humble thatched-roof huts of the slave quarters. He was completely naked and unaware. Only later did he learn that being scantily clad and barefoot was the mark of African slaves, and that a man had to dress and shoe himself properly to affirm his status as a Caribbean-born Creole and be better treated. He learned his lesson well. At the apex of his life, his preferred outfits were the white cotton vest and the tricolor uniform of the two professions he admired the most: planter and officer of the French Army.[8]

Childrearing mores in the black Caribbean, then as now, gave much leeway to very young children, especially since pregnant and nursing slaves were expected to work in the fields. Mothers had little time to spare, but absence did not preclude affection. Some slave mothers re-named themselves after their eldest sons, so it is possible that Pauline changed her identity once more to *Man-Toussaint* (Toussaint's mom) after he was born. Only one thing was nonnegotiable: the respect due to elders, who were known collectively as "aunts" and "uncles" whether they were related or not. This reverence for age (and contempt for young upstarts) remained with Louverture throughout his life.[9]

In the freedom of the early years, every step must have been an ad-venture for a small boy, even one so lightly built that he was known by the nickname of *fatras bâton* (sickly stick). The sharp aroma of roasted coffee in the morning, the distinctive taste of the soursop fruit, and the strange sound of the conch shell used by shepherds to summon their flock (and, much later, by rebel slaves to sound the call to arms): each would have been as puzzling as it was exhilarating. In the evening the sun dropped in a brief red burst that is the privilege of tropical latitudes, and the pitch-dark sky of a pre-electric age lit up with the myriad "children of the Moon," whose nature had not yet been elucidated by science.[10]

Back from a long day's work, the Louverture family would have gath-ered around a fire whose smoke filled the hut for lack of a chimney. To pass time, elders would chat in Fon while the youngest, noted a visitor to another plantation, "lay on the floor, fed the fire with dried cow dung," and listened attentively to tales of the old country. A slave who appeared "gloomy and taciturn" to a white observer during the day was completely different in the privacy of his home: "Now cowering over his fire, he re-cites, talks, gesticulates, reasons, judges, approves, or condemns, both his master and everything around him."[11]

A favorite tale of the young Louverture may have been the story of the warrior king Agassou. He was the son of a princess and a panther (from which he had inherited nails as sharp as claws) and the founder of the clan of the Agassouvi, whose members eventually migrated to the region of Allada and established the kingdom where Louverture's father claimed to have been a king's son. For a young boy like Louverture, it must have been exciting to know that a great warrior like Agassou was his ancestor and that panther blood ran through his veins. As an adult, however, he made no public reference to this or any other African tale, preferring to compare himself to classical European figures like the Greek slave rebel Spartacus.[12]

On special nights, storytelling gave way to dances known as *chicas* or *calendas*, which incorporated African dancing styles as well as the latest quadrille from Versailles. The instruments—banjos, drums, gourds filled with pebbles—were simple, but the singing featured complex harmonics, and the dances were as spirited as they were sensual. Slaves were known to travel for hours from one plantation to another to attend a dance when they had some free time. A favorite meeting spot was La Fossette on the way to the city of Cap. Whites studiously avoided this lugubrious swamp, which made it all the more attractive to slaves looking for a good time away from the master's presence. For a few precious hours, as one dancer challenged another, they could shake off the fatigue of their labors. Louverture probably enjoyed these dances as a child, but as a revolutionary leader he only staged them when he wanted to curry favor with his African-born followers. People often try hard to remember their childhood: Louverture did his best to forget his.

French plantation managers concerned themselves mainly with discipline and production, leaving the slaves free to organize their private lives as they saw fit. Because slaves, and particularly African-born slaves, were so dominant demographically in Saint-Domingue (90 percent of the population, of which maybe two-thirds were African-born), the African imprint was unusually strong there. It mixed with French culture to create a Caribbean hybrid that has given Haiti its unique cultural profile.

Although conversion to Catholicism was slavery's main moral justification and a master's legal duty, planters wasted little money on saving their slaves' souls. Or their own, for that matter: the planters of Saint-Domingue were so impious that the traditional midnight Mass at Christmas had to be banned colony-wide in 1754 because parishioners had used the occasion to turn churches into "houses of debauchery." White spirituality, when it existed, was often heretical. A manager of Haut-du-Cap was known to consult soothsayers; mystical practices, such as Mesmerism, were also popular for a while.[13]

The missionary orders tasked with converting the black population of Saint-Domingue—Dominicans and Jesuits—faced a daunting challenge. There were only 20 missionaries colony-wide at the time of Louverture's birth. As the slave population soared in the following decades, the ratio of priests to slaves diminished from 1 priest for every 315 slaves in 1685 to 1 for every 2,747 in 1752. For lack of priests, Catholic instruction often took the form of a pro-forma baptism, a yearly confession, and little else. But Louverture's exposure to the Catholic religion was more pronounced than what most slaves encountered, as the slaves of the Bréda plantation in Haut-du-Cap were expected to join in a public prayer each day.[14]

French law technically barred non-Catholics from French colonies until 1789, but the law was widely ignored, and Louverture met many Jews and Protestants in his youth. Jews (or "schismatics," as Louverture called them) were particularly active in Cap, where they had their own cemetery. The person selling smoked herring to the Haut-du-Cap plantation was a Sephardic Jew named Aaron Sasportas. The presence of Jews in the colony was an open secret: when one governor made plans in 1765 to expel them from Saint-Domingue, per colonial law, he was reproved by his own king for harassing an economically valuable community.[15]

The original Taino Amerindians of Saint-Domingue had long since vanished, but physical remnants of their culture, which turned up regularly when slaves tilled the soil, played their part in the slaves' religious life. Popular lore held that Taino idols excavated from the ground had been created by lightning, and many blacks kept them in their homes under the belief that lightning would never strike twice in the same place. Some Caribs (another Amerindian group from the Lesser Antilles that had survived European colonization) occasionally ventured as far as Cap, and they must have been an intriguing sight for the young Louverture. Also notable was the embalmed head of a Taino that was later displayed in the museum of the scientific society of Cap. In many ways, colonial Haiti was a land where the Enlightenment met the mystical.[16]

Vodou was the product of this religious hodgepodge. A syncretic faith, it incorporated elements of ancestor and spirit worship from the Slave Coast and the Congo, along with the odd Muslim and Amerindian belief, into the Catholic framework provided by the planter class. Vodou originated in the Allada kingdom of Louverture's father, but Louverture did not care much for a religion steeped in African spiritualism, and available evidence identifies him as a sincere and even ostentatious Catholic. He was baptized as a slave, he served as godfather on multiple occasions, and he was the only person out of the 152 slaves of Haut-du-Cap to be described as "devout" on a plantation register. Even during the Revolution, when it became politically dangerous to appear to be too friendly to the Catholic Church, he made a point of attending Mass every day and even persecuting followers of Vodou.[17]

The most influential people in Toussaint Louverture's early religious life were not *makandals* and *houngans* (sorcerers and Vodou priests), but the members of the Jesuit order who oversaw the Catholic Church in northern Saint-Domingue from 1704 to 1763. The headquarters of the Jesuit mission were a short distance away in Cap; some Jesuits even lived in the hamlet of Haut-du-Cap, right next door to the plantation on which Louverture grew up.[18]

The Jesuits were controversial in Saint-Domingue because they took their role seriously and appointed a "priest of the negroes" who actively ministered to the slaves. Slaves grew more involved in their faith as a result and even began holding services on their own in the church in Cap. "One of them would do catechism or preach to the others," a magistrate complained, and then visit nearby plantations to attract more converts. The name of this self-appointed preacher is not listed in the records, but it is tempting to identify him as Louverture, since a plantation register noted how he was "eager to catechize and proselytize." Years later, as governor, he would quiz young people on their catechism, deliver sermons, and even celebrate Mass as if he were an ordained priest.[19]

For slaves to think and pray on their own was not regarded favorably by colonial authorities; for them to dabble in exegesis also undermined the planters' belief in their intellectual inferiority. When word got out about the independent black services and the wandering preacher in 1761, the municipal council of Cap decided to lock the town's church during lunch hours and at night, effectively preventing slaves from gathering there unsupervised. The Jesuits were blamed for "the enormous crimes . . . committed by the slaves" and expelled from the colony altogether in 1763. Their expulsion ended Louverture's association with the Jesuits but not with the Catholic Church: he also grew very close to the Jesuits' successors, the Capuchins.[20]

Louverture is regarded today as a hero by the people of Benin in West Africa, where his parents were born, but having African roots was considered shameful in eighteenth-century Saint-Domingue. Louverture purposely left behind much of his African cultural heritage as he grew up, from the Fon language to the Vodou religion, so as to embrace the dominant French cultural model. He was no black nationalist: he was trying to fit into a colony where everything African was deemed uncivilized, and lived much of his life as a Creole and an aspiring Frenchman.

THREE

SLAVE
1754

ELIZABETH DE BRÉDA NÉE BODIN, Toussaint Louverture's legal owner since his birth, died in 1752. Two years later her three children reached an agreement on her inheritance: they would divide her estate into three shares and draw lots. Fate put the Haut-du-Cap plantation in the hands of her son Pantaléon de Bréda Jr., who proceeded to "exchange negroes and cattle" with his sisters to even out the shares. Louverture would remain Pantaléon Jr.'s personal property for the next two decades.[1]

A common trope in slave narratives is the awakening: the moment when the slave child realizes that by law he is not seen as a human being but as chattel. The Maryland slave Frederick Douglass took the full measure of his condition when he first saw a woman being whipped. "I was quite a child, but I well remember it. . . . It struck me with an awful force. It was the blood-stained gate, the entrance to the hell of slavery, through which I was about to pass." Though Louverture said no more of his awakening than he did of the rest of his childhood, it may have been on the cursed day of August 26, 1754, as family members were torn from their loved ones to even out the share of an absentee owner he barely knew, that he became fully aware of what it meant to be a slave. His father, proud son of the panther that he was, was property. So was his mother. So was he. Louverture was about ten years old at the time.[2]

Though they owned him by law, the Brédas were largely a footnote in Louverture's life. The typical colonist viewed Saint-Domingue as a place to get rich before returning to one's true home, France, so whites only represented 5 percent of the colony's population. So lopsided was the ratio between slaves and elite whites in rural areas that in the parish of Quartier-Morin, not far from Haut-du-Cap, there were at one time only three resident planters against 7,000 slaves. Surrounded by African-born slaves forcibly brought to Saint-Domingue and European planters longing for France, Creoles (Caribbean natives) like Louverture came to think of themselves as the only true "Americans." "For you all whites, France is your fatherland," explained a mixed-race Creole, "just like Africa is the blacks' and Saint-Domingue is ours."[3]

To prevent colonists from developing an autonomist mind-set, the French government willfully limited the number of schools in Saint-Domingue. This forced colonists to send their children to France so that they could not only "suck on good French milk," but also, potentially, serve as "hostages" guaranteeing their parents' loyalty (Louverture would one day find his own sons in this situation). White children were accordingly a rarity in Saint-Domingue, which was probably for the best, since many of them were overindulged imps whose tantrums could cost the slaves dearly. A slave nanny who dared spank a white child was liable to have her hand cut off, and then be hanged. For his own safety, Louverture, whose primary duties were in the stables anyway, must have stayed clear of the Bréda brats.[4]

As a result, Louverture barely knew the Brédas' three children and eight grandchildren, most of whom spent the bulk of their lives in France. The oldest Bréda child, named Elizabeth after her mother, had married a naval officer at the age of fourteen (her husband is best known for captaining the ship that took Charles-Marie de La Condamine and other scientists to Peru, where La Condamine helped to prove Isaac Newton's prediction that the Earth is not perfectly spherical). Elizabeth bore her husband six children in the 1720s and sent them to France in the 1730s to study, so Louverture never got to know them as a child.

The second Bréda daughter, Marie-Anne, also married a naval officer (he met an inglorious end in a drunken brawl). She left for France with her two children in 1737, six years before Louverture's estimated birth, never to return to Saint-Domingue.

The youngest Bréda child, named Pantaléon after his father, enrolled in the navy in 1730 and spent his adult life at sea. One of his most notable accomplishments, which Louverture must have heard about countless times, involved his role in a 1745 naval battle in Môle Saint-Nicolas (a bay west of Cap) against France's archenemy, Britain. Though Pantaléon's career as a naval officer occasionally brought him back to the Caribbean, and he inherited the Haut-du-Cap estate in 1754, Louverture may never have met him in person.

For slaves like Louverture, the most noteworthy aspect of the Brédas' distant lives is that they had children and then died. Each birth and each death raised the possibility that a sale would divvy up their human assets. The 1754 split, which came after an earlier one in 1744, must have left the young Louverture shocked and bewildered. Family bonds were tentative in this precarious context.[5]

Even after he inherited the Bréda plantation in Haut-du-Cap, Pantaléon de Bréda Jr. continued to serve in the navy, and he settled in France when he retired. His slaves were no more to him than workhorses to be listed alongside mules and cattle on accounting ledgers. He only knew of his slaves through the letters sent by his legal representatives in Saint-Domingue; they knew of him primarily through a portrait that hung in the master house in Haut-du-Cap. By the time Pantaléon Jr. died in Paris in 1786, his assets were so numerous that it took a staggering twenty days for the estate lawyer to read his will. But Pantaléon Jr. left nothing for his slaves, even though it was customary for planters to bequeath cash or freedom to favored slaves. Not once in his surviving letters did he mention Louverture by name.[6]

Because of this pattern of absentee ownership, which was becoming the norm in the plain of Cap during Louverture's youth as the first generation of planters cashed in and moved out, Louverture only knew a few of the third-generation Brédas. Some of them returned to Saint-Domingue to check on their inheritance after spending their childhoods in France and stopped by the Haut-du-Cap plantation to socialize with the appointed manager. The Count of Noé (Pantaléon Jr.'s nephew), who visited the colony in 1769–1775 and 1778, was particularly well known to Louverture—so well in fact that many historians have mistakenly assumed that the count was his owner.[7]

More relevant to Louverture's personal development was the deep impression that elite whites made on him—not just the Brédas and their appointees but local celebrities like Robert d'Argout, a white officer who stopped by the Haut-du-Cap plantation in 1775 and became governor two years later. Collectively, the landed gentry and the bureaucracy were known to the slaves as the "big whites." At once well-born, affluent, and powerful, they carried themselves with an air of innate superiority that was grating but also enthralling. Many years later, after reaching the governorship of Saint-Domingue, Louverture would do his best to imitate their mannerisms and become a "big white" in his turn. After all, did he not descend from aristocracy?

Plantation slavery in French colonies was regulated by the 1685 Black Code. It is rightly decried today for its brutality, but it was actually intended in its time as a paternalistic piece of legislation that balanced the interests of slave owners with their duties toward their wards. Under the Black Code, masters could exploit and whip their slaves, but they could not torture, kill, or rape them, and they had to feed and clothe them appropriately. The very idea that a master could not do as he wished with his property was groundbreaking for its time—so groundbreaking in fact that the Black Code was rarely enforced.[8]

To prevent planters from resorting to excessive brutality, the royal courts were theoretically charged with handling many slave transgressions. Prison time and the "chain" (hard labor on public projects) were common punishments for lesser crimes. Branding words like "theft" on a slave's chest was also a way to keep a permanent record of his misdeeds. The sentences for graver crimes were downright bestial. An official fee schedule informs us that it cost 15 livres to cut a slave's hand or ears, 60 livres to break all the limbs of a slave with an iron bar and leave him to die (the typical penalty for killing one's master), and 120 livres to burn a slave alive (the typical penalty for poisoners). With chilling bureaucratic exactitude, the fee schedule noted that carrying the wood and cleaning up the ashes entailed extra fees. To give the masters of troublesome slaves a financial incentive to resort to royal justice, they were reimbursed a set price whenever one of their slaves was sentenced to death (always eager to profit from their slaves, even dead ones, the Brédas were known to haggle for more money).[9]

There was no way for slaves like Louverture to avoid the gruesome spectacle of "justice." The eighteenth-century legal system did not lock away criminals in a prison for decades, out of sight of the general public, in the belief that the privation of liberty would reform souls; instead, it inflicted punishments that were public, immediate, and physical. Executions were carried out on the main plaza of Cap on market day or at major crossroads so as to make a lasting impression on passersby, and punishments were rendered directly onto the criminals' bodies. At once victims and audience, slaves were also participants because the royal executioner was often a convicted slave whose life had been spared for taking on the job.

These torments differed little from those inflicted against white criminals in prerevolutionary France, so contemporaries rarely questioned whether it was moral for royal courts to torture and execute slaves. Instead, they debated whether masters routinely inflicted extrajudicial punishments as well. Advocates of slavery claimed that private abuse was the exception rather than the norm, and that Caribbean slaves were so coddled that they were "the happy slaves of humane, or rather very mild, masters" and lived better than French and African farmers. But visitors to the colony, who had not yet become inured to plantation cruelty, mentioned illegal private punishments that included mutilation, castration, burning, and death: "The most cruel torment, fire, being buried to the neck, nothing is enough to sate the rage of these infamous executioners," wrote an appalled visitor. Neither side bothered to ask the slaves where the truth lay, but as soon as the Haitian Revolution gave them a chance to speak up, the "happy slaves" revealed that their masters had routinely "mistreated them with all sorts of tortures[,] . . . did not care for them even in times of sickness, and let them die destitute."[10]

There is no indication that Louverture ever personally endured cruel and unusual punishments: "He only knew slavery by name," a well-informed critic later wrote. But he cannot have ignored the violence swarming about him. In the food-growing estates of Vertières and

Charrier, both of them located in the hamlet of Haut-du-Cap, slaves who failed to sell enough vegetables on market day were punished with the *quatre piquets*: they were tied to four stakes, suspended just above the ground, and then whipped mercilessly. Farther away in Plaine-du-Nord, where the Brédas owned another estate, the sugar planter Pierre Chapuizet sewed up cattle drivers inside deceased mules and let them suffocate to death whenever he suspected them of using poison. Owners of nearby plantations burned the limbs of their slaves to force them to confess to alleged crimes. For Louverture and his fellow slaves, who re-enacted Jesus's final hours every year at Easter, life was an endless Passion play. Louverture never forgot "the insults, the misery, the tortures, and the flagellations" that, by his own account, were slavery's daily bread.[11]

In practice, the treatment of slaves varied greatly depending on the work to which they were assigned (labor on sugar plantations was more strenuous than work on other types of plantations, and field work was more demanding than domestic and skilled labor); whether the owner was present (slaves of absentee owners were at greater risk of being mistreated); and the specific period in which they were working (the treatment of slaves seems to have improved over time due to the humanizing effects of the Enlightenment, or more likely, because imported slaves were becoming more costly). The Bréda plantation in Haut-du-Cap fit the pattern deemed most oppressive to slaves: that of an absentee-owned sugar plantation.

Because Pantaléon de Bréda Jr. spent most of his life in France, he appointed an attorney (*procureur*) to represent him legally in the colony and managers (*gérants*) to oversee day-to-day operations on each of his plantations. Louverture's fate was thus highly dependent on the white men who were the Brédas' public face on the plantation. Attorneys had a particularly bad reputation: paid a commission on the value of the sugar shipped to France, they had a vested interest in boosting short-term production at the expense of the slaves' long-term well-being. Judging by the surviving evidence (which is incomplete prior to the 1770s), their record ran the gamut from the humane to the sadistic. Virtually nothing is known of the two attorneys, named Béagé and Faure, who oversaw Haut-du-Cap in Louverture's early years. A third, Gilly, who held the job from 1764 until his death in 1772, was apparently accommodating. "He had the weakness," complained his successor, "of negotiating with the slaves when selecting a new accountant or slave driver, and he believed whatever the slaves would tell him so as not to irk them." Gilly rarely even visited the plantation. His successor, Jean Delribal, resorted to imprisoning slaves and using chains, whipping, and torture during his short tenure in 1773. The next attorney, François Bayon de Libertat (1772–1773, 1773–1789), has a better reputation, but he kept his predecessor's repressive apparatus intact. A later manager named Valsemey was fired in 1790 for using "so much harshness" that a slave died.[12]

These comments were all made by white attorneys, white managers, and white accountants, who only relayed bad news when they wanted to besmirch a rival. Dead slaves could tell no tales. Numbers, however, speak for themselves: life expectancy on the Bréda plantations was a measly thirty-seven. "A few were good," Louverture later wrote in reference to the planter class, "but most of them were truly tormentors."[13]

Louverture had to tread carefully when dealing with "big whites" like the Brédas and their attorneys, because hitting or killing a member of the elite was normally punished by mutilation and a painful death. Not all white employees were worthy of the same level of respect, however. In the colony were many "little whites," who eked out a modest existence because most of the jobs were done by slaves. Some of these white people descended from the pirates who had settled the colony in the mid-1600s, from indentured servants who had come in the late 1600s, or from the vagabonds and prostitutes who had been deported from France en masse in the early 1720s. Others were newer to Saint-Domingue, and more came every year. Most were wrenchingly poor.

To distinguish "big" from "little" whites, slaves also spoke of the "white whites," the rich planters who were the only true whites, and the "white negroes," who had nothing going for them except for the color of their skin. This imaginative slang is indicative of the extent to which race in early Saint-Domingue was defined not simply by biological traits, but also by social status. One could lose the prestige attached to whiteness by being poor; conversely, talented blacks like Louverture could raise their standing through financial success. There was hope still.[14]

The most fortunate of the "little whites" served as specialized workers on plantations. In Haut-du-Cap, a surgeon named Rousseau made regular rounds; an accountant named Valsemey did the books; a carpenter named Cusson helped with construction projects; and refiners named Dupont, Martissans, and Couture oversaw the sugar-making process. In contrast with the owners and managers of the Bréda plantations, with whom Louverture stayed in contact throughout the Revolution, Louverture never mentioned these employees in later years, presumably because he held them in low esteem.

Further down the social ladder, white society crawled with bandits, woodsmen, beggars, smugglers, prostitutes, professional gamblers, and other assorted riffraff whose restlessness would later help bring about the Revolution. Leaving aside the transient sailor community, with which Louverture had few contacts, members of the two colonial regiments were the largest component of the "little white" community in Saint-Domingue. Rank-and-file soldiers were so destitute that for extra pay they occasionally hired themselves out to the Brédas to mine rocks in the hills above the plantation. These men, who had sometimes been recruited against their will in France, toiled alongside African slaves and occasionally ran away with them.

In a curious reversal of roles, the rural police employed black freedmen to chase down white deserters. Once caught, these whites were treated little better than slave runaways. Pantaléon de Bréda Sr. once sentenced a deserter to be branded, to have his ears and nose cut, and to spend the rest of his life doing hard labor. The unfortunate soldier who endured that terrifying treatment truly deserved the moniker of "white negro."[15]

In the end, Louverture's experience of slavery was mixed. Growing up along the plain of Cap, the economic heart of the colony, he was keenly aware of the atrocities committed by judges and planters, but his privileged position as a creole slave spared him from the worst abuses. Slavery, as filtered through his personal experience, must have been less traumatic for him than it was for African-born field hands. This, or perhaps the terrorizing effect of the tortures he had witnessed, may explain why he played no apparent role in the first major labor disturbances that roiled the region of Cap from the 1750s.

FOUR

REVOLUTIONARY APPRENTICE
1757–1773

IT WAS SOMETIME during his teenage years in the 1750s that Toussaint Louverture learned how to ride a horse. According to the story, which we owe to his son Isaac, he taught himself by bravely jumping on an untamed stallion. Maybe he was trying to impress his father, as horse-breeding was a favored pastime of the Allada elite in Africa. After much bucking and neighing, Louverture ended on the grass with a broken femur, but his reputation was made. In time, his horsemanship would become legendary throughout the colony. This self-taught skill earned him the coveted position of caretaker of the plantation's oxen and mules, and ultimately coachman.[1]

The rest of Isaac's story is more surprising. One day, when the plantation attorney, Béagé, took one of the plantation's horses without notifying him, Louverture was so enraged that he cut the girth of the saddle and Béagé tumbled to the ground. Back on his feet, Béagé raised his walking stick high above his head. A defiant Louverture dared him to strike. Time stood still for an instant—until Béagé lowered his cane and left the scene. Hurting one's master was punishable by death under the Black Code, yet Louverture seems to have escaped punishment somehow.

Historians tend to emphasize the brutality and dehumanizing nature of the plantation system of Saint-Domingue. Many atrocities did take place—many were even perfectly legal under the Black Code—but such one-dimensional accounts overlook the extent to which slaves remained agents of their own destiny. As one pores over the day-to-day records of a plantation like Haut-du-Cap, one is amazed by the slaves' capacity to resist their supervisors in so many ways. Chattel they may have been; but human beings they remained, always.

The Haitian slave revolt that broke out in 1791 was described by white contemporaries as a surprise and an anomaly. Central to this argument was the claim that the slaves of Saint-Domingue were gentle beasts of burden who had proved singularly docile in comparison with their Jamaican brethren—and then somehow buckled and launched the most successful slave revolt in world history. The reality was quite different. There were prerevolutionary troubles in Saint-Domingue, as well as a pattern of day-to-day resistance that one can reconstruct by delving deep into plantation records.[2]

The slaves of Haut-du-Cap were a particularly unruly lot. "For many years the plantation has been known to be filled with very bad individuals," an attorney complained. His successor concurred: the slaves were "excessively lazy," he said. "The hamlet of Haut-du-Cap completely spoils them." The accountant agreed: "The workforce has long been infected by all sorts of vices." So did a later attorney, who wrote of the well-established "bad reputation" of the slaves of Haut-du-Cap.[3]

Geography was part of the reason. Located at the foot of the hill of Morne du Cap, on the road from the port of Cap to the plain of Cap, Haut-du-Cap stood at the junction of the colony's three worlds: the commercial centers of the coast, whose large free black population was independent-minded; the plantations of the plains and their slave networks; and the mountainous areas where runaways would go to hide. By visiting the Brédas' sister plantations in Plaine-du-Nord, or spending time on nearby estates to recover from disease or learn a trade, Bréda slaves made valuable contacts: this is most likely how Louverture got to know Jeannot Bullet, the slave of the brother-in-law of a Bréda attorney, who later became one of the leading figures of the Haitian slave revolt.[4]

Slave resistance could take many forms. Slow work and sabotage were relatively safe, as long as one played the expected role of the faithful but foolish slave. Louverture, who was described as loyal and obedient in plantation records, played that game exceedingly well and developed a talent for deceit (what Haitians call "intellectual maroonage") that would serve him well during the Revolution.[5]

Physical resistance was a much graver transgression, but the Brédas, who were legally responsible for any tort caused to a third party, occasionally protected the perpetrator when the victim was not a "big white": Pantaléon de Bréda Sr. once refused to punish a slave who had almost killed a white surgeon. The fact that Pantaléon Jr. spent the bulk of his life overseas also gave his slaves some degree of immunity, since he expected to be consulted before a manager inflicted any life-threatening punishment, and contacting him took time.[6]

The harsh penalties specified by the Black Code no doubt terrified the slaves, but they were not cowed by them entirely. Acts of resistance included the lynching of two royal executioners in Haut-du-Cap in the 1770s, both of them at the hand of local slaves. Louverture must have witnessed the second incident, because it took place just outside the Bréda plantation. Years before the Haitian Revolution, the Bréda slaves were already fighting back.[7]

Louverture was a cautious man who normally avoided opposing authority too overtly, but his emotions occasionally got the better of him. Around 1757, when he was just fourteen, he entered into a brawl with a young white man named Ferret who had insulted him. Louverture fought back, and "Ferret got the worst of it," Isaac later reported. Amazingly, Louverture seems to have escaped punishment that time, just as he did when he unhorsed the attorney Béagé.[8]

Louverture's teenage years were awkward and uncertain times. France and Britain were in the midst of the Seven Years' War (1756–1763), a global battle for colonial supremacy that did not go well for France. In a few years, Britain took Guadeloupe, Martinique, and eventually Québec, as well as French outposts in India and Senegal. Saint-Domingue itself faced a possible invasion when a British fleet threatened the port of Cap.

It was in this tense context that in May 1757 a slave on another Saint-Domingue plantation, owned by the Lavauds, revealed a startling secret: the recent death of his mistress was no accident; she had been poisoned by her domestics. The royal prosecutor found it hard to determine the poisoners' motives, because, "aside from a few negresses, they ferociously withstood bouts of torture without confessing to anything," but his unyielding efforts eventually uncovered a support network reaching all the way to Cap thirty miles away, where a free black had supplied the poison. Arrests led to more torture, more denunciations, and more arrests. Dozens of planter deaths were reclassified as possible murders, and authorities estimated that the poisoners had killed up to 6,000 slaves as well. Far from being an anomaly, the use of poison was apparently rampant among the slaves of northern Saint-Domingue.[9]

Slaves were supposed to be meek and brutish: What, authorities wondered, could drive their animus? Because many planters had been assassinated by the very slaves whom they had promised to free in their wills, authorities concluded that the poisoners simply wished to hasten the dates of their liberation and that they lacked a political agenda. But some fretful planters suspected a far more ambitious plot to kill all whites in Saint-Domingue and seize control of the colony.

The evidence, which was obtained under torture according to the standard practices of prerevolutionary French justice, was far from conclusive. It is not even certain that poison was actually involved, because royal investigators tested the alleged poison on slave convicts and they survived. The spike in mortality among slaves coincided with a British naval blockade that had been compounded by a drought that caused severe food shortages and forced inhabitants to eat tainted meat and flour. In this context, the poison scare of 1757 may simply have been an episode of mass hysteria caused by societal stress.[10]

A different perspective emerges in the deathbed confessions of convicted slaves. The mysterious powders were not poison at all but religious artifacts, they said: the ground bones of unbaptized children, holy water, a crucifix, and nails that had been put into a cloth packet. Holy men had sold the packets to the slaves to serve as protective talismans. They had also organized ceremonies (known as "devil-making") to feed and then "awake" them. The most successful sorcerers were believed to be able to talk to the talismans and the spirits they embodied, which gave them unfathomable magical powers.[11]

This parallel hierarchy of underground religious societies had been operating under the nose of French authorities for years. The leader of the underground movement was a man known as Makandal, a Kreyòl term meaning "sorcerer" or "talisman." Makandal had been a slave himself, toiling on a sugar plantation before losing his hand in a mill accident and running away. For ten years he had been able to hide from authorities: other slaves were deathly afraid of his abilities and dared not denounce him. It was only in 1758 that the French finally managed to capture Makandal, interrogate him, and try him in court.

Makandal was publicly tortured so as to force him to reveal the name of his accomplices. Then, according to his sentence, he had to "make amends, wearing only a shirt . . . in front of the parish church . . . while bearing signs on his front and back inscribed *seducer, blasphemer, poisoner*." He would then be burned alive.[12]

Makandal's final moments proved memorable. As the flames closed in on him, he managed to break his ties in a desperate, superhuman effort. The slaves in the audience, who thought that Makandal had the ability to transform himself into a mosquito at will, gasped "Makandal is free!" A riot seemed near. Authorities cleared the plaza to restore order, forced Makandal back onto the fire, and executed him as planned, but many slaves did not witness the moment of his death and remained convinced that he had flown away unscathed. Proof of Makandal's handiwork came later that year, when the *intendant* (the official who had overseen the investigation) suddenly died, as did his successor. For decades thereafter, slaves whispered that Makandal would return one day to free them— and in at least one sense, he did: mosquito-borne tropical diseases were a main cause of France's defeat during the Haitian Revolution.[13]

The poison scare and the hunt for Makandal must have made a deep impression on the young Louverture. Makandal's original plantation in Limbé was just a few miles from Haut-du-Cap; his roaming grounds as a runaway likely included the hills of Morne du Cap above the plantation. It is even possible that Louverture, who was fifteen years old at the time, attended Makandal's January 1758 execution, which took place just outside the Catholic church that he normally attended. The following months and years were also hard to ignore. Chastened by the episode, French authorities created new regulations limiting slaves' ability to travel without a pass; to bear arms, even to protect livestock; to buy medicine for their masters; or to earn cash on the side. All of these things had been tolerated before.

French officials were not the only ones to be afraid of Makandal's second coming: Louverture developed such a lasting horror of poison during the Makandal conspiracy that four decades later, as governor of Saint-Domingue, he had all his meals monitored for fear that a rival might murder him. He was not one for magic tricks and Vodou rituals, even in the name of freedom.

Short of outright revolt, the most effective form of resistance was to become a maroon, a term derived from the Spanish word for a wild animal (*cimarrón*) that was used to describe slave runaways. The Black Code punished maroonage harshly (branding for a first offense, hamstringing for a second, and death for a third), but such punishments were later lessened to hard labor or prison time. Some slaves, accustomed to the hardships of plantation life, viewed the latter "as a time of rest rather than punishment." Cases of maroonage were accordingly numerous, so much so that a rural police force, composed primarily of free people of color, was set up in 1721 specifically to catch runaways. Even then, there were enough maroons around Cap for a section of the local newspaper to deal exclusively with runaway notices.[14]

The Bréda plantation in Haut-du-Cap was particularly prone to maroonage. "I don't know what to do with four young creole slaves from this plantation," complained an attorney. "When they are not enchained, they run away." A grove of banana trees was a favorite escape route. The hills of Morne du Cap, which abutted the back of the plantation, also made for an easy hideaway. One Bréda runaway, who bore the unusual name of Sans Souci (literally, "no worries"), may have been the same Sans Souci who later led a large rebel group during the Revolution, in which case he and Louverture would have been old acquaintances.[15]

The freedom trail could reach quite far. One Bréda runaway made it all the way to Port-au-Prince; others joined autonomous maroon communities in Saint-Domingue's interior, or, more frequently, crossed the border into Santo Domingo (now the Dominican Republic) to claim asylum. The French negotiated an extradition treaty with Spain in 1776–1777 to curb the practice, but Santo Domingo's reputation as a safe haven was sufficiently well established that many rebels, Louverture included, sought refuge there when the Haitian Revolution broke out. Even more troublesome were the runaways who stayed close to their plantation of origin and, like Makandal, stirred trouble among the enslaved workforce.[16]

Slave runaways foreshadowed the Haitian Revolution in many ways, but they did not yet have a political agenda. They hailed from a world in which slavery was an established part of life on both sides of the Atlantic, so imagining that free labor could be the norm would have required a complete change of paradigm. In Haut-du-Cap, slaves did not flee their plantations to bring slavery to its knees—a ludicrous and even unthinkable idea at the time—but to protest excessive punishments or the lack of food. They then returned to work after they had obtained what they sought. The practice became systematic under the tenure of the attorney Gilly in 1764–1772, when slaves became used to "running away together as soon as [their masters tried] to punish them," in order to put pressure on their overseers and obtain better work conditions. They had discovered the ultimate French institution: the strike.[17]

After Gilly's death in 1772, the attorney's position was briefly held by his protégé François Bayon de Libertat. But Bayon made the mistake of overspending on new buildings without seeking prior permission from the absentee owner, who sacked him in April 1773, and another attorney named Delribal took over. Delribal was convinced that his predecessors had been far too lax, and that it was time to restore discipline. Events gave him an opportunity to showcase his determination. A cattle epidemic had just begun to sweep through the plantations of the plain of Cap, killing dozens of mules, oxen, and cows on the Haut-du-Cap plantation. Veterinarians attributed the deaths to some previously unknown disease, but Delribal, drawing from the Makandal precedent, blamed poison instead. He arrested the slave in charge of the mill's mules, Louis, another slave named Jean-Baptiste, and the sugar refiner Ouanou. He then tortured them to force them to confess that foul play was involved.

A distraught Louis cut his own throat with a broken bottle, but his suicide attempt and the lack of evidence did not discourage Delribal.

He built a private prison on the Haut-du-Cap estate, began to threaten more arrests, and wrote to the absentee owner to let him kill one slave as an example. This must have been a terrifying period for the slaves of Haut-du-Cap. Years later, during the Revolution, one of the rebels' first demands was the abolition of private prisons like the one set up by Delribal. Louverture's name, strangely, is not mentioned in surviving documents, but he must have followed the events closely because cattle and horses were his area of expertise.[18]

Under the Black Code, victims of egregious planter misconduct were supposed to appeal to royal authorities, who would then prosecute the planter on their behalf. But recent attempts by neighboring slaves to do just that had shown that it was almost impossible to overcome the pro-planter bias of the courts (for one thing, slaves could not legally take the witness stand). Slaves typically lost their cases and were sent back to their home plantations to endure whatever vengeance their owners saw fit to inflict. So the Bréda slaves tried a different technique: in September 1773, twenty-five of them absconded, and then appealed to relatives of the Brédas who lived in the area.[19]

Their timing was good. The flight of so many slaves was a major financial blow. Production plummeted, and Delribal, for all his tough talk, had to spare the runaways when they returned as a group in October 1773. Labor frictions were still far from over: one month later, when Delribal ordered a slave whipped for stealing sugar, thirty-six more slaves ran away.

Delribal's tumultuous tenure ended a month after that, when he received news from France that Pantaléon de Bréda Jr. had fired him after just a few months in office—not for brutalizing the slaves, but for his poor financial performance (Pantaléon Jr. had just purchased an expensive residence in Paris and urgently needed cash). François Bayon de Libertat, who had kept the absentee owner informed of his rival's misdeeds throughout the crisis, got his old job back; it is even possible that Bayon had egged on the slaves behind the scenes. Bayon then simply waited until the cattle epidemic died out in 1775.[20]

Historians usually describe Bayon as a gentle master, because Louverture wrote that "his workers loved him like a Father, and in return he treated them with untold kindness." Bayon did treat elite slaves well, which may explain Louverture's fond recollections, but his behavior toward field hands was little better than Delribal's. Like his predecessor, he had to contend with episodic strikes from a slave workforce that was anything but submissive (one Bréda slave was even caught with a loaded gun). Like his predecessor, he employed fear to quell unrest. He shackled troublesome slaves with an iron boot, a kind of metallic brace that made it impossible to bend one's legs, and he kept troublemakers locked up in a small cell for months like some badly behaving dog. Louis and Ouanou, the two slaves abused by Delribal in 1773, spent part of 1775 there. This must have been a trying experience in a tropical climate, and Louis passed away after a four-month stint in the cell. Bayon expressed some regret for his death, but only because Louis had "talent" as a sugar refiner, and his death was a financial setback. He mentioned the death of older slaves with barely disguised glee: too weak to do much work, "they had become a burden." Such was the "kindness" of Bayon.[21]

How much did Louverture involve himself in the various forms of resistance employed by the slaves of prerevolutionary northern Saint-Domingue, both big and small—specifically the Makandal conspiracy in the 1750s and the strike against Delribal in the 1770s? There is no firm evidence tying him to either incident, probably because the first was too closely associated with Vodou, and the second entailed too much physical risk. Instead, he kept his distance and watched on like some apprentice revolutionary learning his trade. He was by nature a cautious man—especially now that he had a family to care for.

FIVE

FAMILY MAN
1761–1785

A SOMBER CEREMONY took place in the swamp of La Fossette, a short distance from the Bréda plantation in Haut-du-Cap, on November 17, 1785: the funeral of a young man named Toussaint, who had just died at the age of twenty-four. His brother Gabriel Toussaint followed the procession. Funerals of prominent slaves were important affairs, possibly because Haitian folklore held that the dead haunted their relatives as zombies if they were not properly buried. "A considerable crowd of African slaves accompany their [deceased] comrades to the cemetery," described a chronicler. "Women sing and clap their hands, followed by the dead, and then the negroes. A negro marches by the coffin and regularly hits a drum in a gloomy manner."[1]

The white priest likely grumbled about having to walk all the way from his church in Cap to the new cemetery of La Fossette in the outskirts of town (the previous cemetery had been unhealthily but conveniently located downtown). But there was no time to lose: in keeping with Caribbean practices, where the warm weather did not allow for extended mourning periods, the young Toussaint was lowered into his grave just hours after he died. Priests usually kept religious rituals to a minimum because authorities paid them no extra fee for black funerals, but perhaps the priest made an exception on that day because the father of the deceased was very well known to him. He was one of his most devout parishioners and a muleteer on the nearby Bréda plantation. His name was Toussaint Louverture.

The burial certificate, tucked away in the French colonial archives in Aix-en-Provence, came as a surprise when it first surfaced in 2011, because neither Toussaint Jr. nor his brother Gabriel Toussaint were known to scholars. Also surprising was the identity of their mother, a black woman named Cécile who was identified as Louverture's wife. For two centuries, historians had only known of another wife, named Suzanne, and two other sons who were born at a much later date. This first family, suddenly rescued from history's void, cast new light on an overlooked but central facet of Louverture's personality.[2]

Saint-Domingue was a terrible place to raise a family. The imbalanced sex ratio made it difficult for men to find a spouse, and disease, overwork, natural disasters, and war meant that deaths far exceeded births. An owner's death could break apart one's family at any time; a master could rape one's wife and daughters with impunity. In this unfavorable context, most male slaves died alone and childless. And yet Louverture managed to marry not once, but twice. He had biological children, illegitimate children, a stepson, an adopted daughter, a stepmother, two biological parents, and two surrogate parents, along with a bewildering collection of nephews, siblings, goddaughters, and in-laws. This sprawling family network allowed him to cope with slavery; much later, it would also form the backbone of his revolutionary regime.

Marriage—a difficult proposition in any slave system—was a rarity among the slaves of Saint-Domingue. The first obstacle was simple arithmetic. African traders preferred to sell their female slaves in Africa or the Middle East, where they were sought after as domestics and concubines, so the majority of the slaves purchased by French traders were males (179 men for every 100 women), who were better suited for the backbreaking toil of the sugar plantations anyway. The ratio was slightly less lopsided on old plantations, where births evened out the population over time; but the Haut-du-Cap plantation's unusually high rate of deaths and slave purchases meant that it still had 152 men for every 100 women as late as 1785. In much of Africa, it was a sign of social success for a man to marry several brides. In Saint-Domingue, polyandry would have made more sense.[3]

The problem was compounded by some masters' blanket opposition to marriage (which had a way of complicating the sale of family units), as well as by reluctance on the part of male slaves to bind themselves to a "form of servitude that is even more onerous than the one they were born into" (or so judged a misogynistic Jesuit author). By choice or by necessity, many slaves, especially field slaves from Africa, entered into temporary informal unions instead of church marriages—that is, if they could find a partner at all.[4]

Louverture distinguished himself from his peers as he embraced the European model of a formal marriage sanctioned by the Catholic Church. Toussaint Jr. was listed as legitimate in his 1785 death certificate, so Louverture must have married Cécile in or before 1761, when he was just eighteen. We know very little of his first wife except that she had a brother, Tony, who was "given to drinking and lazy." Like Louverture, he was a coachman on the Bréda plantation.[5]

Motherhood was not an attractive proposition for slave women like Cécile. Giving birth meant bringing yet another slave into the world. The Black Code specified that family units had to be kept together, but experience taught otherwise. In any event, masters made few efforts to encourage natural reproduction; concluding that it was cheaper to import a ready-made worker from Africa than to feed an infant slave to adulthood, they usually gave no time off to pregnant or nursing mothers. In this context, why add child-care duties to one's long hours in the fields for the sole purpose of enriching one's master? Infanticide and abortion were disturbingly common, and the fertility rate of Dominguan slaves was among the lowest in the world (a quarter of the women never even became pregnant).

Only as the century progressed and the price of imported slaves rose did some masters begin to pursue pro-natal policies to save money. On their plantations, the Brédas began to exempt women from field labor after they gave birth to five children as an incentive to procreate. Results were mixed. "Your negresses in Plaine-du-Nord have not had children for years," reported a Bréda attorney, "but in Haut-du-Cap there are always a few." Two slave mothers in Haut-du-Cap—Hélène and Marguerite—had five children or more by 1778. Another twelve babies were born on the plantation from 1780 to 1785, most of them to domestics and specialized slaves like Louverture, leading the accountant to grumble that "the master house looks like a nursery."[6]

It was in this uncertain environment that the young couple then known as Toussaint and Cécile Bréda began a family of their own. They had three children together, two boys and a girl. The oldest, named Toussaint like his proud father, was born in 1761. Later came Gabriel Toussaint and a girl named Marie-Marthe (aka Martine). If one includes his later marriage and extramarital dalliances, Louverture fathered or adopted sixteen children during his life, an indication of his unusual social prominence. Tragically, he outlived eleven of them, starting with his first-born son, Toussaint Jr.[7]

Enslavement shaped every aspect of marriage and family life. Though masters could not have intercourse with their female slaves under the Black Code, the clause was routinely evaded in a world where white women were few and slave women vulnerable. "Nothing more common than the debauchery that exists between whites and the women of color, both mulattresses and negresses," noted a visitor.[8]

Among the victims was Louverture's daughter Marie-Marthe, who was probably no more than a teenager when she gave birth to a mixed-race

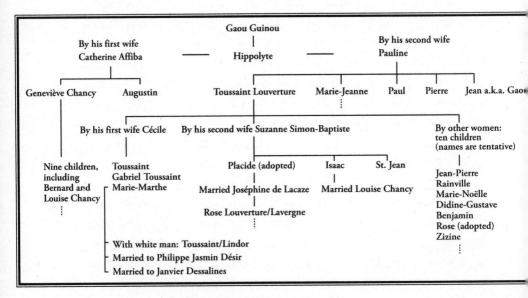

Toussaint Louverture's family tree. Figure by the author.

son whom she named Toussaint after her father and two brothers. Details about the child's background, starting with his white father's identity, are not known to us (the Bréda attorney Bayon de Libertat, whose wife had extended stays in France in the 1770s, is a good candidate); the child's very existence was only discovered in 2013.[9]

So common was interracial intercourse in Saint-Domingue that the free population of color was almost as large as the white population by the time the Haitian Revolution began. In addition to Marie-Marthe's son, there were three other mixed-race children on the Bréda plantation in the 1770s: two boys and a girl. The girl was Louverture's goddaughter. Four mixed-race domestics from other plantations later took up residence in the master's house as well. All of them were living proof of the unchecked power of the white personnel on the plantations.

Contemporary white planters liked to describe themselves as the victims of conniving colored seductresses eager to appropriate their manhood, but it is difficult to describe the union between Marie-Marthe and her sexual partner as anything other than statutory rape, given her young age and the unequal relationship between them. Toussaint's grandchild must have experienced his share of hardships as well: white women could be quite cruel to mixed-race slaves, who were daily reminders of their husbands' philandering ways.

Male slaves were indirect victims, as they had no way of fighting back if a master violated their wives or daughters. Louverture never spoke of his daughter and her mixed-race child, but one suspects that he shared the feelings of a fellow coachman and revolutionary leader who railed against the white planters who "soil our daughters after they barely emerge from childhood." Such powerlessness was emasculating. Many years passed before Louverture finally got his revenge: as governor of Saint-Domingue, he made it his habit to use as mistresses the wives of white planters.[10]

Rather than abort or kill their child, some female slaves chose to make the best of a bad situation. On the Bréda plantation in Plaine-du-Nord, the white manager Rouillan was known for his many liaisons with enslaved women, whom he would then reward with extra rations of food. He also offered to buy and free a mixed-race son, though Pantaléon Jr. demanded such a high price to punish him for impregnating one of his slaves that it took the manager six years to gather the sum. The sugar refiner Rousseau also bought and freed his mixed-race son. In the twisted world of plantation slavery, rape could result in freedom.

Not so with Louverture's daughter. Her white partner took no apparent step to free their child, so it was only years later, after Marie-Marthe married a freedman and obtained her own freedom, that she was finally able to purchase and free the mixed-race boy named after Toussaint Louverture.

Before 1492, Caribbean islands like Saint-Domingue had been a Garden of Eden where contagious diseases were virtually unknown. Their geographic isolation and the dearth of domesticated animals had protected them, but all this changed when the Columbian Exchange introduced all the diseases of the Old World. Within fifty years, most of the Taino Amerindians were wiped out by Eurasian diseases like measles and whooping cough. By the late 1600s, mosquito-borne African diseases like yellow fever and malaria had also found a congenial environment in the swampy plains where sugarcane grew best, making Saint-Domingue very unhealthy for whites as well. Smallpox, so feared in West Africa that it was worshiped as a god, also took its toll: it hit the Haut-du-Cap plantation in 1772 and returned in 1778, 1785, and 1787.

Though newly imported African slaves were less susceptible to tropical fevers than Europeans, their death rate was still estimated at 7 to 14 percent a year. On the Haut-du-Cap plantation, 95 slaves died in 1774–1785 out of a total workforce of 130 to 150 slaves. That meant a 70 percent turnover in a decade's time. Only Caribbean-born Creoles like Louverture, who had been exposed to the colony's deadly microbiological brew all their lives, stood a fighting chance of making it to old age.[11]

The hostile environment of the Caribbean did not make the survivors' lives easy. Each year brought its cataclysm. An earthquake roiled Port-au-Prince in 1770, then Cap in 1785; hurricanes ravaged the colony in 1765, 1772, 1775, 1780, and 1785; the Bréda plantation always seemed to be fighting a drought or a flood. Man-made disasters filled in the gaps, as France and Britain waged seemingly continuous wars for much of the eighteenth century.

Even when accounting for births, the natural growth rate was a *negative* 1 to 5 percent per year, by different estimates, so the slave population only grew because of massive imports from Africa. "More [African slaves] are bought every year to make up for the mortality rate, which is considerable," lamented the accountant of Haut-du-Cap. Louverture barely got a chance to know many of the incoming slaves before they headed for the cemetery. Sixteen Alladas were brought to the plantation in 1774, speaking the Fon language of his parents; six were dead within six months, so twelve Congolese were purchased in 1775. Sixty-four percent of Haut-du-Cap's slaves were African-born by 1785, the highest percentage in the area. As a result, many of the slaves of Haut-du-Cap had only been in Saint-Domingue for a few years by the time the Haitian Revolution began in 1791, which helps explain why creole old-timers like Louverture took over most of the leadership roles.[12]

Two names stand out in this litany of deaths. In April 1774, the Bréda attorney notified the absentee owner of the deaths of "the black woman Pauline and her husband Hippolyte, both of them afflicted with chest disease. They left five creole children." Louverture's parents had died within three months of one another. As the oldest child, Louverture, who had just turned thirty, found himself in charge of the family's future, which included four siblings (two of them still breastfed), as well as a wife and children of his own.[13]

No doubt heartbroken by the loss of his mother and father, Louverture coped by adopting two older slaves as surrogate parents. "The good and virtuous Pélagie" became like a "second mother" to him. Like his biological mother, she hailed from the Aja tribe. Plantation records indicate that she was "robust and dance[d] well, according to the custom of her native country," and that she was a laundress and caregiver.[14]

Louverture's surrogate father, Pierre Baptiste, worked as a carpenter and gatekeeper on the plantation. He was also Louverture's godfather, the father of his second wife, and a man he deeply respected—so much in fact that many historians have mistakenly described him as Louverture's biological father. According to a family tradition, Baptiste "knew French and some Latin . . . and even a bit of geometry," which he had learned from the Jesuits. He passed on some of his knowledge to his godson, a precious gift at a time when slave literacy was a rarity (only 31 percent of black freedmen rich enough to use a notary were literate). But Louverture's writing skills remained basic until the Revolution, which deeply troubled him. Of all the indignities he had suffered during his years of enslavement, his belated education was the one he mentioned most often.[15]

Baptiste remained an important father figure throughout Louverture's life. He lived through most of the Haitian Revolution, eventually dying in 1802 at the remarkable age of 105—a survivor, just like Louverture.

In the eighteenth century, friendships were at once fewer and more meaningful. Louverture spent decades in close proximity with his fellow slaves and family members, rarely traveling more than a few miles from his home. In the process, he developed a close-knit network that served as a mutual aid society when he was a slave, and that later, during the Revolution, became his political base.

Louverture's church family was part and parcel of this relationship network. In 1768, five years after the Jesuits were expelled from Saint-Domingue, the Capuchin order officially replaced them at the head of the Catholic Church in northern Saint-Domingue. The Capuchins were often mocked in the colony for their loose sexual and financial mores, but they were fairly progressive on racial matters. Contrary to the Dominicans and the Jesuits, they did not own plantations (though they employed enslaved domestics). They also continued the Jesuit practice of celebrating special Masses for blacks in the Cap area. Slaves who, like Louverture, were baptized and married formed the most elite group and sat in a special section of the nave. Six of them even led others in prayers under a second skin of cassocks and surplices. Louverture, who may already have dabbled in missionary work under the Jesuits, was presumably one of them, because a fellow revolutionary later described him as an "old Capuchin." Slaves who were merely baptized sat in a different section of the church, and catechumens in yet another; runaways and abortionists knelt at the church's threshold as a form of penance, as if crimes against one's master were also crimes against God. Unbaptized slaves were denied entry into the church altogether.[16]

For Louverture, Sunday rituals were familiar and comforting. "On Sundays and holidays, we would go to Mass, my wife, I, and my relatives," he later recalled. "Back to our home, after a pleasant meal, we would spend the rest of the day together, which we would finish with a prayer." His involvement in the Church provided some solace in the difficult circumstances in which he lived, but it also allowed him to bypass the planter hierarchy and form independent bonds with black parishioners and white priests. He made so many allies in that manner that many priests sided with him when the slave revolt broke out in 1791.[17]

Two lists of the slaves of Haut-du-Cap, dated April and December 1785, are our main source on the identity of the people who toiled on the Bréda plantation alongside Louverture in the first decades of his life. In keeping with colonial practices, their names were drawn from the Bible, Greco-Roman antiquity, and Africa in accordance with each slave's social status. The man who worked with Louverture as a carriage driver bore the Christian name of André, while their assistants had French nicknames, including Janvier and Jeudi ("January" and "Thursday"). The sugar makers to whom they delivered sugarcane stalks also had Christian names, such as Laurent and Augustin, and proud classical names, such as César and Alexandre. Many field hands had to content themselves with African names, like Azor and Zaïre.[18]

The April 1785 roster gives us little information beyond each slave's age, ethnicity, and occupation, but the December roster, discovered in 2013, also describes each slave's idiosyncrasies, bringing out something of their individual characters—albeit from the perspective of their overseers. We thus learn that Louverture's colleague André was "debauched, libertine, plagued with venereal disease, insolent and dangerous" (or so thought the accountant who annotated the roster); that Janvier was "prone to drinking rum, sleepy and lazy"; and that Jeudy "wears irons that are wounding him and is a bad subject living of thievery."

Other acquaintances of Louverture leap from the page, from Rémy (Congolese, nineteen, "rather good subject") to Flore (Congolese, seventeen, "maliciously maintains an ulcer on her leg" so as to be assigned to the chicken coop in lieu of the master's house, presumably because she was getting too much attention there). The accountant often emphasized the slaves' flaws, but he described Louverture as a "sweet" and "intelligent subject, knowing how to care for injured animals." The future leader of the Haitian Revolution, on the surface at least, was a model worker.[19]

For Louverture, these were not mere names but coworkers, friends, neighbors, and cousins. These were the people who greeted him in the morning as he left his home; these were the people who shared stories with him at night. Many were relatives. His godfather's progeny included the laundress Suzanne (whom Louverture later married) and the mason Gilles, himself a father of six. Louverture's two goddaughters were the nieces of his colleague André.

Many of the relatives of Louverture listed on the roster later became important figures in his regime. His brother Paul, listed as a personal servant and cook ("good domestic, sweet and obedient"), later became a general. His other brother, Pierre, listed as a field hand, died fighting by his side in 1794. His nephew Moïse was a mason apprentice and later became a general. Charles Bélair (usually described as Louverture's nephew) was a shepherd and later became a general. Louverture's illegitimate son Jean-Pierre served as colonel, his stepson Placide as sublieutenant.[20]

Other relatives, not living on the plantation, included Louverture's brother-in-law Claude Martin (later a colonel), his step-nephew Bernard Chancy (an aide-de-camp), his step-nephew Jacques Chancy (a captain), and his cousin Félix (a battalion chief). Step-nieces also married into the families of the revolutionary generals André Vernet, Jean Villatte, and Jean-Jacques Dessalines. These family ties were not coincidental: in the unstable context of a slave revolt, Louverture preferred to rely on people he had known for decades. "These are the only ones I can trust," he later wrote.[21]

One historian has compared the leaders of the American Revolution to a "band of brothers": so it was with Haitian revolutionaries, most of whom, in the northern province, were related by blood or marriage to Toussaint Louverture. By cultivating this network of relationships, he was not just establishing himself as a leading figure of the Haut-du-Cap plantation: he was unwittingly laying the groundwork for the revolution to come.[22]

SIX

FREEDMAN
c. 1772–1779

ON APRIL 7, 1776 (a Sunday), a mixed-race baby girl was baptized under the name of Marie-Josèphe in the church of Le Borgne in northern Saint-Domingue. Her godfather was Toussaint Louverture. A church attendant had to stand at the font in his stead because Le Borgne is thirty-five miles distant from Haut-du-Cap and Louverture could not make it to the ceremony, but being asked to serve as godfather was an honor that reflected Louverture's piety and his high standing in the black community. A few years later in the church of Cap, he again took on the role of a godfather, this time for Marie-Josèphe's black half-sister Marie-Egyptienne. Both of Louverture's goddaughters were slaves on the Bréda plantation of Haut-du-Cap, as was their mother.[1]

The original baptismal record of Marie-Josèphe was lost during the Haitian Revolution, but a copy survived in the French colonial archives in Aix-en-Provence, where it was discovered in 1977 (and then, apparently, lost as well). Two letters in the document startled the researchers who first encountered it: Louverture's first name was followed by the mention "n.l.," short for *nègre libre* (free negro), indicating that he was no longer a slave by the time of Marie-Josèphe's baptism. This was the first conclusive evidence that, fifteen years before the outbreak of the great slave revolt of 1791, the godfather of the Haitian Revolution was legally free—or at least claimed to be.

Manumissions (the legal term for freeing a slave) were relatively rare in Saint-Domingue, so the chance of being freed over the course of a lifetime was less than 1 percent. Most of these manumissions benefited a planter's sexual partner and their mixed-race offspring, as was the case when Geneviève, Louverture's stepsister from his father's first marriage, married a white planter in southern Saint-Domingue and obtained official freedom papers in 1776. By contrast, male manumissions were tied to exceptional deeds like military service, so black men represented less than 11 percent of all manumissions even though they formed the majority of the slave population. Louverture had won the lottery.[2]

Louverture's release from bondage was surely one of the most meaningful events in his life, and yet it remains shrouded in mystery. Who freed him? When? Why? Answering these questions is exceedingly difficult because he found it politically convenient during the Haitian Revolution to hide that he had been a freedman for decades, so as to preserve his credibility as the champion of the enslaved masses. "Twenty years ago the heavy burden of Slavery was lifted from my shoulders": this passage in a confidential 1797 report to the French government was the only reference he ever made to his liberation.[3]

The most likely scenario for Louverture's manumission is provided by a family tradition reporting that "a rigorous punishment convinced Toussaint to flee his earliest masters." He may have timed his escape for the summer of 1772, since one of the Bréda attorneys, Gilly, died in August of that year, and for a time no one was officially in charge in Haut-du-Cap. That September, a five-foot-tall, thirty-year-old creole black man named Toussaint was listed as a runaway in Cap, where he had lived for two months while pretending to be free.[4]

It was difficult for Louverture to remain in hiding when his name appeared in runaway ads in the local paper. He was soon captured and sent back to his plantation. Gilly's successor as attorney of Haut-du-Cap, François Bayon de Libertat, could have inflicted a severe punishment, but he recognized Louverture's potential and instead offered him a promotion. After Louverture was recaptured, the family tradition goes on to explain, "Bailly [Bayon] bought him and made him his coachman," and then manumitted him. "My former boss, the virtuous Bayon," Louverture later explained in the 1797 report, "decided to fulfill his duties toward humankind rather than benefit from the labor of a wretched Being." The event must have taken place between the beginning of Bayon's tenure in 1772 and the baptism of Marie-Josèphe in 1776, by which point Louverture described himself as free.[5]

As best we can tell, this is how history's most famous slave earned his freedom: by forging a special bond with a "big white." Manumissions often functioned as motivation, implanting in the most loyal slaves some hope of being freed if they collaborated with the plantation system. This would explain Louverture's closeness to the planter class and his political moderation just as, coincidentally, authorities were trying to reduce the number of manumissions and the rest of the slave population was becoming increasingly desperate as a result.

An important question remains: What happened to the evidence? No official manumission deed (or reference to one) has been found, which is surprising, because the manumission process was very formal and should have left a lengthy paper trail. It would seem, then, that Louverture was never formally freed in the manner required by law. Perhaps Bayon wished to avoid paying the manumission tax, which was raised to 1,000 colonial livres in 1775. Perhaps he had defrauded Louverture's legal owner, Pantaléon de Bréda Jr., who lived in Paris and was apparently never informed that Louverture was no longer his personal property. Neither possibility should surprise us: Bayon was a shifty individual who was eventually sacked for embezzling plantation funds and slaves.[6]

As a result, instead of citing the specific date of his official manumission, as required by law, Louverture simply introduced himself as a "free negro" whenever his name appeared in church or notarial documents, as if he could become a freedman merely by asserting that he was one. Friendly notaries and church clerks went along with the deception, but only a manumission deed could prove one's freedom in court. This left Louverture in a precarious legal position. The governor could re-enslave a freedman if his owner had not followed the proper procedure. Nominally but not formally free, Louverture had not completely severed his ties to slavery.

Despite the lack of formal recognition, Louverture joined the community of free people of color in Saint-Domingue, which was unusually large by Caribbean standards. From 6,897 free people of color around the time of his manumission, the size of the community would jump to 27,548 by the time of the Haitian Revolution. By then free people of color were almost as numerous as whites (30,826), who had outnumbered them 20 to 1 just a century earlier (both groups were dwarfed by the enslaved population, which stood at 465,429 in 1789). By comparison, there were only 4,093 free people of color in British Jamaica, a colony that otherwise closely resembled Saint-Domingue.[7]

Just as there were "big whites" and "little whites," there were "big" and "little" free people of color. Some were the mixed-race descendants of white colonists whose skin color was described by a rich racial vocabulary, ranging from *mulâtre* (mulatto) to *quarteron* (quadroon) and *métif* (octoroon); others, such as Louverture, were blacks of pure African ancestry. Some came from families that had been free for several generations; others, including Louverture, had been freed during their own lifetimes, sometimes unofficially. Some had inherited plantations from their French fathers; Louverture and others owned little or nothing. A member of the plantation elite when he was a slave, Louverture now found himself at the lowest rung of the free community.

Collectively, free people of color claimed to own one-third of the plantations of Saint-Domingue. The figure was probably closer to 10 percent, but there is no doubt that they were active participants in the plantation economy. Like whites, they traded, owned, and exploited crops, land—and human beings.[8]

Louverture was typical in this regard. In or before 1776, he acquired a slave named Jean-Baptiste, a native of the West African coast.[9]

Louverture's slave-owning past came as a shock when it was first made public in 1977: How could the future leader of the Haitian Revolution have exploited slaves? The evidence is a bit less damning when set in its proper historical context. We only know of Jean-Baptiste because Louverture legally freed him so that he could marry. Louverture may have simply bought and then freed someone he cared about, a common practice among free people of color. The only mystery is why Louverture chose to free Jean-Baptiste, who had no known family tie to him, rather than his many relatives who were still enslaved. Perhaps Louverture owed a moral debt to Jean-Baptiste, who had been tortured by the attorney Delribal during the cattle epidemic of 1773, and may have protected him in some unknown way at the time.[10]

A freedman with limited financial resources, Louverture faced a moral dilemma that is unfathomable to us: Which slaves should he help free? A child or an old person? Both were relatively cheap to buy, but their freedom would be largely symbolic, because they did relatively little work and lived at the master's expense. Or a woman of childbearing age, who was far more expensive to free, because of a punitive manumission tax, but who would otherwise continue to produce enslaved children, because slavery was matrilineal?[11]

Aside from Jean-Baptiste, the first person Louverture bought was apparently his wife Cécile, whom he freed "so that the children to be born of their marriage could be free," according to a later account. Cécile immediately tried to buy the liberty of her brother Tony, a coachman on the Bréda plantation. She may also have bought a slave of her own.[12]

Cécile and Toussaint Louverture's children were next. Their daughter, Marie-Marthe, was married by 1779 to an affluent free black, who presumably bought her freedom if Louverture had not already done so. Their sons, Toussaint and Gabriel Toussaint, were freed sometime between 1778 and 1785.[13]

Louverture also had siblings and relatives to think about. His brothers Paul and Pierre were still listed as slaves on 1785 plantation registers, and they likely remained enslaved until the Haitian Revolution. But his sister, Marie-Jeanne, was not on the registers, so perhaps by then she was free. So was Marie-Rose, the mother of his goddaughters. Then, in 1789, Louverture arranged for his surrogate mother, Pélagie, to be freed. Ladies, as potential bearers of slaves, came first in his mind.[14]

Fully extirpating slavery from one's family tree was difficult. Although Louverture's daughter Marie-Marthe was free by 1779, her mixed-race son was not, because he had been born when she was still a slave. So in 1783 Marie-Marthe had to buy her own son and then petition to have him legally freed.[15]

Louverture also found time to think about his own financial future. In 1779, he bought a small lot in Haut-du-Cap. He was probably planning to raise crops to earn extra cash or even build a house of his own.[16]

Louverture's manumission was an opportunity for him to expand his personal network, which had once been limited to fellow slaves from the Bréda plantation but now came to encompass many free blacks from the Cap region. Every carriage ride was an opportunity for Bayon's coachman to broaden his horizons. Work, church, family, city: he gained friends in every venue.

The archives hint at some of the stops on Louverture's rides. His boss, Bayon, liked to dine at La Charité, a religious hospital that had a reputation for terrible care but great food, and Louverture was spotted serving guests at the main table. This is probably how he met the future revolutionary leader Georges Biassou, whose mother was enslaved at the hospital. One can almost picture the two revolutionaries-to-be whispering to one another in the courtyard while their masters sip postprandial liqueurs with the hospital's monks.[17]

Reconstructing Louverture's personal network in a more systematic manner is a difficult but not impossible task. Church and notarial records list witnesses, godparents, and business associates, so by sifting through old registers it is possible to identify the people known to Louverture, many of whom were destined for great things. The ties seem coincidental at first, but when all the index cards are pinned to the wall, they converge on one man who seems to appear, as if by magic, at the center of it all. One or two steps are usually enough to connect Louverture to every major revolutionary figure in the northern province.

Detailed maps and tax censuses of Cap also bring to life the city that Louverture visited countless times as Bayon's coachman before the Revolution, down to the address of many of his acquaintances. The layout of the streets has not changed in three hundred years, so one can literally walk in Louverture's footsteps, tax census in hand, and follow him as he built up his network.[18]

The diminutive town where Louverture's parents had landed on a slave ship in the 1740s was barely recognizable by the time Louverture

Map of Cap showing Louverture's possible itinerary while visiting the town in the late 1770s and 1780s (north is to the right). Drawn by the author after René Phelipeaux, "Plan de la ville du Cap Français et de ses environs" (1785), Caribbean Map Collection, University of Florida, Gainesville.

obtained his freedom in the 1770s. In thirty years, municipal authorities had raised and paved the streets, traced new squares, and erected public buildings and fountains. Because a fire had burned the original city to the ground, by law most houses in Cap were now made of stone (twice destroyed by an earthquake, Port-au-Prince was purposely rebuilt in wood and had a more ramshackle look).

During their visits to Cap, Louverture and Bayon would have approached the city from the south, leaving the cemetery of La Fossette (where Louverture's son was later buried) to their left and the swampy mouth of the Haut-du-Cap River (which served as a disposing ground for animal carcasses) to their right. That area remains so unappealing today that the slums of modern Cap are concentrated there. They then entered Cap proper through Espagnole Street, then and now the city's central thoroughfare. On their way, they passed by La Couronne Inn, whose chef was a free black named Henry Christophe, who later became one of Louverture's leading generals and a king of Haiti. Their association presumably went back to the 1770s, when Louverture first noted his potential while stopping at the inn.[19]

Espagnole Street was the widest and least shaded in Cap, so Bayon would have asked Louverture to hasten on to Montarcher Square, in the political center of Cap, to drop him off before it got too hot. Louverture liked to push his mounts hard (he purposely kept them half-tamed so that they would gallop faster) and was always happy to oblige; perhaps it was one of Louverture's joy rides that prompted the city of Cap to pass a municipal ordinance barring black coachmen from galloping inside city limits. From Montarcher Square, Bayon could walk up to the government house to his left to meet royal officials, or he could go down the street to his right to the office of Éloi-Michel Grimperel, his favorite notary.[20]

After leaving Bayon at the square, Louverture would have had a few hours to himself. Just opposite the square was the recently expanded theater of Cap. Acting was considered a "criminal profession" worthy of excommunication, and the theater was a raucous place known for its fistfights (a government clerk once bit the soldier who guarded the entrance). But it was also the focal point of the city's social life (the son of the king of England once attended a play), so Louverture, who could recite lines from *Othello* from memory, must have attended plays there. If nothing else, it gave him an opportunity to connect with friends and acquaintances.[21]

The most logical destination after leaving the theater was the church of Cap, three short blocks downhill on Notre Dame Street. It was a beautiful edifice rebuilt at great expense in 1772–1774 after an earthquake destroyed the previous building. Louverture was a frequent visitor, in part because Mass allowed him to hone his skills as a public speaker and to befriend parishioners and priests, which would serve him well during the Revolution.

Coming out of the church's dark recesses, Louverture would have stood in the midday glare at the south end of the Place d'Armes, the largest public square in town. He had no reason to linger on the plaza, where the poisoner Makandal had once been burnt alive, and where public executions of white criminals still took place regularly (black criminals were now executed on the market square, in keeping with a growing emphasis on racial segregation). These executions were not only gruesome but also rowdy and even dangerous: once in 1777, a criminal fought back, and the crowd sided with him. A riot ensued, and it was the executioner who died that day.[22]

From the church, Louverture could have crossed the Place d'Armes on his way to the arsenal and the neighborhood of Carénage, at the town's northern tip, or even trek all the way to Fort Picolet a few miles north of town, which is still standing and offers a beautiful panorama of the Bay of Cap. But he had no business in these elegant neighborhoods, where the presence of an unattached black man could attract unwelcome attention; nor would he have any desire to run into his old tormentor, Delribal, who managed a few houses nearby. Instead, he would most likely have turned around and headed south toward Cimetière Street, where the notary François Bordier often did legal work for Louverture and other free people of color.[23]

From Bordier's office it was only a short walk to the city's waterfront docks, where longshoremen unloaded cargo in a maelstrom of activity. "A jetty reclaimed from the sea extended quite far," marveled a visitor. "Storage houses on Capitaines Street were filled with the richest goods, and the amount of business done there defies description. One could see a forest of ships from the jetty, and the sea was covered with small craft

Street scene in Cap. From La Cauchie, *Un marché à Saint-Domingue* (c. 1800). Personal collection of the author.

loading and unloading them." But the scene's allure would have been lost on Louverture, who did not like ships, presumably because of his parents' traumatic experience during the Middle Passage.[24]

Heading away from the docks on Trois Chandeliers Street, Louverture would have passed by the house of Aaron Sasportas, the Jewish merchant who supplied food to the Haut-du-Cap plantation. It was probably there that Louverture first met Aaron's young son Isaac Sasportas, who later played a notable role as a radical firebrand during the Revolution. Farther down the street, Louverture must often have stopped at the house that stood at the corner of Trois Chandeliers and Vaudreuil streets: it was rented to Corneille Brelle, a white priest who later became a trusted confidant.[25]

Just across from Brelle's residence was the busy expanse of Clugny Square. First opened in 1764, then paved in 1781, it was (and remains) a sight to behold. Up to 15,000 people attended its market on Sundays. Meat, both butchered and live, fish, and countless other products were sold by black women who tried to lure passersby like Louverture with an inviting laugh. Perhaps it was on Clugny Square that Louverture first befriended Marie Mouton (aka Fanchette Estève), a black merchant who later became his mistress. Her common-law husband, Joseph Bunel (a French immigrant who also dabbled in commerce), later became Louverture's treasurer and diplomatic envoy.[26]

Moving away from the market's hustle and bustle, Louverture would likely have stopped in nearby Chantier Street at the home of Vincent Olivier, a centenarian who was the unofficial leader of the community of free people of color in the town. He did not live to see the Revolution, but he had many stories to tell, going back to the raid of Cartagena in 1697, at a time when Saint-Domingue was still a base for buccaneering expeditions, and where his bravery had earned him his freedom.[27]

Two blocks over, on Boucheries Street, lived another prominent free black named Blaise Bréda, who was very well known to Louverture. Like Louverture, Bréda was a freedman of Allada ancestry who had been a slave on the Bréda plantation. Freed earlier than Louverture, he already owned property worth as much as 50,000 livres, including two houses in Cap. He now bought slaves, sold and leased slaves, and hunted down the slaves who ran away from his home. But he also used his influence to facilitate manumissions, thus providing a blueprint as a financially successful black freedman who had not completely forgotten his roots.[28]

Just a block away, where St. Nicolas Street met Espagnole Street, lived another affluent free person of color, the building contractor Pierre-Guillaume Provoyeur, whom Louverture knew well because he often did construction work on the Haut-du-Cap plantation. But Provoyeur showed untoward interest in Louverture's wife, Cécile, in the late 1770s, so Louverture had every reason to quickly cross Espagnole Street to the black neighborhood of Little Guinea, in the highest part of town, where Cap's signature stone houses gave way to rickety wooden huts.[29]

For Louverture, always accustomed to being on his guard, Little Guinea was a different world. Whites were few and urban blacks were assertive: black freedmen alone represented 46 percent of the population, and even slaves could live quasi-independently, as long as they found employment and paid a monthly fee to rent their own bodies from their masters. It was likely in Little Guinea that Louverture first met César Thélémaque, a free black who lived in a house on Taranne Street, not far from a Masonic Lodge, and who later became the mayor of Cap during the Revolution.

On the way down from the Little Guinea neighborhood, wedged in between army barracks, lay the oddest street in Cap's orderly geography. Just one block long, it was nicknamed "Ha Street" by surprised pedestrians who ventured into it by mistake. There lived the freedman Jean Jasmin, who was revered in the free community for setting up a charity hospital for people of color. In the close-knit world of Cap's free population, where everyone was seemingly related to everyone else, Jean Jasmin was likely the adoptive father of Philippe Jasmin Désir, an affluent free black and Louverture's son-in-law.[30]

From street to street and block to block, in a few hours' time Louverture could have visited a dozen individuals known to have played a notable role in the Haitian Revolution. Many others lived nearby on plantations connected to the Brédas by business and family ties. In traditional accounts of the Revolution, it often seems as though rebel leaders pop up like rabbits from a magician's hat—but in the northern province, most of them were actually known to Louverture long before the Revolution. Did he realize at the time that his rides and strolls through the region and streets of Cap were the first steps on the road to the Haitian Revolution? We cannot tell. As he looped around and headed back to Montarcher Square to pick up Bayon and drive him home to Haut-du-Cap, he again donned the mask of the loyal servant.

SEVEN

SLAVE DRIVER
1779–1781

TOUSSAINT LOUVERTURE ELBOWED his way into Conseil Street in Cap. The streets were even more packed than usual because a fleet of French warships was about to sail for North America to join in the US War of Independence. It was August 17, 1779, and merchants, steve-dores, and prostitutes worked overtime to accommodate the expedition. So did notaries: many free men of color from Saint-Domingue who had volunteered for the expedition were drafting their wills before embarking for a war from which they might never return.

But Louverture was not in Cap to plan for death and destruction. When he finally broke through the throngs and entered the office of the notary Jean-François Doré on Conseil Street, it was to finalize the terms of a business deal with his son-in-law Philippe Jasmin Désir. For 1,000 colonial livres a year, Louverture agreed to lease a sixteen-acre coffee es-tate that Désir owned near Grande-Rivière, about ten miles southeast of Cap. The transaction included the estate's land and buildings as well as thirteen of Désir's slaves, who could be mortgaged and leased in Saint-Domingue like any piece of property.[1]

Louverture never mentioned this deal thereafter, to avoid damaging his revolutionary credentials, but it was a turning point in his life, more

View of Cap from the southeast. The plantation of Haut-du-Cap was located at the foothills of the Morne du Cap, to the left of this picture. From Taylor, *Vue générale du Cap-Haïtien* (nineteenth century). Personal collection of the author.

meaningful in some ways than his recent manumission. He had become a freedman, and then a slave driver. He was one of *them*. A general law of emancipation was unthinkable at the time, so making money by any means necessary was the only way he could free his relatives. Money was liberty.

Unfortunately, Louverture had not picked the best time to go into business. Racism toward free people of color was becoming increasingly institutionalized in Saint-Domingue and the war made for a difficult economic context. The experience was a sobering one. Within two years, Louverture lost his money, his lease, his wife, and, for all practical purposes, his freedom.

Saint-Domingue's free people of color were not rebels: they were strivers. Despite their full or partial African ancestry, they looked up to white planters—and ultimately to France—for inspiration. They thought more highly of standard French than of Caribbean Kreyòl; they publicly rejected the Afro-Caribbean religion of Vodou in favor of Roman Catholicism. They also wanted to get rich the same way every white Frenchman wanted to get rich: by buying and exploiting slaves.[2]

Their strategy paid off early in Louverture's life, when race was defined as much by one's financial success as by the color of one's skin: some wealthy mixed-race planters managed to be listed as white in legal documents. But as the years passed there were increasing efforts to treat any amount of African blood as a stain that could not so easily be erased. By the 1760s, so-called scientific racism, a biological definition of race that was less flexible than the socioeconomic definition that had preceded it, was becoming the norm.

There was nothing preordained about the rise of racism in Saint-Domingue. The word "race" did not even exist in the French language until the fifteenth century, and even then it often referred to one's class background rather than the color of one's skin. Racism began as a man-made historical phenomenon in the aftermath of the Seven Years' War, when French authorities purposely fostered tensions between free whites and free people of color for fear that they might unite in a common bid for independence. White planters quickly embraced racism for their own practical reasons: they hoped that slaves would be more docile if they were "intimately convinced of the white man's infallibility." Because people of color outnumbered whites twenty to one, a white colonial author argued, "safety demands that we treat the black race with such contempt that anyone who descends from it, until the sixth generation, must be indelibly stained." Down the social ladder, "little whites" welcomed the notion that the color of their skin somehow made them superior to mixed-race planters who outranked them in every other aspect. In time, racial theorists developed the pseudoscientific theories white people needed to rationalize their self-interest.[3]

Louverture did not have to look far for evidence of racism's growing hold. The most famous racial controversy in 1770s Saint-Domingue involved none other than his old boss François Bayon de Libertat and a neighboring planter named Pierre Chapuizet. Chapuizet's great-great-great-grandmother was apparently an African slave, but one's racial background had been less important in the early 1700s, so many legal documents had failed to mention his mixed ancestry. Things changed in 1778, when Chapuizet applied for an officer commission in a white militia unit. Local white planters, spurred on by Bayon, rejected his application because "there are certain stains that a court decision cannot erase perfectly . . . or whiten sufficiently." Suits and countersuits flew back and forth until July 1779, when the appeals court in Cap affirmed that Chapuizet was legally white, sentencing Bayon to a fine of 150 livres and a public apology for suggesting otherwise.[4]

Free people of color (including, apparently, Louverture) loudly celebrated the court's decision in Chapuizet's favor, but their joy was misplaced. The court did not outlaw racial prejudice when it declared that Chapuizet was legally white: it merely left open a path by which a handful of light-skinned individuals like Chapuizet could repudiate their African ancestry and pass as white. The principle remained that African ancestry was to be considered shameful and that people of color could only be declared equal by special dispensation (such was also the norm for the Jews of Saint-Domingue, one of whom spent the same summer of 1779 petitioning for individual citizenship rights). Only the French and Haitian revolutions would make all men free and French regardless of their race or creed.[5]

Such a radical concept was still unthinkable in the Caribbean of the 1770s. Racism so permeated society that people of color, instead of rejecting its underlying principles, instead made it their own. Mulattoes and quadroons resented being excluded by whites, but they kept their distance with black freedmen like Louverture, who in turn treated their African-born brethren as less civilized. The chain of contempt ended with the newly imported slaves, the *bossales*, a term derived from the Spanish *bozales* (muzzled, or shackled), but that was often rendered in French as *peau sale* (dirty skin).

Louverture's own relationship to race was a complex one. He was sensitive to any racial slight, but he also longed to be accepted by white planters, who were held up to him as a model for the first half-century of his life. He was envious and critical of mixed-race mulattoes, and he favored his mixed-race stepson over his biological black son. He was a product of his age.

The growth of racial prejudices had important consequences for Louverture and his fellow black freedmen, who were supposed to be equal to free whites under the 1685 Black Code, but were progressively subjected to discriminatory colonial laws. After 1767, free people of color could no longer claim noble status or hold public office, and in 1774 white men married to women of color were placed under similar restrictions. Authorities began to require that a person's race be listed on legal documents, and in 1773 they denied people of color the right to use a French last name, in a move to emphasize their African ancestry. By 1779, free people of color could not even wear clothes as luxurious as those of whites, and they could not stay out dancing after 9 p.m., as if they were slaves on the lam. For the mixed-race offspring of white planters, who had always thought of themselves as French, the rejection took on Oedipal tones. "O, my fathers!" one of them lamented. "Because you had us with Africans, you think we cannot feel and think like you?"[6]

Some of these laws hit close to home for Louverture. When his daughter Marie-Marthe freed her mixed-race child, by law she had to pick an African name for him, so that he could not be mistaken for a "real" Frenchman. Initially named Toussaint after his grandfather, the boy had to change his legal name to Lindor. One generation earlier, Louverture's parents had been stripped of their African identity and given new Christian names; French authorities now insisted that the next generation could never escape its African roots. Neither African nor French, Caribbean Creoles like Louverture were cultural nomads.[7]

Every interaction with whites became fraught with danger. In 1780, the coachman of a Bréda heir who was returning home from work was shot on sight by rural policemen, who were out "hunting maroon negroes" and suspected him of being a runaway. The penalty for this wrongful death was a simple fine.[8]

The most prominent free people of color did not stand hapless. They ignored the laws that did not benefit them and were not afraid to sue to implement those that did, sometimes successfully (suing one's neighbor was a favored pastime in Saint-Domingue). The Bréda family alone lost no fewer than five civil lawsuits against mixed-race neighbors around 1780: Bayon's attorney, already hard at work on the Chapuizet case, must have been a busy man and a bad lawyer. But Louverture did not have the legal resources or social standing to fight back in court and simply learned to respond to white harassment with meek submissiveness.[9]

In this already tense racial context, news that the thirteen British colonies in North America had formally declared their independence hit Saint-Domingue in the summer of 1776. The American rebels found it "self-evident, that all men are created equal": for free people of color in the Caribbean, these stirring words seemed to foretell a new era in which one's legal status would be based on universal ideals rather than crass calculations about profit and loss. But the US Declaration of Independence had been written by a slave owner, so maybe this revolution would not lead to meaningful change.[10]

The reaction of the white colonists hovered between dread and jubilation. A French war with Britain, which seemed likely, would disrupt trade links and cause food shortages in Saint-Domingue, a worrisome prospect, since a drought had already pushed the Bréda slaves to the edge of starvation. "It would be a shame for us if we had a war," worried Bayon, who wondered how he was going to export molasses to New England past British warships. But there was something enticing about white planters setting up a government of their own while keeping intact the plantation system that had made them rich. After all, were Dominguan Creoles not Americans as well? "Everyone here believes very strongly that . . . this country [the United States] will be independent," Bayon wrote excitedly after receiving news of the rebel victory at Saratoga, evidently having changed his mind about the risks involved.[11]

Paris balanced its options carefully. On the one hand, if the North American rebels succeeded, it would set a bad precedent for France's own colonies. On the other hand, anything that was bad for Britain was good for France. France also feared that a reconciliation between the United States and Britain would be sealed by a joint attack on Saint-Domingue. After thinking the matter over, King Louis XVI decided to support the rebels, declaring war on Britain in February 1778. Spain followed suit a year later.

The war's impact was felt acutely in Cap. A British squadron blockaded the port in the fall of 1778, making it virtually impossible to export goods and forcing Bayon to stockpile sugar. Fearing an invasion, royal authorities demanded that the slaves of local planters help overhaul the colony's fortifications. As the plantation located closest to Cap, Haut-du-Cap was hit particularly hard by such requisitions.

Who should defend the colony was another contentious issue. France had long wished to supplement its regular regiments from Europe with local recruits who were less susceptible to tropical diseases, but white colonists were averse to any type of military service. It was only after overcoming an armed white uprising that colonial authorities had been able to create a militia in the mid-1760s. The issue rose again during the US War of Independence, when, in 1779, Admiral Charles d'Estaing headed to Cap with a large fleet. He made urgent requests for troops to replace the 1,500 men he had lost to disease since reaching the Caribbean, and the governor of Saint-Domingue set out to create volunteer units of colonists. Both whites and free people of color could enlist, but they would be assigned to different units.[12]

The public response was mixed. Only 156 white Dominguans offered to join d'Estaing's force; most other whites viewed military service as a dishonorable and unrewarding profession good only for "little white" ruffians. By contrast, no fewer than 941 free people of color volunteered. They saw military service as a way to prove themselves as French patriots at a time when they were being relegated to second-class status by law. The Saint-Domingue volunteers were incorporated into two units: whites formed a unit of elite assault troops, the *Grenadiers volontaires*, while people of color formed a much larger unit of light infantrymen, the *Chasseurs volontaires*.[13]

Many of the Chasseurs were destined to become famous in the Haitian Revolution. Jean-Baptiste Chavanne, who would lead an important uprising in 1790, was among them. So were André Rigaud, who would become a general and Louverture's main rival in the 1790s, and Jean-Baptiste Belley, who later served as deputy in the French parliament. According to Haitian traditions, the expeditionary force also included Henry Christophe, who went on to serve as general under Louverture. Louverture's son-in-law Philippe Jasmin Désir likely joined as well, as did his future son-in-law Janvier Dessalines.[14]

Louverture, meanwhile, stayed put. He had a more lucrative plan in mind.

It was in August 1779, just as the fleet was preparing to set sail for North America, that Louverture signed the lease to rent Désir's coffee estate and thirteen of his slaves. The document did not provide the rationale for the transaction, but the historical context strongly suggests that Désir had hired Louverture to serve as a caretaker during his absence.[15]

This was the riskiest and most ambitious business venture that Louverture had ever attempted. In addition to 1,000 colonial livres of yearly rent, he pledged to reimburse Désir for the cost of the slaves, valued at 16,500 colonial livres in all, who might die under his care or flee. The deal clearly stretched his resources. To pay the first year's rent, Louverture had to sell part of a small plot of land he had bought just six months earlier. He also put up the rest of his assets as collateral.[16]

To manage the estate, Louverture had to leave Haut-du-Cap, where he had spent all his life, and move ten miles south to the hamlet of Petit Cormier, which stood on the left bank of the Grande-Rivière (Great River) as one traveled upstream from the town of the same name. Lying south of the sugar-making plain of Cap, the county of Grande-Rivière was a hilly area dotted with 329 coffee estates. The region was known for producing centenarians, including the famed black veteran Vincent Olivier, whom Louverture had probably met in Cap (he died in 1780 at the alleged age of 119).[17]

Coffee was a new but booming crop in Saint-Domingue, on a path to supersede sugar as the colony's signature export. The low up-front costs involved made it particularly attractive to an undercapitalized freedman like Louverture, but it required a cultivation process that someone who had spent his life on a sugar estate would have found arcane. After the coffee cherry was harvested from the bushy trees, it had to be cleaned, dried, milled, husked, and sorted. The profitability of Louverture's venture would depend on getting every step right.

Louverture knew how to manage workers, but now there was one key difference: he was no longer an elite slave supervising fellow slaves, but a freedman exploiting slaves he had rented from their owner. The fact that all thirteen of Désir's slaves—a man, his four sisters, and their eight children—belonged to the same family must have made for a strange work environment as well. Picking coffee was not as physically demanding as harvesting sugarcane, but the death rate from lung afflictions could be high on coffee plantations on account of the cooler air of the hill country, a frightening prospect, considering that Louverture was financially responsible for the life of each of the slaves.

Among the eight young slaves of the family, the costliest was Jean-Jacques, valued at 1,500 livres. It came to light in 2012 that he was none other than the person known to us as Jean-Jacques Dessalines, who later became the first leader of independent Haiti. Dessalines is Louverture's equal in the eyes of many Haitians, so their prerevolutionary ties came as a jolt, as if it had suddenly been revealed that Thomas Jefferson had once been George Washington's indentured servant. The complex dynamics of Louverture and Dessalines's relationship—at once close, unequal, and contentious—likely originated during the period when the young Jean-Jacques toiled as a slave under the freedman Toussaint Bréda on the coffee estate of Petit Cormier.[18]

When Admiral d'Estaing's fleet left Cap in August 1779, its mission was to seize the British-held town of Savannah, Georgia. But the experience of war proved less exhilarating than the volunteers of the Chasseurs unit had hoped. Though many of them were socially prominent in Saint-Domingue, they were assigned menial tasks, such as digging trenches. Only during a final French assault on Savannah were they able to prove their mettle: the British counterattacked, and the Chasseurs successfully defended the French camp. The siege itself was inconclusive, however, and the French expeditionary force withdrew after a few months.[19]

Leaving the French Army proved to be more difficult than joining it. The Chasseurs considered themselves civilians, and they expected to return home after the siege, but the French high command was reluctant to let go of trained men in the midst of a war. It would be three years before some of the men would again see Saint-Domingue. When they did, they received no hero's welcome: the Chasseurs had hoped to be accepted as French citizens through military service, but they returned to the same segregated colony they had left. Within a decade, their disappointment would morph into a movement for racial equality.

Although it was a military failure, the Savannah expedition served an important long-term political purpose. Free people of color, who already served in the rural police (maréchaussée) and the militia (milice) in Saint-Domingue, learned in Savannah that they could be a fighting force equal to any white army. The lesson was not lost on the various Savannah veterans who later participated in the Haitian Revolution.

The war had not been a boon to Saint-Domingue's economy in the Chasseurs' absence. As French and Spanish troops flooded the colony, demand and prices for foodstuffs rose precipitously, as did the cost of every item needed to run a plantation. Meanwhile, few tropical crops were exported, because of frequent British naval blockades, so sugar and coffee piled high in the warehouses of Cap while their prices plummeted. A hurricane hit in November 1780, followed by torrential rains, leaving a trail of devastation, particularly in the Grande-Rivière area. By the following spring, drought was a concern. Then the flooding returned. "The colony is devastated: we need peace," wrote Bayon in March 1781.[20]

This difficult environment proved deadly for Louverture's fledgling business. Two of the thirteen slaves under his care died, costing him 3,000 colonial livres in penalties, as well as, one hopes, some moral qualms about his involvement in plantation slavery. In a desperate effort to raise cash, in May 1781 he sold another strip of land from his small lot in Haut-du-Cap, which netted him a meager 175 colonial livres. In July, Louverture and Désir (just back, presumably, from the Savannah expedition) agreed to cancel the lease on the coffee plantation, which was initially scheduled to last for nine years.[21]

After it first came to light in the 1970s that Louverture had rented slaves from his son-in-law, some historians began to argue that his values were virtually interchangeable with those of a white planter of the Old Regime, a view as extreme as the idealistic paradigm it tried to displace. Some biographies made the most outlandish claims: that Louverture was worth 648,000 livres by the time the Haitian Revolution began (an extraordinary sum); that he traveled to France as the business associate of the Bréda attorney (the evidence is thin); that he was a Freemason (the evidence is thinner). We were suddenly introduced, complained a skeptic, to "a wealthy planter but also a Freemason . . . who hob-nobbed with the island elite."[22]

Anointing Louverture as an abolitionist saint is a mistake, but so is depicting him as an elite individual completely cut off from the realities of slavery. Mixed-race planters who had inherited land from their fathers could be very rich, but the typical black freedman occupied a low rung in the colonial hierarchy. By default, many whites assumed that a black man was a slave until proven otherwise—which, assuming that Louverture had not properly registered his manumission, was technically true. He was no "big white": he was a "little black" of limited means embarking on a new life at a late age, which explains why so few people knew of him when he first burst onto the scene during the Haitian Revolution.

Historians have also sought to account for what happened to Louverture after the lease on the coffee plantation ended in the summer of 1781.

Did he start another business? If so, where? A slave register uncovered in a private collection in 2013 provides a sobering response: Louverture simply headed back to the Bréda plantation in Haut-du-Cap, where he resumed the duties that had been his as a slave. Though a freedman, he lived among slaves and enslaved relatives; his name appeared on plantation documents as if he had never been freed.[23]

Louverture returned to a plantation in upheaval. During the war, Haut-du-Cap was used to garrison French and Spanish soldiers, whose rowdy behavior did nothing to foster discipline in the workforce. In addition to stealing and damaging property, the soldiers started an epidemic of venereal diseases among the slaves that took years to extinguish. (Elderly nuns from the convent of Cap were housed on the nearby plantation of Charrier, but were probably not subject to the same treatment.) Also notable was the visit of Bernardo de Gálvez y Madrid, the former governor of Louisiana, who spent a year on the nearby Charrier plantation while overseeing a Spanish attack on the Bahamas. His presence must have made an impression on Louverture, who had a penchant for bright uniforms and impressive titles.[24]

In the summer of 1781, Admiral François de Grasse dropped anchor in Cap with a massive force of 26 ships of the line and a convoy of 200 sails. Taking 3,000 soldiers from the local garrison with him, he set sail in August for the United States, where his men took part in the two battles—the Battle of the Capes and the Battle of Yorktown—that sealed Britain's defeat and the independence of the United States. Peace negotiations began in Paris in 1782.

Before leaving for North America, de Grasse had left behind his sick, who were admitted to a makeshift hospital in Haut-du-Cap that housed up to 400 souls. The staggering death rate of European soldiers stationed in Saint-Domingue was not lost on Louverture. Many years later, he would make the deadly epidemiological environment created by the Columbian Exchange a centerpiece of his military strategy.[25]

The war years claimed another casualty: Louverture's marriage. In 1777, the Bréda attorney Bayon had hired a contractor named Pierre-Guillaume Provoyeur to expand the sugar mill of Haut-du-Cap. Provoyeur was a free mulatto, a slave owner, and a successful entrepreneur worth almost 70,000 livres, which put him in the upper tier of the free population of color in Cap. He apparently developed a close bond with

Louverture's wife, Cécile, while working on the Bréda plantation, which was no doubt facilitated by Louverture's lengthy absences while managing the coffee estate in Petit Cormier. A suspiciously generous man, Provoyeur promised Cécile the sum of 1,800 livres in 1778, along with a house that he would build for her in Haut-du-Cap. He then bought lots in Haut-du-Cap in 1781 (presumably so that he could build the house for Cécile) and reiterated his financial promises in a 1782 will. Louverture, who was desperately trying and failing to keep his coffee estate afloat at the time, could not match his rival's munificence.[26]

Louverture's marriage to Cécile broke down, and he never mentioned her thereafter. Perhaps his wife's betrayal was too great a humiliation; or perhaps he wished to hide the fact that his relationship to his second wife began while he was still technically married to Cécile, divorce being illegal in France until the French Revolution. He was either a cuckold or a sinner, and neither was flattering.[27]

Louverture's first family quickly disintegrated. His son-in-law Désir died in 1784, aged forty-five. His firstborn son, Toussaint, followed Désir into the grave in 1785, aged twenty-four. His other son, Gabriel, simply disappeared. His widowed daughter, Marie-Marthe, briefly returned to the Bréda plantation and then remarried in 1787.[28]

Louverture's new son-in-law, like his previous one, was a free black and a slave owner who had served in the Savannah expedition. Named Janvier Dessalines, he bequeathed his last name to Marie-Marthe and to the slaves she had inherited from her first husband, which is how the slave Jean-Jacques came to be known to history as Jean-Jacques Dessalines.[29]

The demise of Louverture's first marriage coincided with the end of a period that had proved anything but tranquil for the colony, free people of color, and Louverture. Thankfully, the 1783 Treaty of Paris brought peace at last. France's victory over Britain avenged the military humiliation of the Seven Years' War, the colony's economy rebounded, and Louverture began to rebuild his personal life.

EIGHT

MULETEER
1781–1789

TOUSSAINT LOUVERTURE SPENT the last years leading up to the Haitian Revolution on the Bréda plantation of Haut-du-Cap, his birthplace. It was the first plantation that travelers encountered when leaving Cap on the road to Port-au-Prince. Though it was not the largest or the most valuable of the Bréda estates, it was usually there that their attorney resided because it was close to Cap, breezy, and scenic. The view from the balcony of the main house during an early Caribbean morning, when the rising sun bounced off the dewy leaves of a balisier, enchanted many a visitor. "It is one of the most beautiful panoramas in the world," marveled one.[1]

The view of the lowlands below the plantation was less pleasing. Malnourished slaves, their steamy skin glistening in the early light, were already at work cutting cane. A train of carriages, their axles creaking under heavy loads, snaked up from the fields, across a crumbling bridge, and over the river of Haut-du-Cap to the plantation's main production buildings, from which the acrid smoke of burning cane soared to the sky. Louverture straddled both processes: listed as a "master miller and muleteer" on a plantation register, he oversaw the mules that hauled the canes from the fields and then powered the mill that crushed them.[2]

The scene—industrial machinery, harnessed nature, and economic success—brings to mind mid-nineteenth-century British landscapes in which painters proudly showcased the steel mills and coal pits of the modern age. This is no coincidence. Saint-Domingue underwent its own agro-industrial revolution in the 1780s as it combined slave labor with the latest capitalist innovations. The heyday of the plantation system would forever remain Louverture's economic point of reference. Whether the entrepreneurial spirit of the planters and the exploitation of their slaves were enough to wrest a fortune from the island's unforgiving climate, however, remains an open question.

Sugarcane had been the main moneymaker in the plain of Cap since the beginning of the eighteenth century. Each decade, new production records were set. Frequent wars with Britain entailed financial setbacks, particularly the Seven Years' War (1756–1764), which cost France its claims to Canada and Louisiana. Luckily, quipped Voltaire (who had never visited Louisiana), these were just "a few acres of snow." Saint-Domingue, which was far more valuable to France than the rest of North America, forged ahead in the war's aftermath. By the 1780s, sugarcane had spread to the valley of the Artibonite and the plains of Port-au-Prince and Cayes. Saint-Domingue was the world's largest sugar exporter.[3]

Sugar is such a cheap and undistinguished commodity today that it is difficult to understand its eighteenth-century cachet. Like coffee, it was a luxury item consumed by the rich and the aspiring middle classes. It was also rare. In the 1780s most of Europe's sugar came from cane grown in the Caribbean and Brazil. Small Caribbean islands, such as Saint Lucia and Martinique, became economic powerhouses. With its 793 sugar plantations, Saint-Domingue was in a class of its own. The total value of its exports reached 137 million livres in 1788, putting it far ahead of Jamaica (45 million livres), Martinique (26), Guadeloupe (23), and the Spanish Caribbean (18).[4]

Little remains of the Haut-du-Cap Bréda plantation today, but its physical footprint, judging by contemporary maps and surviving foundations, was typical of the sugar estates of the era. At the center of the estate stood the master's main house, a hospital, a prison, a kitchen, slave quarters, and stables. Farther away were workshops, such as the forge and the lime kiln, along with the buildings required for the transformation of sugarcane: a mill (to crush the cane), vats (to boil cane juice), a purging house (to purify raw sugar), a drying tower (to dry purified sugar), and storehouses. Just across the road, pottery works owned by the Bréda family manufactured the clay molds used to purify sugar, fragments of which can still be found on the site today.

Sugar plantations like Haut-du-Cap were the largest and most heavily capitalized agricultural estates in the New World. Because they required expensive facilities like aqueducts and mills in order to operate, they also required significant initial investment. At a time when a manual laborer earned 1 or 1½ French livres a day in France, the total value of a single estate could top 1 million colonial livres. At a time when a typical US planter might own half a dozen slaves, Haut-du-Cap employed 150, its sister plantation in Plaine-du-Nord 200, and the Manquets plantation, the crown jewel of the Bréda empire, 400. Because of the many processes needed to transform the cane, plantations were as much industrial as agricultural in nature.[5]

Cane grew best on the level, well-watered fields of the alluvial plain of Cap. Farther up the slopes, as the plantation merged into the gravelly hillsides of Morne du Cap, cane fields gave way to individual gardens, where slaves were expected to grow their own food in their spare time, a practice that was illegal yet commonplace. A banana grove on an islet of the Haut-du-Cap River supplemented their diet (bananas were grown for local consumption only; they did not become an export crop until the advent of fast refrigerated ships in the late nineteenth century). Other areas were left uncultivated, often as grazing grounds.

Sugarcane cultivation was physically demanding. Slaves first had to clear old-growth jungles. Even on established plantations like Haut-du-Cap, they often undertook labor-intensive improvements, such as digging drainage ditches or renovating buildings. The wooden bridge over the Haut-du-Cap River was often damaged by floods and had to be repaired countless times. Some plantations used an aqueduct or a windmill to power the sugar mill (one colonist even suggested using the steam produced by boiling the sugarcane juice as a source of energy), but in Haut-du-Cap mules and slaves were the only source of mechanical power.[6]

Growing cane was a never-ending process. Slaves first plowed the fields by hand before planting the cane. The seedlings were then carefully weeded and watered until the mature stalks were cut about one year later, also by hand, and stripped of their razor-sharp leaves. Throughout, slaves were pushed and pulled by the threat of the driver's lash and a call-and-response chant (the practice has endured in Haiti as *kombit*, a form of communal farm labor accompanied by singing).[7]

Growing the cane was just a starting point. On a typical plantation, about half the slaves toiled in the fields; the rest, including a majority of the men, served as blacksmiths, wheelwrights, carpenters, coopers, and sugar refiners. Because sugarcane juice sours fast, Louverture and other muleteers rushed the freshly harvested stalks to the plantation for further processing. After they had milled the canes, a refiner boiled the juice to separate the gooey molasses from the brown sugar, which was then dried and purified into "clayed" sugar. It was not rare, during the harvest period, for slaves to work well into the night and then wake up before dawn for the next day's labors. Injuries due to overwork and exhaustion, such

On the plantation of Haut-du-Cap, Toussaint Louverture worked at a mule-driven mill of this type. From Anon., "Moulin à sucre" (painted version of an engraving originally published in Denis Diderot's *Encyclopédie*). Personal collection of the author.

as losing one's hand in the drums of the sugar mill or getting scalded by boiling cane juice, were common. Sugar was a bitter crop.

Entrusted with the comparatively undemanding task of caring for the plantation's mules, Louverture was a lucky man. The imaginative names he chose for the animals of Haut-du-Cap also suggest that he had a sense of humor: *Trahison* (treason) worked alongside *L'argent bon* (money's good), *Ça yo voir* (let's see), and the cheekily named *Nègre maître* (negro master) and *Gouverneur* (governor).[8]

Saint-Domingue on the eve of the Revolution was a blend of Enlightenment progress and antiquated labor exploitation. In April 1784, just six months after the world's first demonstration of a hot-air balloon in France, the first balloon to fly on the American continent took off from the Gallifet plantation a few miles from where Louverture lived. It may have represented the latest advances in chemistry and physics, but it flew over slaves who were among the most poorly treated in the colony. Later that year, a scientific society started meeting in Cap, and its members began to exchange findings with scientists in Philadelphia; but the meeting room was located a short distance from the spot where slave ships unloaded their African cargo.[9]

Saint-Domingue stood at the center of a busy trading network that stretched from the slave-trading outposts of West Africa and the banking center of Amsterdam to Newfoundland cod fisheries, the cattle ranches of Santo Domingo, the wharves of Bordeaux, the silver mines of Mexico, contraband havens like Curaçao, and the plantations where African slaves transformed black sweat into sweet gold. This was no triangular trade; this was a mercantile octagon.

Though they depended on slavery, sugar plantations bore all the characteristics of a modern capitalist enterprise: a large workforce, the division of labor, industrial processes, large capital investments, complex financial transactions, and long-distance trade. "Each planter is, strictly speaking, an industrialist," proudly noted the colonial assembly.[10]

The sugar economy's far-reaching connections gave Louverture a cosmopolitan outlook that would have been uncommon among the parochial European peasantry of the time. This may explain why, when he took over the reins of the colony in the 1790s, he seemed equally at ease writing letters to a US president and negotiating with African-born laborers in their native tongue. He was, in many ways, a citizen of the modern, capitalist world.

The attorney who oversaw Haut-du-Cap when Louverture returned to the plantation in 1781, François Bayon de Libertat, had occupied the position almost continuously since 1772. So close were the two men that some early historians described Bayon as a "friend" who went on "sexual escapades" with Louverture, though the yawning social gap between the "big white" and the black freedman probably precluded such close intimacy.[11]

A native of Aix-en-Provence in southeastern France, Bayon oversaw multiple estates for the Brédas and other absentee owners. It was a lucrative occupation. He received 10 percent of the overall income whether the plantation ran a profit or not. He also owned a coffee estate for a time, and in 1777 he purchased a sugar plantation of his own in Limbé. Along the way, he managed to finagle his way into a title of nobility, hence the fancy "de Libertat" that he tacked onto his last name.[12]

A landowning family man and an adept networker, Bayon embodied Louverture's aspirations. He lived in Haut-du-Cap's main house with his wife, Marie-Jeanne de Saint-Martin, and their two daughters, born in 1773 and 1774. He had married well: his wife's father was the dean of the court of appeals in Cap and her many sisters had all wedded prominent lawyers, officers, and planters. He sent his daughters to complete their education in a French convent in 1780 and immediately began planning their marriages to ensure that they would get a more suitable match than their mother had. They had not yet turned ten.[13]

His views on race marked Bayon as a product of his time. He described an employee as "more negro than white" to illustrate his incompetence, and he waged a legal battle for years against his neighbor Pierre Chapuizet over his application to become an officer in a white militia because he suspected him of having a black ancestor. The prevalence of maroonage on the plantations that he owned or managed also suggests that he was not popular with field hands—for good reason. Under his management, living conditions in Haut-du-Cap were downright primitive. A twenty-foot-deep ravine caused by soil erosion bisected the slave quarters. The hospital was no better, especially after Mrs. Bayon, who played the role of unofficial nurse, went to France for an extended stay. The sick were left to fend for themselves: "What an inhumane spectacle to see a poor fellow lying on a cot, without a mattress or sheets, almost naked, longing for a quick death!" lamented the accountant.[14]

Despite Bayon's shortcomings, Louverture maintained friendly relations with him well into the Haitian Revolution, probably because of his willingness to grant skilled employees like him (as opposed to field hands) a remarkable degree of impunity. In the Bréda plantation of Manquets, a slave driver named Hippolyte and a sugar refiner named Jean-Jacques once walked off of their jobs, inciting dozens of others to do the same, in order to protest extended hours and an unpopular manager. Bayon punished them lightly, most likely because slave drivers were influential and sugar refiners were costly. He simply put Hippolyte off-duty and sent Jean-Jacques back to work, eventually rewarding him with two gold coins for good behavior.[15]

House slaves—a group that included Louverture's brother Paul and his surrogate mother, Pélagie—also fared well under Bayon's management. There were no fewer than 20 slaves attached to the master house of Haut-du-Cap out of a total workforce of 152. An additional 27 slaves belonging to Bayon and neighboring planters lived there at the Brédas' expense as well—a remarkable number considering that the total of 47 domestics only had to care, at most, for a family of four (Bayon's wife often visited spas in France, where their daughters also studied in 1780–1784). One domestic was solely employed to make jams and wigs. By contrast, the much larger plantation of Gallifet, which employed 407 slaves, only assigned 7 to domestic duties. The accountant of Haut-du-Cap fretted about the Bréda domestics' "taste for laziness, independence, and libertinism." They had little else to do.[16]

Coachmen like Louverture normally lived in the carriage house, but the building was falling apart by the 1780s on the Bréda plantation, so perhaps he built his own lodging on a little parcel of land he owned near the plantation. This is where he began a new life after the breakdown of his first marriage. The exact date remains a mystery: by his own account, Louverture began a relationship with his second wife around 1778, had a son by her in 1784, and considered himself "married" to her by 1785, even though his first wife was actually still alive. Unable to obtain a divorce, he probably kept his marital status unclear so as not to draw attention to the adulterous or bigamous nature of his second union. Afraid of being tagged with illegitimacy and losing their inheritance, his children by his second wife similarly tiptoed around the issue, vaguely explaining that their parents were living in "the creole way" before making their common-law marriage official.[17]

Louverture's second wife, Suzanne Simon-Baptiste, was a laundress on the Haut-du-Cap plantation. She was apparently the daughter of Pierre Baptiste, the elderly gatekeeper of the Bréda plantation and Louverture's godfather. She was also the sister of the slave driver Bruno and the mason Gilles, which placed her at the center of the established families that formed the backbone of the plantation. Born around 1746, she proved to be a dependable wife. Louverture grew very attached to her, though he still carried on the occasional affair. Like her husband, she was a devout Catholic. Pragmatic and businesslike, she stayed away from politics during the Haitian Revolution, preferring to accumulate and manage landholdings instead.

Suzanne already had a mixed-race son before marrying Louverture, as well as possibly a mixed-race daughter. Her son, Placide, also known as Séraphin, was born in 1781 to a *mulâtre* (mulatto) named Séraphin Clerc, which made him a *griffe* (three-quarters black), according to the meticulous racial nomenclature of the colony. Though Placide was not Louverture's biological son, he always treated him as if he were, and even displayed a marked preference for him. It is difficult to know whether this bias reflected Placide's personal qualities or some deeply buried desire to whiten the family line.[18]

Suzanne and Toussaint Louverture had two sons together, Isaac (born in 1784) and Saint-Jean (born in 1791). Both appeared as slaves on Bréda plantation rosters alongside their mother. Most likely, Louverture could not afford to buy their freedom after the failure of his coffee business, and so they remained enslaved until the Haitian Revolution. Their continued bondage underscores the extent to which he navigated two worlds: he was a freedman who had rented slaves, but he was now raising an enslaved family on the plantation of his former master. After the heady period of the late 1770s, when he had been able to free several relatives, the 1780s marked a long pause in his social ascent.

Louverture raised his second family in a difficult environmental context. Deforestation and soil erosion, two woes of modern Haiti, were already becoming an issue. Colonists cut forests haphazardly to harvest exotic woods like mahogany and to make room for fields (an attorney of Haut-du-Cap even cut down all the guava trees). Tropical downpours, known locally as *avalasses* (a Kreyòl term derived from "avalanche"), then washed the soil away, leaving the hill of Morne du Cap bare and stone-dry. As a result, the Bréda plantation was often hit by droughts and flash floods that destroyed bridges, carved ravines, and ruined crops.[19]

Plagues of biblical proportions hit Haut-du-Cap in rapid succession. After a major flood in 1784, followed by a lengthy drought in 1785–1786, smallpox returned in 1785, taking the life of Bayon's cook and prompting him to vaccinate all the young children on the plantation—a frightening prospect at a time when vaccination was nearly as dangerous as the disease itself. Isaac Louverture was just a few months old. Bayon had suffered heartbreak of his own when one of his daughters died in 1784, just weeks before she was due to return from France.

The death in Paris in July 1786 of Pantaléon de Bréda Jr., the absentee owner of the Bréda plantations, was more significant in Louverture's life than the death of his boss's daughter. Because Pantaléon Jr. had died childless, he had divided his fortune among his four nieces and nephews. Word quickly got out, terrifying all those—including Louverture—whose families had been owned by Pantaléon Jr. "Slaves no longer wanted to work the land, because they had gotten it into their head that they would be split and even sold," reported Bayon. "I had to use all my influence to calm them." Freak incidents—such as a rainless lightning storm that killed a slave—did nothing to soothe fretful nerves. Altogether, eight slaves died in Haut-du-Cap in the summer and fall of 1786.[20]

Fortunately for Louverture and his relations, Pantaléon Jr.'s absentee heirs had trouble coordinating a sale, in part because of the bad reputation of the slaves of Haut-du-Cap. After years of confusion and delays, the heirs abandoned the partition plan they had drawn up. Instead, they decided to continue operating the Bréda plantations in Haut-du-Cap and Plaine-du-Nord together and to split the proceeds—or rather losses, since the estates turned out to be far less lucrative than they had expected.

According to colonial statisticians, the plantations of Saint-Domingue were veritable gold mines. By 1790, Saint-Domingue was exporting 70 million pounds of white sugar a year by weight, plus 93 million pounds of brown sugar, 68 million pounds of coffee, and 6 million pounds of cotton. The total value of these goods topped 200 million colonial livres (133 million French livres), or more than the production of all of Britain's Caribbean colonies combined. In return, France sold 80 million French livres' worth of goods in its Caribbean colonies, a market that kept 3 million French workers busy. The 600 French ships plying the Saint-Domingue trade also served as a training ground for 12,000 sailors who could be enrolled in the French Navy in the event—the certainty—of yet another war with Britain.[21]

Generations of historians have cited these numbers ever since, but by doing so they have been unwittingly recycling the propaganda of the planter lobby. Colonial bookkeeping was not meant to enlighten scholars but to evade taxes and defend slavery. Because far-sighted economists like Adam Smith and Pierre du Pont de Nemours argued that slavery was no cheaper than wage labor when accounting for the slaves' high cost and low productivity, slavery's apologists felt compelled to prove that slavery was, if not morally defensible, at least highly profitable.

Accordingly, contemporary estimates of slavery's profitability varied dramatically depending on the source's political leanings. One of the best works on the matter was a two-volume study published in 1775 by Michel Hilliard d'Auberteuil, who was sympathetic to the plantation system but also eager to reform it. According to his careful accounting, each year a typical slave produced 600 to 1,800 colonial livres more than it cost to feed him or her. When accounting for the initial purchase price and other costs, this made for an 8 to 10 percent return on investment, or slightly more than the cost of credit. But Auberteuil was deeply concerned that the main cost variable, labor, was trending upward, and that profit margins were getting ever thinner as a result. At the time of his writing, it was virtually impossible for a newcomer to get rich on borrowed money, although hundreds of young men flocked from France every year hoping to do just that. Ten years later, the declining fertility of the soil and the rising price of imported slaves brought down profit rates further and put the sustainability of the entire plantation economy in doubt. Investments from France kept pouring in anyway, but the Saint-Domingue sugar boom was increasingly taking on the trappings of a financial bubble.[22]

Measuring profit rates on French plantations is a mammoth task that has yet to be undertaken, but the example of the Haut-du-Cap plantation suggests that sugar plantations were no longer moneymakers by the 1780s, at least for absentee owners. The correspondence of the Bréda attorneys reveals a litany of woes. Bayon was a master of the genre: "Drought has entirely ruined Haut-du-Cap" (1776). "No one here has ever witnessed such a hurricane and so much flooding" (1780). "This is the worst weather in thirty-four years" (1784). "We had the worst weather in forty years" (1788). Revenue in other estates he managed for the Brédas, such as the pottery works and the Manquets plantation, was subpar as well.[23]

In lengthy but anecdotal letters that offered no clear view of the overall financial picture, Bayon attributed these setbacks to problems like bad weather, but third-party accounts indicate that the deficit was actually structural. When subtracting production costs, Haut-du-Cap and Plaine-du-Nord ended 1787 with a combined loss of 34,495 colonial livres. The following year, with a loss of 15,653 livres, was only marginally better. So was 1789, with a loss of 3,289 livres. The gold mine was a money pit.[24]

As years passed, the Bréda heirs increasingly complained of Bayon's lackluster performance, not only in Haut-du-Cap, which, plagued by labor unrest and recurrent drought, was unlikely to ever produce enough to cover its costs, but also in the potentially more lucrative Plaine-du-Nord and Manquets plantations. Bayon's habit of blaming bad weather grew thin over time, especially at a time when tales of Saint-Domingue's wealth circulated freely in France. Were the Bréda heirs not supposed to be, as the expression went, "rich like a Creole?"

Against Bayon's wishes, in 1789 two of the Brédas traveled to Saint-Domingue to get a firsthand look at their inheritance. What they saw appalled them. Bayon's recordkeeping was poor, his management style lackadaisical. He would spend funds on a new dovecote or on ferrying his surviving daughter to her dance lessons instead of more productive purposes. He was often gone for business or pleasure, so sugarcane was cut late or never, and field slaves died in large numbers for lack of proper care, leading to constant and costly purchases of new slaves from Africa. And yet the proportion of sick and elderly slaves on the Bréda plantations remained stubbornly high for a simple reason: after enduring cost over-runs on the sugar plantation that he had purchased in his own name in Limbé, Bayon routinely employed the Brédas' healthy slaves on his estate. He also sold molasses to local merchants below the going rate (presumably in exchange for kickbacks) and could provide no receipts for a full year's worth of sugar sales. Such shenanigans were common on absentee-owned plantations, but Bayon's brazenness stood out even by local standards. The heirs sacked him.[25]

Sugar production began to recover under new management, but increased productivity was not necessarily a good thing for the slaves, whose own toil was responsible for it. To maximize profits, the Bréda heirs refused to invest in new laborers and kept extending working hours. Ambitious infrastructure improvements, notably irrigation works on the Plaine-du-Nord plantation, also added to the workload. The understaffed plantations could not conceivably continue operating in this manner indefinitely—nor did they: the Bréda slaves were among the first to revolt in 1791.

Hard-pressed for cash, the Bréda heirs eventually consigned all their sugar exports to a Bordeaux merchant, who was charged with reimbursing their debts and giving them a fixed allowance. But the merchant complained that sugar shipments from their plantations barely covered interest on their debts and cut down their allowance accordingly. Everyone from the planters to the merchants was losing out financially, and the slaves were suffering.[26]

According to the mercantilist economic theory that underpinned the French empire, the well-being of colonial planters and merchants was a moot point, since the sole purpose of the colonies was to enrich the mother country—but Saint-Domingue's overall value to France was questionable as well. The department of the navy and colonies consumed 45 million French livres a year in peacetime, and wartime expenses were far higher: the Seven Years' War cost the French government the staggering sum of 1.8 billion French livres; the US War of Independence cost another 1.3 billion livres. Saint-Domingue, France's largest colony, only contributed 5 million colonial livres a year in royal taxes. The French government could only hope to recoup its losses through trade monopolies, but colonists dutifully evaded them. A royal official aptly described Saint-Domingue as a colony "sustained by France, fed and defended by

France, and expecting France to pay for its deficits." The cost-benefit ratio only got worse with the Haitian Revolution.[27]

A dominant narrative today asserts that Europe's surge into the industrial age was financed in part by the profits it made off slavery. However, given the amount of blood and treasure wasted by France in Saint-Domingue, it may well be that in the Haitian case, colonialism was a losing proposal for all involved. Buying slaves in Africa so that they could die in the Caribbean was not only inhumane, but also may have been bad business.

By the time Bayon was forced to relinquish his job as attorney of the Bréda estates in the first days of July 1789, the Haut-du-Cap plantation was a combustible mix. Its slaves were at once abused, malnourished, and restive. Maroonage, disobedience, and slow work were rampant. Owners and managers were squabbling. The Bourbon monarchy had bankrupted itself fighting for an American colonial empire whose economic value was questionable. At this very moment, a mob was running through the streets of Paris on its way to the Bastille prison. The ripple effects of the French Revolution would soon be felt across the Atlantic.

NINE

WITNESS
1788–1791

IN MARCH 1788, Toussaint Louverture heard a shocking story of labor abuse. It involved a white planter named Nicolas Lejeune who owned a coffee estate near Plaisance, thirty miles southwest of Cap. Convinced that his slaves were trying to poison him, Lejeune had tortured several of them to force them to confess. The rumor mill spoke of unspeakable acts. For Louverture, the episode may have brought back painful memories of the cattle epidemic of 1773, when the attorney Delribal had also tortured alleged poisoners. At the time, the Haut-du-Cap slaves had appealed to nearby Bréda relatives for redress. Lejeune's slaves took a different route: as provided by royal law, they notified local officials and begged them to intervene.[1]

A magistrate visited the Lejeune plantation and stumbled across a horrific scene. Two women were shackled inside a makeshift cell, their limbs a charred mess of black flesh. Lejeune had partly burned them off. The women later died. Lejeune's actions clearly violated the Black Code and recent royal ordinances that outlawed the torture and murder of slaves. Penalties for slave abuse rarely exceeded a fine in practice (Lejeune and his relatives had already gotten away with similar crimes in the past), but the governor of Saint-Domingue concluded that such impunity, if allowed to continue, would encourage slaves to revolt and imperil the whole colony. He demanded that the Lejeune case be brought to court to make an example.[2]

An uproar ensued. White masters could never be proven wrong, colonists claimed, even when they were; otherwise the entire racial foundation on which the colony was built would collapse. Moreover, the right to dispose of one's personal property, including of the human variety, was a sacred and inviolable right of man; protecting sadists like Lejeune was really a crusade for individual liberty. The court in Cap sided with the planters and acquitted Lejeune. Royal officials brought the case to the appeals court in Port-au-Prince, where Lejeune again narrowly prevailed.

The beginning of the Haitian Revolution is usually associated with the great slave revolt of August 1791, but disputes like the Lejeune case were already pitting white colonists against royal authorities by the late 1780s. These political controversies may be regarded as the first steps of a revolutionary process that eventually culminated with the slave revolt. Strangely, one could argue that Saint-Domingue's first revolutionaries were not black slaves but the colony's free white colonists and free people of color. Louverture was not apparently involved in these early stirrings: instead, he observed them from afar as an interested witness learning how not to wage a revolution.

No French king ever traveled to the Caribbean, so in Saint-Domingue, as in other French colonies, royal power was exercised by a *gouverneur* (the political and military leader) and an *intendant* (the chief financial and legal officer). In theory, these two men made all the important decisions on behalf of the absolute monarch of France. In practice, Versailles and its appointees exercised barely any control in the colony.[3]

White restlessness harked back to the very beginnings of Saint-Domingue, at a time when it was an independent settlement of pirates who switched their allegiance from one country to another based on their strategic interests. The colonists eventually picked France as their colonial overlord, but they continued to view the colonial bond as a voluntary contract between two equal parties. Many rejected the moniker of "colony" altogether, arguing that they were really an "allied state" of France. Because the colonists' allegiance was contingent on France's military protection, every war raised the possibility that they might throw in their lot with a more powerful patron—as would eventually happen during the Haitian Revolution.[4]

This social contract was not a happy one. First on the list of colonial grievances was the *exclusif*, the set of trade laws that theoretically excluded most foreign merchants from colonial ports and forced colonists to buy overpriced French products. Trade restrictions had helped spark a violent white revolt in 1722–1723, and hatred of the *exclusif* endured.[5]

Taxation was another point of contention, just as it was in the American and French revolutions. Saint-Domingue only began to pay royal taxes in 1713, and then under the condition that a colonial assembly set the rates, an unusual arrangement in absolutist France. The assembly regularly tried to expand its powers into the legislative arena, particularly during power vacuums created by the deaths of King Louis XIV in 1715 and Governor Armand de Belsunce in 1763. The assembly's power grab failed, but complaints about excessive taxation and lack of representation remained part and parcel of the colonial mindset until the Haitian Revolution.

The Superior Councils of Cap and Port-au-Prince were other outlets for autonomist claims. Their main task was to serve as courts of appeal, but they also had to register royal laws before they could take effect, and they used this role as an excuse to claim some legislative powers (their counterparts in France, the *parlements*, did the same). The councils' activism peaked during the militia controversy of 1768–1769, the second of Saint-Domingue's three great white revolts, which only ended when the governor deported all the magistrates of the Port-au-Prince Superior Council and replaced them with cronies. But other colonial courts continued to defy royal authorities until the Revolution. The acquittal of Nicolas Lejeune was just one example.[6]

Over time, the Enlightenment critique of absolute monarchy provided the colonists with the theoretical framework to challenge colonial rule more directly. Concepts like the separation of powers (from Montesquieu), constitutional monarchy (Voltaire), and the popular will (Rousseau) ran against the top-down, authoritarian nature of the French colonial empire. Because the *gouverneur* and the *intendant* were appointed by the secretary of the navy in Versailles rather than elected, colonists complained of being subjected to a kind of "ministerial dictatorship."

All-powerful when dealing with their slaves, "big whites" like the Bréda attorney François Bayon de Libertat felt powerless when confronting royal appointees. "The current administrators, who are despots, only want us to submit blindly and unquestioningly to their authority," Bayon complained.[7]

In practice, colonists stripped royal authority of its substance through passive resistance. They falsified census forms to avoid paying the capitation tax due on each slave. They bribed royal officials to skirt the law. As for the trade regulations of the *exclusif*, legal loopholes abounded, contraband was rampant, and governors threw open the ports of Saint-Domingue whenever there was a war or a natural disaster—which was often.

All this changed in the 1780s, when France made a concerted effort to run its empire more efficiently, in keeping with the Enlightenment's focus on reason and order. Though well intended, these reforms rekindled white unrest by upsetting the various methods that colonists had developed to cope with absolutism (similar efforts to bring North America under British laws helped bring about the US War of Independence, while Spain's Bourbon Reforms constituted a leading cause of the Latin American wars of independence).

As part of these reforms, France allowed foreign merchants in 1784 to sell timber and foodstuffs in some colonial ports and then reduced rates on US imports. But France took this opportunity to increase enforcement against smuggling, which revived old grudges against all trade restrictions. Colonists looked enviously at the complete freedom of trade that American revolutionaries had achieved after waging their own war against Britain's Sugar Act and Townshend Acts.

In 1785, François Barbé-Marbois took over as *intendant* of Saint-Domingue and made the peculiar decision to perform the duties expected of him. A capable and honest administrator, he vigorously collected overdue taxes and debts so as to balance the colonial budget. He even had the gall, Bayon complained, to confiscate the slaves that owners had not declared in their machinations to evade the capitation tax. The *intendant*'s ambitious infrastructure projects also meant that the slaves of Haut-du-Cap were requisitioned to work on the road that passed through the Haut-du-Cap plantation; it was enlarged and extended all the way to Port-au-Prince.[8]

Equally grating to the "big whites" was a growing movement in France to improve the lives of slaves. Early Enlightenment philosophers had spent little time discussing the implications of their egalitarian principles in the colonial context, but in the 1770s and 1780s a new generation of more radical activists, such as Denis Diderot and the Marquis of Condorcet, began to attack slavery as an affront to civilized society. Abolitionist societies were founded in Philadelphia in 1784, in Britain in 1787, and in France in 1788, the last known as the Society of the Friends of the Blacks. These societies coordinated their efforts in a kind of abolitionist international whose goals were the immediate abolition of the slave trade and, ultimately, slavery itself.[9]

Royal administrators were sympathetic to the abolitionists' call for reform. They feared that unchecked labor abuses would cause a general slave uprising. Accordingly, in December 1784, King Louis XVI of France signed an ordinance allowing slaves to appeal to public officials if they were subjected to excessive forms of cruelty, such as severe whippings and mutilation. Though the ordinance merely reiterated clauses already found in the 1685 Black Code, it angered Saint-Domingue's planters, who felt that reminding their slaves that they had rights was as dangerous as it was outrageous. "The last edict did much harm," erupted Bayon. "Soon, we will no longer be the masters of our negroes anymore. They will denounce us to county commanders and to the rural police." (Bayon probably also resented clauses in the ordinance that outlawed the various tricks he and other attorneys had used to defraud absentee owners.)[10]

Repurposing the rhetoric of the Enlightenment to defend their economic interests, planters described themselves as "slaves" who sought to preserve their "liberty" (by which they meant their property rights) from an abusive government. Alternatively, proslavery authors presented themselves as realists who knew better than bleeding-heart abolitionists. Surely, slavery was not a perfect system, but it was a necessary one: there was no other way to produce crops in the tropics. Without slaves, there would be no sugar to export, and thus no merchant navy, and thus no sailors for the French Navy. Without slaves, France would fall behind Britain. Abolitionists were not just a public nuisance: they were enemies of the state.[11]

In an unprecedented act of defiance, the appeals court in Cap summoned the governor and the *intendant* from the colonial capital in

Port-au-Prince to defend the royal ordinance of 1784 in person, and then refused to enforce it anyway. The court eventually backed down after receiving a watered-down version of the ordinance a year later, but to punish the court for its insubordination, Versailles shut down Cap's appeals court altogether in 1787. This move forced colonists to travel all the way to Port-au-Prince, several days' sailing away, for their legal business. "Discouragement is general, this colony will slip away," lamented Bayon. His father-in-law, the court's senior member, resigned his position soon afterward.[12]

Slaves and freedmen like Louverture did not take part in these political debates, but they knew of them. Bayon feared "an awful disorder among our negroes, who are already quite independent. . . . Negroes know what is in [the December 1784 ordinance]. It is printed and many can read." It was possibly during that period that Louverture, who had learned the basics of reading from his godfather, first became aware of a famous passage attributed to Guillaume Raynal that warned of an impending slave revolt. "The negroes only need a chief courageous enough to lead them to vengeance and carnage. . . . Where is he, this great man . . . this new Spartacus?" the passage asked in reference to the Greek slave who had almost vanquished Rome. According to one possibly apocryphal account, Louverture read and reread the passage many times while dreaming that he might one day become the black Spartacus of the prophecy.[13]

Slaves took note of Louis XVI's efforts on their behalf and began to view the reformist Bourbon king as their best advocate. Meanwhile, white colonists were toying with secessionist ideas so as to nullify French slave regulations. Concerned that their masters would give free rein to their worst instincts once they were freed of royal officials' moderating influence, slaves viewed the colonial bond as their first line of defense. In time, they would revolt with the avowed goal of defending the French monarchy. In Saint-Domingue, advocates of independence were reactionaries, while rebel slaves were staunch royalists.[14]

White Saint-Domingue was a society always teetering on the edge of chaos. The white lower class included descendants of the unruly pirates who had founded the colony, indentured servants, and a sizable contingent of petty criminals that France had exiled to the colony in

1721–1722. As slavery came to underpin the agricultural sector, these landless whites found it increasingly hard to make a living. Late colonial Saint-Domingue was beset by social strife between slaves, landowning "big whites," and unemployed "little whites." And yet more migrants came every year, drawn like moths to a flame by exaggerated accounts of the colony's riches. Twelve hundred men arrived in a single convoy in 1785 with few prospects of finding either a job or a bride. "Disease will sweep clean the lot of them," Bayon noted crassly. Either that, or their restlessness would sweep the colony away.[15]

A city of 20,000 patrolled by a mere 12 policemen, Cap was not known for its attachment to law and order. Duels caused 80 deaths a year in the garrison of Cap alone. It did not take much to set people off. In 1785, fistfights and duels erupted in Cap's theater. The cause? Theatergoers disagreed over whether there should be a play or a ball that night.[16]

Already accustomed to fighting for no reason, whites found a worthy cause when the monarchy tried to reform slavery in the 1780s. Each new royal ordinance led to protests, riots, and even talk of independence. Elite whites encouraged the restless lower class to get to the streets to defend their rights. "Little whites," who had adopted the rhetoric of self-government, were happy to play along. The example set by the victorious American rebels suggested that it was possible to gain political autonomy while maintaining racial inequality—though local separatists seemed to forget that slaves represented 90 percent of the population of Saint-Domingue, a far higher proportion than had ever been the case in any of the thirteen US colonies. Extremists were openly considering rebellion by 1787, when they threatened to set the colonial capital of Port-au-Prince on fire to protest the closing of Cap's court of appeals. "It is horrifying that people are willing to burn a whole town to seek vengeance against administrators they do not like," reported a suddenly chastened Bayon. "The remedy is worse than the disease."[17]

The situation in the mother country was, if anything, even more flammable. French public expenses, exacerbated by the costly intervention in the US War of Independence, vastly exceeded income. Eighty percent of tax receipts went to pay interest on existing debts. One obvious solution to the fiscal crisis would have been to eliminate the tax-free privileges of clergymen and nobles, but Louis XVI was too irresolute to make such an unpopular decision. Instead, in 1788, he summoned deputies from all corners of the kingdom in the hope that the resulting assembly, known as the Estates-General, would balance his budget for him. His decision unwittingly led to the French and Haitian revolutions by bringing into the open two fundamental questions: Who belonged to the French nation, and who were its legitimate representatives?

Louis XVI viewed colonies as moneymaking ventures more than French provinces, so he did not have them in mind when he summoned the Estates-General. But the richest white colonists of Saint-Domingue unilaterally selected eighteen deputies to represent their cause in Versailles. In a ploy that evoked the three-fifths clause of the US Constitution, they justified the large size of the delegation by counting Saint-Domingue's total population, including slaves and free people of color, even though they had no intention of granting either group political rights. To appease the colonists, France eventually agreed to seat six white planters as deputies. The Count of Noé, the absentee owner of one-fourth of the Bréda estates in Saint-Domingue, served as a deputy alternate. Other Bréda heirs joined the Club Massiac, an influential group defending the interests of white planters in Paris.[18]

Summoning a representative assembly was a dangerous step for Louis XVI. In June 1789, bourgeois members of the Estates-General, seeing themselves as the embodiment of the French nation, formed a National Assembly and began work on a constitution. In the months that followed, they passed ever bolder measures that far exceeded Louis XVI's limited goals of fiscal reform. On August 4, they abolished the privileges of the nobility and the clergy; on August 26, with assistance from the US ambassador, Thomas Jefferson, they passed the Declaration of the Rights of Man and of the Citizen, which began with the radical claim that all men were born "free and equal in rights." The French Revolution had begun.

When some liberal deputies argued that the first article of the Declaration implicitly abolished slavery—as indeed it did—the Saint-Domingue delegation in Paris panicked. "THEY ARE DRUNK WITH LIBERTY," the deputies reported to their constituents. A formal abolition of slavery seemed imminent. Rather than defending slavery itself, colonial deputies cleverly invoked the ideal of self-government, begging the National Assembly to let colonies pass their own laws on internal matters. The ruse worked. Distracted by local events, the National Assembly eventually delegated all colonial matters to a legislative committee dominated by colonial lobbyists, which buried or watered down racial legislation for the next two years (women, men without property, and Jews were initially excluded from the full benefits of the French Revolution as well).[19]

By October 1789, a Bréda absentee owner was marveling at the "inconceivable revolution" that had just taken place in Paris. "Stay where you are," he wrote to a cousin who was in Saint-Domingue to settle the inheritance of Pantaléon de Bréda Jr. But events in the colony were following a parallel course. In Cap and Port-au-Prince, street clashes pitted advocates of self-government against partisans of Louis XVI. White separatists saw no danger in yelping about liberty while surrounded by slaves, but the attorney who oversaw one of the Bréda estates was more astute: "There exists a kind of anarchy that hurts commerce a lot," he wrote. "I hope to God it will end soon, because all of this sets quite a bad example for our workforce."[20]

In the heated context of a transatlantic revolution, few paid heed to these cautionary notes. In 1789, Saint-Domingue's white colonists secretly elected assemblies in each of the three provinces of the colony to enshrine racial discrimination in colonial law before the French National Assembly could legislate on the matter. Things quickly got out of hand. In October 1789, the provincial assembly of Cap forced the unpopular *intendant*, François Barbé-Marbois, to flee the colony. It then arrogated to itself legislative and executive powers normally reserved for the king. An even more radical assembly, which claimed to speak for the entire colony and was dominated by radical "little whites" eager to defend their racial privileges, took up residence in the city of Saint-Marc in the spring of 1790. In a matter of weeks, it banned all royal interference in racial matters, outlawed future manumissions, and disenfranchised white men who had married women of color. All these decrees at least dealt with domestic issues; but the assembly of Saint-Marc also eliminated the trade restrictions of the *exclusif* and claimed for itself the sole right to legislate in the colony, both of which encroached on France's basic prerogatives as a colonial power. The assembly's efforts culminated in May 1790, when it passed a constitution that effectively made Saint-Domingue independent from France. It was Haiti's first constitution, though few Haitians today would recognize it as such because it was drafted by racist settlers.[21]

By this point, some wealthy whites were growing concerned that the assembly of Saint-Marc and the "little white" rabble had gone too far. "A decree just demobilized all royal troops" and incorporated them into a colonial army, a Bréda attorney marveled. The crew of a ship of the line that had recently arrived from France had mutinied and embraced the autonomist cause because the French sailors felt a sense of kinship toward the "little white" population. Such chaos could not be allowed to continue. Sensing a change in mood, Governor Antoine de Peynier—whom the assembly of Saint-Marc had fired for good measure—sent loyal troops in August 1790 to disband the runaway legislature. He then banished its deputies to France so that they could be put on trial for sedition.[22]

The victory of the forces of order and tradition was short-lived. Tired of the colony's tumultuous politics, Peynier left in November 1790. The only man willing to take his job in such circumstances was a relatively obscure officer named Louis de Blanchelande. It would have taken a strong-willed and skilled leader to prevent the colony from exploding, but Blanchelande, like the genial Louis XVI, was neither. When two French regiments mutinied in Port-au-Prince in March 1791 and attacked his headquarters, Governor Blanchelande—who officially bore the title of "general" of the colony and was primarily charged with its defense—ingloriously snuck out through a rear window and let the local commander handle the situation. The troops lynched the commander, after which Port-au-Prince, the colonial capital, effectively became an independent white republic beyond the reach of French administrators.[23]

Blanchelande found refuge in Cap, which was traditionally more Francophile due to its close commercial ties with the mother country, but the city was only slightly less restive. "Surrounded by mulattoes and negroes, [colonists] indulge themselves in the most imprudent discussions on liberty," remarked a visitor, who chose to leave Saint-Domingue before imprudent discussions turned into imprudent actions.[24]

Saint-Domingue's second-most-affluent community, free people of color, was the second group to join the Haitian Revolution. Their main objective was not emancipation, since many owned slaves, but the repeal of the discriminatory laws passed since the 1760s. The wealthy mixed-race planter Julien Raimond was in France as early as 1784 to demand equal rights for his kin, but it was the outbreak of the French Revolution in 1789 that really brought the issue of free-colored rights to center stage. In Paris, Raimond received the support of the Society of the Friends of the Blacks, which focused its initial efforts on enfranchising free people of color rather than the more distant goal of abolishing slavery. Even this modest proposal was considered heretical by the colonial lobby, which adamantly opposed the admission of free people of color as deputies to the French National Assembly, even when they were rich, mixed-race, and slave-owning. Afraid of pushing white colonists into open secession, the National Assembly chose not to intervene. French deputies did not formally list free people of color as voting citizens in a March 1790 law, and then explicitly excluded them from the body politic in October of that year.[25]

Advocates of racial equality in Saint-Domingue were no more successful than their allies in Paris. Racist "little whites" seized upon the political chaos to harass or kill people of color with impunity. Louverture came close to the same fate while walking back from Mass one day with his prayer book. According to the story, which he shared ten years later, "a white man broke my head with a wooden stick while telling me 'do you not know that a negro should not read?'" Louverture prudently begged for forgiveness and slipped away, a decision that likely saved his life. But he kept his blood-soaked vest as a reminder and neither forgot nor forgave. Running into the same man years later, after the outbreak of the slave revolt, he killed him on the spot.[26]

Louverture was not alone in thinking that racial slights warranted physical retaliation. So did Vincent Ogé, a light-skinned coffee planter and merchant of substantial means who spent the first two years of the French Revolution in Paris lobbying for voting rights for free people of color. He also tried to convince absentee owners that some labor reforms were needed, "lest the Slave raise the standard of revolt." He failed on both counts.[27]

Unwilling to wait for the National Assembly to finally take a stand on racial equality, Ogé vowed to resort to force when politics failed (one suspects that he got his fighting spirit from his mother, a forceful and defiant woman). "I begin not to care whether the National Assembly will admit us [as deputies] or not," he told the British abolitionist Thomas

Clarkson, with whom he was dining at the home of the Marquis of Lafayette, another early opponent of slavery. "We can produce soldiers on our estates who are as good as any found in France. Our own arms shall make us respectable." Ogé purchased a fancy uniform and a colonel commission and secretly headed back to Saint-Domingue to begin the revolutionary struggle.[28]

Upon landing in Cap in October 1790, Ogé met up with Jean-Baptiste Chavanne and other free people of color from the towns of Grande-Rivière and Dondon, both a few miles southeast of Cap. Chavanne, who had served in the 1779 Savannah expedition, was a radical figure who had named his son after the French-American abolitionist Antoine Bénézet. He further radicalized Ogé, and the two young men wrote to Governor Blanchelande to demand the right to vote.

Blanchelande's response was to send the mounted police to arrest them. Ogé eluded his pursuers, set up a fortified camp with four hundred followers, and encouraged free people of color in other provinces to join him. His initial moderation had melted away. "We will participate in elections," he insisted. If not, "we will fortify ourselves. We will use force to defend ourselves." To avoid scaring away mixed-race planters, he added that "advocating . . . for enslaved negroes" was not on the agenda for now.[29]

In Haut-du-Cap, the Bréda attorney immediately saw the risk that Ogé's limited uprising might spread colony-wide. "If we only have to face these enemies we have nothing to fear, but shouldn't we also fear those who surround us [the slaves], who have as much right as Ogé to ask for the rights of man? The entire French part of the island will experience similar upheavals because the timing seems favorable: whites are politically divided."[30]

But Ogé made a strategic mistake: unwilling to incite slaves to revolt, because he was "trying to be assimilated to whites," he decided that he would only "encourage black slaves to rise against their masters" if his forces were overwhelmed. He never had a chance to follow through on this claim. His men held their ground at first when the royal troops attacked them, but they had to retreat when reinforcements arrived from Cap. Ogé, Chavanne, and a few followers crossed the border into Santo Domingo (today's Dominican Republic) and asked for asylum. But French authorities demanded that these "brigands" be extradited, and Spanish authorities complied.[31]

Louverture must have personally known several participants in the Ogé rebellion from the two years he spent managing the coffee estate in Grande-Rivière, from which most of Ogé's followers came. He probably also knew Jean-Baptiste Cap, a free black from Cap who tried to arm slaves and free Ogé from prison after his capture. He surely heard of Ogé's trial, which was major news on the Haut-du-Cap plantation. In all likelihood, he personally witnessed Ogé's final moments in Cap.[32]

By quickly giving up their fight, Ogé and Chavanne had hoped for mercy. They received none. "They shall be led to the main square of this town," their sentence went, "where, on the side opposite the one used for the execution of whites, they shall have their arms, shins, thighs, and pelvis broken while alive on a scaffold erected for this purpose. The High Executioner shall then place them on wheels with their faces turned toward heaven for however long it pleases God to maintain their lives." Their execution was meant to be not only painful but also humiliating, since the breaking wheel was normally used in Saint-Domingue to execute slaves who had revolted against their master, not elite mixed-race planters. More gruesome executions followed in ensuing weeks, including that of Ogé's brother Jacques.[33]

Louverture was accustomed to the horrors of eighteenth-century justice, but he found Ogé's death particularly troubling. Louverture admired Ogé for giving his life for the "liberty" of free people of color, though he later came to resent his failure to include slave emancipation among his immediate goals. "Toussaint's hatred for the city and inhabitants of Cap was born on the day this poor Ogé was executed," a colleague of his would write in 1801. Tactically, the lessons to be drawn from Ogé's defeat were similar to those from the Makandal conspiracy in 1758: the white planters would not give up their privileges without a fight, and any revolt would have to be successful, lest its perpetrators meet a gruesome end.[34]

French deputies, who had failed to take a stance on free-colored rights when Ogé was in Paris, were horrified when they learned of his death; executions by the breaking wheel were in the process of being banned in France. In a kind of legal eulogy to Ogé, the National Assembly passed a law allowing people of color born of two free parents to vote in May 1791. Recent freedmen, including Louverture, remained disenfranchised, as did all slaves. "I'd sooner see the colonies perish than betray a principle," Maximilien de Robespierre, a leader of the French Revolution, allegedly proclaimed. The French government prepared to send three commissioners to Saint-Domingue to enforce the law and bring an end to "displays of disorder that are singularly dangerous in the colonies, where they cannot be hidden from a class of men [the slaves] that can only be cowed by force."[35]

News of the May 1791 law reached Saint-Domingue in June. The outcry was unprecedented. However modest in scope, the law established the precedent that the French National Assembly could legislate on the status of people of color in the colonies: What could prevent it from abolishing slavery in the future? White separatists advocated "massive resistance," and a US consul predicted "civil war." Governor Blanchelande immediately promised that he would not enforce the law in order to appease radical racists, but an all-white electorate selected yet another colonial assembly that was scheduled to convene in Cap in August 1791. Some deputies spoke of declaring independence outright.[36]

Louverture and the slaves of northern Saint-Domingue had other plans. For two years they had stood by while whites and free people of color had fought their revolution. It was now their turn to set the colony afire. After spending most of his life as a passive witness, Louverture was finally ready to make his mark on history.

TEN

REBEL
1791

JUST AS FRENCH revolutionaries were preparing to assault the Bastille prison in Paris on July 5, 1789, an event took place in the office of the notary Éloi-Michel Grimperel in Cap that had more immediate relevance to the life of Toussaint Louverture. This was the day the four Bréda heirs fired François Bayon de Libertat, the crooked attorney who had overseen the family affairs since 1772, and Louverture lost a longtime ally who had done much to mitigate the effects of slavery in his life.

To revive their fortune, the Bréda heirs had a clever idea in mind, which they did not put in writing because it was so dishonest. Since the Haut-du-Cap plantation showed no sign of ever being profitable, they planned to transfer twenty to thirty able-bodied slaves to their other plantation in Plaine-du-Nord and an equal number of young and elderly slaves from Plaine-du-Nord to Haut-du-Cap, so that each work-force remained the same on paper. They would then sell Haut-du-Cap to some unsuspecting buyer who would be burdened with an unproductive plantation staffed by the weak and the troublesome. Alternatively, they discussed selling the land piecemeal and disposing of the slaves at auction.

Both plans would have fragmented Louverture's family network. He was so concerned for the fate of his surrogate mother, Pélagie, that he negotiated a deal with the Bréda heirs: he gave them "a young negress of the Aja nation, age 22," whom he must have purchased for the occasion, in exchange for his mother. The deal, first uncovered in 2013, was the second documented instance in which Louverture had owned a slave. The morally ambiguous nature of the arrangement—one woman's freedom for another's enslavement—was made even clearer when the young slave provided by Louverture died in childbirth just a few months later. This was Louverture in all of his complexity: at once opposed to and complicit in the slave system. And yet, it was the same man who, two years hence, would help launch the greatest slave revolt in the history of the world.[1]

Who or what incited Louverture and the slaves of Saint-Domingue to rebel was and remains a matter of great controversy. Unwilling to admit that their slaves had any reason to complain, contemporary white authors generally argued that they had been manipulated by outside agitators: free people of color, the British, the Spanish, Freemasons, abolitionists, or monarchists. It is customary today to reject such conspiracy theories and emphasize the agency of the slaves, so most historians now depict rebel leaders like Louverture as heroic idealists inspired by the principles of the Enlightenment. Others cite practical demographic factors, such as the size of the colonial garrison, to explain why the slaves picked this particular moment to revolt.

There is actually evidence for all three theories: the revolt stemmed from an alleged royalist plot, the impact of the French Revolution, and worsening living conditions for the slaves. All these strands converge in one place, the Bréda plantation of Haut-du-Cap, and one man, Toussaint Louverture. He was about forty-seven years old.

In 1789–1791, as white Saint-Domingue sank into political anarchy, life in Haut-du-Cap became ever more unbearable for the Bréda slaves. Food production, already meager, declined in a context of recurrent droughts followed by flooding. So dire did the situation become that the attorney who replaced Bayon in Haut-du-Cap, Sylvain de Villevaleix, took the unusual step of buying imported food to feed the workforce. But he did not reduce the workload, and the resulting mortality was "frighteningly" high by his own recognition.[2]

The plantation was rife with discontent. There were so many runaways by the end of 1789 that authorities had to stage a "hunt" in the hills above the plantation to round them up. Then, in 1790, a slave died after being mistreated by the manager who ran the plantation's day-to-day operations. Villevaleix launched a discreet inquiry among the workforce—starting, presumably, with old-timers like Louverture—which revealed that bad treatment was the norm. Villevaleix promptly fired the manager. After nine runaways returned the next day, he reported that all the slaves now "seem[ed] perfectly happy." Or so he thought: within a few months, twenty-seven more slaves had absconded.[3]

The slaves' mood colony-wide was equally volatile. Given the unstable situation in France, royal authorities begged masters to avoid undue cruelty lest the slaves start plotting a revolt. But the colonial assembly of Saint-Marc refused to curtail the masters' property rights, instead banning manumissions altogether in 1790. When this traditional safety valve disappeared, even people who had previously been willing to collaborate with the planters, such as Louverture, were left with only two options to free their loved ones: flight or fight.

Despite all evidence to the contrary, the white extremists did not think their uncompromising policies were ill-advised: to them, wild talk of liberty and equality in France was the root problem. What would happen, they wondered, if news of the racial debates taking place in Paris reached the colony, or worse, if some liberal hothead slipped into the colony to spread his views? To forestall this scenario, the Saint-Domingue delegation in Paris urged its constituents to "ARREST SUSPICIOUS PEOPLE AND SEIZE DOCUMENTS THAT MERELY MENTION THE WORD OF LIBERTY." Colonists in Saint-Domingue began to screen incoming passengers and denied entry to any agitator tied to the Society of the Friends of the Blacks. "Ports and piers are so well guarded that it is nearly impossible for proselytizers to put their projects into action," Villevaleix reported confidently. "Wiser than the whites, the negroes only think of working. Maybe they even laugh at our ever-increasing folly." Another Bréda appointee was not so sure: the endless political quarrels of the white minority "set a very bad example for our workforce," he wrote. "We had several alerts already." "As soon as unrest began in Saint-Domingue," Louverture later explained with the benefit of hindsight, "I saw that the whites could not last, because they were divided and heavily outnumbered."[4]

It was impossible to hide the news from France in a port like Cap that was visited by hundreds of ships each year. The French Revolution was on everyone's lips; political tracts proliferated. As a partly literate man who regularly visited Cap, Louverture was one of the channels through which information about the revolution in France reached the enslaved population in the plain. "Despite all the efforts of our masters to hide from us this happy event [the French Revolution], the most astute among us began to see a glimmer of hope," he later wrote. One source even claims that he subscribed to French newspapers, or more likely, obtained some bootleg issues. Domestics, like his brother Paul, could also learn much from dinnertime talk. "Indiscreet conversations held in their presence and then obviously repeated to others have informed them of the reforms planned in their favor in France," complained the governor. The visit of Lord Dunmore, who was best known for freeing the slaves of his political enemies in Virginia during the US War of Independence, must also have caused some heated dinnertime conversations in the presence of enslaved servants.[5]

Uneducated slaves could not philosophize on the Rights of Man, as elite free people of color were prone to do, but they got the gist of it: "The white slaves killed their masters," is how they understood the French Revolution. Louverture's analysis was even more perceptive: he saw the inconsistency of colonists who cited the Enlightenment to defend their own privileges, "but who would not let the Revolution destroy the prejudices against the free people of color, nor the enslavement of the blacks."[6]

The only tangible effect of censorship measures was to provide a fertile ground for rumors. The political situation in France and Saint-Domingue was confusing enough, but some colonists purposely spread rumors of an upcoming slave revolt to discredit their enemies. As a result, the slaves of Haut-du-Cap learned of major political developments through hearsay, in the manner of today's *telediol* (rumor mill) in Haiti. Every few weeks, someone would burst onto the plantation with some incredible news. Slaves had revolted in the island of Martinique (August 1789). Members of the provincial assembly were on their way to

Port-au-Prince to overthrow the *intendant* (December 1789). The garrison of Cap had mutinied (April 1790). Whites in Cap had just expelled envoys sent by the assembly of Saint-Marc (June 1790).

However outlandish they seemed at first, all these rumors turned out to be true. This gave credence to the most persistent (though inaccurate) rumor of all: that the king of France had granted slaves three days of rest a week, or maybe even freed them, and that planters were hiding the royal decree. Louverture was probably shrewd enough to distinguish between gossip and fact, and guess that Louis XVI had signed no decree of abolition, but the rumor could be put to good use when the time came to stir the slaves into action.

By 1791, the slaves of Saint-Domingue seemed ready to act. In January, a small revolt broke out in the southern town of Port-Salut. Others followed near Port-au-Prince in July. The strategic situation was promising: one of Saint-Domingue's two colonial regiments had revolted, many men of color in the militia had been disarmed after the Ogé uprising, and most of the sailors had left the colony for the hurricane season. The slaves only needed a political colossus to inspire the huddled masses and mold them into a viable revolutionary movement. If none was available, a short and wily coachman would do.[7]

The slave revolt of August 1791 was uniquely successful because it was a carefully planned operation overseen by the elite of the slave population. Louverture's exact role in that operation has been the focus of much speculation. Did he personally instigate the revolt? Or did he stay at the margins for several months to see how events would unfold? It is difficult to reach a definite conclusion when Louverture carefully hid the exact nature of his involvement, but the most likely answer is "both": he was apparently the revolt's mastermind even though he remained behind the scenes for four months to protect himself and his family.

Louverture's most daunting task as he planned the revolt was to convince the slaves to rise up despite the very real risk of defeat and death. For that he employed the clever trick of implying that he was acting on behalf of the king of France. He spread a story that his former boss Bayon, now living on his sugar plantation in Limbé after being fired by the Brédas, had personally asked him to organize a revolt on behalf of "big whites" close to Governor Louis de Blanchelande. Their goal was to scare the colonial assembly away from any plan to declare independence. In return for rising up in his name, a grateful king would grant the rebels three days of rest a week. This convoluted story was not as outlandish as it seemed, since Louis XVI had just tried to flee Paris to ask for help abroad.[8]

The tale, which reduces the Haitian Revolution to a royalist conspiracy gone laughingly awry, may seem preposterous today, but a century of progressive royal regulations had convinced the slaves that the mysterious French king who lived across the ocean was their most loyal defender. Reassuringly, the uprising would not truly be a revolt but a counterrevolution. There were historical precedents aplenty: mentions of an alleged royal emancipation decree had played a role in virtually all Caribbean slave revolts to that point.[9]

The mysterious power of the written word gave credibility to Louverture's claims. "He was the only one who knew how to read and write," reported a well-informed French officer. "This made him an oracle. He was, or claimed to be, in possession of documents that authorized the rebellion. . . . He had a repertoire of princely letters, gubernatorial orders, and royal edicts and proclamations . . . which he cleverly used to encourage the Africans, who had a natural affinity for monarchy." So successful was Louverture's deception that some of the rebellion's own leaders were convinced that they were indeed part of a royalist conspiracy, as were many contemporary royal officials.[10]

On August 14, 1791, two hundred slave foremen (most of them Creoles) from the plain of Cap met on the Lenormand de Mézy plantation in Morne-Rouge. According to a slave who was present at the meeting, one of the participants showed some official documents and "told us that the king had granted us three days [of rest] per week and that white [planters] were opposed to this; but that the king and the National Assembly would send troops to uphold our rights." One of these documents may have been an inflammatory pamphlet by the French abolitionist Henri Grégoire that had just reached the colony. Another was probably a forged letter in which royal officials allegedly asked Louverture to start a revolt.[11]

Louverture did not put his name forward when it came time to select a leader. Known popularly as *fatras bâton* (sickly stick), he argued that he did not have the requisite physique to head a revolt. Best to appoint more towering figures, such as Georges Biassou, the son of a slave at the nearby Charité hospital. "Hidden behind the curtain," Louverture would play the role of coordinator while others carried the rebel standard into battle. Rounding out the rebel leadership were Jeannot Bullet, the slave of Bayon's brother-in-law; Dutty Boukman (aka François Bouqueman), a fellow coachman from the Clément plantation; and Jean-François Papillon (aka Petecou), a runaway whose original owner was a merchant in Cap. Louverture had probably befriended all of them while crisscrossing the region as coachman. The network of friends and partners he had built over the previous decade was now proving invaluable.[12]

Louverture had good reasons to be wary of publicly taking the helm of the revolt. A slave uprising, even one ostensibly fought on behalf of the king of France, was a dangerous undertaking. Throughout his life, he had seen many a rebel die a horrible death for opposing the planter class. Just six months earlier, the bones of Vincent Ogé had cracked open under the executioner's blows in nearby Cap. His young boys and his many relatives might also pay the ultimate price. But Biassou saw Louverture's reticence as cowardice more than common sense: Louverture "proposed to me that we mobilize our comrades, but when the time came to get started, no one could convince him to act," he noted mockingly. "Not daring to put himself at the head of our group, Toussaint begged me to make myself chief."[13]

Louverture's elusive way of opposing authority, which continued to characterize his political activism throughout the Revolution, meant that few people were initially aware of his role—or even his existence. He was initially a secondary figure in the public eye, choosing to wield power through his influence over leaders like Biassou rather than in person. It was only two years after the 1791 slave uprising that he finally revealed that he had helped initiate it. "Have you forgotten that I was the first to raise the standard of insurrection against tyranny?" he declared. Most people had.[14]

Some firebrands called for immediate action at the August 14, 1791, planning meeting, but the general consensus was to wait until the new colonial assembly gathered in Cap on August 25, which also happened to be the feast day of Saint Louis, Louis XVI's namesake and ancestor. This way, the rebels could strike in the plain and the town simultaneously and decapitate the colony's entire power structure at once. This was a clever plan, but events took on a momentum of their own. On the night of the 17th, some overeager slaves set fire to a building of the Chabaud plantation in Limbé. On the 20th, others attacked the manager of the Gallifet plantation in La Gossette. Suspects were captured and tortured, and on the 21st, one of them revealed an ambitious plot to "set the plantations on fire, cut the throat of the whites, seize their arms," and march on the city of Cap. Fortunately for the revolutionaries, Governor Blanchelande did not immediately realize that these early stirrings were the omen of a much larger upheaval, and he failed to take the necessary precautions.[15]

On August 21, a second gathering took place on the Choiseul plantation. We know little of the Bois-Caïman ceremony, as this second meeting is now known, except that it was a Vodou ritual that was probably designed to inspire African-born field hands. Louverture's presence is not mentioned in the few available sources, which is logical, as a pious Catholic would not have been comfortable with these rituals. According to Haitian lore, which has grown ever more elaborate over the years, a priestess sacrificed a black pig to the spirit of war, and one of the rebel leaders, Boukman, asked all the people present to take a sacred oath. Boukman then made a call to action: "Let us start a nobler vengeance! . . . May the plantations turn to ashes and ruin!" The crackle of a lightning bolt punctuated his last words and a tropical storm unleashed its fury. Drenched in blood and sweat, the attendees disbanded to their home plantations and prepared for the great battle to come.[16]

One day after the ceremony, the 22nd, the impetuous Boukman, concerned that the rebellion would fail if they waited any longer, decided to act. Workers from a few plantations in Acul county, including the Clément plantation on which Boukman was a coachman, gathered silently in the night. The Manquets plantation, which Louverture knew well because it belonged to a Bréda heir, was their first target. "The plantation staff was making sugar while an apprentice watched on," wrote a contemporary witness:[17]

> A sugar-maker grabbed him by his hair and told him that all whites would die, then killed him with a machete. Several slaves then went to slit the throat of the refiner, who was in his bed. The attorney (M. Dumesnil), hearing all this noise, got up, ran to the balcony of the

main house and asked what was going on. A gunshot killed him on the spot. The surgeon [Monge] was spared on the condition that he take care of the sick negroes.

This outburst forced other rebels, including those of the Bréda plantation in Plaine-du-Nord, to follow suit in haphazard fashion. One after the other, the sugar estates that had made Saint-Domingue famous went up in smoke. The rebels broke machinery, burned buildings, and killed or captured planters, managers, and their families. Within a month, the tally of burned estates in the plain of Cap rose to 1,400, including 172 sugar plantations.[18]

Survivors fled to the city of Cap, where the atmosphere hovered between denial, panic, and bloodlust. But the hundreds of roaring black columns of smoke, which rose from the horizon before blanketing the city under a layer of ashes, gave evidence enough that the revolt was real. It finally dawned on colonists that they faced a general uprising, and that Cap could easily be overrun. It only had sea fortifications, to defend the city in the event of a British assault.

The white inhabitants of Cap were terrified of the slaves and freedmen in their midst, who far outnumbered them. There was no segregation in Cap: blacks were on every block, in every home and every bedroom. A white mob took preemptive action, massacring seventeen free people of color in the street. Then, as the legal system took over, two wheels and five scaffolds were erected on the market square. In a gruesome ritual, day after day, suspected conspirators were broken or hanged while women and men looked on from nearby balconies.[19]

Louverture probably heard of the slave revolt when some haggard refugee from the plain stopped on the plantation of Haut-du-Cap on her way to Cap with a tale of destruction. Pretending to be shocked was not difficult for Louverture: this is not how things were supposed to happen. The initial plan had called for a coordinated attack on the 25th, just as the colonial assembly began its session. Instead, on that day, colonial authorities were already on high alert and dispatched 250 royal troops from Cap to Haut-du-Cap to guard the main road. Governor Blanchelande personally paid a visit to the Bréda plantation to inspect the camp. A hastily built palisade soon surrounded Cap on the landward side, making any surprise attack against the town impossible. The revolt was the largest ever in Caribbean history, but the impatience of hotheads like Boukman had ruined the rebels' blueprint for a quick victory.[20]

Bloodshed was relatively limited at first as rebels killed a few plantation managers while taking other whites prisoner, especially women, priests, and surgeons. Atrocities became more common as the weeks passed, either in response to the tortures inflicted on black suspects in Cap, or because rebel leaders found it increasingly difficult to contain those whom they nominally commanded. White contemporaries were quick to emphasize these atrocities, especially when the victims were white women and children. "Young and virtuous women perished while being ravished by brigands between the corpses of their father and spouse," recounted a planter. "Young children impaled on bayonets were the bloody flags that accompanied this horde of cannibals." In retribution for the sexual exploitation that had been their lot, some female rebels also forced their male prisoners to serve them naked or to smell their genitals. In all, the immediate aftermath of the uprising claimed the lives of about three hundred white planters and their families, a tally that seemed staggering at the time but that would eventually represent only one-thousandth of the Haitian Revolution's total human cost—a rounding error.[21]

Personal bonds and simple humanity could still prevail at this early stage. Even as some slaves tortured and killed whites, others denounced the rebel agitators and saved the lives of their masters. Louverture's attitude was most ambiguous of all. He did not overtly take part in the rebellion, most likely because he feared for himself and his family now that the governor had set up an army camp next to the Bréda plantation. Instead, when rebels came to set the cane fields on fire, he repulsed them and made a show of finishing the harvest. "The loss was not considerable," he explained apologetically to the manager of the plantation.[22]

Louverture then headed to the plantation of his former boss Bayon, in Limbé, and helped Bayon and his family hide in a wood. He brought them food from the nearby rebel camp that he had joined. He may have done some reading as well: a Frenchman later found among the ruins of the rebel camp a copy of Raynal's history of the Caribbean, which, in dramatic fashion, had been left open at the page predicting the second coming of Spartacus. A month after first hiding them, Louverture helped Bayon and his family escape to safety because he was "afraid of being discovered." In later years, Louverture continued to assist the Bayons financially as they relocated to the United States and France. Humanity probably underpinned his conduct, but also personal interest. Who knew? If the French won, Bayon was the only one who could vouch for Louverture and prove that he was a freedman.[23]

When leaving Haut-du-Cap for the rebel camp near Limbé, Louverture had probably left his wife Suzanne and his children behind him. ("When the Revolution broke out, the most painful thing I had to do was to leave my wife," he later recalled.) His youngest son, Saint-Jean, was just eight months old at the time. This would explain why a rebel force led by "coachmen and foremen" attacked the Haut-du-Cap plantation on several occasions in early September: Louverture was most likely trying to rescue stranded relatives.[24]

His family in tow, Louverture must then have migrated south to the area of Grande-Rivière, where he had once been a coffee planter, and where the main rebel camps were located by that time. There, he joined a leadership wracked by dissent and ideological chaos. "Sometimes they ask for the rights of men, liberty, the Old Regime, three days off a week and to be paid," reported a French merchant. "Sometimes they say they want no master since the whites want no king." Those who were swept up in the fervor of the nascent revolution were already considering a radical agenda of general emancipation and fought under the motto "liberty or death," which had been used in other Atlantic revolutions. They might have learned their politics from the few white liberals who fought alongside the rebels, some of them in blackface. Boukman was among the hardliners, as was Jeannot Bullet, who was quickly acquiring a ghastly reputation for cruelty as he whipped, burned, or hanged white prisoners from hooks.[25]

By contrast, Louverture, Jean-François Papillon, and to a lesser extent Georges Biassou eschewed random acts of violence, probably because they wished to leave some room for a negotiated settlement if the revolt failed. Louverture, who had owned and leased slaves (as had his daughter and his sons-in-law), made no call for universal emancipation at this time. As for Jean-François, he insisted that he was fighting for labor reforms, not "general liberty," and he would continue to do so until his death. Rebels literally wore their politics on their sleeves as they proudly showcased the paraphernalia associated with the Old Regime, including white cockades (the king's color) and crosses of Saint Louis (a royalist medal). They described themselves as "generals of the armies of the king" in their correspondence. These king-loving and God-fearing slaves bring to mind the conservative peasants of the Vendée region, the *chouans*, who also rebelled against the French Revolution in the name of their Catholic king in the 1790s. Everyone had expected the slaves to stage a second Bastille; instead, Saint-Domingue was turning into a black Vendée. It would take another three years for Louverture to develop a true revolutionary agenda.[26]

Angry at the French National Assembly for speaking of liberty and poisoning the slaves' minds, the colonial assembly of Cap did not initially notify the French government of the slave revolt. Instead, it appealed to Jamaica, Cuba, Santo Domingo, and the United States. Money, food, weapons, and above all, soldiers: urgent help was needed to prevent the conflagration in northern Saint-Domingue from bringing down the entire plantation system with it.

It is generally assumed that the Haitian Revolution terrified white planters throughout the Americas, but Saint-Domingue's neighbors actually felt no sense of urgency and sent little help, beyond a Jamaican envoy who was eager to witness his rivals' woes for the "gratification of my curiosity." Surely, other Caribbean colonists thought, their own slaves were better treated than French slaves and could not possibly revolt. A Cuban booster even described the revolt in Saint-Domingue as "the hour of our happiness," because it removed an important competitor from world markets. When it became clear that Saint-Domingue could not expect significant assistance from its neighbors, the colonial assembly finally informed the French government that its most important colony desperately needed help.[27]

Because of the delay in contacting France, no troops were likely to arrive until 1792, and colonists rushed to shore up the defenses of Cap. Temporarily putting their disputes on hold, they enrolled all civilians, sailors, foreigners, and royal troops to guard the city. They also struck an alliance with free men of color, a pact that was formalized in September when whites grudgingly granted free people of color the political rights they had been requesting since 1789 in exchange for their military assistance. In case this was not enough, whites also took the families of free men of color hostage, so as to guarantee their loyalty. France went one step further in April 1792, when all free people, regardless of their race or colony of origin, became formally equal under French law. This was the Haitian Revolution's first tangible achievement—but the alliance between free whites and free people of color, who had chosen limited gains over a more profound reordering of colonial society, seemed to condemn the slave revolt to failure.

The slave rebels were no more successful when trying to expand their revolt to the rest of the colony. In the North, the French established a military cordon that effectively sealed off the plain of Cap. In the South, a conspiracy involving several plantations was foiled when faithful slaves denounced it; another was diffused when white colonists concluded an alliance with free people of color. In the West, a serious crisis erupted when free people of color armed some of their slaves and demanded voting rights. But white colonists granted their demands in exchange for deporting their armed slaves to Central America. Tensions continued to flare up episodically: most of Port-au-Prince even burned in November 1791 during a riot led by racist "little whites" and mutinous soldiers, but there was no large black-led uprising akin to the northern revolt, just an escalation of the previous years' factional disputes. Slaves in the West and South, though they were as oppressed as their northern brothers, apparently lacked a leader able to plan a large-scale revolt.[28]

Once the initial crisis had subsided, the garrison of Cap organized sorties to disband nearby rebel camps and destroy the crops that fed them. A raid on the rebel camp of Charitte on September 19, 1791, resulted in "horrible carnage." Another sortie on the 27th forced the rebels to evacuate their biggest camp, located on the Gallifet plantation.[29]

The French counteroffensive stung. There were possibly 50,000 rebels in the North, one hundred times more than in the largest slave revolt in US history. Ultimately, the Haitian Revolution would engulf the totality of the colony's slave population and add another zero to that number. But the rebels, many of whom had originated as prisoners of war in Africa, knew little of European-style warfare. They did not know how to load the cannons they had captured from the French. Encouraged by their creole leaders, they attacked en masse, hoping to be protected by their talismans and war chants, only to be cut down by the disciplined fire of French troops. "Their chiefs were careful to send ahead of them the African-born negroes, fresh off the ship and stupid," snickered a French observer. "Gun and cannon fire would mow down scores of them." Three thousand rebels died in the first month of combat, ten times more than their French foes.[30]

The strategic picture was no brighter. Although Louverture and his allies had organized the largest slave revolt in Caribbean history, its premature start meant that it had failed to take Cap or spread beyond the neighboring plain. By October 1791, they were relegated to the swath of mountains south and east of Cap, alongside the border with Santo Domingo. Victory was impossible in such conditions. With time, as colonial authorities were pleased to inform the rebel leadership, French reinforcements would reach the colony and crush the revolt with the help of free people of color. Then they would punish the leaders with the utmost cruelty. The giddiness of the early days was gone. The rebels were now a weary group plagued by food shortages, battle deaths, and doubt. Some hungry rebels began to flee to French lines and beg their previous owners for forgiveness.[31]

It was time for the rebel leaders to reevaluate their options. As a freedman, Louverture could have joined the French, who had begun to offer legal equality to free people, but he had good reason to fear that the white colonists would renege on their promises as soon as the military emergency subsided (which they did). Also, many of Louverture's relatives were still enslaved, so it was essential to obtain their freedom before he laid down his arms. He had to negotiate a deal. So did Jean-François, whose family had been taken prisoner in Cap, and Biassou, who feared for his mother, a slave at the Charité hospital.[32]

After some initial overtures by Governor Blanchelande, the gears of peace cranked into action on November 1. Though Jean-François and Biassou nominally acted in the rebels' name, because Louverture was still hiding his involvement in the revolt, Louverture's influence is discernible throughout—after all, it was All Saints' Day, his feast day. Jeannot, whose vicious treatment of white prisoners was a roadblock to any reconciliation, was arrested, put on trial, and shot. Boukman's serendipitous death in combat a few days later only left moderate figures in charge. A formal offer followed: the rebels demanded official freedom papers for themselves and their families and a general amnesty, in exchange for which they would send their followers back to work. The deal, which benefited all the parties except the slaves, may have been inspired by a similar one recently signed with free people of color in the western province. It was neither the first nor the last time that Saint-Domingue's laboring masses were betrayed by their elites.[33]

Just then, three French commissioners landed in Cap. It was difficult to keep up with revolutionary events when it took up to three months for sailing ships to cross the Atlantic, so the commissioners' orders were woefully out of date. They brought news that the French National Assembly, informed of the white planters' opposition to the May 1791 law enfranchising some free people of color, had repealed it to appease white colonists. Upon landing, they learned that a slave revolt had broken out in the interval and that white colonists had actually decided on their own to ally themselves with their mixed-race rivals. Casting aside their orders, the commissioners refocused their energies on a more pressing agenda: extinguishing the slave revolt, preferably by political means, since they had brought relatively few troops with them.[34]

It was at this juncture that, for the first time in the archival record, Louverture unambiguously came out as one of the rebel leaders—not to expand the slave revolt but to bring a negotiated end to it. On December 12, when the rebels yet again offered terms, a hesitant and misspelled "Tousaint" appeared at the bottom of the document, the earliest confirmed sample of his writing found so far. A prisoner of the rebels also noted that it was "the negro Toussaint, belonging to Bréda," who convinced his fellow leaders to reduce the number of family members to be freed from three hundred to just fifty to increase the likelihood of a deal.[35]

On December 21, Jean-François met the French commissioners in the outskirts of Cap to finalize an agreement; Louverture may have been part of the peace delegation. Frantic about the fate of his common-law wife, Charlotte, who had been taken prisoner by the French, Jean-François threw himself on his knees and begged for a pardon. His act of contrition moved the commissioners, but convincing his followers to return to work proved difficult: "We worked ceaselessly to appease the negro slaves, who are very worked up," he noted. The slaves feared being "betrayed" after surrendering; memories of the "bad treatments" they had suffered at the hands of their masters were still too fresh in their minds. Biassou, who reported that "the negroes are in a general state of effervescence," was no more successful. The chasm between the Revolution's rank and file and its leadership would continue to complicate Louverture's political agenda for years to come, and become the Haitian Revolution's main subtext. It was not only social but also gender-based: Biassou specifically listed "negresses" as the most apt to be sent back to work in the fields. Black women, who were often the most radical of the rebels, begged to disagree.[36]

In the end, Louverture's first foray into politics proved futile when the planter-dominated colonial assembly refused to grant the necessary manumissions and criticized the French commissioners for even negotiating with the rebels. An outraged Biassou prepared to execute his white prisoners, only to change his mind when Louverture counseled moderation. Instead, in January 1792, the rebels launched a surprise raid on Cap. Moving stealthily, they swam across the Haut-du-Cap River near Louverture's old plantation and seized Fort Bélair, one of Cap's main strongpoints. Their goal was apparently limited to freeing Biassou's mother, and they prudently retreated when the French counterattacked.[37]

Pressured by French sorties, the rebels fell back to Ouanaminthe along the border with the Spanish colony of Santo Domingo. There, they made yet another attempt at compromise: Why not bypass the colonial assembly, which had blocked all negotiations so far, use Spain as a go-between, and appeal directly to Louis XVI, in whose name they had ostensibly rebelled? Spanish authorities, whose monarch was a Bourbon cousin of the French king, were interested. But renewed factional disputes in Cap meant that French military pressure was light for the next few months, and the rebels eventually shelved their proposal.[38]

For the remainder of 1792, the military situation remained evenly matched. A large group led by the rebel leader Candi joined the French side in January, while a slave rebellion broke out near the town of Port-de-Paix west of Cap in March. The French nearly pacified the western province over the summer, only to suffer a major defeat when attacking the rebel camp of Platons in the South. Overall, the French retained control of most of western and southern Saint-Domingue, but they failed to annihilate the rebel army in the interior of the northern province—nor did they really try, since they were too busy fighting each other again now that the crisis had ebbed. This temporary lull gave Louverture some time to pause and regroup after the turmoil of the past few months.[39]

ELEVEN

MONARCHIST
1792

AN AIDE-DE-CAMP hand-delivered to Toussaint Louverture an in-
vitation from Georges Biassou, his fellow rebel and longtime acquain-
tance, on August 24, 1792. In highly formal French, Biassou's secretary
requested that Louverture and all "messires the colonels and commandants" of the army present themselves at 2 p.m. to observe the feast day
of their king, Louis XVI. They should see to it that their troops were
"well armed and equipped" and that they arrived on time. The setting
was Grande-Rivière in northern Saint-Domingue, but it could just as
well have been Versailles.[1]

It was exactly one year since the initial outbreak of the slave revolt.
For twelve months, white colonists had disparaged Louverture and other
rebel leaders as uncivilized brigands; for twelve months, Louverture and
his colleagues had tried their utmost to prove them wrong. Even the word
"rebel" was insulting in their eyes. Labeling him an insurgent was pure
"calumny," Biassou complained, when he was actually fighting for his
king. Echoing Jean-Jacques Rousseau, Louverture also railed against those
who described as "brigandage" what was truly "resistance to oppression."[2]

Eager to show that they were more than a pillaging mob, the rebels took on all the trappings of a European army of the Old Regime,

complete with aides-de-camp, laissez-passers, and fancy officer brevets. Formal ceremonies like the one held by Biassou on August 24 were meant to counteract the colonists' slurs; so were the grandiose titles the rebel leaders adopted. Jean-François Papillon, who was particularly irked when his French adversaries continued to address him by his first name, as if nothing had changed since the days when slaves were confused with "the vilest animals," went by the title of "grand admiral" (though the rebel force had no navy). Biassou called himself "general of the army of the King" and "knight of the military royal order of Saint Louis" (though he had received no such royal commission). Louverture went more humbly by "Monsieur Toussaint," which was still a step up from his previous monikers of "Toussaint belonging to Bréda" and "Toussaint, free negro," since the title of *monsieur*, equivalent to "sir," had been reserved exclusively for white men in prerevolutionary times.[3]

Because relatively little fighting took place in the middle of 1792—an unusually restful period of the Revolution—Louverture used these months to complete his personal transformation and convince his white foes to take him seriously. He was no brigand, he insisted, but a bona fide revolutionary, a military man, and a fellow human being. This struggle for recognition would occupy him for the next decade—and, tragically, it would fail.

When trying to encourage the slaves to revolt in August 1791, Louverture had spread rumors that he was acting on Louis XVI's orders. The claim was spurious, but it took on a life of its own; loyalty to the Bourbon dynasty became the hallmark of the rebel forces fighting under Biassou and Jean-François. Whether they were celebrating Louis XVI's feast day or flying the white flag of royalist France, the rebels who served with Louverture made it clear that they had taken up arms "to support the rights of the king our master as well as our religion."[4]

The Bourbon kings and the Catholic Church were so closely intertwined in eighteenth-century France that to fight for Louis XVI meant to pray to his God. Eschewing the Vodou ceremonies popular among other rebel groups, Biassou and Jean-François ostentatiously portrayed themselves as fervent Catholics. Neither could out-pray Louverture, who, when no priest was available, even officiated a Mass in his eagerness to put his faith on display (a sacrilegious practice, since he was not ordained). Louverture forged a close bond with several white priests, most notably a Spanish priest named Josef Vásquez and a French one named Jacques Delahaye. The latter, who had been ministering in Cap and Quartier-Morin since the 1760s, must have been known to him for decades.[5]

To cultivate the support of the Catholic Church, rebels were willing to condone the very slave system against which they had supposedly rebelled. When two slaves fled from Father Delahaye, who owned them, Biassou personally intervened to have them arrested and returned to the priest (the rebels extended similar courtesies to their Spanish neighbors). "As for the rest of your domestics," Biassou told the priest, "Monsieur Toussaint ordered them to return to their duty."[6]

The plantation system was not yet dead. Louverture offered "to go on an inspection tour every week to restore order" among field laborers, a policy also embraced by his colleagues ("All these negresses should work," explained a rebel leader). Some rebels even sold black women and children to Spanish slave traders from Santo Domingo. Their behavior had a precedent: in the eighteenth century, independent black communities in border areas had often agreed to return runaways to their French and Spanish owners in exchange for pacts of nonaggression. The 1791 slave revolt was large enough to turn into a real revolution, but Jean-François and Biassou seemed happy to live as petty chieftains on the margins of a slave-based plantation society. Life was good when one could frolic in a carriage with "*demoiselles*," as the handsome Jean-François liked to do.[7]

Though he forced field hands to continue working, Louverture did not sully his name by trading slaves the way his associates did. Perhaps it was he who convinced Father Delahaye to add an addendum to his will to free his slave Françoise. These were the first signs of an ideological evolution that would quicken over the following two years.[8]

On August 25, 1792, just one day after Biassou had summoned his commandants to a ceremony in Louis XVI's honor, a strange battle erupted in the city of Ouanaminthe, along the border with the Spanish colony of Santo Domingo. It began as rebel soldiers fired on their leader Jean-François and expressed their preference for Biassou. Biassou was far away in Grande-Rivière, probably recovering from the previous day's party (for he was as loyal to kegs of rum as he was to the king of France), so Jean-François was able to regain control of Ouanaminthe.

The one-day civil war in Ouanaminthe stemmed from a simple but intractable question that Louverture's equivocal attitude during the 1791 slave revolt had failed to answer: Who was in control? When the fighting ended, Biassou remained in command of the region of Grande-Rivière directly south of Cap, and Jean-François retained his base farther east in Ouanaminthe, but each continued to claim that he was senior to the other. The status of *Monsieur* Louverture, who sided with Biassou in the feud, was even less clear. Though Biassou described him as a major general (*maréchal de camp*) and his subordinate, Louverture later insisted that he had in fact led his own independent force all along.[9]

The rebel army was still a long way from becoming effective. Rebel leaders did their best to play the parts of European officers, but most were former plantation foremen and domestics who lacked basic military skills. Louverture's expertise was animal husbandry.

Always eager to improve himself, Louverture used the inconclusive year of 1792 to learn the art of soldiering, which would remain his primary occupation for the rest of his career. A black veteran of the militia taught him basic drills, while a French prisoner he had spared gave him fencing lessons, but the learning curve was steep. Some rebels learned to love the powdery smell of the battlefield, most notably Louverture's daughter's former slave, Jean-Jacques Dessalines, who joined Louverture's personal guard as a guide and grew into a formidable warrior. But Louverture's personal skill set was better suited for politics, and his body became a running log of his military setbacks. "I received a bullet in my right hip that is still in my body," he later wrote. "I suffered a violent concussion to the head caused by a cannonball that so shook my jaw that most of my teeth fell out and that the few that remain are still very wobbly. Finally, I suffered on different occasions seventeen wounds, of which I still bear honorable scars."[10]

Slaves were slowly becoming aware of their potential. Throughout their lives they had been told by their masters that whites were few but innately superior and even invincible; the slave revolt had put that notion to rest. What made the Revolution so dangerous to the plantation system was the rebel slaves' realization that they had no reason to cower before their former masters. In Limbé, just west of Cap, black women demanded that their female prisoners serve them during dinner "as if they were their servants," a Frenchman marveled. As far away as Port-au-Prince, where the slave revolt had not yet taken hold, slaves no longer showed their masters any "respect."[11]

From the white point of view, whether the process was reversible grew more doubtful with each passing month. "The magic [of racism] has disappeared, how will we replace it?" lamented a nostalgic planter. According to a neighbor of the Brédas, planters might have to "sacrifice half of our workforce" to stop the "epidemic" and start fresh with a new batch of imports from Africa. As these genocidal fantasies became more commonplace, defeat came to entail extermination for Louverture and his fellow blacks.[12]

Jean-François was sufficiently shaken by the August 25 civil war in Oua-naminthe to ask Spanish authorities across the border for their support. Louverture countered with a letter on Biassou's behalf. Santo Domingo's governor, Joaquín García, thought little of Jean-François, who "doesn't know how to write," but he was impressed by the letter from Louverture, of whom he had never heard before. Here evidently was a man with "better character." Though Biassou's name appeared at the bottom of the letter, García had a hunch that "other hands and heads" with more intellectual ability labored in the background. He wondered who in the rebel army truly held "the reins of their government."[13]

Louverture quickly understood that his white peers would never treat him as an equal as long as he could not express himself as well as they did. Though he had learned the basics of writing from his godfather before the Revolution, he was still functionally illiterate as late as the fall of 1791, when he was about forty-eight years old. Other rebel leaders simply relied on secretaries, but Louverture, always eager to control his own destiny, was unwilling to settle for white mediation. He studied with various educated whites and blacks, including a French tutor whom he ostensibly hired for his sons because he was too proud to be the young man's pupil (he snuck in at class time and listened to the lesson from the back of the room).[14]

The word proved even trickier to master than the sword, but Louverture, a gifted learner, made significant progress over time. To showcase his erudition, he built up an extensive library of ponderous tomes on military history and Greek political thought, though it is unlikely that he had the time to read them all. Within a decade, he was able to write a lengthy memoir largely on his own. His handwriting remained hesitant, possibly because he badly hurt his right hand during one battle and had to use his left hand thereafter; his grammar was wayward, his spelling phonetic. Concerned that his limitations as a writer might reflect poorly on his intellect, he employed secretaries to draft all but his most sensitive letters and contented himself with adding his signature. But he had his secretaries pen multiple copies and then spent his nights comparing them under the flickering light of a candle to ensure that no one had misrepresented his thoughts.[15]

By mastering the art of writing, Louverture had entered the historical record. He could at long last begin to tell his story.

By the time Biassou summoned Louverture and his other officers to celebrate Louis XVI's feast day on August 24, 1792, their king was actually no longer ruling France. Unbeknownst to them, two weeks earlier in Paris bloody street battles had led to his downfall and imprisonment. The end of the Bourbon monarchy made a great impression on Louverture when he finally heard of it. For the rest of his life, he would refer to the events of August 10, 1792—not Bastille Day in 1789, or, amazingly, the 1791 slave revolt—as the true beginning of the Revolution.[16]

The news of Louis XVI's demise reached Saint-Domingue in October 1792, shortly after a relief force of 6,000 French troops landed in Cap. These were two heavy blows for the rebels. After six months of relative calm, the French went back on the offensive and recaptured the towns of Ouanaminthe (Jean-François's headquarters) and Dondon (in Biassou's area of command). They then launched a coordinated assault on the rebel camp of Morne-Pelé. Surrounded and almost captured in the whirlwind of a defeat, Louverture had to consider himself lucky to survive the battle, though he was wounded.[17]

At this difficult juncture, the rebels could have forsaken their allegiance to Louis XVI and laid down their arms. They did not. On Christmas Day 1792, feast day of his other Lord, Biassou gathered his army in his "royal palace" and had the throngs recognize him as "viceroy of all conquered lands" who would rule Saint-Domingue in the Bourbons' name while awaiting the restoration of the monarchy in France. He promoted Louverture to general of the royal army-in-exile for the occasion.[18]

Biassou then charged Father Delahaye with organizing a proper coronation ceremony and setting up a constitutional arrangement. "Please draft a speech to thank the people for their trust," he instructed the priest, and "establish a law, which is to say a form of government to restore order while we await the orders of the king our master." Unfortunately, no copy has survived of the document, which was in effect Haiti's second constitution after the one drafted by the white deputies of Saint-Marc in 1790.

With time, Biassou's vice-royalty could have evolved into an autonomous polity allied with Spain and nominally loyal to the French monarch. Indeed, a runaway community in that mold had existed for hundreds of years in Maniel, in the borderland between Saint-Domingue and Santo Domingo. But momentous events in France and Saint-Domingue would send the Revolution in a new direction. The year about to begin, 1793, would prove more cataclysmic than even 1791.[19]

TWELVE

SPANISH OFFICER
1793–1794

WHEN THE NEWS REACHED Saint-Domingue, in September 1792, that a French relief force of 6,000 was about to land in Cap, a wave of panic swept through the rebel army. The rebels had lost their chance to beat the French colonists when they were weak. Now, with France's support, the planters would go on the offensive and destroy them. However large and well planned at its inception, the Saint-Domingue slave revolt would join the countless failed Caribbean uprisings.

The situation was so dire that the rebels put their internal disputes aside and jointly pushed for a negotiated settlement. Louverture (acting as Biassou's representative) and Jean-François contacted Spanish officials in Santo Domingo and asked them to pass on an offer to the king of France: they would send their followers back to their plantations by assuring the rebel slaves that they would now work "as free people and with a daily or weekly pension." Then the rebels would be disarmed and put back under the "yoke of slavery." As a reward for betraying their followers, Jean-François and Louverture would get "protection and freedom papers signed by the King." Their proposal went nowhere. If it had, Louverture would have gone down in history not as the great liberator of the slaves of Saint-Domingue, but as an accessory to their re-enslavement. This was

Louverture a year after the slave revolt had begun: a secondary figure, still living under the shadow of Biassou and Jean-François, though of superior intellect; and an ambivalent revolutionary.[1]

Much happened over the next two years. White political infighting and the slave revolt continued like a fever that would not break; meanwhile, Louis XVI was executed in France, after which Britain and Spain invaded Saint-Domingue. In a few short months, to everyone's surprise, emancipation became the law, not only in Saint-Domingue but in the rest of the French colonial empire as well.

In this changing landscape, Louverture followed a sinuous path that took him from the rebel army to the Spanish Army and eventually the French Army. These two years were for him a time of political maturation as he shook off the trappings of the Old Regime to don the new revolutionary mantle of universal liberty. Out went the old, in came the new, including a last name full of promise: it was during this period that he took the name Louverture. This personal journey reached its endpoint in 1794, when, for the first time in his life, Louverture unambiguously and publicly embraced the cause of liberty for all.

After debating for months whether to relieve the beleaguered colonists, France decided in the spring of 1792 to send a second group of commissioners and an army to Saint-Domingue. Their primary mission was to disband the all-white colonial assemblies that had toyed with independence and enforce a law passed in April 1792 granting political rights to free people of color. The commissioners' instructions said remarkably little of the slave revolt itself; the French government assumed that it would be easily subdued once the conflict between free whites and free blacks was brought to an end.[2]

After the fleet reached Saint-Domingue in September, the French commissioner Léger-Félicité Sonthonax, a rotund man of twenty-nine, took over the northern province, while his colleague Etienne de Polverel, a lawyer from Bordeaux, headed for Port-au-Prince in the West (the third commissioner, who was supposed to oversee the South, left as quickly as he arrived). One of the commissioners' first acts was to dismiss the pusillanimous governor Louis de Blanchelande and send him back to France to account for his conduct. There, he was put on trial and guillotined for his failure to contain the slave revolt. The nagging suspicion that he had secretly encouraged the slaves in the first place, which Louverture had done much to cultivate, sealed his fate.[3]

The new French commissioners expected the worst from white colonists, but the colonists proved surprisingly pliant. In short order, they accepted the dissolution of the colonial assemblies and the enfranchisement of free people of color. In exchange, the commissioners promised to launch a major offensive against rebel positions. The 6,000 men they had brought from France, who were later reinforced by an additional 3,000 men, brought the garrison of Cap to a total of 11,000 men. France had sent fewer men across the Atlantic during the US War of Independence.[4]

Victory seemed imminent, but the political unity only lasted a month. The French soldiers the commissioners brought with them began quarreling over revolutionary dogma before they even set foot in Saint-Domingue. The fall of Louis XVI in France then gave white colonists an excuse to denounce the commissioners' appointment as invalid. Sonthonax, a formidable figure with a short fuse, had little patience for those whom he called "the aristocrats of the epidermis," and would not let himself be bullied like his predecessors. Chaos followed. Sonthonax deported Jean-Jacques d'Esparbès, Blanchelande's successor as governor, because he considered him too attached to the old monarchy; three more governors came and went over the following eight months.[5]

France took an even more radical turn when, on January 1793, Louis XVI was put on trial and guillotined in Paris. As a new regime, called the National Convention, seized power, civil war broke out between partisans and enemies of the king. Already at war with Austria and Prussia, France was also attacked by Portugal, the Netherlands, Britain, and Spain, each of them eager to stamp out the radical experiment that was Jacobinism.

Britain, the largest naval power in the world, was a formidable foe. Louverture, who had already experienced three Anglo-French wars in his lifetime, knew that previous conflicts had caused crippling food shortages in Cap. The newly arrived French regiments would probably go hungry, and France was unlikely to reinforce them as long as the European war lasted. His own troops, by contrast, could live off the land or smuggle cattle from Santo Domingo. They could also attract new recruits from the colony's vast black population.

Spain was past its heyday as a world power, but its entry into the war, news of which reached Saint-Domingue in May 1793, was nevertheless significant because Spain controlled Santo Domingo. The possibility arose of a formal alliance with the rebels. What if, despite the odds, the rebels were to prevail after all?

Because their troops were not yet proficient on the battlefield, the rebel leaders employed what we would call today guerrilla tactics. Success in such conflicts depends on the support of the civilian population, access to food and ammunition, and the assistance of sovereign neighbors willing to offer a safe haven in times of peril. Without Spain's help, the rebels could be cornered and starved; with it, they might outrun and outlast their enemy.[6]

Within two months of the initial August 1791 uprising, the rebels were already in contact with someone they described as "the Spanish man," who was probably a merchant. Commercial exchanges multiplied when the rebels took control of the border town of Ouanaminthe

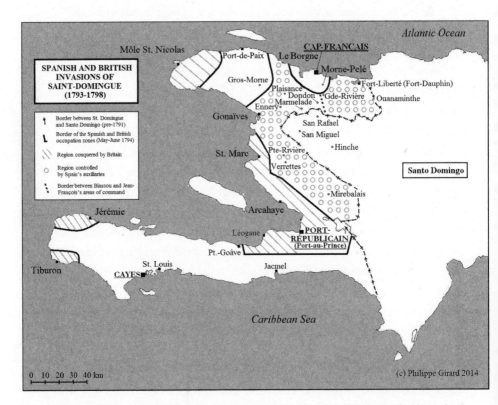

The Spanish and British invasions of Saint-Domingue (1793–1798). Map by the author.

in January 1792. Though Santo Domingo's governor, Joaquín García, officially adopted a neutral stance to avoid upsetting French authorities, in practice local Spanish officials condoned the contraband trade (the rebels even sent García a thank-you note). This accommodating policy ran against instructions from Madrid that called for "perfect neutrality" regarding the slave revolt, but who would reprove the governor of Santo Domingo when it often took nine months for his dispatches to travel from his colonial backwater to Spain and back? At any rate, García lived in Santo Domingo's capital and did not visit the border regions until 1794, so local Spanish commanders did as they pleased. And it pleased them very much to make easy money by trading with the rebels.[7]

The contraband trade aside, Governor García was careful not to be drawn into the tumultuous politics of his neighbor. He sealed the border and turned away black rebels so that his colony would not be "infected" by the revolutionary virus. Even more concerned by the radical republicanism of the French, he turned away male white refugees as well.[8]

The rebels made their first official overtures to Spain in February and September 1792, at times when their military position was weak. Nothing came of them, but they tried again when the French commissioners launched their offensive during the winter of 1792 to 1793. Feeling "hounded like a ferocious beast," Louverture concluded that the rebels needed a powerful patron. Upon learning of Louis XVI's death in March 1793, "a black man sent by Biassou" (probably Louverture) went to see the Spanish commander in the border town of San Rafael and offered to integrate the rebel forces into the Spanish Army.[9]

The timing was impeccable. Spain had just declared war on France in Europe, and Madrid had ordered Governor García to recruit allies in Saint-Domingue, whether they were royalist whites or "brigands, negroes, and mulattoes." García chose to rely primarily on the latter: he only wanted "well-disciplined troops," and the rebels, who had spent 1792 shaping themselves into a respectable army, seemed more reliable than the white colonists who had subjected Saint-Domingue to endless political convulsions. The rebel leadership's yearlong effort to gain the respect of powerful whites was paying its first dividends.[10]

The French commissioners made their own attempts to woo the rebels by promising them manumissions and cash rewards if they joined the French Army. The Spanish offers were no better, but Louverture,

Jean-François, and Biassou decided to accept them. Their decision may seem surprising: Spain was a slave-owning power, whereas revolutionary France had just made its first tentative steps toward racial equality. But the rebels had a hard time trusting French promises when no one knew who was in charge from one day to the next. So unstable was the situation in French-controlled areas that Commissioner Sonthonax had to wage two urban battles in April and June 1793 to wrest Port-au-Prince and Cap, the colony's two largest cities, from the hands of white rivals.

By contrast, Spain, the oldest colonial power in the Americas and a Catholic kingdom governed by a relative of Louis XVI, represented respectability and legitimacy in the rebels' eyes. "To die for my King and for Freedom: this is my motto," explained Louverture. "Give the Spaniard some credit: he fears his God and his Prince." Having made up his mind, in June 1793 Louverture raised the Spanish flag over the town of Dondon and began yet another stage of his life as a major general (*mariscal de campo*) in one of the so-called "auxiliary units" of the Spanish Army.[11]

In the first half of 1793, almost two years after the outbreak of the slave revolt, slavery was still well entrenched in French Saint-Domingue. A planter opening the paper in Cap could read ads for a slave-trading ship fresh from Africa and a "negro tailor: for sale or lease," as if the revolt had never taken place. Granted, a rebel army was active in the interior of the northern province, but the reinforcements sent by France would surely bring them to heel. In the end, it took the leadership of a single man to end slavery in the colony. His name was not Louverture but Léger-Félicité Sonthonax.[12]

Sonthonax had long harbored reservations about slavery. A friend of the founder of the Society of the Friends of the Blacks, he had judged in 1790 that it was useless to oppose "the principles of universal liberty." He was also a member of a Jacobin club agitating for the abolition of slavery in France. In a bizarre twist, it was this closet abolitionist that France had entrusted with the mission of ending the slave revolt.[13]

After landing in Saint-Domingue, Sonthonax warred against the slave rebels because his orders required him to, but his heart was clearly not in it. He begged French legislators to pass some measure in the slaves' favor, because "the slaves of the New World fight for the same cause as the French armies" in Europe. By May 1793, he concluded that sub-duing slave rebels would be both impossible (he lacked the troops) and counterproductive (Why kill the colony's workers?). He also reaffirmed the old regulations of the Black Code, which, in a novel act, he translated into Kreyòl so that slaves would be better informed of their rights. In early June, he began to offer "universal liberty" to the rebels who joined the French side. His colleague Etienne de Polverel, also a closet abolition-ist, took similar steps in the western province.[14]

This gradual move toward abolition gained new momentum on June 20–22, 1793, when Sonthonax fought on the streets of Cap against the fourth governor in a year, François Galbaud. Facing defeat, Sonthonax issued a proclamation promising that all black warriors who joined his side would get their freedom in return. With the assistance of two nearby rebel chiefs, Sonthonax prevailed, and he kept his promise.[15]

The three days of intense street fighting destroyed most of the city that Louverture had come to know as a coachman. Estimates of the num-ber of people killed ranged from 3,000 to 10,000. Most of the white survivors fled Cap along with some free people of color and slaves. In time, the Dominguan community-in-exile would grow to more than 20,000 people, most of them in Cuba, Jamaica, Santo Domingo, and the eastern United States. Local planters feared that copycat slave revolts would break out wherever they landed. But the real impact was back in Saint-Domingue: the departure of so many white colonists meant that the demographic imbalance that already favored the black majority now became overwhelming.[16]

There was no turning back for Sonthonax after the battle for Cap. The troops he had brought from France were decimated by disease during the summer of 1793. The remaining white colonists hated France for killing their king and enfranchising free people of color. The nascent war with Spain and the threat of a British invasion, which materialized in September, made the commissioner's situation truly desperate. Free people of color aside, Sonthonax could only count on one group: the colony's enslaved majority.

Over the summer, Sonthonax repeatedly urged Biassou and Jean-François to join him, but they eventually refused. Louverture, whom Sonthonax also contacted, replied that he "wanted a king." Sonthonax sneered at African monarchists who fought "to avenge our good king

Louis XVI," but the concept of a republican government seemed nebulous to the rebels. It was not made any clearer by the fact that Sonthonax, after dismissing the colonial assembly and Governor Galbaud, essentially ruled as a dictator in the manner of the Committee of Public Safety in Paris.[17]

Pressed by the black population of Cap to proclaim "general liberty," Sonthonax, on July 11, offered to free the spouses of any black soldiers who joined the French Army. By defecting, Louverture could have gotten France to recognize his second wife, Suzanne, as free, which had been his goal all along. And yet, he again turned down French offers, because he blamed the "republican traitors" for beheading Louis XVI.[18]

Undeterred, Sonthonax continued to expand his policy of emancipation for the rest of the summer. Unlike previous French colonial administrators, who had often purchased plantations or married creole heiresses, he had no financial or personal stake in slavery. In fact, he took on a mixed-race partner whom he eventually married. Interracial marriages had not been technically illegal in prerevolutionary Saint-Domingue, but they carried such a social stigma that it was unthinkable for a prominent official to marry across the color line. Sonthonax's personal life offered a powerful illustration of the changing times and of his commitment to racial egalitarianism.[19]

Louverture saw the slave rebellion that he had midwifed slip out of his control as Sonthonax became the embodiment of black liberty. On Bastille Day 1793, Sonthonax organized a ceremony in Cap in which he planted a tree of liberty topped by a liberty pike and a liberty cap, a triptych that symbolized freedom and that would later become the centerpiece of the Haitian coat of arms. Rumor had it that he intended to abolish slavery altogether, which would secure his place in history as Saint-Domingue's Great Emancipator. Meanwhile, in an attempt to be recognized as commander-in-chief of all the black auxiliary units of the Spanish Army, Biassou was spreading stories that he was the Revolution's true father because Louverture had been too cowardly in August 1791 to claim that role for himself. Two years into the Revolution, few knew that he had conceived it.[20]

Concerned by Sonthonax's and Biassou's attempts to upstage him, Louverture publicly announced for the first time that the slave revolt was his brainchild. "I was the first to favor [liberty], a cause I always upheld," he revealed in August 1793. It was also apparently during this period that he acquired the cryptic nickname of "Louverture," his misspelled rendering of the French for "the opening." Theories on the origins of his name abound: authors have variously attributed it to his battlefield exploits, the gap between his teeth, and Vodou tradition. In fact, remembered a comrade-in-arms, he simply wanted to publicize that "he was the first who stepped forward to get the slaves of the North to revolt." The nickname was a way to brand himself as a revolutionary trailblazer.[21]

There was also an element of personal vindication in Louverture's belated naming. For five decades he had been known as Toussaint Bréda after his owners. Though legally required to adopt an African-sounding name after his manumission (such as Guinou, his grandfather's last name), he had not done so, most likely because he wanted no reminder of his African roots. Only after 1791 did he acquire a full French identity, first as "Monsieur" Toussaint, and now as Toussaint Louverture. This was a proud moment in his life. He now had a name that he could pass on to his offspring. He would introduce himself as "Toussaint Louverture" consistently for the rest of his life, often in the face of racist enemies who persisted in calling him "Toussaint" as if he were still a slave.[22]

Sonthonax's ever more sweeping proclamations forced Louverture to hasten his political evolution. In August 1793, he wrote several letters to introduce himself to the world. One of these became known as the proclamation of Camp Turel, after the place from which it was written, and is often quoted to underline his supposed lifelong commitment to black liberty: "I am Toussaint Louverture, my name may be known to you," he began. "I want liberty and equality to reign in Saint-Domingue. I worked from the beginning for its existence."[23]

Read in isolation, this passage implies that Louverture was and had always been an advocate of general emancipation; the rest of the document, however, implies that the letter was addressed to free people of color and whites, not slaves, and that the term "liberty" referred to the political rights of a privileged minority, not universal emancipation. Other letters he wrote around the same period are marked by ideological inconsistency, mixing God, monarchy, and the rights of men.[24]

On August 29, the same day that Louverture delivered his ambiguous proclamation in Camp Turel, Sonthonax put an end to four years of French equivocation. After asserting, per the French Declaration of the Rights of Man and of the Citizen, that "MEN ARE BORN AND REMAIN FREE AND EQUAL IN RIGHTS," he abolished slavery in northern Saint-Domingue altogether. Polverel did the same in the West and South of Saint-Domingue in October, at which point all the slaves of the colony became officially free under French colonial law.[25]

Sonthonax publicized his decree widely. He translated it into Spanish and Kreyòl and sent printed copies to the rebel leaders in Spain's employ. Louverture got his own copy. No other European power had abolished slavery in the Western Hemisphere, and only a few states in the northern United States had. Even the physical document itself was exciting: at a time when Louverture's patrons in Santo Domingo had no printing press at their disposal and relied exclusively on handwritten manuscripts, the public proclamations printed in Saint-Domingue looked very modern by comparison.

And yet Louverture was not completely won over. The idea of general liberty clearly intrigued him, but his loyalty to the Bourbons was just as strong. "His politics, character and conduct are easy to understand," remembered his son. "A former slave, he loved freedom passionately. The grandson of an African king, he could not hate kings and nobles."[26]

Louverture's sharp political instincts also gave him pause. How could he trust a man like Sonthonax, who had come to Saint-Domingue to end the slave revolt and had once "sworn before the Supreme Being to maintain slavery forever"? The governor of Saint-Domingue immediately denounced the emancipation decree as null and void because it violated Sonthonax's instructions. Sonthonax could not even get his decree implemented in Gros-Morne, an area nominally under his control. It was not clear, for that matter, whether he was still a commissioner: the man who had appointed him, Louis XVI, was dead, and there were persistent (and, as it turned out, accurate) reports that the French government had recalled him. His enemies did their best to further undermine Sonthonax by spreading rumors that he had died and that his fellow commissioner Polverel was about to join him in the ground. The very future of France, which was at war with most of Europe's monarchies, seemed bleak; Louverture heard that France had already lost the war in Europe. "There is a big ruckus in France," an old slave replied when he was approached by Sonthonax's envoys. "When it is over, they'll come to take away this liberty at gunpoint."[27]

Better, then, to wait and determine whether abolition was here to stay before committing to the French camp. Sonthonax's decree was a "trick" and a "chimera," warned Biassou. "This liberty is good for nothing," agreed another rebel leader, echoing a common belief among the rebel ranks that no one but a master or a king had the legal right to free a slave. Makaya and Pierrot, two relatively minor leaders, were the only ones who took up Sonthonax's offer—only to have second thoughts later.[28]

The rebels' entry into Spanish service proved highly beneficial to their Spanish patrons. They brought 10,000 warriors with them, a formidable army by Caribbean standards. Jean-François led the largest force (6,000), but Louverture, who served under Biassou, was the most active. In a few months, he carved out a territory that encompassed the towns of Dondon, Marmelade, Verrettes, Petite-Rivière, and Plaisance in the interior of the northern province; he capped off his achievements in December 1793 by conquering the port of Gonaïves on the western coast, which cut French Saint-Domingue in two and gave the Spanish access to the Caribbean Sea. More skilled as a politician than as a soldier, Louverture often won his victories by convincing his foes to join his side. This would always remain his preferred strategy, along with his willingness to pardon his adversaries—including white planters, whom he would then enlist in his army. Louverture's handler Matías de Armona, the Spanish commander of the central border region, was usually wary of black auxiliary troops, but he was so impressed by Louverture's achievements that he rewarded him with ornamental swords and bullfights in his honor. This delighted a man who had longed for recognition all his life.[29]

Governor García requested that Madrid manufacture three engraved gold medals for Jean-François, Biassou, and a now-forgotten rebel leader named Hyacinthe to show his gratitude for the rebels' help. By the time the medals arrived, Hyacinthe had been hanged for double-crossing the Spanish, but García had become so taken with "the good deeds of another black named Toussaint Louverture," who "worked with efficiency and skill, unlike those of his color," that García selected him to receive the third medal.[30]

The rebel force's transformation from marauding slave band to professional army intensified under Spain's leadership. The Spanish colony of

Cuba sent officers to drill the troops, while Biassou's general staff drafted formal regulations and job descriptions for the entire chain of command, all the way down to child drummers. Meanwhile, Jean-François married his common-law wife, Charlotte, so that it could not be said that a Spanish general was living in sin. She received silk stockings from Governor García as a wedding present; he received a stern lecture from Father Josef Vásquez about marital fidelity. No more *demoiselles* for him.

One thorny issue—Who led the rebel army?—remained. In the summer of 1793, Jean-François visited Biassou's encamped army and distributed cash to his troops in an overt attempt to steal them. Biassou countered by sending a personal envoy to Governor García to denounce Jean-François as a man of "many words but few deeds." He wanted to get himself recognized as "generalissimo" of all the conquered territories. A Spanish officer noted that Biassou's "only job is to drink *aguardiente* [hard liquor]," so one suspects that Louverture was orchestrating this political maneuvering behind the scenes. Tensions between the two rebel factions reached a point that Jean-François briefly had Louverture imprisoned in retaliation.[31]

Afraid of losing the war due to infighting among the rebel factions, Spain organized a formal reconciliation ceremony in November 1793. The experience must have been awe-inspiring for men just two years removed from the sugar fields of Saint-Domingue. Standing at attention in front of an audience of Spanish officers, translators, and witnesses, Biassou, Jean-François, and Louverture declared that they were "honored to be the faithful vassals" of the king of Spain and swore "never to speak again . . . of past disputes." The Spanish formally delineated the border between Biassou's and Jean-François's territories, and their feud eased thereafter. But the ceremony left one issue unresolved: Louverture's status. Though he was asked to pledge his personal loyalty to Spain, as if he led his own force, the document listed no area under his command, which implied that he served at Biassou's discretion.[32]

Louverture's decision to join the Spanish Army transformed the lives of his wife and sons, who established their residence in the town of San Rafael while he campaigned in the central region of Saint-Domingue. Aside from occasional forays to Cap to attend Mass, the Louvertures had spent their entire lives in Haut-du-Cap; they now lived in another colony altogether. They had been nobodies; now they were the family of one of the most powerful figures in Santo Domingo. They had been slaves, but Spain had now likely provided them with official freedom papers. Louverture was away for months at a time because of the war, but this period marked the first time, after the subjugation of slavery and the upheavals of the slave revolt, that he could lead a family life that was almost normal.[33]

Louverture, who a decade earlier did not have enough money to buy back his relatives' freedom, began accumulating significant wealth in real estate. He and Suzanne acquired plots in San Rafael, San Juan de la Maguana, and Bánica, as well as a cattle ranch near Hinche. They later bought or leased several coffee plantations near Ennery and Gonaïves on the French side, making them one of the richest couples in Hispaniola. Louverture estimated his personal wealth around that period at over half a million francs (the new name for the French livre), an impressive sum when the death of two slaves worth 3,000 colonial livres had doomed his coffee-growing venture at an earlier stage of life.[34]

During the winter of 1793–1794, local colonists encouraged Britain to invade Saint-Domingue and nullify the emancipation decree. In short order the British took over the main ports of the western and southern coasts. Jérémie, Môle Saint-Nicolas, and Saint-Marc fell one after the other. The Spanish received reinforcements from Cuba and Puerto Rico and seized the major port of Fort-Dauphin (today Fort-Liberté) in the North, after which they prepared to launch an amphibious assault on France's main stronghold in Cap. Sensing that victory was within grasp, Governor García traveled from the colonial capital of Santo Domingo to Fort-Dauphin to witness it firsthand.

Yet a crisis was brewing. It did not seem fair to Louverture that Jean-François and Biassou, whom he had recruited into his plot in August 1791, were his seniors in the Spanish Army. He claimed that they were lightweights who lived well at Spain's expense while he did most of the actual fighting. Spanish expense reports indicate that there was some truth to his recriminations: when selecting gifts for their allies, the Spanish chose fine muslin and scarlet cloth for Jean-François, and barrels of wine and rum for Biassou, while Biassou's staff—which is to say Louverture—received quills, ink, and paper. Why should he bow for a fop and a sot?[35]

Louverture's relationship with Jean-François had been frayed since the incident at Ouanaminthe in August 1792; the white colonists of

Santo Domingo made sure that his relationship with Biassou, a boisterous but endearing character, eventually soured as well. One evening, when Biassou and Louverture were dining together, Biassou received a letter from a planter named Laplace, which the illiterate Biassou handed to Louverture to read. As he deciphered the letter, Louverture was "surprised to learn that Mr. Laplace, who was writing, was urging [Biassou] to be careful and that I was an old Capuchin who would supplant him while praying to the good Lord." Biassou assured Louverture that he paid no attention to Laplace's persiflage, but Louverture did not forget the incident. Over time, he came to view his old friend as "a weak man, fragile, and ignorant," as well as "impetuous, disorganized, and forgetful."[36]

Laplace was one of the many exiled French planters who returned in 1793–1794 to the Spanish-controlled areas of Saint-Domingue where slavery was still legal. Their arrival upset a balance of power that had tilted heavily in favor of black officers. Some of the planters, whose political common sense remained remarkably deficient from the start to the end of the Revolution, expected to recover their slaves and immediately send them back to the fields upon their return. In Le Borgne, planters tried to reinstitute the use of the whip; in Petite-Rivière, a local commander recommended killing all foremen and one-tenth of the workforce whenever a crime was committed on a plantation. Louverture's officers also complained that the Spanish soldiers who were supposed to "offer us protection" were involved in the "vile commerce" of buying slaves in Saint-Domingue and exporting them to Cuba. The feud between Louverture and Biassou, which had begun as a simple clash of egos, turned into a profound ideological dispute over the morality of the slave trade and, ultimately, the goals of the Revolution.[37]

A trusted adviser of Biassou proposed to institute a type of serfdom enforced by rebel soldiers that would offer an alternative to the extremes of slavery and emancipation. Though he would adopt a similar labor system ten years later, Louverture did not think the political climate was right for it presently. If plantation work was restored too quickly, he feared, the independent rebel groups whose loyalty was still up for grabs would surely side with the abolitionist French.[38]

The cost of these disputes became evident in March 1794, when some of Biassou's men re-enslaved the wives and children of some of the soldiers in Louverture's army and then blamed Louverture. Louverture insisted that he had taken no part in this "odious trade," but one of his subordinates blamed him nonetheless and staged an ambush. Eight men died by Louverture's side, including his brother Pierre.[39]

Louverture fled to the Spanish headquarters in San Rafael and asked for redress, but he received little sympathy. Juan Lleonart, who had replaced Matías de Armona as commander of the border region, had long been convinced of Louverture's "perfidy." A proud noble with forty-one years' service in the army, Lleonart also disliked having to cater to former slaves. When new upheavals broke out among black auxiliary units, Lleonart blamed Louverture, jailed his nephew Moïse, and put his wife and sons under house arrest.[40]

Louverture's loyalty to his kin was one of the few nonnegotiable principles in his long and complex life. By killing his brother Pierre and imprisoning his relatives, his rivals had crossed a line. He chose to defect.

Spanish contingents were few in the border regions, but battalions from Cuba were expected shortly and there was no time to lose. In April 1794, Louverture opened negotiations with the French, armed plantation slaves opposed to Biassou, and even made plans to assassinate his old friend. These were dangerous gambits. Angered by the defection of some minor rebel chiefs, Governor García had recently decreed that anyone communicating with the enemy would be sentenced to death, and Biassou was known to "chop off heads like the Emperor of Morocco."[41]

In early May 1794, after evacuating his family from San Rafael, Louverture handed over the city of Gonaïves to the French. He had his men murder many white planters in the process. Details are hazy, because Louverture did his best to hide his involvement in the massacre, but he probably intended to permanently weaken the colonists' camp by culling their numbers. Jean-François carried out a similar massacre of white colonists a few months later in Fort-Dauphin; in that incident, Louverture's old boss François Bayon de Libertat, who had just returned from exile in the United States, was almost killed.[42]

In August 1791, Louverture had played the role of the dutiful slave while planning a slave revolt; in May 1794, he defected to the French Army while assuring his Spanish overlords that he was still on their side. Amazingly, he managed to continue this charade for five months, which he spent assuring both France and Spain of his loyalty while also encouraging the British to court him, for good measure.[43]

France itself was wracked by political disputes. After abolishing slavery in August 1793, Commissioner Sonthonax had sent a six-man delegation to France to get his government's approval. Three of the delegates absconded on the way to France for fear of retribution; the others were assaulted by conservative exiles during a stop in Philadelphia, and then briefly imprisoned when they landed in France. As they finally approached Paris, the deputies wondered whether they would be met with garlands or the guillotine: aside from abolishing the slave trade, the French National Convention had not been particularly forward-thinking when it came to racial equality.[44]

In the event, when the three members of the Saint-Domingue delegation—one white, one black, and one of mixed race—entered the legislative chamber in February 1794, they were welcomed as heroes. The black delegate, Jean-Baptiste Belley, who had been part of Louverture's extended circle in Cap prior to the Revolution, became the first black deputy to serve in the French parliament. His personal journey, Belley told French deputies, had taken him from Senegal in West Africa to Saint-Domingue, to Savannah in 1779 as a soldier, and now to Paris. He had known three continents and three revolutions. He had been a slave, a slave owner, and a slave emancipator. The story seemed almost too good to be true—and to some extent it was: Belley, who is listed as a native of Saint-Domingue on other documents, likely invented his African birth to reinforce the symbolism of his election as deputy.[45]

Sonthonax's bold decision to abolish slavery without obtaining France's prior permission was ratified by the Convention. Not only that, but France declared that slavery was now abolished in all French colonies, not just Saint-Domingue, and that freed slaves would become full-fledged citizens of France, not just freedmen with a lesser legal status. Contrary to many other abolition laws passed over the next one hundred years, this decree did not provide for a transition period or for financial compensation for the planters. Encouraged by the slave revolt in Saint-Domingue, French revolutionaries had finally put behind their equivocations and brought the Declaration of the Rights of Man and of the Citizen to its logical conclusion. Commoners, Jews, and people of color now all shared the same rights under French law in keeping with the revolutionary motto "liberty, equality, and fraternity." (Sisterhood was not on the list: women, whether they were white or black, remained disenfranchised until 1944.) The law proved popular in France, where many stories about labor abuse on plantations had circulated in recent years, and where public opinion was hostile to the planters.[46]

Granting freed slaves French citizenship was particularly significant. Many abolitionists viewed emancipation as a humane gesture toward a suffering group, but they did not necessarily see blacks as their intellectual equals. As a result, free people of color retained a subordinate legal status in the Americas even after emancipation became the norm in the nineteenth century. In France, by contrast, black males entered the body politic outright after they were freed.

Because the February 1794 law of universal emancipation in France and Louverture's May 1794 defection from the Spanish to the French in Hispaniola happened around the same time, he was later able to present his volte-face as an idealistic act motivated by his love of freedom. In reality, news of the abolition law only reached him in July, so the passage of the law cemented rather than triggered his decision. This is not to say that Louverture's growing unease with slavery played no role in his abandonment of Spain; rather, as so often in his life, he carefully considered his personal career, which had reached a dead end in the Spanish ranks, and his political goals, which also pushed him toward France. Surviving while defending one's ideals: such is the difficult task of individuals caught in a revolution.[47]

THIRTEEN

FRENCH PATRIOT
1794–1796

A SHIP ARRIVED in the south of Saint-Domingue bearing formal orders to recall the commissioner Léger-Félicité Sonthonax in June 1794. He was accused of having overstepped his authority by unilaterally abolishing slavery. In a curious two-step, the National Convention had confirmed Sonthonax's abolition of slavery in 1794 and then demanded that he come to France to answer for his actions. Accordingly, the man who welcomed Louverture into the French Army was not Sonthonax but Etienne Laveaux, a native of eastern France who had served as governor of Saint-Domingue since 1793.[1]

Laveaux would eventually become very close to Louverture, but the first letter he sent him after he joined the French Army was rather cold. Concerned by Louverture's monarchist past, Laveaux began with a little refresher on French civics and reminded him that he now fought for a republic committed to the rights of man. "Thank God, you have now understood your mistake and have rejoined your fatherland. You must serve it with fidelity and attachment." Unsure how valuable Louverture's defection would prove to be, Laveaux also asked him to provide a detailed report on the size of his army and the territories he controlled.[2]

Over the next two years, Louverture assuaged all of Laveaux's concerns as he fought and defeated Spain, Britain, and various internal enemies. But war was a continuation of politics at a time when France stood alone in defense of universal liberty. Because of his social background and newfound embrace of emancipation, Louverture's military successes made him a lodestar of the abolitionist cause in the French Republic and, ultimately, around the world. In return, he fully imbibed its ideals as he strove to become something that had been denied to him all his life: a Frenchman.

With his new post came new colleagues. Louverture's boss, Governor Laveaux, was stationed in Port-de-Paix, a town located west of Cap on the northern coast of Saint-Domingue. His two main peers were the mixed-race officers Jean Villatte, who commanded the North from his headquarters in Cap, and André Rigaud, who commanded the South from his headquarters in Cayes. Laveaux entrusted Louverture with the cordon of the West, a strategic region abutting the territories controlled by Spain and Britain in central Saint-Domingue, but he demoted him from general to colonel. Louverture, who had already undergone the indignity of losing his generalship when joining the Spanish cause, would have to prove himself yet again.

To overcome Laveaux's initial suspicion, Louverture insisted that he had been drawn to the French ranks by his love of liberty rather than political expediency. More important, he brought a formidable force with him. Because of disease and combat, in the North and West only 1,000 French troops remained of the 12,000 who had been sent in various installments since 1791. Louverture, who commanded 4,000 black soldiers, immediately made his mark. The towns of the western province that he had conquered for Spain, including Gonaïves and Dondon, were the first to fall back into his hands. Most of the northern province soon followed. Then, in October 1794, he moved into Santo Domingo proper and captured the towns of San Miguel and San Rafael, where his family had lived when he was in Spanish service. So many recruits flocked to his side that he was able to add two new regiments to his command. As usual, he relied on brains rather than brawn—or, to use his terms, "cabals" and "ruses." His crowning achievement was the capture of Mirebalais in July

1795, which fell "without a drop of blood" after he spent three months secretly encouraging the town's inhabitants to switch sides.[3]

Spain could call on few professional troops to stop Louverture. Santo Domingo's garrison mostly kept to the Spanish side of the border, and regiments sent from Cuba in 1794 were decimated by an epidemic that almost claimed the life of Governor Joaquín García as well. The losses forced Spain to rely on the auxiliary units of Jean-François and Biassou, who did not command a large following among the black population because they traded slaves.

Jean-François tried to seduce some of Louverture's officers by warning them that "the type of liberty mentioned by Republicans is false": liberty was an individual privilege that could only be granted by one's master or king. After consulting Louverture, the officers replied that they were "free by natural right" per the universalist principles of the Enlightenment, but the concept was lost on Jean-François.[4]

Within a year of defecting, Louverture had retaken almost all the French towns he had previously conquered for Spain. These and other military setbacks in Europe forced Spain to sue for peace. Signed in July 1795, the Peace of Basel stipulated that Spain would cede Santo Domingo, which had been in Spanish hands since the second voyage of Christopher Columbus in 1493, to France. Spain was the first major European power that Louverture had defeated; two more would follow.

After learning of the Peace of Basel, Governor Laveaux made plans to take possession of Santo Domingo and apply the 1794 French law abolishing slavery, marking the first time that the principles of the Haitian Revolution had been exported outside French territories. To that end, Laveaux appointed three envoys (one black, one white, and one of mixed race), who distributed a "decree of liberty" about the upcoming abolition of slavery as they made their way from Saint-Domingue to Santo Domingo to take possession of the colony. Freedom was on the march—literally.[5]

Being absorbed by a black-dominated, abolitionist colony was inconceivable to Governor García and his white countrymen in Santo Domingo, especially since the radical ideas planted by Laveaux's envoys seemed to prompt a slave revolt in Oyarzábal, the colony's only modern sugar plantation. García brutally suppressed the revolt and did all he could to delay the French takeover. Louverture did not involve himself directly in the negotiations, but with newfound republican fervor he noted reproachfully that "Spanish inhabitants do not want to hear of general liberty." In the end, France was in no rush to administer a colony that depended on Spanish subsidies and decided not to push the issue. A few border towns aside, the takeover of Santo Domingo did not occur until Louverture took the matter in his own hands six years later.[6]

The fate of Spain's black auxiliary units was a more pressing issue in the short term. Louverture was keen to enlist privates into his army, but he insisted that their officers, especially his rivals Jean-François and Biassou, leave the island at once. He got his wish. The Spanish, who were equally eager to rid themselves of their black allies now that they no longer had any use for them, abruptly deported eight hundred leading auxiliary troops and their families in December 1795—so fast, in fact, that Biassou's mother was left behind. The black auxiliaries headed for Havana, where Cuban authorities, fearing for the safety of their own slave system, broke up the so-called "French negroes" into smaller and more manageable groups and dispatched them to the Isle of Pines and various spots along the Central American coast. The British would similarly exile many of their own black auxiliary units in 1798, as would the French in 1802, creating a wide-ranging diaspora of Haitian veterans and deportees throughout the Americas and Europe.[7]

Biassou headed for Saint-Augustine in Spanish Florida, where he died in 1801, while Jean-François ended up in Cádiz, Spain, where he died in 1805. Louverture never saw them again, though he remained in contact with members of their families whom he had known before the Revolution. The obscure ends of these once-formidable leaders confirmed to Louverture that he had gambled smartly in aligning his fortunes with those of the French Republic.[8]

Though he had defeated Spain, Louverture still had to face Britain, the preeminent colonial and naval power of the day. During the winter of 1793–1794, white colonists had handed over many ports of western and southern Saint-Domingue to the British. Britain initially lacked the troops to garrison them effectively, but in 1794 and 1795 it sent two large expeditions to the Caribbean in an attempt to destroy French power in the region. Saint-Domingue's administrative capital of Port-au-Prince fell in June 1794.

Fresh from defeating the Spanish, Louverture headed for the region of Port-au-Prince in 1795 and directly engaged the British, but it quickly became clear that he was not yet ready to face a large professional European army in the field. He chose to lift the siege of Saint-Marc when his hand was crushed under a cannon's wheel. During a later campaign near Mirebalais, his battalion was cut to pieces when it was surprised by British cavalry in the open field. By the fall of 1795, so many British soldiers had landed in Saint-Domingue that Louverture had to fall back to a defensive line established along the Artibonite River.[9]

For the next two years Louverture maintained a defensive posture, relying on the most potent weapon in his arsenal, disease. It did not disappoint. British commanders failed to push their initial advantage and remained camped in coastal areas, where their soldiers, many of whom landed at the height of the rainy seasons of 1795 and 1796, were decimated by yellow fever. In 1794, the British lost 10 percent of their troops to disease *per month*, a rate that rose to 15 percent in 1795 and hovered between 5 and 10 percent throughout 1796 and 1797.[10]

Such losses are easily understood today: we now know that epidemics spread fastest when nonimmune hosts live in close quarters, as was the case of the British soldiers garrisoned in mosquito-infested ports. But at the time, most doctors blamed yellow fever on "miasmas," a kind of foul air. One wonders how Louverture made sense of the providential plague. Throughout his life, and particularly during the Revolution, he saw European invaders die by the tens of thousands while local residents like him were spared. According to one estimate, European powers lost a staggering 180,000 men in the Caribbean during the period of the Haitian Revolution. The last two years of the Haitian Revolution alone saw more French general officers (twenty-seven) die than any other campaign of the Revolutionary and Napoleonic wars. A large majority of them died of disease rather than in combat.

Did Louverture conclude that Saint-Domingue was a natural home for native Creoles, and that white colonists were short-lived interlopers? Or did he view these epidemics as evidence that God was fighting by his side? He did not say, but his subordinate Jean-Jacques Dessalines, who had followed him from Spanish into French service, had his own theory on the matter: "Our vengeful climate is proof enough that [the whites] are not our brothers and never will be," he later explained.[11]

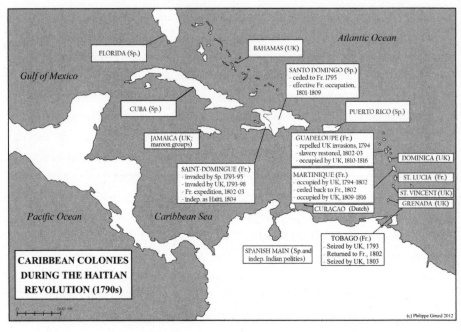

Caribbean colonies during the Haitian Revolution. Map by the author.

To compensate for their losses, the British supplemented their forces with locally raised regiments of black and mixed-race auxiliary troops, but it was clear to everyone that they were the defenders of the old order. In the areas they controlled, they showed no intention of abolishing slavery and in fact reestablished racial inequality between whites and free people of color. Louverture publicized the French laws on racial equality (April 1792) and abolition (February 1794) to fortify his support among the people of color, who represented the overwhelming majority of the colonial population.

Events in the Lesser Antilles, where Britain also sent sizable contingents, underlined the power of revolutionary slogans. The British easily took Martinique, Tobago, and Guadeloupe in 1794 with the support of white colonists, but a French agent armed with a copy of the decree of abolition retook Guadeloupe in 1794 when he freed the slaves and enrolled them as soldiers. French freedmen then joined with local slaves and the so-called Black Caribs (mixed-race Afro-Amerindians) to attack the British in Grenada, Saint-Vincent, and Saint-Lucia, while upheavals roiled Jamaica and Dominica and a French-inspired slave revolt broke out in Dutch Curaçao. Louverture was not involved in any of these events, but he watched them from afar with clear pleasure. "I hope that our new brothers will achieve their goal," he explained after learning that the Maroons had revolted in Jamaica. "I desire it with all my heart."[12]

Chasing the British from Saint-Domingue was a more daunting task because Britain had committed extraordinary reserves of manpower and treasure to occupying it. But Louverture could afford to wait while his enemies could not. "Slowly goes far and patience beats force," his favorite proverb, guided him. By 1796, a clamor was growing in Britain to bring an end to its Caribbean ventures, which cost Britain 20,000 casualties in Saint-Domingue alone. France, despite sending no significant forces to the Caribbean in 1794–1798, was eventually able to repulse the British everywhere except Martinique and Tobago. Former slaves like Louverture who became citizen-soldiers fighting for the cause of liberty were the

Temple commemorating the abolition of slavery in Cap. M. Rainsford and J. Barlow, *View of a Temple Erected by the Blacks to Commemorate Their Emancipation*, reprinted from Marcus Rainsford, *An Historical Account of the Black Empire of Hayti* (London: Albion Press, 1805), 218.

main reason for this miraculous turn of events. For once, idealism and political expediency walked hand in hand.[13]

Liberty in Saint-Domingue left an imprint that was both symbolic and tangible. Port-au-Prince was renamed Port-Républicain; Fort-Dauphin became Fort-Liberté. A neoclassical monument dedicated to the law of emancipation was erected in Cap, and images of liberty replaced the fleur-de-lys on coins, monuments, and letterheads. The white flag of monarchy gave way to the flag of the French Revolution, with the added twist that the blue, white, and red stripes of the French tricolor (which normally referenced the Parisian National Guard) were intended to symbolize blacks, whites, and mixed-race people in the colonial context.

From time to time, the colony's leadership organized revolutionary celebrations where they planted trees of liberty and made speeches celebrating the new era of freedom. Most notable was the 1794 Bastille Day ceremony, during which Laveaux officially presented the French law of abolition. Fireworks and a rollicking party guaranteed that the day would never be forgotten. The last dancers only disbanded with the dawn of the new era, at 7 a.m.[14]

French revolutionaries sought to remake time itself when they replaced the Gregorian calendar of the popes with a new Republican calendar. Avowedly secular, it began with a September 1792 French military victory instead of Jesus's birth. Traditional Catholic holidays disappeared, so All Saints' Day, Louverture's feast day, was renamed after the oyster plant, a European vegetable he had never seen. Sunday gave way to décadi, the last day of a new ten-day week that was dedicated to some nondenominational "Supreme Being" rather than the Catholic God. This was too much for the pious Louverture. He dutifully employed the revolutionary calendar in his official letters, but he never warmed to it, and abandoned it as soon as he got the chance.[15]

Louverture remained friendly to priests, a courageous move at a time when the Catholic Church had become controversial in revolutionary France because of its associations with the monarchy. But he was also careful to adopt the lingo of the French Republic and named one of his regiments the "Sans-culottes" in reference to the radical revolutionary group. The term, which meant "without britches" in French, could be taken literally, since many of Louverture's men wore no uniform and went "naked as worms."[16]

Louverture knew how to adapt his rhetoric to his audience. He ended his letters to Governor Laveaux and other French officials with patriotic "salutations in the name of the fatherland," but the term "abolition" disappeared from his vocabulary when he tried to convince white planters to join his side. When it came time to court a group of African-born plantation runaways, he rediscovered his Allada roots and addressed them in their native tongue. A political shape-shifter, he prompts a question that is ultimately unanswerable: Who among his multiple incarnations was the real Louverture?[17]

This former leader of a slave revolt and convert to the Republic remained friendly toward aristocratic planters, partly to convince them to throw off their allegiance to Britain, but also because he had always dreamed of joining the rarefied world of the "big whites." When the Marquis of Espinville was taken prisoner during the fall of Mirebalais, French patriots demanded that he be put on trial as a traitor. But Louverture begged Governor Laveaux to spare d'Espinville's life because he had promised him "protection." "I would sooner abandon my command than break my word," Louverture said. Indeed, an officer's word of honor was central to his sense of self; to ask Louverture to break it would have implied that a black man lacked the requisite character needed to wear an epaulet. Laveaux relented, and a glowing Louverture was feted by d'Espinville's grateful friends. This was one of the proudest moments in his life: "I remember being complimented by all these gentlemen who were present for having defended the honor and the dignity of my government," he later explained in considerable detail. "Yet I never received an education nor instructed, but my big common sense made me understand that a man must keep his word."[18]

Defending aristocrats like d'Espinville was politically risky: these were the kinds of counterrevolutionaries who were routinely sent off to the guillotine in France. But Louverture, eager to dispel stereotypes of black rebels as bloodthirsty African savages, avoided unnecessary bloodshed whenever he could. Meanwhile, he also kept silent about his early manumission and his slave-holding past so as to protect his reputation as a revolutionary. Only through this delicate balancing act could he build a broad coalition in these fractious times.

The person Louverture most needed to seduce was Governor Laveaux. After three months of epistolary courtship, the two men first met in person in August 1794. Laveaux was immediately won over. He concluded after their conversation that Louverture was a true abolitionist. Not only was he "trusted by all negroes," but by some miracle, he also managed to be "respected and venerated" by "at least 600 planters." Louverture's slave roots gave him credibility, while his record of moderation toward whites gave him wide appeal. To Laveaux, he was the perfect revolutionary hero, at once genuine and nonthreatening.[19]

Over time, Louverture's military successes and personal charisma earned him a special place in Laveaux's heart. In October 1794, Laveaux offered him the feathery plume of a grenadier infantryman, which Louverture proudly displayed thereafter on his hat. In 1795, Laveaux described Louverture as a man "filled with virtue, courage, military talent, obedient toward his superiors . . . knowing how to read and write, and even better how to think." In response, Louverture nicknamed him "Papa Laveaux," although Laveaux was younger than him. He wrote that he "kissed" him "with all my heart," assuring his "dear papa" that "I often dream of you" and that "I will forever be your affectionate and submissive son." Men of that era occasionally described their friendship in baroque terms; an officer once wrote to Laveaux's predecessor, "I love you like the lover idolizes his mistress." But such displays of affection were unusual for Louverture. The two men must also have socialized outside of work, because they frequently made inquiries about their spouses in their correspondence. Officer status, universal abolition, the planters' gratitude, and the governor's ear and heart: these were heady times for a muleteer just three years removed from the sugar mill of the Bréda plantation.[20]

Whether France was as committed as Laveaux to the cause of abolition remained an open question. The Convention had confirmed Sonthonax's abolition of slavery in 1794, but it had then recalled him. Sonthonax was eventually cleared, but Louverture might have wondered how long the Convention would last.[21]

As it turned out, not long at all. In July 1794, the main architect of the Reign of Terror, Maximilien de Robespierre, was sent to the guillotine, after which a more conservative regime, calling itself the Directory, replaced the National Convention. Exiled planters smelled blood. For the first eight months of 1795, a rancorous debate over the colonies raged in the French parliament, where conservative deputies denounced the law of abolition as rushed and ill-advised. Echoes reached Saint-Domingue in the summer and fall. Louverture, who was waging hard-fought defensive battles against the British Army at the time, had good reason to fear for his and the colony's future.[22]

The uncertainty proved short-lived. In October, an envoy arrived from France with good news. Peace with Spain had been ratified, and conservatives had lost the colonial debate. The military successes of Louverture had proved instrumental: when planters had decried abolition as an economic disaster, their opponents had countered that black freedmen had saved Saint-Domingue from foreign occupation. This contest between France's economic and strategic interests would continue to pull the abolitionist debate in opposite directions. Louverture's freedom was safe—as long as he continued being useful to France.[23]

To influence future policymaking, Louverture sent three deputies to Paris and asked them to remind everyone of his "great and memorable services to the fatherland" and to combat "the enemies of the liberty of the people of Saint-Domingue." They were the vanguard of a public relations operation that would become ever more sophisticated over the years.[24]

As evidence of its gratitude, France promoted Laveaux to division general and Louverture to brigadier general in 1795. Such rapid promotions were not uncommon during the French Revolution, when constant wars and the exile of aristocratic officers gave men of talent many opportunities to rise through the ranks; the most famous example was Napoléon's elevation to brigadier general at age twenty-four. Color was no longer an obstacle. There were three mixed-race brigadier generals in Saint-Domingue and one mixed-race division general in France, the father of the famed novelist Alexandre Dumas. But Louverture still stood out as the highest-ranking *black* officer in the French Army.

Because voting rights under the Directory were restricted to males who owned property or served in the army, officers of color and landowners like Louverture were the main beneficiaries of the Republic's racial egalitarianism in the colonies. His wife Suzanne had likely been freed when her husband was in Spain's service, and then again as part of France's general abolition law, but by law she could not vote. War, a male endeavor, was the main form of social promotion during the Revolution; freedwomen remained on plantations, where they eventually formed the majority of the workforce and as such were the main victims of attempts to keep freed slaves in the fields.

With the fall of the Convention and the advent of the Directory came a new French constitution, the third since 1789. It stated that French colonies were now *départements*, basic French administrative units. This seemingly minor clause had profound implications. In 1790, autonomist planters, to protect their racial privileges, had insisted that colonies were distinct territories operating under special laws. Integrating Saint-Domingue into the French legal system now meant that former slaves had as strong a claim to citizenship as any Frenchman from Lille to Lyons.[25]

The black population of Saint-Domingue saw close bonds with the former country as an asset and welcomed the colony's ascension to *département*. The American Revolution's slogan, "No taxation without representation," led logically to independence; the slogan of the Haitian Revolution, "Liberty or death," was better achieved by cultivating ties with revolutionary France. This explains why a declaration of independence was the Haitian Revolution's closing act, and why Louverture, who is often seen as a precursor to Haiti's independence, actually spent much of the Haitian Revolution voicing his loyalty to the French Republic. He felt, he explained, "a sense of duty and gratitude toward those who gave liberty to his brothers." As long, of course, as France continued to support emancipation.[26]

Even the most idealistic revolutionaries understood that one could not transform African-born slaves into French citizens overnight by legal fiat. In France, where provincialism ran strong, a true sense of a unified national identity did not emerge until the development of railways, the institution of the draft, and the establishment of universal primary education in the late nineteenth century. In post-emancipation Saint-Domingue, education and the army were also major instruments of integration as colonial authorities strove to turn freedmen into Frenchmen.

Prerevolutionary authorities had once limited educational opportunities for people of color on the grounds that "our security derives from the ignorance of people of their ilk." All this changed after the abolition of slavery. Colonial officials established a public school in Cap and asked for teachers to be sent to France so as to promote an effective program of universal education. It would serve two purposes: educating the voting citizenry, and teaching freedmen that hard work was a republican virtue.[27]

Louverture, who had only learned recently and imperfectly how to read and write, paid great attention to educational matters. Gabriel Toussaint, one of his sons by his first wife, Cécile, could sign his name, but his daughter, Marie-Marthe, could not (his older son, Toussaint, died without leaving a written record). Louverture saw to it that Placide, Isaac, and Saint-Jean, his sons by his second wife, Suzanne, were properly educated, hiring private tutors for them.[28]

Suzanne had also learned to read and write by 1794, presumably from the same teacher as her husband, because the two shared the same handwriting and phonetic spelling. But very few letters by her have survived, and those that have focus on mundane matters that tell us little about her inner life. Her earliest surviving letter is dated July 13, 1794, two months after her husband's defection to the French side, and one day before the Bastille Day ceremony in which the law of abolition was formally presented to the population of Saint-Domingue. Yet in the letter she merely reminded her husband that his laundry was ready.[29]

Despite their lack of political content, this and other letters by Suzanne are revealing: she and her husband addressed each other in standard (if misspelled) French, not Haitian Kreyòl. Because French carried more social cachet than Kreyòl, members of the Haitian elite traditionally employed French in official settings, but they typically still used Kreyòl in everyday family life. The Louvertures went one step further: French crept into their everyday life in a manner that must have come across as snobbish to their contemporaries. "I was poorly received one day when I tried to speak to Louverture in the local patois," a white visitor noted in reference to Kreyòl. "He only used it to harangue laborers and soldiers."[30]

In the summer of 1795, as his campaign against Spain drew to an end, Louverture moved his family to Gonaïves in the western province in order to be closer to British lines. At Suzanne's request, he purchased yet another estate, the Sansay plantation in nearby Ennery, which remained the Louverture family's home for the rest of the Revolution. Louverture was a northerner born and raised in the outskirts of Cap, but for reasons that are not clear, he disliked that city and developed a particular affinity for the region of Gonaïves. He would eventually establish the area as its own province and name it after himself.[31]

Louverture offered the ultimate proof of his loyalty to the Republic when he announced in June 1796 that he wished to send his sons Placide and Isaac, whose "existence . . . make my life happy," to finish their schooling in France. In doing so, he followed the example set by white colonists like the Brédas and the Bayons before the Revolution. He also wished to keep up with his colleague and rival General André Rigaud, who had recently sent his own son to France to be educated. Louverture's youngest son, Saint-Jean, who was just five, remained in Saint-Domingue and attended a school in Port-de-Paix.[32]

The prospect of her sons traveling to France deeply worried Suzanne Louverture. Placide and Isaac were only fourteen and eleven, respectively. After many delays, they finally left on the seventy-four-gun ship of the line *Wattigny* in July 1796. Choosing such a large warship for the trip was intentional. A ship of the line could weather a storm better than a smaller ship; it was also less likely to be captured by enemy privateers, who could have re-enslaved the sons of the most promising officer in the French empire. Saint-Domingue may have been in the throes of a revolution, but the outside world was an even more dangerous place for two young black men.[33]

Louverture's sons spent some time in Paris with Jean-Baptiste Belley and Louis Dufaÿ, the two deputies from Saint-Domingue who had secured passage of the law of abolition in 1794. They then headed for the Liancourt school, a dreary and underfunded boarding school where they spent a few miserable months before they did what the slaves of Haut-du-Cap had taught them: they ran away. Informed of their dissatisfaction with the school, the French government then transferred them to the more congenial environment of the National Institute of the Colonies in Paris (aka Collège de la Marche). It was run by a stern but caring defrocked priest named Jean-Baptiste Coisnon who became the boys' father-in-exile.

Placide and Isaac's education was paid for by the French government, which hoped to endear itself to Louverture but also wanted collateral, should General Louverture ever lose his patriotic fervor. The boys studied alongside the sons of prominent colonists, both white and of color. It must have been awkward for white boys orphaned by the Haitian Revolution to share rooms with the sons of the black generals who had launched it. The Louvertures also dined regularly at the residence of

Joséphine Bonaparte, the daughter of creole planters from Martinique and the wife of Napoléon. Her husband was then in the process of conquering Egypt. They received from her the maternal love they missed so much; in return, Louverture arranged to rebuild a plantation that Joséphine had inherited in Saint-Domingue.[34]

The Louvertures made rapid progress at the Institute of the Colonies. "They could not read in the year V [1797]," marveled their teacher Coisnon in 1800. "Now they can analyze Quintus Curtius Rufus and they have studied equations of the second degree and Newton's binomial theorem." They displayed their achievements every year in public ceremonies attended by the minister of the navy, who urged them to "bring back to the tropics the example of devotion to the Fatherland and the love of liberty and equality."[35]

The absence of the boys, which eventually stretched to more than five years, was hard to bear for their parents, but it was a necessary price to pay to secure the long-term success of the Louverture line. "Of all the gifts it gave to me, the education that the French government was kind enough to provide for my children is the one that touched me the most," Louverture later wrote. "If I cannot leave them a personal fortune, then they will have a fine education that is worth more than the largest fortune. If I had not myself received a Christian education . . . I might be lost among the crowd today." As always in Louverture's life, the personal and the political overlapped. He regularly ended his official letters to the minister of the navy with a plea to take good care of his sons; meanwhile, he urged them in his private letters to meet the famous abolitionist bishop Henri Grégoire and to "pay close attention to what he will tell you."[36]

Isaac and Placide did not disappoint their father. They were soon able to write to him in perfect French. He replied accordingly, though he had to use a secretary to match their level of proficiency. In time, they fulfilled their father's most ardent wish: full acculturation. "Raised among the French and their customs, we imbibed their principles," Isaac proudly noted. "They really were two young Frenchmen," wrote someone who met them in France—leaving aside, he added ominously, "their color." Such racial prejudices, inherited from the prerevolutionary era, would do much to sour Louverture's attachment to the French Republic over the following years.[37]

FOURTEEN

POLITICIAN
1796–1798

ON THE MORNING OF 30 VENTÔSE in year IV of the French Republic (March 20, 1796), Etienne Laveaux began his 890th day as governor of Saint-Domingue. His office, located in the government house of Cap (the former headquarters of the Jesuit order), overlooked the city and the shimmering bay below. He still had, he later wrote, his slippers on.

Laveaux's morning was brusquely interrupted when six mixed-race officers barged into his office and assaulted him. The first of the group landed a punch; Laveaux fought him back, yelling, "No, you do not represent the people! I see no black or white citizens among you, you are assassins!" His foes overpowered him, grabbed him by his hair, and dragged him from his office. Before he could understand what had happened, the governor of Saint-Domingue was in a prison cell alongside his chief financial officer and two black army officers. Haiti's presidential seat is cursed, Haitians like to say; so was, apparently, the governor's chair.

Laveaux soon learned that the plot to unseat him had originated with General Jean Villatte, the mixed-race commander of the northern province. The coup attempt did not entirely surprise Laveaux, since his relationship with the mixed-race elite had been steadily deteriorating for over a year. Luckily for him, black officers in nearby towns remained on his side. Within two days, they demanded and obtained his release, after which Laveaux fled to the hamlet of Haut-du-Cap and prepared his counterattack. To Toussaint Louverture, who was in Gonaïves fighting the British, he made an urgent plea: "My friend, you need to send me forces at once so that I can subdue the rebels."[1]

There was little question which side Louverture would support. Villatte and his coconspirators were known in the colony as the "formerly free" community because they had been free before the Haitian Revolution. Louverture was technically a member of their group, as he had been freed in the 1770s, but he claimed to be one of the "newly free," the slaves who had been emancipated by the Haitian Revolution and who represented the majority of the colony's population. Louverture had fought a clandestine battle with Villatte and the "formerly free," going as far as arresting a mixed-race friend of Villatte's who had then died of a mysterious "bilious choler" in his cell, or so Louverture claimed.[2]

Villatte's arrest of Governor Laveaux was the most daring episode of their political rivalry yet. Villatte apparently had acted with the knowledge and support of André Rigaud, the mixed-race commander of the southern region, so Louverture had reason to fear that the "formerly free" elite was planning to band together and relegate recently minted black freedmen like himself to subordinate roles. Villatte and Rigaud could not be allowed to succeed; otherwise, Louverture's area of command in the central region of Saint-Domingue would be surrounded by enemies, his political future compromised.

Louverture likely learned of the Villatte plot ahead of time thanks to his network of informers in Cap, which included his ally Father Jacques Delahaye and his son-in-law Janvier Dessalines, who now worked as a concierge in the government house. But he let Villatte proceed and then took his time before intervening in order to give Villatte enough rope to hang himself. It was only one week after Laveaux was attacked that Louverture finally sprang into action. Taking with him Jean-Jacques Dessalines, Moïse, and Charles Bélair (all of them relatives or old acquaintances), he headed for Haut-du-Cap, where he issued a proclamation to the population of Cap to win them to his side. Then he entered the city with an imposing force. Villatte, whose leadership throughout the crisis had been less than forceful, stepped down at once, and Laveaux reclaimed the governorship.[3]

To the victor went the spoils. On April 5, 1796, Laveaux held a public ceremony in Cap to publicly thank Louverture for saving his seat. Just two years earlier, Laveaux had treated Louverture's defection to the French Army with suspicion; he now made him his lieutenant governor. He also celebrated Louverture as "the Man predicted and foreseen by Father Raynal"—that is, the black Spartacus who was destined to liberate the slaves of the Caribbean. Louverture would purchase several busts of Raynal and place them in his various residences to remind everyone of the prophecy he had come to fulfill.[4]

"After God comes Laveaux," a beaming Louverture declared to the crowd gathered before him as the ceremony drew to a close. The Villatte affair was indeed a godsend for him. It underscored the vulnerability of French officials, who had no local power base and had to rely on his military support for survival. The ill-advised coup attempt also wiped out mixed-race power in the North. Villatte lost his generalship, and then, at Louverture's insistence, was deported to France and court-martialed. Within two months, France promoted Louverture to division general and three other black officers to brigadier general to thank them for saving the French governor. The era of the black generals had begun.[5]

Political feuds like the Villatte affair were frequent occurrences from 1796. Though Louverture had yet to defeat the British, he was already planning for their withdrawal, when Saint-Domingue would be up for grabs. Mixed-race officers like Rigaud, French administrators like Laveaux, the "newly free" majority—who would prevail was an open question. It was not even certain that Louverture would emerge as the champion of the "newly free": to eliminate black rivals, he fought several campaigns that year against Joseph Flaville, who was popular with plantation workers near Port-de-Paix, and Pierre Dieudonné, who commanded significant support among plantation workers near Port-Républicain. This slave turned freedman turned rebel turned general had begun yet another career, that of a politician of the French colonial empire.

Shortly after Louverture's triumphant promotion to Laveaux's second-hand man, an unwelcome guest sailed into the harbor of Cap. It was

Léger-Félicité Sonthonax, the commissioner who had abolished slavery in Saint-Domingue in 1793. After being cleared in France for abolishing slavery without authorization, he returned in May 1796 as one of five members of yet another French commission.[6]

Louverture could not help but fear Sonthonax, not because he was an enemy of racial equality, but precisely because he embodied it. Sonthonax never let anyone forget what he had done. "I founded liberty in Saint-Domingue and I have returned to strengthen it," he grandiosely declared after landing in Cap to the former slaves he had freed. He was a master at using proclamations in Kreyòl to reach out to black field hands, to whom he also distributed 20,000 muskets so that, he explained, they could defend their freedom. Louverture found his appropriation of a revolution he had initiated deeply grating. "I am white but I have the soul of a black man," Sonthonax once told Louverture. "And I am black but I have the soul of a white man," Louverture replied testily. He tended to be unusually candid when was he was angry, which probably explains this rare moment of introspection.[7]

Sonthonax's return brought Louverture's political rise to a sudden halt. Although Louverture retained his rank of division general, he had to yield his lieutenant-governorship and his political duties when the new commissioners claimed primacy over civilian affairs. The leadership structure of French colonies, with its *gouverneur* and its *intendant*, had always been prone to internal conflicts; it only became more so during the Haitian Revolution. The groups of commissioners sent by France frequently clashed with the *gouverneur/intendant* duopoly as well as with the black generals, who had become powerful figures in their own right.

Concluding that it was too soon to use force to impose his authority, Louverture discreetly positioned his pawns on the chessboard. When the colony held legislative elections in the summer of 1796, he arranged for Governor Laveaux to be selected as deputy of Saint-Domingue in the Council of Ancients, the upper chamber of the Directory in Paris. He wanted "a true friend of the Blacks" to defend the cause of abolition in the French legislature. The promotion conveniently required that Laveaux leave the colony at once. Louverture reminded Laveaux that France was his "true fatherland" and that he had not seen his wife and children for years. A homesick Laveaux agreed and left for France in October 1796.

What became of Marianne, the common-law wife who had shared his life since 1792, is unknown.[8]

In September 1796, Sonthonax announced that he would also leave for France to become deputy to the Council of Five Hundred, the Directory's lower chamber. Louverture must have been overjoyed to rid himself of his rival so easily, but Sonthonax quickly recanted. He was so popular with the black population of Saint-Domingue that they could not bear to see him leave—or so he claimed.

Sonthonax and Louverture maintained an outwardly cordial work relationship at first. They shared a commitment to abolition and a distrust of mixed-race generals, most notably Rigaud, who had set up a quasi-autonomous regime in the southern province. In February 1797, Sonthonax publicly handed to Louverture a ceremonial saber and two pistols; he promoted him to general-in-chief of the colonial army three months later, Louverture's third promotion in as many years. But Sonthonax's blunt style had a way of irking Louverture. It had become fashionable during the French Revolution to address one another as "citizen" instead of "sir," and to use the informal *tu* instead of *vous*. In keeping with the egalitarian spirit of the times, Sonthonax addressed Louverture by his first name, but Louverture, who had fought long and hard to become a *monsieur*, considered this insulting. He smiled and seethed.[9]

British military setbacks sparked new tensions because they allowed Sonthonax to shift his attention from the short-term urgency of war to the long-term recovery of the colonial economy. As the French conquered the last British-held areas and colonists fled with them, Louverture and other officers were eager to lease their vacant estates cheaply and to benefit financially from the revolution they had sponsored. But the incorruptible Sonthonax insisted that they pay market rates, and the would-be planters had to dance to his tune while dreaming of a day when he would leave and they could enrich themselves in peace.

A doctrinaire Jacobin, Sonthonax refused to let exiled planters return to the colony, seeing them as counterrevolutionaries. This position put him at odds with Louverture, who was more inclined to cultivate alliances with the exiles. The matter came to the fore when Louverture's former boss, François Bayon de Libertat, returned unexpectedly in July 1797. Louverture begged Sonthonax to allow him to settle in the colony, but Sonthonax refused to pardon a person so tied to the old royalist clique; he even told Louverture that he ought to have Bayon shot as a counterrevolutionary. Bayon, who had already tried to return during the Spanish invasion, only to have a close brush with death during the July 1794 massacre of Fort-Liberté, had to leave the colony yet again. In the new Saint-Domingue, the label of "big white" was no longer a desired one.[10]

The friction between Sonthonax and Louverture increased. As the five commissioners sent from France divided their responsibilities, Sonthonax took on the task of overseeing military affairs. That gave him an excuse to appropriate some of Louverture's troops, and he sent instructions to Louverture's subordinates in an infuriating breach of the chain of command. Sonthonax also re-created the national guard and the rural police, both of which could challenge the supremacy of the regular army, which was headed by Louverture. In July 1797, Sonthonax even proposed to disband one of Louverture's regiments as a cost-saving measure.

It is not clear which one of these events pushed Louverture over the edge: Bayon's exile? The dissolution of the 2nd Regiment? Rumors that France would soon send an army to Saint-Domingue? Or, more simply, personal ambition? But in August 1797, Louverture decided to rid himself of the overbearing commissioner. Sonthonax received advanced warning of Louverture's intentions, but he disregarded it. He thought that Louverture was a man "of limited intellect" and the puppet of royalist conspirators.[11]

All those who underestimated Louverture during the Revolution did so at their own risk. When Louverture traveled to Cap in August 1797 for the commemoration of the fifth anniversary of Louis XVI's overthrow, he brought a contingent of troops with him, ostensibly for a general review. Then, once his men were positioned all over town, he informed Sonthonax that it would be best if he left for France at once to finally take up his seat as deputy in the French parliament. Any delay, Louverture warned ominously, would lead to unrest, "which might cause some bloodshed." Sonthonax left two days later, taking his mixed-race wife and children with him.[12]

Louverture feared that Sonthonax might land somewhere else in the colony and start a civil war, but Sonthonax headed straight for France and caused no further trouble. Perhaps he missed his French daughter enough to make the best of a bad situation. That officials like Sonthonax (and Laveaux before him) had no personal connection to Saint-Domingue greatly facilitated Louverture's political rise. A strong nudge was often enough to convince rival officials to leave the war-torn, disease-ridden colony and rejoin their loved ones in France.[13]

Because Louverture's own sons were in France, he immediately set to work on presenting Sonthonax's forced departure in a positive light, lest they find themselves paying the price for their father's actions. To that effect, he published a verbatim transcript of his conversations with Sonthonax, which he claimed to remember word for word because "they have remained etched in my memory." According to the transcript, Louverture had deported Sonthonax after learning of a most extraordinary plot: the French commissioner planned to kill white planters and proclaim the independence of Saint-Domingue.[14]

> **Sonthonax**: "We should declare our independence from France. What do you think? Such is my project."
>
> **Louverture** (surprised and embarrassed): "That's too much. . . . Give me some time to think before I respond."
>
> [During a later meeting]
>
> **Sonthonax** (embracing Louverture and kissing him): "Blacks here are always worried about their liberty; there are some suspicious white colonists here, we need to kill them all; all is set, I only need your agreement."
>
> **Louverture**: "Why would you want to kill all the whites? Aren't you white yourself?"
>
> **Sonthonax**: "Yes. Not all the whites, only the enemies of liberty."
>
> **Louverture** (with barely disguised impatience): "Let's switch the topic."

The transcript read like a play, complete with scene breaks and stage directions. It was, in many ways, a work of fiction. It defies imagination that a passionate revolutionary like Sonthonax would advocate independence and re-enslavement; and it is doubtful that Louverture could remember every word of conversations held over several months. The style was awkward, the wording suspicious. "Toussaint only speaks Kreyòl, he barely understands French," Sonthonax protested upon reading the flowery phrases attributed to him in the transcript. But the forgery allowed Louverture to portray the expulsion of a French representative not as an act of defiance, but as a desperate measure to save the colony. It worked. The Directory bought the story (or at least pretended to) and reaffirmed its confidence in Louverture. His legacy erased by Louverture, Sonthonax, the first man to abolish slavery in an American colony, became a footnote in history.[15]

Of the five members of the third commission, only one, the mixed-race planter Julien Raimond, remained in Saint-Domingue by the time of Sonthonax's exile. He was no threat, being primarily interested in enriching himself through land speculation, but Louverture eventually sent him back to France as a deputy anyway. The black general Etienne Mentor, who had dared criticize Louverture's treatment of Sonthonax, also followed the well-trodden path from rival of Louverture to deputy of Saint-Domingue. Louverture also expelled Etienne Desfourneaux, a French officer and the only other division general left in the colony; he became the French agent in the island of Guadeloupe. Since Sonthonax had aggressively deported his own rivals during his tenure, no one remained in northern Saint-Domingue by 1798 who could realistically challenge him. France, however, was another story.[16]

After his friend Laveaux left for France, Louverture received no letter from him for much of 1797. Laveaux's silence gave him no inkling of the political situation in France, where the conservative colonial lobby, after suffering major defeats in 1794 and 1795, was again resurgent. In May 1797, Vincent de Vaublanc, a "big white" and a deputy from Saint-Domingue, declared to the French parliament that the colony had fallen under the yoke of "ignorant and brutish negroes" and that emancipation had been an economic disaster. His speech had a tremendous impact in conservative circles. By the summer of 1797, there were rumors of a counterrevolutionary coup in Paris.[17]

Louverture was only informed of the threat in September when a copy of Vaublanc's speech finally reached him via the United States. He "became somber and silent" after reading it, wrote a witness. "He was no longer the open and even gay man we had known earlier." "The speech seems designed to upset the blacks," Louverture immediately complained to Paris. Rumor had it that France intended to send an expedition to Saint-Domingue to restore slavery.[18]

Laveaux did his best to defend Louverture's name in France, but his enemies invoked technicalities to prevent him from taking his seat as deputy for most of 1797. It was up to Louverture to become the public voice of emancipation.[19]

Louverture, for whom the world of print was uncharted territory, published a lengthy justification of the Haitian Revolution in October 1797, engaging with many of the central questions posed during the Enlightenment. It was the most sophisticated document he ever penned. One by one he listed Vaublanc's accusations; one by one he took them apart. Blacks were not lazy and ignorant savages: slavery had made them so. Some violence had indeed taken place in the Haitian Revolution, but violence had also taken place in the French Revolution, he reminded his readers; the slaves had in fact proved remarkably merciful toward the planters who had so cruelly oppressed them. Black officers were not disloyal: they had defended Saint-Domingue while Vaublanc and his clique were encouraging Britain to invade the colony. In closing, Louverture reaffirmed black freedmen's "right to be called French Citizens" and their desire to live "free and French." He also warned that he would not hesitate to wage a new war for liberty if France ever dared to restore slavery.[20]

Louverture did not have to act upon his threats. By the time he made them, French liberals had already arrested the main royalist conspirators in Paris, including Vaublanc, and deported seventeen of them to French Guiana, a backwater colony at the northern end of the Amazon rainforest that France used as a penitentiary. The French government immediately reassured Louverture that emancipation was still official policy and that he had nothing to fear.[21]

Though it ended well, the episode made clear that eliminating rivals in Saint-Domingue was not enough to secure Louverture's political future: he also had to shape public opinion in Paris. His initial forays into lobbying (three deputies sent to Paris after the 1795 colonial debate, another three sent after Sonthonax's expulsion) now became systematic as Louverture established a permanent presence on the Parisian political scene. Every time a boat sailed from Saint-Domingue, it took with it letters to the French government that emphasized Louverture's achievements. Every time he made a controversial decision, which was often, he distributed printed reports justifying his actions and dispatched trusted associates to the colonial ministry in Paris.

Equally effective were the fluff pieces planted in the French and US press that outlined Louverture's genius and moderation. One article, ostensibly based on the testimony of a person who had recently met Louverture in Saint-Domingue, described his life in idyllic terms to the Parisian reading public. "It is I," Louverture explained, "who picked my wife. My masters wanted to marry me to young and alluring women," but he was more interested in a "happy marriage," and so selected Suzanne as his bride. Louverture made of course no mention of the fact that he was still legally married to Cécile. The article did much to soften Louverture's public image at a time when he was starting to challenge French authority. "This is how public opinion is shaped," one of Louverture's envoys reported triumphantly from Paris. "We defeated [your enemies] and easily remained masters of the battlefield."[22]

After the departure of Sonthonax, Louverture governed northern Saint-Domingue for seven months with minimal interference from France. He also scored a great coup when the British, whose invasion of Saint-Domingue had proved one of the worst fiascos in British military history, appointed a new commander to oversee an orderly withdrawal. Victory, both domestic and international, was on the horizon.

Then, as March 1798 was drawing to an end, yet another French representative arrived. Gabriel de Hédouville bore the official title of "agent" of the French Republic, which gave him broad authority over all matters in the colony. Accompanied by fewer than two hundred troops, he immediately wrote to express his goodwill, but Louverture took his unannounced arrival and his decision to land on the Spanish side of the island as proof of France's lack of trust in his loyalty. Still reeling from the painful colonial debate of 1797, he had begun to second-guess every French policy move. The fresh-faced idealist of 1794 was gone; suspicion and recrimination were now the order of the day.[23]

Hédouville was a veteran of the republican civil war in the Vendée and a genuine son of the French Revolution, yet Louverture disliked him from the outset, most likely because he resented the presence of a civilian who officially outranked him. He found one excuse after another not to meet Hédouville. He had to fight the British, he wrote; a flood had cut off the road; he was simply too busy. It was only after he had overseen the British evacuation from Port-Républicain and nearby Saint-Marc that in June 1798 Louverture finally visited Cap, where Hédouville had been awaiting him for well over a month.

Hédouville presented Louverture with fine gifts—a carbine, a scarf, and a saddle from the best workshops in France—but Louverture remained on his guard, remembering that experience had taught him that "some men seem to love liberty on their lips, even though they are its sworn enemies inside." To a French frigate captain who suggested that he might enjoy retiring in France, Louverture allegedly replied, "Your boat is not large enough for a man like me." He later added, while pointing to a shrub, "I will only leave when this provides enough wood to build a ship-of-the-line."[24]

Hédouville was careful not to offend Louverture, whom he viewed as the most capable of all the black officers who had been promoted during the Revolution, but political and financial quarrels soon began to emerge. A decree preventing officers from leasing vacant estates below their market value did not go well with the black officers, Louverture included, who wished to invest in the plantation economy. Appalled by the embezzlement of army funds, Hédouville also proposed to reduce the size of the colonial army to 6,000 men as the war with Britain wound down. "If there are no soldiers, there won't be any more generals," complained Louverture's nephew Moïse. Louverture "reacted strongly to this project," Hédouville reported in code back to Paris. "He fears that the government will send forces to restore slavery." Far from demobilizing his troops, Louverture incorporated into his army two regiments of men of color left behind by the British during their evacuation.[25]

In keeping with French revolutionary doctrine, Hédouville took a hard line against the nobles who had collaborated with the enemy or fled Saint-Domingue (the so-called émigrés). But Louverture disobeyed him and issued blanket amnesties to most of the planters who stayed behind when the British evacuated Port-Républicain and Saint-Marc in May 1798. One of them was none other than Bayon de Libertat, who had snuck back to Saint-Domingue for a third time. Louverture jumped at the opportunity to become the patron of his former boss and unilaterally allowed Bayon to settle in the colony so that "this poor old man will finally enjoy the happiness that has eluded him for so long."[26]

The émigré controversy reemerged in August 1798, when Britain evacuated the southern town of Jérémie, and planters flocked to Port-Républicain to beg Louverture for his forgiveness. Defying Hédouville's orders, he again issued a general amnesty. "You are guilty in the eyes of the Republic," he told the repentant whites from the pulpit one Sunday after Mass. But "I will imitate Jesus Christ who is being worshiped in this temple. He forgave in the name of his Father, I will forgive in the name of the Republic."[27]

Louverture's magnanimity gave Thomas Maitland, the general overseeing the British evacuation, a clever idea: what if he could turn Louverture

Louverture negotiating with General Maitland during the British evacuation of Môle Saint-Nicolas in 1798. [François Grenier?], *Le Gal Toussaint-L'Ouverture* . . . (c. 1821), courtesy Library of Congress, Prints and Photographs Division.

against Hédouville and salvage something from Britain's disastrous invasion of Saint-Domingue? When the time came to evacuate the port of Môle Saint-Nicolas, the last position still in British hands, Maitland insisted on negotiating directly with Louverture instead of Hédouville's envoy. To drive a wedge between the two men, Maitland treated Louverture as if he were royalty and showered him with gifts and honors. "I was not expecting such deference," Louverture wrote glowingly.[28]

By September 1798, the rupture between Louverture and Hédouville was complete. Their letters read like shouting matches. Louverture did not attend the Feast of the Republic in Cap, a celebration commemorating the beginning of the Republican calendar year, and instead prepared his next move. Hédouville had few French troops and even fewer local supporters, which made it relatively easy to oust him, but Louverture prepared the ground thoroughly anyway. He first offered to resign so as to deceive Hédouville; meanwhile, to ingratiate himself to the black population, he spread rumors that Hédouville's labor regulations were a first step toward the restoration of slavery. Relying on the power of Vodou for the occasion, Louverture let cultivators organize dances and ceremonies in which priests made "horrible imprecations" in front of an ox's skull.[29]

Unwilling to break with France openly, Louverture sought some indirect means of exiling Hédouville. The French agent provided him with just the excuse he needed when in October 1798 he abruptly disbanded Moïse's regiment in Fort-Liberté. Within days, 10,000 irate black soldiers and field hands were at the gates of Cap demanding justice. A terrified Hédouville appealed to Louverture, who declined to intervene; he had probably encouraged Moïse to revolt in the first place. Instead, he asked another subordinate, General Dessalines, to march on Cap to put even more pressure on Hédouville. Only after Hédouville set sail for France to save his own life did Louverture providentially appear to restore order.[30]

To Moïse, whose brother had died during the incident of Fort-Liberté, Louverture began hinting at declaring independence outright. "Hédouville claims he will pick up troops in France and return; does he think he scares me?" he told his nephew. "I waged war with three countries, and I vanquished all three." He reaffirmed his loyalty to France, however, and insisted that the departure of Hédouville was simply a misunderstanding. To defend himself, he sent envoys to Paris bearing copies of a memoir printed at his request and personal letters addressed to every person he knew in the city. He also asked each town of the colony to write a petition in his favor.[31]

Louverture's written offensive worked. The minister of the navy expressed his "surprise" that a second French representative had been forced to leave in a year, but after much lobbying by Louverture's emissaries, the minister eventually condoned his conduct. As long as the war with Britain continued in Europe, France could not do much against its wayward general in Haiti anyway.[32]

In two years, Louverture had defeated his most serious rivals: a mixed-race general (Villatte), three colonial officials (Laveaux, Sonthonax, Hédouville), one French deputy (Vaublanc), and half a dozen lesser local rivals of all colors. For the first time in his career, in northern and western Saint-Domingue he had no superior to answer to and no local enemy to defeat. Over the next two years he would also eliminate the mixed-race general governing southern Saint-Domingue and the last of the French agents, systematically removing all his rivals until there were none.

FIFTEEN

DIPLOMAT
1798–1800

JOSEPH BUNEL ARRIVED at the Philadelphia residence of US Secretary of State Timothy Pickering the day after Christmas in 1798. Bunel was the personal envoy of Toussaint Louverture—in effect, his ambassador. Pickering was hosting a dinner party; other guests included two congressmen and the Speaker of the House, but it was Bunel whom Pickering really wanted to see.[1]

The diplomatic background to Bunel's visit was a sensitive matter. The alliance between France and the United States dated back to the American Revolution, but the relationship had recently deteriorated after questionable seizures of US merchantmen by French privateers. Neither country had declared war; but by 1798 they were waging an unofficial conflict known as the Quasi-War.

Most of the fighting took place in the Caribbean, where the US Navy waged and won the first battles in its history. French officials considered a daring response: invading the United States with an army of freedmen from Saint-Domingue. The continental army had melted away after the War of Independence, so Haiti was the superior land power at the time. A panic ensued when word got out that a black army might soon ravage the US South. In retaliation, the US Congress passed an embargo that banned all trade with France and its colonies, and commerce to and from Saint-Domingue came to a standstill.

The timing of the Quasi-War was particularly bad for Louverture. Now that the last of the British had finally left Saint-Domingue, he was eager to begin the arduous process of rebuilding the plantation economy. Meanwhile, a civil war with his mixed-race rival André Rigaud seemed increasingly likely, and he needed to restock his arsenals. He could not pursue either of these goals without the commercial support of the United States, which had replaced France as the colony's main trading partner during the French Revolution.

Convincing the United States to lift its trade embargo was the mission of Louverture's diplomatic envoy to Philadelphia. In a personal letter Bunel brought to President John Adams, Louverture expressed his "great surprise and utmost sadness to see the ships of your nation abandon the ports of Saint-Domingue." Well aware of the causes of Adams's ire, Louverture promised that "orders will be given to our privateers to protect the flag of the United States." He also opposed French plans to invade the United States.[2]

Bunel's arrival caused a stir. Louverture had selected a white man as his ambassador to avoid offending local racial sensitivities, but Bunel was married to a black woman and represented the first black leader in the Americas, either of which was controversial enough on its own. Yet Adams, who was neither a Virginian nor a slave owner, proved more willing to engage Haitian revolutionaries than his predecessor, George Washington, and his successor, Thomas Jefferson.[3]

One week after dining with Pickering, Bunel obtained a personal audience with the president. It went well, and in February 1799 the US Congress authorized Adams to exempt from the trade embargo any French territory that did not harass US commerce. The law was so transparently intended for Saint-Domingue and Louverture that it was nicknamed "the Toussaint clause."[4]

As winter gave way to spring, Pickering selected a Caribbean-born doctor, Edward Stevens, as the first US consul general to Saint-Domingue, sending him off to Cap to negotiate a formal treaty with Louverture. Stevens brought with him a full cargo of items for sale, which, in these days of fiscal restraint, would finance his stay in Saint-Domingue. He also carried his government's official response to Louverture's letter. President

Adams had not drafted the response himself—this was precisely the kind of snub that Louverture was quick to notice—so Secretary of State Pickering had taken on the task, indicating that he was open to "a renewal of commercial intercourse." He closed with an arresting flourish: "I am with due considerations, Sir, your obedient servant." To a former slave, the niceties of diplomatic language must have had a peculiar ring: Louverture was not used to hearing prominent white men refer to themselves as his "obedient servant."[5]

Saint-Domingue was not officially independent, but the next two years saw Louverture conduct high-level negotiations with British Jamaica and the United States as if he were the master of his own domain. His diplomatic partners had yet to abolish slavery and the slave trade, or even give free blacks a political role, but Louverture proved so uniquely talented as a diplomat that they agreed to deal with him on almost equal terms—a remarkable achievement considering that the United States would not again establish formal diplomatic relations with Haiti until 1862. Meanwhile, Louverture targeted the last local rivals who stood between him and absolute power. He had to betray his abolitionist principles along the way, but by 1800 his status as all-powerful leader of Saint-Domingue would be secure.

While Bunel was in Philadelphia, a new French agent, Philippe Roume, arrived in Saint-Domingue to take the post left vacant by Hédouville's exile. Roume was a moderate white creole planter who had embraced the cause of abolition. He was, in short, the kind of man Louverture could live with. Louverture had in fact requested Roume's presence for fear that France might appoint a more troublesome figure instead. Roume was nonconfrontational by taste and by necessity: instead of opposing Louverture head-on as his predecessors had done, his strategy was to channel his ambition by "deserving and earning his trust."[6]

Louverture had a plan of his own. As Roume made his way from Santo Domingo to Port-Républicain to meet him, demonstrators physically threatened him all along the route; each time, they stopped when Louverture sent orders to spare his life. By the time Roume completed his journey, he had gotten the point: he only lived at Louverture's discretion. The agent immediately announced that he would "do nothing" without first consulting Louverture, thus upending the normal hierarchy between civilian and military authorities.[7]

In an effort to placate Louverture, who often decried the colony's libertine ways and wished to break down racial barriers, Roume formally divorced his estranged French wife, so that he could marry his longtime mixed-race mistress Marie-Anne Rochard. Louverture served as witness for the wedding as well as for the baptism of their daughter, which took place nine months later to the day. Their personal ties notwithstanding, Louverture did not ease up the pressure on the French agent. He again organized popular demonstrations to intimidate Roume when he left Port-Républicain to take up his post in Cap. Roume was cowed and powerless from the beginning of his tenure—and, judging by the rambling style of his letters, a little unhinged.[8]

Over the previous months, France had sent instructions to Saint-Domingue officials to export the ideals of the Declaration of the Rights of Man, just as France had done on European battlefields. Specifically, Louverture was to attack the southern United States or Jamaica. The French agent in Guadeloupe had successfully invaded neighboring islands with black freedmen, and the French were hoping to continue the strategy elsewhere. But Louverture had a different reading of the diplomatic situation. He did not want to risk his life in some harebrained adventure overseas, even one that offered the promise of altering the course of world history. His long-term goal was not universal emancipation but abolition in Saint-Domingue, his political rise, and the colony's economic recovery, none of which could take place if he needlessly provoked the two main naval powers of the Caribbean. He chose to pursue cooperation instead.

Although French colonies like Saint-Domingue were not normally allowed to conduct diplomacy independent of the imperial capital, Louverture welcomed Stevens with open arms when the US consul general reached Cap from Philadelphia in April 1799. Roume reluctantly agreed to cancel the commissions of French privateers so that trade with the United States could resume. His mission completed in a matter of days, Stevens took up residence in Cap, where he rented a house owned by Louverture and developed a warm relationship with him. The French agent in Guadeloupe, who tried and failed to negotiate a similar treaty with the United States during the same period, could only admire Louverture's diplomatic acumen.[9]

Just then, Thomas Maitland, the British officer who had negotiated the British evacuation in 1798, returned to Saint-Domingue with orders from Britain to sign a formal treaty of amity and nudge the colony toward independence. Negotiating with the United States, a longtime ally with which France was not officially at war, was one thing; negotiating with archrival Britain was another matter altogether. Roume vociferously opposed any agreement. The very act of meeting a British envoy was seditious, he informed Louverture.

Louverture proceeded discreetly. Leaving Roume in Cap, he headed for the city of Gonaïves, where in June 1799 he signed a secret agreement by which he promised not to invade Jamaica as long as Britain agreed not to interfere with Saint-Domingue's commerce. Well aware that Paris would react strongly if word of his private diplomacy ever got out, Louverture asked that British ships trade under a neutral flag and that the man appointed to represent Britain's interests not bear the official title of consul.

Roume learned of the agreement nonetheless and warned Louverture that he was veering dangerously close to high treason. Louverture's retaliation was swift. Within days, Stevens wrote, Roume was "no better than a dignified prisoner at the Cap." From then on, Louverture only kept him as agent so that he could sign his decrees in France's name and write sycophantic reports to Paris. In case his forceful advocacy on behalf of Louverture seemed suspicious, Roume's reports ended with mentions that he had written them "entirely in my hand," with "my handwriting," and "my signature."[10]

The US and British governments were each convinced that they had scored a major diplomatic coup. Soon, Pickering insisted to his superiors, Louverture would drop all pretense of serving France and declare independence under Anglo-American tutelage. Alexander Hamilton, a native of the Caribbean island of Nevis and the presumed half-brother of Consul Stevens, even began drafting a constitution for an independent Saint-Domingue. Louverture "is taking his measures slowly but securely," Stevens wrote. "He will preserve appearances a little longer. But as soon as France interferes with this colony he will throw off the mask and declare it independent."[11]

Stevens spent many hours discussing independence with Louverture and was convinced that it was an end he sought. But this was the same

Louverture who consistently assured France of his loyalty and confided that he was "proud to be [France's] adoptive son." It is not rare when reading Louverture's correspondence to find two, three, or even four letters written on the same day on the same topic but addressed to different recipients, each one convincingly making a different argument for the recipient's benefit. Deceit was his forte: he liked to quip that if his left arm ever became aware of what his right arm was doing, "then he'd have it chopped off."[12]

While assuring his various partners that he was on their side, Louverture followed his own plan of action, which was to reduce France's authority without completely severing his ties with the mother country. Going any further on the path to independence would have put his sons in danger. Independence would also have been too politically sensitive at a time when he faced the most serious crisis of his political life.

The last official act of Roume's predecessor, Hédouville, before leaving Saint-Domingue had been to denounce Louverture as a "rebel" and encourage André Rigaud, the commander of the southern region, to reject his authority. General Rigaud, who had been freed by his white father prior to the Revolution, was the leader of the "formerly free" community and Louverture's last major rival in Saint-Domingue. A goldsmith by trade, he had traveled to France, Guadeloupe, and the United States (as part of the 1779 Savannah expedition) when Louverture was still a homebound muleteer in Haut-du-Cap. Rigaud was of mixed race, while Louverture was black. Rigaud disliked priests, whereas Louverture courted them. Rigaud was a southerner; Louverture was a northerner. At once racial, religious, social, and regional, the Rigaud-Louverture dispute was first and foremost personal: each of these two ambitious generals aspired to govern all of Saint-Domingue now that white power had almost vanished. Britain's final departure and Hédouville's ouster, both of which took place in October 1798, brought into the open a rivalry that had been largely private for years.[13]

Shortly after taking over as French agent, Roume brought Rigaud and Louverture together in a final attempt to avoid an armed conflict. The date, February 4, 1799, was well chosen: it coincided with the five-year anniversary of the French law of abolition and reminded the two rivals of their shared ideological agenda. The two men made a public show of reconciliation, but the war of words resumed as soon as Roume left for Cap. To the mixed-race population of Port-Républicain, which Louverture suspected of pro-Rigaud sympathies, Louverture warned that "he only had to raise his left arm and they would be done for." This was no empty boast. Louverture, who could draw from the superior demographic resources of the North and West, amassed an army of 15,000 to 20,000 men in Port-Républicain; Rigaud was only able to muster about 5,000. The only thing Louverture lacked was supplies, which explains his eagerness to sign a commercial treaty with Britain and the United States in the spring of 1799. Accounting for ratification delays, commerce was scheduled to resume on August 1, 1799.[14]

Rigaud chose not to wait. In June, he struck first and attacked the town of Petit-Goâve, located southwest of Port-Républicain, at the junction of the western and southern provinces. Although Louverture's army vastly outnumbered Rigaud's, his men were poorly equipped, and Rigaud had the superior strategy. While Louverture's lumbering army marched south to meet the enemy, Rigaud sponsored insurrections all along the northwestern coast, deep inside Louverture's territory.

When Rigaud's supporters threatened Cap itself, Louverture had to double back to avoid losing the war before it had even started. For the first time since 1792, he was in real danger of being on the losing side. As he approached Gonaïves, he narrowly escaped an assassination attempt when two bullets passed through his hat; two of his followers were killed by his side. Outraged, he ordered the suspects torn to shreds by cannon fire on the town square. He also ordered mass executions of Rigaud sympathizers, many of them of mixed race. Shooting, bayoneting, drowning: the War of the South, also known as the War of the Knives, had started as a power struggle between two generals, but was now turning into a racial war of untold brutality. A desperate Roume reminded everyone that Dominguans were united in their diversity and that he was himself the white "husband of a mulattress, the father of a quadroon, and the son-in-law of a negress." His plea for unity fell flat, and the colony sank under a sea of blood.[15]

Hoping to put Louverture's martial spirit to more productive uses, Roume next tried to revive long-standing French dreams of attacking

British Jamaica. A young merchant named Isaac Sasportas provided him with just the plan he needed. The scion of a wide-ranging family of Sephardic Jews, Sasportas revered the French Revolution because it had proclaimed the civil emancipation of the Jews. He felt proud to "fight for liberty and the French" at a time when discrimination was the norm for Jews in the Americas and Europe. Sasportas presented Roume with a radical idea: not only should France invade Jamaica, but it should also start a slave revolt there. Roume was initially concerned by the fate of Jamaica's white planters, but Sasportas's enthusiasm won him over.[16]

Over the following months, Roume put together a 4,000-man expeditionary force. Meanwhile, Sasportas traveled to Jamaica to gather information and cultivate contacts. Sasportas planned to poison the governor's coffee on Christmas Day 1799, at which point Jamaica's slaves, the powerful Maroon communities of Jamaica's Blue Mountains, the many French exiles living in Kingston, and the town's Irish community would rise simultaneously. The French expeditionary force would then make the short dash from Saint-Domingue to Jamaica, proclaim the general emancipation of the slaves, and seize the colony for France and freedom.

The plan was on the verge of being put into effect when Louverture leaked it to his US and British contacts. Louverture's active opposition to a slave revolt in Jamaica is perplexing but well documented: "Toussaint may fairly claim credit for affording to [British agent Charles] Douglas the perusal of the several projects for the attack on Jamaica," noted the governor of Jamaica, who immediately ordered Sasportas arrested in Kingston and put on trial. He was convicted of treason and sentenced to death.[17]

For several days, Sasportas was left alone in his cell next to a coffin. "Nature shuddered within me when I learned of my upcoming destruction," the young man wrote touchingly. The governor of Jamaica rejected his pleas for clemency, and Sasportas was hanged two days before Christmas 1799. The French invasion quickly unraveled. Jamaica's slaves would not be fully freed until 1838.[18]

Louverture's betrayal of the Sasportas plan was the clearest violation of his abolitionist ideals to date, but it was consistent with his diplomatic and political priorities. He only pretended to go along with Roume's plans because he wanted an excuse to ask Spain and France for weapons, which he really intended to use against Rigaud. He denounced the invasion of Jamaica to endear himself to British and US authorities and obtain their commercial support, but he kept the denunciation secret to avoid offending France and his black supporters. The measures he took to hide his actions were so effective that they even deceived later generations: while celebrating the two hundredth anniversary of Louverture's death in 2003, a Haitian president cited the Sasportas plot as an example of Louverture's "solidarity with all the slaves, no matter what countries they were in," without realizing that Louverture had actually been responsible for the plot's failure.[19]

Louverture's political skill was worthy of a Machiavelli or a Talleyrand, but his decision to pursue revolution in one country alone, which remained a bedrock principle of the postindependence Haitian state, meant that Saint-Domingue's slave revolt never exported itself beyond the shores of Hispaniola. From Brazil to the United States, planters feared a second black revolution of the same scale. But the impact of the Haitian Revolution was actually limited, and the willingness of black statesmen like Louverture to trade pledges of nonaggression for diplomatic acceptance is largely responsible for that.[20]

Louverture did not have time to second-guess his strategic choices. As the War of the South raged on, he and Rigaud each appealed to the French government and the population of Saint-Domingue for support. Printing presses spewed out a slew of proclamations in French in which each side accused the other of being an enemy of liberty. As a former slave, Louverture had more credibility than Rigaud, but his closeness to the British left him vulnerable to accusations that he was secretly favoring slave owners. He did not hesitate to resort to racially charged rhetoric to win the argument. "Like you I was a slave," he explained in a proclamation to the black population on July 19. Rigaud and his ilk wanted "the enslavement of the blacks and the unchallenged domination of the men of color," he added on July 30. Rigaud massacred babies still "sucking on their mother's tits," he continued on August 23. Rigaud had rebelled because "he felt humiliated, as a mulatto, to obey a black man," he concluded on September 9.[21]

Remembering his roots, Louverture also turned to oral culture to reach out to black laborers in the South. "Am I not a negro like you?"

he asked one group in Kreyòl. "We are all brothers. . . . It is Rigaud, it is the mulattoes who want to make slaves of you. They had you as slaves and they are unhappy to see you free, not me, who was a slave just like you." After promising an extra weekly day of rest to plantation workers to boost his popularity, he organized *calendas* (parties) and looked on as African-born Igbos staged war dances for him. Meanwhile, he organized processions and Masses to win fellow Catholics to his side.[22]

But his mobilization efforts encompassed much more than propaganda and high ceremony. Louverture drafted every man above the age of sixteen and bought food, uniforms, and weapons from US merchants. One by one his generals extinguished the rebellions that Rigaud had started in the North, until, in November 1799, Louverture was finally able to shift his focus back to the southern part of the colony.

Because the southern peninsula is narrow and its interior mountainous, there were only two gateways from Port-Républicain to the South: Léogane and Jacmel, towns located on the peninsula's northern and southern coasts, respectively. Heavily fortified by Rigaud, Léogane held out for months. The siege of Jacmel proved bloody and equally indecisive.

To break the stalemate, Louverture dispatched the flotilla initially intended for the Sasportas expedition to take Jacmel by sea. But the British, who proved remarkably ungrateful for Louverture's help in forestalling the invasion of Jamaica, seized the ships before they could reach Jacmel. "Long ago they did not cease telling me that the English were deceivers, their promises, their words were never to be depended upon," an aggrieved Louverture exploded with unusual candor.[23]

Louverture realized over time that the British, despite all their declarations of support, actually wanted Rigaud to fight on so that Saint-Domingue would be ravaged by an endless civil war. They never considered Louverture a partner worthy of their respect: their main negotiator feared compromising "the character of the British nation" by dealing with a black man, while the admiral of the Jamaican squadron denounced "the ambition of this man with thick lips and frizzy hair."[24]

Fortunately for Louverture, Consul Stevens and the US Navy proved more accommodating. The fabled USS *Constitution* and other warships transported Louverture's troops, captured Rigaud's barges, and blockaded his ports. Then, in March 1800, in the first case of US military meddling in another country's internal affairs, the USS *General*

Greene bombarded the forts of Jacmel and finally forced its starving defenders to surrender. An ecstatic Louverture gave the captain of the *General Greene* 2,500 pounds of coffee to thank him for his assistance; the captain returned the favor by inviting Louverture on board with full honors. Louverture, who had only stepped foot on a ship once before, was so impressed by the influence of sea power that he repeatedly tried in ensuing months to buy a frigate from Britain or the United States. Unwilling to give him the ability to project his forces overseas, both countries declined.[25]

A three-man delegation arrived from France just after the fall of Jacmel. Its timing was poor. The delegates had been instructed to bring an end to the civil war, but Louverture had no interest in ending a conflict that was finally turning in his favor. Increasingly willing to employ force against France's representatives, he arranged for the envoys to be heckled and roughed up. One of them, who had dared to criticize Louverture in the past, was subjected to three mock executions.[26]

After the fall of Jacmel, Louverture's generals, particularly the fearless Dessalines, swept across the southern peninsula, taking Rigaud's positions one by one. By June 1800, they were besieging the southern capital of Cayes, from which Rigaud fled in July. The war was over. Louverture had emerged victorious from the bloodiest conflict in Saint-Domingue's history.

Louverture's triumphant entry into Cayes was not only of political significance. Many years before, his half-sister Geneviève, the daughter of his father's first wife, had been sold to a white planter and taken south. This old wound had apparently never healed: Louverture went searching for his half-sister as soon as the War of the South finally gave him the opportunity. She was still alive and had in fact done quite well, having married a white planter who had freed her. She had borne him nine children. She and Louverture spent many hours reminiscing about the bad old days, after which Louverture hired one of her sons as his personal aide-de-camp. He also asked her daughters to move in with him, and his niece Louise Chancy eventually married his son Isaac. While in Léogane, Louverture also fathered an illegitimate son with the wife of a local notable, his family network expanding alongside his military conquests.[27]

The reunion did not soften him. At the end of the war, he presided over a second wave of massacres that eliminated the last remnants of

Rigaud's regime. Louverture delegated the task to Dessalines, who had a taste and talent for this sort of thing, and then made a public show of criticizing him for his bloodlust: "I told you prune the tree, not uproot it!" But in a clear indication that he approved of Dessalines's conduct, he later promoted him to division general and commander of the western province. Nineteenth-century Haitian historians, many of whom were of mixed race, put the total number of Louverture's victims during and after the War of the South at between 5,000 and 22,000. The higher estimates were likely inflated, since the free population of color was less than 30,000 at the outbreak of the Revolution, but the actual number was no doubt significant.[28]

One Sunday before Mass, Rigaud's last surviving supporters were lined up before Louverture. In a public display of contrition, they stood entirely naked. A delegation of young white women interceded in their favor. Louverture quizzed the women on their catechism (a habit of his) and delivered an impromptu sermon on the value of Christian forgiveness. He then turned to his prisoners and delivered his verdict: "Forgive us our trespasses, as we forgive those who trespass against us. Return to your duty, I have already forgotten everything." Saint-Domingue's lord and master was ready to move on.[29]

Louverture's foray into the world of diplomacy in 1798 and 1799 underscored the complexity of a man who was a former slave, a father, a brother, a planter, and a diplomat. A master of the gray area and the white lie, he pursued multiple goals simultaneously and had to make morally ambiguous compromises to achieve them all. One of these goals was the defense of emancipation in Saint-Domingue—as long as that liberty could be reconciled with the economic recovery of the plantations. It was a delicate balancing act that would occupy him for the next two years.

SIXTEEN

PLANTER
1800–1801

ON 25 PLUVIÔSE of the year IV in the French revolutionary calendar (February 14, 1796), Toussaint Louverture learned that soldiers and workers from the region of Port-de-Paix were in open rebellion. Leaving his headquarters in Gonaïves, he made his way north, picking up troops along the way, until he reached the Andro plantation. There he met the commander of the rebellious troops, Etienne Datty, who had come with five hundred armed men and field workers to confront him. Louverture was undeterred by their menacing presence. "I entered the circle and, after preaching to them morals and reason and reproaching them for the murders they had committed, I told them that if they wished to preserve their liberty they needed to obey the laws of the Republic, be docile, and work." If they had any grievances, they should have contacted him first instead of rebelling. "God said: ask and you will receive, knock and the door will be open to you."[1]

A spokesman for the rebels stepped forward and explained that their leader, Datty, had been unjustly stripped of his command. Datty was the one "who ate misery to win our liberty" during the slave revolt, he said. Also, no one had paid the field laborers for their work, and they were convinced that a restoration of slavery was at hand. All present nodded in agreement.

Louverture listened attentively and sympathized with the workers' plight, but he could not help but fault them for resorting to violence. By rebelling, he said, they were helping the enemies of liberty, who thought that "blacks are not made to be free," because then "they don't work anymore and commit thefts and murders." Instead, they should prove "to the whole universe that Saint-Domingue can become rich again with free laborers." The argument struck a chord, and the rebels agreed to go back to work. They vowed to become "so good that everyone will forget what we just did."

Leaving the Andro plantation, Louverture crisscrossed the region of Port-de-Paix to negotiate with other rebel groups, give more speeches, and arrest some of the troublemakers. After five days of this, he was nodding off during a celebratory dance organized by local cultivators when he received word that another commander had revolted during his absence from the western province. Galloping into the tired night, he headed south to suppress the uprising.

Over the next few weeks, Louverture had to deal with the unruly leader Makaya (February 23, 1796); other unruly leaders named Paul Charrite, Thomas André, and Noël Artaud (April 5); upheavals in Gros-Morne (April 7) and Marmelade (April 9); and then another one in Gros-Morne (April 11); before another revolt broke out near Port-de-Paix, led by none other than the ever-troublesome Etienne Datty (April 14). After putting down three more revolts in Bombarde, Môle, and Saint-Louis du Nord, he finally had had enough: "My African brothers! How long will you let yourselves be manipulated by your most dangerous enemies like blind men?" He got his answer on May 11 when he faced another insurgency in Gros-Morne—and then one in Jean-Rabel—and on and on for most of 1796, and 1797, and the rest of his life.[2]

This pattern of unrest was unsurprising in a colony beset by years of revolutionary upheavals. Only with the end of the War of the South in July 1800 did Saint-Domingue experience something it had not known for a decade: peace. For almost two years thereafter, with the exception of the occasional cultivator uprising and an attack on Santo Domingo, the colony enjoyed an unusually restful period. The reprieve gave Louverture an opportunity to focus on an issue that was of particular interest to him: the recovery of the plantation sector.

His main obstacle was how to convince former slaves—such as the rebels of the Andro plantation—to get back to work. His solution—to enforce a labor status halfway between slavery and complete freedom—was typical of his desire to reconcile the interests of the planter class and the aspirations of former slaves. His efforts were unceasing, but the results were disappointing. The colonial economy bounced back, but only partly, and the many compromises he had to make along the way enraged his black base without gaining him the full acceptance of the white planter class.

Whether sugar colonies could function without resorting to forced labor was a long-standing debate in Europe and the Caribbean. Apologists of slavery had long argued that no one worked in the tropics unless they were forced to do so, least of all lazy and childlike Africans, so abolishing slavery would lead to economic ruin. Abolitionists had replied that plantations could flourish with free workers, but aside from one inconclusive experiment by the Marquis of Lafayette, who had purchased a clove plantation in French Guiana in 1785 and then freed its slaves, this had not been demonstrated.[3]

The Haitian Revolution was the abolitionist movement's greatest test case—and an economic embarrassment. As soon as they had the chance, field hands fled their plantations in droves (sometimes killing their master first), and the colonial economy collapsed. In the weeks that followed the August 1791 slave revolt, in the region of Cap alone, 1,400 sugar- and coffee-growing estates were reduced to ashes. With a major commodities exporter suddenly out of world markets, prices skyrocketed while other producers (most notably Jamaica and Cuba) scrambled to make up for the shortfall.[4]

When France formally abolished slavery two years later, abolitionist societies in the United States waited eagerly for the result of an experiment that, in their view, could prove or disprove their claim that free blacks could become productive members of society. They were disappointed. According to free-market economists, the promise of a salary should have been enough to entice black laborers back to work. But former slaves associated plantation labor with servitude: they preferred growing subsistence crops on a plot of their own to working on a former master's estate, even as a salaried employee. The total production of colonial crops plunged 98 percent, declining from 226 million colonial livres in 1789 to 4 million in 1796. The Spanish and British invasions (1793–1798), the War of the South (1799–1800), and a major flood of the Artibonite River (1800) destroyed what the slave revolt had spared. In this context, Louverture did not so much seize power as inherit an economic wasteland. A planter who visited the plain of Cap in 1799 described it as a "desert."[5]

If the colony was going to be a major economic power, sugar was the only option. With the exception of pottery works and rum distilleries, Saint-Domingue had no manufacturing sector. Unlike Spanish colonies like Mexico and Peru, it had no silver mines. Nor was it a trading center like Curaçao or a privateering haven like the Bahamas. Saint-Domingue's wealth derived from one thing and one thing only: the exportation of sugar, coffee, and other tropical crops. As Louverture, put it, "our mines are our plantations."[6]

Without sugar production on a massive scale, Saint-Domingue could not pay for imports of flour and gunpowder, and without flour and gunpowder it was exposed to famine, foreign invasion, and re-enslavement. If he could not get the plantations operating again, Louverture's regime, which was financed by taxes on the production and exportation of tropical crops, could not function. His government came dangerously close to bankruptcy during the last months of the War of the South: the colonial treasury had to suspend all payments, raise taxes, fire half of the public servants, and cut the salaries of those who were left in order to avoid immediate default.[7]

One way or another, Saint-Domingue needed plantations: large ones, too. Former slaves could conceivably have grown coffee on small plots (this became the norm in postindependence Haiti), but yeomanry was incompatible with the cultivation of sugarcane. Sugar plantations required large capital investments, so a sugar plantation could not hope to turn a profit without achieving economies of scale. Breaking apart large estates and distributing the land would have pleased Louverture's supporters, but it would have forced him to abandon the colony's iconic crop.

The barrier was not only economic but psychological. Louverture was not nursed on the Jeffersonian ideal of an independent citizen-farmer. He came of age in a region of the globe where social prestige was bestowed upon large landowners—the "big whites"—and specifically, sugar planters like the Brédas. Despite (or because of) his servile past, Louverture desperately wanted to re-create a planter class, albeit one in which he and his fellow black generals would play the leading role, so that he could become what Haitians today call a *gwo nèg*, a "big black" or "big shot." The most enthusiastic white converts to the Revolution were known as "white blacks"; in many ways, he was a "black white" who had made the economic worldview of his former masters his own.[8]

Louverture saw many reasons to foster the recovery of the plantations, but ultimately the most compelling of them was that he stood to benefit financially. Prior to the Revolution, he had only owned a small plot of land in Haut-du-Cap, slivers of which he had sold in 1779–1781 to finance his failed foray into coffee-growing. After the outbreak of the slave revolt in 1791, during the years of his military and political ascent, his landholdings had multiplied. He acquired a cattle ranch in Santo Domingo (probably when he served Spain in 1793–1794), plantations around Gonaïves (possibly when he conquered the area for France in 1794), a house in Môle Saint-Nicolas (which Britain gave him when evacuating the town in 1798), and coffee estates near the southern town of Jérémie (which he leased after the War of the South). Toussaint and Suzanne Louverture eventually owned or leased a staggering thirty-one estates across Hispaniola. This self-made man, who did not even own his own body as a child, was now the richest individual in the colony. If he could only get his plantations to achieve their full potential, he could be the richest in the Americas.[9]

It would have been impossible in ordinary times to acquire so many plantations. A single sugar estate could be worth more than a million colonial livres before the Revolution, so even the princely salary of 300,000 colonial francs a year that Louverture awarded himself as leader of the colony would not have sufficed to buy a single estate. "I never had much cash," he later insisted. "I had many animals, I was rich with land, but I never had much cash."[10]

Louverture owed his landowning prowess to the peculiar circumstances of the Revolution. As violence spread, thousands of planters left Saint-Domingue. The colonial administration seized their assets, so by the late 1790s over half of the colony's plantations were under state control. The colony then leased sequestered estates to private managers who paid a share of the production as rent. Here was an endless opportunity to enrich oneself off an exiled planter's land.[11]

A January 1798 French law specified that public servants and army officers could not lease plantations from the state. The law was designed to prevent them from using their influence to negotiate favorable terms. Louverture, however, simply used front men, such as his brother Paul, to circumvent the law. When the French agent Hédouville required that leases be awarded at public auctions to avoid any backroom deals, Louverture freed himself from the constraints by ousting Hédouville. In the months that followed, he rented numerous plantations in the western province that Britain had recently evacuated, and he did not hesitate to use his influence to lower his rent. It was easy to ignore the law when one had an army. Other officers of color did the same.[12]

Louverture's acquisitiveness put him on a collision course with his usual allies, the white colonists. They had hoped that he would help them contain the revolutionary impulses of the black population; they had worried that if he died, some uncouth radical like Moïse or Dessalines was next in line. With time, however, the white planters realized that Louverture had deceived them, and that he had no intention of giving back the estates that he had leased in their absence.

Most of the exiles who returned to Saint-Domingue during Louverture's ascendance experienced only frustration. Begging Louverture for a personal favor was the only way to recover one's land, and even that humiliating experience was not always enough. One such planter, Pierre Chazotte, who returned from the United States in December 1800, endured months of delays; finally he concluded that Louverture had a "scheme of appropriating to himself the kingly revenues of all the estates belonging to absentees." Broke but not yet broken, Chazotte went to Louverture's personal residence to push his claims in person. Louverture made him wait all day in the parlor before peremptorily sending him away. "Get yourself away from my presence! Away! Away!" Louverture told him. Rather than settle for a subordinate role in the new Saint-Domingue, Chazotte left the colony and waited for better days to come.[13]

Confiscating the plantations of exiled planters was just a first step. Outside the plain of Cap, which had been settled early in Saint-Domingue's history, land was relatively plentiful, and it only became more so as white colonists died or fled. Far more valuable than land was the labor force needed to operate a large plantation: dozens of workers for a coffee plantation and hundreds for a sugar plantation. The challenge was to get field hands to work, now that slavery was no longer there to force them.

After declaring emancipation in 1793–1794, French colonial administrators had tried hard to convince former slaves to keep working. Luxury goods were desirable, former slaves were told, and they could only acquire them if they earned a salary: idleness was evil, work was a moral duty, and freedmen should do their part to enrich a republic that had welcomed them as citizens. "Do not think that liberty . . . is a state of laziness and idleness," Commissioner Sonthonax had warned them on the day he abolished slavery. Racists everywhere were convinced that "a freed African will no longer work," he had said. "Prove them wrong."[14]

No one argued these two points better or more often than Louverture. "Work is necessary, it is a virtue" (March 1795). Disprove "the enemies of liberty . . . who think that blacks are not ready to be free" (February 1796). "No! Man cannot be free if he does not work" (July 1798). "Prove to the enemies of liberty that Saint-Domingue, cultivated by free hands, will recover its former splendor" (October 1798). "Liberty imposes more obligations on you than slavery did" (November 1798). "The *safety of liberty* imperiously requires it" (October 1800). "Shun idleness, it is the mother of all vices" (July 1801).[15]

Louverture employed every tool at his disposal to deliver his message to every segment of the population. He outlawed the practice of Vodou, a religion he described as "an utterly vicious doctrine, because it only breeds disorder and idleness," and promoted Christianity instead. He used his fluency in Kreyòl and a stock of parables, many of them borrowed directly from the Gospels, to reach out to the black population. After throwing a handful of white corn kernels into a jar filled with black corn kernels, he would remind his audience that they formed the vast majority of the colonial population: they had nothing to fear from a handful of white planters. At other times, he would mix water and wine, and ask field hands to separate one from the other. When they replied that it was impossible, he pointed out to them that this was precisely the point: whites and blacks were now inseparable.[16]

By and large, former slaves turned a deaf ear to these admonitions. When propaganda failed them, Louverture and other French colonial officials switched from the proverbial carrot to the stick to keep laborers in the fields. They did not restore slavery, which was morally objectionable and politically unfeasible; instead, they designed an intermediate system. Former slaves became "cultivators," for whom paid work was both a right and an obligation. We are accustomed to think of slavery and freedom as polar opposites today, but in the Caribbean, where labor forms like *repartimiento* (for Amerindians) and indentured servitude (for whites) had once been the norm, slavery and freedom were two endpoints on a continuum. The roots of the cultivator system can be traced back to the immediate aftermath of the slave revolt, when rebel leaders like Georges Biassou first outlined its main principles in an effort to contain the radicalism of their base. Sonthonax formalized it in French-controlled areas as soon as he abolished slavery in 1793. He announced that cultivators were no longer "someone else's property," could not be whipped, and had to be paid—but he also required that they sign one-year contracts on a plantation, because "in France, everyone is free but everyone works." Every colonial official, from Etienne de Polverel to Etienne Laveaux, André Rigaud, and Gabriel de Hédouville, maintained Sonthonax's restrictive cultivator system, which was also employed in the French colonies of Guadeloupe and Guiana.[17]

Louverture served French officials until 1798 and then vied with Rigaud for popular support, so it was only after winning the War of the South in July 1800 that he could truly make his mark on the cultivator system. He lost no time. On August 4, he complained that cultivators in the South were "merely running to and fro and taking absolutely no care of cultivation," and he ordered them back to work. The cultivator system of his predecessors, which he had occasionally criticized for political advantage, was here to stay. In a novel move, he asked the army to enforce labor regulations. This militarization of plantation work would become the hallmark of his rule.[18]

In October 1800, Louverture unveiled a comprehensive set of labor regulations that remained in place for the rest of his career. It was arguably the most important piece of legislation of his career because it clarified his thinking on the Revolution's signature issue, labor. When it came time to pick between two extremes—slavery and unfettered freedom—Louverture stopped well short of the latter. By order of General Louverture, all former field slaves, even those who had settled in urban areas during the Revolution, would return to their original plantations, sometimes under their former masters. Those who refused would be *"arrested and punished as severely as soldiers,"* which implied that plantation runaways could be shot as deserters. He thereby merged the two worlds he knew best—the sugar plantation and the army camp—into a kind of military-agricultural complex.[19]

Although women had been a minority on prerevolutionary plantations, they now formed the bulk of the labor force. The reason was that so many men had died in the Revolution or were still serving in the army. The demographic shift was not lost on Louverture, who went out of his way to use both the masculine and the feminine versions of the French word for "cultivator" in his labor code. He expressly forbade female field hands from entering army camps, presumably so they could not forge alliances with the men charged with enforcing the new labor laws. He also railed against women who moved to towns and cities to live of "libertinage." Equal work did not bring equal pay: when the plantation's crop was distributed as salary, female field hands received two-thirds of the share their male counterparts got. Women were also denied the higher-paying jobs, such as sugar refiner (which paid double the usual male share) and foreman (three shares).[20]

In a nod to black public opinion, Louverture did ban the use of chains and the whip, and he expelled a planter who was accused of branding one of her young cultivators. But these measures were not always enough to quiet his critics. Days after he issued the October 1800 regulations, some planters told their former slaves, "I will command you as in the past, and you will see that you are not free." The claim traveled like wildfire among the black population. Louverture had to threaten any planter making such "incendiary" remarks with jail time to avert a revolt.[21]

More regulations followed. In February 1801, Louverture banned land sales of fewer than 50 *carreaux* (about 160 acres) to prevent plantation laborers from establishing subsistence farms. In July, he declared that cultivators, who had once been able to sign one-year (then three-year) contracts and change employers, would now have to work on the same plantation for life, which essentially turned them into serfs. In September, he decreed that cultivators would need his personal authorization before marrying someone from another plantation, a rule that had been in place under the Old Regime. Some cultivators wondered if Louverture's strict labor regulations had brought the Revolution back full circle to the days of the Black Code.[22]

Louverture emphasized that being sent back to the fields was not the same as being re-enslaved, but the legal distinction between a cultivator and a slave seemed overly theoretical to many freedmen. For them, true liberty was more tangible: it meant cultivating one's own land, settling in town if one wished, and being allowed to marry someone from a different plantation without having to seek prior authorization. The harsh manner in which Louverture's officers implemented his regulations did nothing to allay their fears. The ten-day week of the new revolutionary calendar also meant that laborers only got three days of rest for each thirty-day month, instead of the four or five days a month they had been entitled to under the old seven-day week. This was a notable change for people who had begun their slave revolt as a fight for three days of rest *a week*.

Had the Revolution's true purpose been to end labor exploitation, former slaves asked themselves, or had they fought a revolution so that rebel leaders could confiscate the plantations of white colonists? Had they traded one master for another? Surely they hadn't fought so they could be herded into the fields to work at gunpoint. The social struggle that emerged was in many ways a reprise of the rivalries that had pitted African-born field hands against Caribbean-born skilled workers on pre-revolutionary plantations. The African-born freedmen who formed the vast majority of the plantation workforce had the nagging suspicion that the creole elite and the formerly free had used them as a "stepping stone" and hijacked the slave revolt for their own purposes.[23]

The cultivators did not give in. They groused and they grumbled; they disobeyed; they rebelled; they threatened to kill their managers; they ran away. In short, they used all the modes of resistance that they had developed as slaves. During one of the many social upheavals that roiled post-abolition Saint-Domingue, an agitator killed a plantation supervisor and spread the word that Louverture was planning to restore slavery. Louverture rushed to the scene and tried to reason with the cultivators, but "they took up arms against me and my only reward was a bullet in my leg," he protested. In a fit of anger, he decreed that stealing plantation produce was henceforth punishable by death. That was a penalty harsher than the one prescribed by the old Black Code.[24]

The passage of time diminished neither the cultivators' obstinacy nor Louverture's willingness to use force to impose his economic model. Just one month after he issued his October 1800 regulations, a major revolt broke out in western and southern Saint-Domingue. Over 1,000 cultivators died in the ensuing repression. Another uprising hit Cayes in May 1801, and then an even larger one took place near Cap in October 1801, after which Louverture had 5,000 cultivators put to death. As was his habit, Louverture delegated purely repressive tasks to his subordinates, who had acquired plantations of their own and had a vested interest in forcing the laborers back to work. Jean-Jacques Dessalines, who served as inspector of cultivation in the western province, was particularly feared. He was known to strike and even kill the laborers and the foremen who did not meet their production quotas.[25]

To Louverture, the level of violence was justified. The only material consequence of the 1791 slave revolt had been the destruction of the plantation economy, which was replaced by chaos and thievery, a point that buttressed the arguments of the critics of abolition. Louverture was trying to build a functioning state that the rest of the world would see as a model. In curtailing the cultivators' individual freedoms, so as to defend emancipation's good name, he saw himself as safeguarding liberty for all.

Regulating labor was bound to achieve little as there were not enough laborers in the first place. The age-old problem of the shortage of workers in Saint-Domingue only became more acute after 1791: the war ravaged the black population, planters took some of their slaves with them into exile, the slave trade ended, and the army drafted all the able-bodied males. "The Revolution was a prodigious reaper," wrote the French agent Roume, who estimated that the population dropped by one-third (to 400,000) between 1791 and 1800. In addition to plantation laborers,

Louverture needed a standing army of about 20,000 soldiers to maintain internal order and protect Saint-Domingue against foreign invasion.[26]

Like the rulers of prerevolutionary Saint-Domingue, Louverture looked overseas for a solution to his labor shortage. He asked the planters who had taken their slaves with them to the United States to send them back. After an incident in which a US merchant tried to kidnap a black man, he began to search outgoing vessels. He accused Spanish traders of taking black laborers to Santo Domingo. Most importantly, while negotiating with a British diplomat, Louverture confided that he was eager to encourage "the importation of negroes from Guinea who are to be purchased as formerly." Louverture would free them "after the labour of a certain number of years" in a system reminiscent of indentured servitude. That was arguably better than the fate Africans would endure if they were sold in another colony, but the fact remained that he was willing to sign a Faustian bargain with British slave traders to import African flesh by the boatful. The project was so politically sensitive that Louverture kept it a closely guarded secret; we only know of it through British sources. His own son thought his father actually had a "vast project" to "fling himself, with a handful of brave men, on the African continent, to abolish the slave trade and slavery."[27]

Louverture formally legalized the restoration of the slave trade in July 1801 and then sent his trusted diplomatic envoy, Joseph Bunel, to Jamaica to purchase laborers. Bunel probably did not have the time to buy anyone, because the British broke off diplomatic negotiations during his visit. But Louverture's willingness to do business with slave traders underlines how far he was willing to go. It had been a long time since Louverture had denounced his colleagues Georges Biassou and Jean-François Papillon for their willingness to trade slaves in Santo Domingo, and even longer since his parents had left their homeland as part of the Atlantic slave trade.[28]

The exact state of the Dominguan economy was the subject of fierce debates in Europe in the late 1790s. Critics of emancipation described Saint-Domingue as a backwater, arguing that restoring slavery was a prerequisite to the colony's revival. Well aware that Saint-Domingue's economic record would reflect on the merits of emancipation, and more generally his worth as a colonial administrator, Louverture countered that the plantation sector was actually booming. "The cultivators' zeal is as satisfying as can be hoped," he wrote in 1797. He hoped to "live long enough to see the colony brought to a degree of prosperity unknown before the Revolution." By 1802, he proudly declared his mission accomplished: "Cultivation and commerce were flourishing and the island had reached a degree of splendor never seen before."[29]

The reality was more complex. Saint-Domingue never matched past production levels under Louverture, let alone exceeded them, but the economy did recover from the low point it had reached during the Revolution. Exports, from an estimated 93 million French livres of sugar and 76 million livres of coffee in 1789, dropped to nearly zero in 1794–1795, but bounced back to 18 million and 43 million livres, respectively, under Louverture's leadership. Plantations in the West and South performed relatively well, as did the coffee sector in general, but the sugar plantations of the northern plain, which had borne the brunt of the revolutionary upheavals, were still in shambles. A full recovery would take years.[30]

The finances of Louverture's regime remain something of a mystery to this day. Public expenses were exorbitant because of the large peacetime army he maintained to protect himself from his enemies, both internal and external. To raise revenue and balance his budget, he had to increase production taxes and export tariffs several times in 1800–1801. When planters and merchants complained that a convalescent economy could not bear the fiscal burden, he backed down. Officially, his treasury was losing money, but Louverture paid his troops little and late, so there were persistent rumors that he was secretly accumulating a war chest. These rumors were apparently true: in 1802, French forces found stashes of money worth several million francs in various locations.[31]

The incomplete recovery of the colonial economy under Louverture was not a reflection of his limitations as an administrator. Louverture spent every waking hour maintaining order, investing in plantations, and urging laborers to work. The main obstacles were the same ones the Brédas had faced in the 1780s: the field hands' reluctance to work and the staggering investments needed to rebuild the sugar plantations. One French expert estimated that it would have taken anywhere from 40 million to 4 billion colonial francs to get the plantations back into working order after the ten years of constant warfare that had ravaged the colony.

Whether the sugar sector would ever be financially sustainable remained an open question.[32]

Louverture knew this as well as anyone. One of the plantations he had taken over during the Revolution was the Manquets plantation near Cap, which had once been the largest of the Bréda estates. He invested an immense amount of money into it in an attempt to revive its operations, including over 4,000 gourdes (30,000 colonial francs) to renovate the water mill, but its output amounted to a mere 45,000 colonial francs in 1800 and 97,000 in 1801—an improvement, but still just a fifth of the prerevolutionary revenue. To save funds, Louverture delayed distributing shares to workers, forcing the plantation manager, Jean-Baptiste (possibly the same man Louverture had freed in 1776), to beg him to send some cash. Jean-Baptiste had not been paid for two years, he reminded Louverture, and "the cultivators are always pestering me about their pay." If they were not paid for their labor, they asked, what differentiated them from slaves?[33]

For most of his life, Louverture had been forced to contend with events beyond his control: as a slave of the Brédas, as a subordinate of Biassou, and as a general serving French commissioners, he could not do as he wished, and that makes it difficult for historians to understand his real aims and intentions. The period after 1800 is instructive because for the first time in his life Louverture's powers were almost limitless. Revealingly, he did not use his newfound authority to fully extirpate slavery from Saint-Domingue; nor did he attempt to export abolition to other shores. Rather, he used it to send former slaves back to work under a reformed labor system. Louverture's equivocation was representative of an age that had to reconcile Enlightenment principles and the labor requirements of plantations. Like three other great figures of the Age of Revolutions—Thomas Jefferson, Simón Bolívar, and Napoléon—he had conflicted views on the delicate matter of human bondage. As a rebel leading a population of self-emancipated slaves, Louverture could not and would not renounce the ideal of universal freedom. But as a planter and a statesman, he would not and could not let the island's plantation-based economy founder for lack of workers. He never adequately solved the problem of marrying individual liberty with economic development, not even in 1801, the most successful year of his career.

SEVENTEEN

GOVERNOR GENERAL
Early 1801

IN THE EARLY DAYS OF APRIL 1800, Toussaint Louverture formally asked the French agent Philippe Roume to authorize him to take over Santo Domingo. The unresolved status of the Spanish colony had vexed him for years. Spain had ceded it to France in 1795 under the Peace of Basel, but no official accession had taken place owing to the opposition of Governor Joaquín García. Then, as Louverture's power grew, France concluded that it was wise not to add to the territories under his control. France wanted to retain independent access to Santo Domingo's ports in case it decided to send an expedition to remove Louverture from office. As months turned into years, Santo Domingo thus remained in Spanish hands.[1]

It was Louverture who revived the Santo Domingo issue in 1799–1800. Theoretically, seizing Santo Domingo would have enabled him to abolish slavery in a colony where it was still the law of the land. But slavery as practiced in Santo Domingo was considered comparatively benign by the standards of the time, whereas Louverture was enforcing an increasingly strict cultivator system on Saint-Domingue's plantations, so the contrast between Spanish slavery and French liberty was not a clear one. Louverture actually complained that many cultivators were "fleeing to the Spanish part to avoid work or punishment." The young men who refused to be drafted into his army also fled there.[2]

Strategic considerations other than abolition were foremost on Louverture's mind. As André Rigaud began to lose ground during the War of the South, many of his supporters found refuge in Santo Domingo, where they received a warm welcome from Governor García and from the French agent in Santo Domingo, who was a mixed-race supporter of Rigaud. Only by seizing Santo Domingo could Louverture forever rid Hispaniola of Rigaud's clique.[3]

In April 1800, after the fall of Jacmel made clear that victory in the War of the South was imminent, Louverture asked Roume to give his blessing to an immediate takeover. He expected Roume's assent to be a formality, since he held him prisoner in the government house of Cap. But Roume refused, in keeping with his instructions from France. To put pressure on him, Louverture asked various towns of the colony to write petitions demanding his dismissal, a tactic he had employed against Hédouville in the past, but this action did little to sway Roume, who by this point only wanted to return to France.[4]

Louverture did not relent. On April 10, 1800, 5,000 cultivators and soldiers marched to the outskirts of Cap and demanded to see Roume. General Moïse, who was at their head, had an intimidating reputation. Everyone dreaded a repeat of the June 1793 riot, which had led to the burning of Cap and the death or exile of thousands of its white inhabitants. To save the city, Roume agreed to follow Moïse to Haut-du-Cap and address the demonstrators. Insults, accusations, and death threats awaited him there. The demonstrators bitterly reproached Roume for opposing the takeover of Santo Domingo. Roume remained calm throughout the ordeal, guessing from past experience that the protest had been staged by order of Moïse's uncle, a native of Haut-du-Cap. The threats continued for eight full days; Roume, the official representative of the French Republic, spent much of that time locked up in a chicken coop.

Louverture had to come in person to deliver the final pitch. When he arrived, he demanded imperiously that Roume present himself at once and account for his obstinacy. Defiant as ever, Roume replied that he was France's representative and protocol dictated that Louverture come to *him*. "So much firmness surprised Toussaint, who agreed to appear below the second-floor gallery where Roume was awaiting him with singular aplomb," wrote a witness. "Without leaving his horse, Toussaint spewed out reproaches and threats," again without apparent effect. Only when it became clear that the safety of his family and that of the white population of Cap hung in the balance did Roume grudgingly sign the document authorizing Louverture to take over Santo Domingo.[5]

Louverture lost no time. In May 1800, he sent a delegation to take possession of the colony. To allay Spanish fears about black rule, Louverture selected the white general Pierre Agé to head it and promised not to abolish slavery. Santo Domingo "will continue to be treated and governed as in the past," he instructed Agé. "We have often discussed the poor way in which universal liberty was proclaimed in the French part [without a transition period], and how it would be wise to implement it in this part without causing tremors: so we must not change anything to the system that exists."[6]

These reassurances were not enough to convince García. The governor replied that he needed to ask Madrid for guidance, which guaranteed several months' delay. Next, a Spanish mob chased Agé from Santo Domingo, after which Roume informed García that his approval of the takeover had been extracted against his will, and countermanded it. Word then came that a messenger was on his way from France with orders that Louverture could not have Santo Domingo.

A few years earlier, Louverture probably would have backed down in the face of such determined opposition. But he increasingly saw himself as an autonomous leader rather than a general subject to military discipline. He was also concerned by reports that France would soon launch an expedition to oust him from power, and that it would first make landfall in Santo Domingo.

The situation in France had indeed changed dramatically. In November 1799, Napoléon had seized power and made himself first consul. The Directory that had ruled France since 1795 came to an end; the era of the Consulate began. Napoléon ordered a general review of French colonial policy. His views remained tentative at first, but after hearing of Louverture's treasonous diplomacy with Britain, he assembled an expeditionary force in the port of Brest. Because of various practical hurdles and

Louverture's victory in the War of the South, Napoléon eventually chose to send the fleet to Egypt instead of Saint-Domingue; but to confuse the British, he ordered Louverture's son Placide out of his school and onto the fleet. Louverture's spies in France informed him that Placide was on his way to Brest: "It seems self-evident," they said, "that the expedition is destined for the Spanish part of Santo Domingo."[7]

Louverture chose to invade Santo Domingo at once before Napoléon could strike. To avoid an open break with France, he did not publicly reveal his rationale, instead emphasizing the problems stemming from Santo Domingo's sanction of slavery. Spanish slave traders, he claimed, were routinely crossing the border with Saint-Domingue to capture black laborers and sell them as slaves in Santo Domingo. Only by putting all of Hispaniola under his control would it be possible to safeguard his countrymen's freedom. It was a story designed to resonate with his black followers and French progressives.[8]

Early in January 1801, two army columns began their march. The first, under Moïse, left Cap and headed for the city of Santiago in northern Santo Domingo. The second, under Louverture's brother Paul, left Port-Républicain and headed for the colonial capital, also known as Santo Domingo, on the southern coast. Louverture did not normally supervise military campaigns in person, but this time he left with his brother's column. The French envoy carrying official orders not to proceed with the takeover was expected to arrive in Cap at any time, and he did not want to be there when he did.[9]

Spanish authorities in the city of Santo Domingo learned of the invasion as they were gathering to celebrate the Feast of the Epiphany. They were stunned. Terrified that the horrors they associated with the Haitian Revolution would soon be repeated in their colony, they hurriedly prepared to defend themselves, but their forces were hopelessly outmatched. Paul Louverture's southern column promptly brushed aside 1,500 Spanish troops at the Nizao River, after which the road to the capital lay open. Just two weeks after Louverture's army set out, it made camp outside the gates of Santo Domingo. So swiftly had his infantrymen traversed Hispaniola's mountainous terrain, he noted gleefully, that they had been forced to pause to give the cavalry time to catch up.

After the Spanish agreed to a cease-fire, Louverture triumphantly entered Santo Domingo, the oldest European city in the Americas.

Louverture had once served as a black auxiliary of the Spanish Army. He cheekily reminded Governor García that, had the Spanish crown treated him better in 1794, he "would still be in its service." Local inhabitants hovered between shock and panic. To be governed by a black general and ex-slave was unthinkable for elite Dominicans, whose society was structured along racial lines. Always the first to confront racial prejudices head-on, Moïse organized balls in which the proud Spanish nobles were expected to dance with their black slaves. Spanish colonists prepared to depart for Venezuela and Cuba en masse.[10]

Most historians take it for granted that Louverture formally abolished slavery in Santo Domingo, but contemporary sources are remarkably un-clear on the matter. No emancipation decree has been found; none was included in a detailed account of the invasion printed on Louverture's or-ders. To prevent an exodus of colonists and their slaves—that is, taxpay-ers and workers—he tried to convince the Spanish planter class that he was no radical, even as he wished to be celebrated as a liberator by their slaves. His proclamations were contradictory. "The Republic does not want your assets, only your hearts," he reassured Spanish planters before the invasion. Then, after the invasion, he told Dominican slaves that they would enjoy their "liberty" and receive a fourth of the crop as salary, just like the cultivators of Saint-Domingue. But he immediately insisted "that they work, even more than before; that they remain obedient; and that they do their duty with diligence, being fully determined to punish severely those who do not."[11]

Freeing the slaves of Santo Domingo should have been a landmark moment in the history of the Caribbean, but Louverture's version of wage labor was so strict that the difference between it and slavery was lost on many contemporaries. "General Toussaint Louverture did not proclaim the liberty of their slaves during the takeover," Spanish planters remembered many years later. Even legal experts were confounded: man-umission documents issued in Santo Domingo in 1801 hint at a chaotic situation in which layers of Spanish and French law overlapped while slavery effectively remained in place.[12]

Louverture's refusal to radically transform Santo Domingo's so-ciety left a gaping hole in his political legacy. He had been absent for the abolition of slavery in Saint-Domingue in 1793, when he was in the Spanish Army; his equivocation in 1801 meant that his name would not be associated with the abolition of slavery in Santo Domingo either. Dominican slaves were only fully freed during a later Haitian invasion in 1822, and it was in honor of "Papá Boyé," Haitian president Jean-Pierre Boyer, that the slaves sang.[13]

Louverture's actions did serve his short-term goal: it averted a mass exodus. Out of a total population of 125,000, only 10,000 people left for other Spanish colonies (among the emigrants were the remains of Christopher Columbus, which were taken to Cuba and later Spain). With his customary vigor, Louverture proceeded to develop a colony that was twice the geographic size of Saint-Domingue but had never matched its agricultural output. In an effort to foster large-scale plantation agriculture, he improved roads, lowered export taxes, and banned sales of small plots of land.[14]

Leaving his brother Paul in charge, Louverture headed back to Port-Républicain. Sitting on a throne draped with silk, he attended an elaborate ceremony in his honor. Golden letters placed above his head proclaimed to the world, "God gave him to us, God will preserve him for us." He then proceeded to the next item on his agenda: annihilating the last remnants of political opposition.[15]

One of Louverture's foremost goals during his political ascent was to arrogate to himself the powers traditionally ascribed to France and its representatives. He proceeded cautiously at first: he had encouraged Laveaux and Sonthonax to leave the colony to become deputies in the French legislature. But Louverture became bolder with time. To force Hédouville to embark in 1798, he asked his nephew Moïse to threaten him with a popular uprising, a tactic he employed again in 1800 to force Roume to accede to the takeover of Santo Domingo.

By his own admission, Roume was no more than a "puppet" after the April 1800 chicken-coop incident in Haut-du-Cap, but his very presence implied that Louverture was a subordinate figure who needed France's representative to countersign his decrees. Louverture treated him ever more harshly, eventually imprisoning him and his family in the town of Dondon. No longer pretending that the agent—that is, France—was the source of his authority, Louverture began to legislate under his own name. From that point forward, he was effectively an independent ruler.[16]

The philosophical justification for a ruler's right to govern and the limitations of that power were two central questions of the Enlightenment. The Bourbon kings had once claimed that their unlimited authority stemmed from their exalted birth, and ultimately from God. To this, Jean-Jacques Rousseau had retorted that only the popular will could legitimize lawmaking. In the 1789 Declaration of the Rights of Man and of the Citizen, the French National Assembly had also enshrined certain inalienable rights that no legislating body could take away. But Louverture, like Napoléon in France and Simón Bolívar in South America, did not trust the people's ability to make informed choices. Though he paid lip service to the republican principles of liberty and equality, he effectively instituted one-man rule. Enlightened dictatorship was his model, not the Enlightenment. Unlike John Locke, he did not advocate a representative government based on a social contract with the people. Instead, he styled himself after Plato's philosopher king.

Following the invasion of Santo Domingo, Louverture felt strong enough to let French authorities know where their relationship with Saint-Domingue now stood. In February 1801, he informed them that he had deposed the agent Roume, a fact that he had kept secret until then. When sidelining previous officials, he had taken pains to accuse them of various wrongs, to print reports, and to dispatch envoys to Paris to justify his conduct. This time, he merely sent a batch of letters in which he accused the minister of the navy of "not doing him justice enough." His tone verged on impertinence. Roume spent much of 1801 in captivity, and his health became so precarious that Louverture sent him to the United States, so that he would not die on his hands. France had no representative in Saint-Domingue thereafter, even in a purely symbolic role.[17]

In another letter sent in February 1801 and addressed to Napoléon, Louverture announced that he had just absorbed Santo Domingo in direct violation of his orders. Black troops had shown during the invasion that "they are capable of the greatest things," he boasted. "I hope that, better disciplined, they will be able in the future to hold their own against European troops." The subtext was clear: I may have disobeyed you, but if you ever try to overthrow me I will stand my ground.[18]

Louverture also explained in his letters that he intended to draft a constitution for Saint-Domingue. He was probably responding to the new constitution of the Consulate, a clause of which had proven controversial in Saint-Domingue: under the Directory, overseas territories had been treated as standard French provinces where French law applied by default, which guaranteed former slaves the same rights as all Frenchmen. Napoléon's new constitution, by contrast, held that French colonies would be governed by distinct—but as yet unspecified—laws. Louverture and others in Saint-Domingue feared that Napoléon wanted to make possible the future restoration of slavery in some of the French colonies. These fears, it turned out, were well-founded. By preemptively enshrining emancipation in a constitution of his own, Louverture hoped to ensure that slavery could not so easily be restored in Saint-Domingue.

Under Louverture's watchful eye, two deputies were elected in each of the five provinces of the colony: his native North; his adopted West; the South, which he had conquered from Rigaud; and two new provinces carved out of Santo Domingo. To play down the radical nature of the gambit, Louverture only picked white and mixed-race deputies, and he was careful not to describe the resulting constitutional assembly, which gathered in Port-Républicain in April 1801, as a fully sovereign body. He also avoided taking a public role in the deliberations. But there was no mistaking who was in charge: Louverture presided over the opening ceremony and ordered the deputies "not to divulge any of the legislative measures you plan to adopt before your work has been approved [by me] in its totality." When Louverture left the city in May 1801, the constitutional deputies obediently followed their master from Port-Républicain to Cap.[19]

Louverture finalized the text of the constitution in June 1801, sent it off to the printer before France or the people of Saint-Domingue could weigh in, and then formally presented it to the population of Cap. That day, July 7, 1801, when he officially became governor of the island where he had once been a slave, was the most celebratory of his life. If we are to believe a nineteenth-century Haitian depiction of the ceremony, God Himself—depicted as an old white man—watched over the proceedings. Parades, adulatory speeches, a grand Mass, and a banquet for six hundred guests: the festivities matched those that had accompanied the arrival of a new French governor before the Revolution, a time when Louverture had observed the proceedings from afar as a slave. He was overwhelmed with a sense of pride and vindication. The official account of the ceremony noted in a flurry of capital letters that he had been "the Conqueror of his Country" before becoming its "Legislator," and that his mind was now filled with the "memories of what he was and what he had become through the sole strength of his character."[20]

Louverture's conflicted approach to forced labor was a central theme of his constitution. It forcefully stated that slavery was forever abolished—a principle first introduced by a French commissioner in 1793, then approved by a French assembly in 1794, but one that Louverture had never personally proclaimed. "My fellow citizens," he declared to the assembled masses, "whatever your age, class, or color, you are free, and the constitution handed over to me today is meant to safeguard this liberty forever." But other articles of the constitution buried deeper in the text condoned his more reactionary policies, including the cultivator

The July 1801 constitutional ceremony as reimagined in a nineteenth-century Haitian engraving. [François Grenier?], *Le 1er Juillet 1801, Toussaint-L'Ouverture . . .* (c. 1821), courtesy Library of Congress, Prints and Photographs Division.

system and the importation of laborers from Africa. "Cultivators," he admonished them for the hundredth time when presenting his constitution, "avoid sloth, the mother of all vices!"

Though it referenced democratic principles like the separation of powers, the constitution turned Saint-Domingue into a de facto military dictatorship, foreshadowing the political culture of postindependence Haiti. Gone was the *intendant* who had shared power with the governor in prerevolutionary times; gone, too, were the gaggles of commissioners and agents whom France had sent during the Revolution. Gone were the warlords who had controlled various parts of Saint-Domingue during Louverture's rise to power. There was now only one man in charge, who bore the title of governor general for life and oversaw both civilian and military affairs. "The Governor seals and promulgates laws; he appoints all civilian and military officials. He is commander in chief of the armed forces. . . . He sees to the internal and external security of the colony," Article 34 explained. The seven articles that followed gave him extensive powers over lawmaking, the judicial process, censorship, taxation, trade, and finances. In another break from prerevolutionary practices, the colonial church also fell under the governor's purview.

Summoning a constitutional assembly was Louverture's most daring step yet, more daring even than the humiliation of Roume. A constitution was the social contract of a sovereign body: as such, it was incompatible with the colonial bond. The sole local precedent, the 1790 constitution passed by the assembly of Saint-Marc, had been widely interpreted in its time as a first step by white colonists toward Saint-Domingue's independence. Tellingly, several veterans of the assembly of Saint-Marc served in Louverture's constitutional assembly.[21]

Louverture's constitution might still have passed muster in France if he had limited himself to delineating a semi-free status for former slaves and concentrating power in the hands of an executive branch that answered directly to Paris. Instead, several clauses directly challenged French sovereignty. Although Article 1 insisted that Saint-Domingue was "a colony that belongs to the French empire," the rest of the constitution allowed Louverture to implement laws (starting with the constitution itself) without France's prior approval. It also gave him a lifetime appointment with the right to appoint his successor, despite the fact that all previous governors had been appointed by France. Not even Napoléon, who was then the most prominent of a triumvirate of consuls, had yet dared to claim so much power for himself.

Coming so soon after the imprisonment of Roume and the invasion of Santo Domingo, Louverture's constitution was viewed as a declaration of independence by all those who read it. "There seems to be no doubt left that the black Toussaint Louverture is mulling over projects of independence," the French ambassador to the United States had said after visiting the colony in the spring of 1801. When he read the constitution two months later, he concluded that his assessment of the situation had been correct: Louverture was now "in open revolt against France."[22]

But was he? Louverture discussed forming "a black independent government" in a conversation with a British envoy, but he had mastered the diplomatic art of telling his partners what they wanted to hear. Anglo-Americans hoped that he would break from France, so he let them believe that this was his intention. Meanwhile, he repeatedly emphasized his loyalty to France when writing to Paris, as was expected of a French colonial official. This, too, was a lie. Louverture most likely had other designs: to gain as much autonomy from France as possible without crossing the threshold into outright independence. The strategy made sense in the current political environment. The British and the Americans became increasingly difficult diplomatic partners in 1801, so he had no reason to throw himself at their mercy. France retained its popularity with the black population as the homeland of emancipation, so he did not wish to give credence to the accusations of his enemies that he intended to forsake France and restore slavery.[23]

Finally and most importantly, Louverture had a very personal tie to France: his sons Placide and Isaac. By sending them to France to study, he had hoped to provide them with the kind of educational opportunities he had been denied as a child. He came to regret his decision as the years passed and his relationship with France soured. His sons became hostages guaranteeing his good behavior. "As long as you second the views of the government in Saint-Domingue, we will be pleased to fulfill your wishes regarding your children," warned an official of the ministry of the navy. If not . . .[24]

Being separated from their sons was hard for Toussaint and Suzanne Louverture. It took one to three months for a ship to cross the Atlantic, and more in wartime, because most ships had to transit through neutral ports in the United States. As a result, letters from Isaac and Placide were few and far between. Worse, Louverture suspected that his sons' letters were "dictated" to them by his French enemies, because they dwelt at length on the shortcomings of his policies.[25]

When Louverture set in motion his plans to annex Santo Domingo and sideline Roume, he simultaneously began a desperate campaign to repatriate his sons. "My intention would be to get one of them back . . . to offer me a bit of happiness and consolation, as well as to his sweet mother," he implored, even offering to send his youngest son, Saint-Jean, as a replacement at a future date. But the first consul would not let go of his sons when his spies' reports informed him that "Toussaint is very attached to his children." Napoléon had no other means of pressure at his disposal.[26]

In 1800, Louverture sent two trusted envoys, Augustin d'Hébécourt and Christophe Huin, to France. As they passed through Philadelphia, the French consul learned that their mission was to bring Louverture's sons back to Saint-Domingue by any means necessary, which would "entirely free this general of his ties to France." At the consul's urging, Huin and Hébécourt were placed under surveillance as soon as they reached France and prevented from getting anywhere near the school where Placide and Isaac were studying. Napoléon's extensive police network later uncovered two other plots to abduct the boys.[27]

After the kidnapping plots were foiled, Louverture begged Napoléon again and again in 1801 to send his children back. His sons pled their own case, too, but to no avail. His letters took on a sorrowful tone when he realized that his sons would remain in France indefinitely. "Your mother wishes, just as I do, for you to return, and kisses you tenderly," he wrote. "I kiss you with all my Heart and will remain your good father for the rest of my life." He could not declare independence as long as there was a glimmer of hope that his sons might return.[28]

Another moderating influence as Louverture flirted with independence in the summer of 1801 was Charles de Vincent, a white fortifications expert who had served him loyally over the years while refusing at the same time to forsake his native France. After learning of the main clauses of the constitution, Vincent warned Louverture that he was being "dangerously ambitious against the interests of our mother [France], to which you owe far more than I do." All that was left for France to do was to appoint "chargés d'affaires and ambassadors," Vincent quipped, because Saint-Domingue was now effectively an independent dominion. No longer accustomed to brooking any dissent, Louverture reacted with anger and explained that some "occult force" was pushing him onwards and that nothing could hold him back.[29]

But Louverture soon concluded that Vincent, who had gone back and forth between France and Saint-Domingue many times during the Revolution as an official envoy and knew the first consul personally, might have a point. He ordered that printed copies of his constitution, which he had presented to the public with so much fanfare during the July 7, 1801, ceremony, not be distributed to avoid bringing too much attention to its content. He then sent Vincent to France with a manuscript copy of the constitution and a most delicate mission: to obtain Napoléon's blessing.[30]

In three successive strikes, each of them brilliantly executed over the span of six months, Louverture had invaded Santo Domingo, ousted Roume, and passed a constitution making him governor general for life. He would soon enough learn whether France would forgive him for his actions, as it had so often done in the past, or if he had overreached. After accomplishing so much in so little time, he could have rested on his laurels. Instead, he spent the second half of 1801 exercising a power that was as absolute as it was tenuous.

EIGHTEEN

GOD?

Late 1801

TOUSSAINT LOUVERTURE VISITED Port-Républicain in the fall of 1801 to set up one of the tribunals specified by his new constitution. An impressive ceremony in his honor awaited him there. The town's notables in tow, he marched between rows of soldiers clad in full dress uniform and proceeded under a triumphal arch, as if he were a Roman emperor back from campaigning against the Gauls. He then took his seat on a gilded chair worthy of a king's throne, where he listened to speeches as fawning as those intended for a prerevolutionary governor. He was Hercules, the new Spartacus, and Alexander the Great, his admirers explained. He was the black Napoléon. The day ended with a Te Deum Mass, which was fitting for a man who had begun to compare himself to Jesus Christ. "Man proposes and God disposes of him," he liked to say. In many ways, he was now God made man.[1]

Just three years earlier, when visiting the same city, Louverture had reprimanded the population for celebrating his arrival with too much fanfare. "Only God," he replied, "should be venerated like that." By 1801, he expected elaborate ceremonies in every town that he graced with his lofty presence. "I took flight among eagles," he explained, so "I must be mindful when returning to the ground." Louverture no longer inhabited the realm of mere mortals.[2]

As Louverture's career reached its climax in the second half of 1801, the sheer range and scale of his activity is hard to grasp. The series of accomplishments began in the days after he presented his constitution to the public: On July 12 (a Sunday), he settled a dispute over the quartering of troops in Cap and requested new officers from France. On July 14 he celebrated Bastille Day, reproved his nephew Moïse for his troops' indiscipline, and redrew the internal borders of Saint-Domingue. He then met with Charles de Vincent several times to discuss his constitution. He wrote a letter on the matter to Napoléon on the 16th, making sure to raise the issue of his sons' return one more time. The same day, he sent a report to the minister of the navy on his ongoing efforts to revive plantation agriculture. He negotiated with a new US commercial agent on the 16th and 17th. By the 18th, he was back to debating his constitution with Vincent before dashing off to the town of Saint-Marc on the 19th for wide-ranging negotiations with a British envoy. On and on it went. "His movements are very rapid and uncertain," marveled the US agent on the 20th. "He is certainly an extraordinary man." "Those who view General Toussaint Louverture as an ordinary man have been grossly mistaken," agreed his secretary on July 21. "He is even more astonishing seen up close than from a distance."[3]

With the constitution in place he began legislating at a fast clip, passing no fewer than eighteen laws between July 18 and August 12, 1801. These ranged from the mundane (regulating the uniform of colonial officials) to the spiritual (making Catholicism the official religion of Saint-Domingue, just as it had been before the French Revolution). Most dealt with his central project, the restoration of the plantation economy. Debts, deeds, property lines, tribunals, and absentee ownership: no detail escaped his attention. Louverture also claimed for himself the right to appoint priests and bishops, normally the prerogative of God's representative in Rome.[4]

Even racist contemporaries who were quick to disparage former slaves' capacity for self-government were impressed by Louverture's intellectual abilities. Like Napoléon, to whom he was often and aptly compared, Louverture was a micromanager who made his influence felt at all levels of government. He was not formally educated and wrote with difficulty, but with the help of secretaries he drafted letters at all hours of the day and night. He personally decided on all matters in the colony, no matter how trivial. "Cabinet work . . . is for him a pleasure as sharp as enjoying a meal or possessing a woman would be to most men," wrote his secretary. "Seeing everything for himself, crossing the colony like lightning, and answering 100, 200, 300 letters in a day are for him an ecstasy, a need." To accommodate the workload, he employed multiple secretaries at once. To ensure secrecy, they each wrote a portion of his most sensitive letters, which he then assembled in private like an alchemist synthesizing a dangerous chemical compound.[5]

No one was beyond his reach. When his maid stole cash from his cabinet with the collusion of his aide-de-camp, the court sentenced the woman to prison and the man to hard labor, which the judges thought was punitive enough since she was pregnant and he was a mere accomplice. Louverture did not agree. The man was shot on his orders, as was the woman, once her fetus was disposed of "by people skilled

Louverture dictating a letter to a secretary. Lacoste Jeune, *Toussaint Louverture*, nineteenth-century engraving. Personal collection of the author.

with this trade." He subsequently changed the law to ensure that military tribunals, which directly answered to him, had jurisdiction over all thefts, even those committed by civilians. He also issued a penal code that stipulated the death penalty for crimes as diverse as rape, conspiracy, arson, breaking and entering, and—appropriately enough for a former coachman—horse theft.[6]

Over the years, Louverture had constructed an elaborate public relations operation in Paris to lobby the French government and spin the news in his favor. At the height of his power he went further: he tried to learn everything that happened in France and Saint-Domingue and to eliminate rival viewpoints outright.

He was everywhere. This tireless horseman continually crisscrossed Saint-Domingue on his stallion, Bel Argent, and appeared unannounced in the most remote locations to conduct surprise reviews. When listing the areas of command of the various generals of Saint-Domingue, a French officer jotted down this revealing note next to Louverture's name: "everywhere (his locomotion was surprising)."[7]

He knew everything. He read his mail at all times of day and night, often in his bath, a routine he shared with Napoléon. He subscribed to every newspaper in Paris. He also had the habit, going back to Laveaux's tenure, of opening the mail of other French officials as it passed through his office. More controversially, he sent his men to intercept French couriers before they could deliver sensitive dispatches to his rivals. Three aides-de-camp died in one such incident, news of which he proceeded to suppress.[8]

He controlled everybody. He screened incoming visitors and their luggage to prevent unwelcome news from reaching the colony. He read outgoing mail to censor unflattering accounts. He issued a blanket embargo on commerce whenever he wished to prevent specific events from becoming known at all. "You have no idea what would happen to me if people here learned of the opinions I communicated so boldly to you," a terrified planter wrote in a letter addressed to a French correspondent. General Moïse had just forced a departing captain to hand over a bag of mail at gunpoint. "Several inhabitants of Cap, whose letters were intercepted, had expressed their opinion on the current regime and were thrown into a cell where they will suffer for a long time," the planter wrote. Basic rights like privacy and free speech did not exist under Louverture's rule.[9]

Whites were a small but not negligible presence in Saint-Domingue in 1801. Some had remained in the colony despite the Revolution; more had returned from exile after the War of the South in the hope of recovering their plantations. What to do with them was one of the most sensitive matters Louverture had to settle as governor.

Several of Louverture's generals urged him to deal with the "white problem" once and for all. His nephew Moïse, whom he had promoted to commander of the northern province during the War of the South, was the loudest of the radicals. A French general overheard him say at the dinner table that "if General Louverture did not finish off the rest of the whites . . . then he would start by killing the general himself." Jean-Jacques Dessalines, the commander of the western and southern provinces, similarly told his men that they had just won a "small war" (the War of the South) but still had two more wars to wage: "one with the Spanish [of Santo Domingo], who have to be chased from the island, and one with the French, who will return when peace is declared in Europe to steal our liberty." This was the same Dessalines who eventually massacred most of Haiti's white population after independence.[10]

Louverture rejected Moïse's and Dessalines's calls for white blood. As he proceeded to rebuild the colony after 1800, he welcomed the expertise of white secretaries, white merchants, and white planters, because people of color "don't have enough education to fill such jobs." Accordingly, the man who drafted many of his laws was a white planter from Port-Républicain. His diplomatic envoy and paymaster was a white merchant from Normandy. Most of his secretaries were white, as were his priests, the comptroller general, and the administrator of public estates. Louverture and other generals had sent their sons to France to be educated: the next generation would finish the Revolution.[11]

Employing whites did not mean deferring to them. The white exiles who returned to Saint-Domingue under Louverture were quick to notice the collapse of the old racial hierarchies. During a stay in Cap, a British officer was astonished when a "fat negro" sat next to him at his table and allowed himself to eat from his plate. Such was the way, he surmised, that things were now done in Saint-Domingue. Some whites chose to "laugh when seeing the negresses . . . wear wigs like those of our ladies" and ride carriages as if they were "princesses," but most were not so amused: "Whites are obliged to submit to the blacks and dare not complain," lamented an officer after his return to France. "The blacks are extraordinarily insolent toward them."[12]

Having spent most of his life genuflecting before white colonists, Louverture thoroughly enjoyed deflating their egos. One day, when his former boss François Bayon de Libertat headed to the government house to embrace him, Louverture stopped him before he could get too close. "Slowly, Mr. manager," he said, loud enough for all to hear. "There is more distance between you and me today than there was in the past between me and you." Louverture must also have felt elated when the Count of Noé, the Bréda heir who had once owned a fourth of the Haut-du-Cap plantation (including Louverture's wife and children), wrote from his British exile with a feigned tone of familiarity. "I just learned, my dear Toussaint, that you provided financial assistance to Mr. Bayon our former attorney. . . . This proves that you have not forgotten those to whom you were bound for so many years." Noé was of course asking for money. The "big white" was now a beggar.[13]

Five feet and two inches in height, Louverture did not have an impressive physique. With "very prominent cheekbones, a flat nose, but quite long . . . and a toothless upper jaw," he was not particularly handsome, either. But he had the aura of a man too big for his island. When he entered a town on one of his powerful stallions, holding a gold-tipped cane in lieu of a whip, his personal guard galloping by his side, other men felt very small in his presence.[14]

Louverture was not bound by terrestrial appetites. He was frugal and even stingy. Horses were his one luxury. He slept little and ate quickly. His guests sat awkwardly at his table while he raced through a wordless meal. He preferred water to drink and unpeeled fruit to eat because he feared being poisoned. Judging by his grocery lists, a few of which have survived, specialties like *saucisson* and *petit salé* (cured sausage and salted pork) were his only indulgences. Like many natives of sugar colonies, he also had a sweet tooth and bad teeth.[15]

His ego was his sole weakness. A town near the Artibonite River already bore his name, as did a street in Cap. In July 1801, he carved a whole new province in the region of Gonaïves and named it after himself. He liked to organize elaborate receptions worthy of a European court. Keeping lower-class blacks at bay, he mingled with white colonists, who played along. When one of his white guests made a particularly well-crafted compliment, he beamed and whispered to his entourage: "You negroes should try to learn these manners. This is what you get from being raised in France. My children will be the same."[16]

Few white colonists were genuinely committed to Louverture as a leader and to the racial equality he embodied. They bowed as expected and then snickered behind his back about his ridiculous aspirations and the pidgin Latin he spoke to impress them. Louverture understood that their praise was insincere and that they would forever be "the enemies of the blacks." Yet he remained a prisoner of the racial preconceptions he had known in his youth.[17]

His desk contained a secret compartment where he kept "hair braids of all colors, rings, golden hearts struck with arrows, little keys, boxes, souvenirs, and a multitude of love notes that left no doubt as to the immense success the old Toussaint had enjoyed with the ladies." His critics lambasted him as a hypocrite who pontificated about the sanctity of marriage between rendezvouses with a mistress—but there was probably more to Louverture's philandering than mere sexual gratification. He had once watched helplessly as his daughter Marie-Marthe carried a mixed-race child. In a colony where masters had expressed their power by raping their slaves, interracial intercourse was a way for Louverture to avenge past slights and publicize the new racial order.[18]

An oft-repeated anecdote holds that Louverture finished his letters to Napoléon with the send-off "the first of the blacks to the first of the whites." There is no archival evidence for this (Louverture used the traditional Haitian greeting, "Salutations and respect"), but his craving for recognition was real. He wrote directly to the first consul when protocol dictated that he write to the minister of the navy, his immediate superior. He also wrote to the US president, the Cuban governor, and the British premier as if he were the head of a fellow independent state. He was deeply pained when they refused to personally write him. "I would have been utterly contented if [your envoy] had brought me a little note written by you," he wrote Napoléon in 1800. One year later, no response had come, and Louverture was growing restless. "I wrote several letters to you already and I never received a response from you."[19]

The specter of racial prejudice was never far from Louverture's mind as he pondered these slights. When the slave-owning Thomas Jefferson took over as US president, he downgraded the rank of the US consul general in Cap to commercial agent and gave no accreditation letter to his new appointee. Louverture noted in disgust that "his color was the cause of his being neglected and not thought worthy of the usual attentions." White statesmen were willing to strike a pragmatic alliance with him, but they continued to view him as a negro parvenu. "If I were white I would only receive praise," he complained. "But I actually deserve even more as a black man."[20]

Louverture was also very alone. Because he continuously had to hide his innermost thoughts, even the members of his entourage could not say that they truly knew him. "He is excessively leery," noted his secretary. "Surrounded by rebel slaves since the beginning of the revolution, double-crossed by the Spanish, fought by the French and the English, deceived by all, he understood very early that he had to make himself impenetrable." Louverture had navigated the troubled waters of the Revolution through caution and deceit, but in the process, the people around him had concluded that they could never trust or love him. His brother Paul addressed him with the formal *vous* normally reserved for strangers and social superiors. Even Jean-Jacques Dessalines, whom he had known for decades, was but a lackey to him. He had close relationships only with a handful of family members, including his wife Suzanne and his godfather Pierre Baptiste, who was still alive at the venerable age of 104, and whom Louverture visited every time he passed by his old plantation in Haut-du-Cap. Among whites, the only people he seems to have genuinely appreciated were his former boss Bayon, who had helped him gain his manumission, and Laveaux, who had presided over his early career in the French Army. But Laveaux was no longer writing to him, and his brother Paul was off governing Santo Domingo; his other brother, Pierre, was long dead, as were most of his children. He was estranged from his first family; his sons Isaac and Placide might never return from France. Men who have no equal are condemned to live a lonely life.[21]

Louverture's dealings with and affinity for whites provoked anger among his supporters. "A furious storm is gathering against him," predicted the former agent Philippe Roume from his US exile at the end of September 1801. "The first officer of known merit who will put himself at the head of the malcontent will get the entire colony to rise in less than two weeks."[22]

Roume's prediction became reality a month later, when Louverture left on a tour of the southern province. Shortly after his departure, the commander of Cap, Henry Christophe, uncovered a conspiracy to kill all the whites of the town. Christophe quickly arrested the plotters, but in the ensuing days groups of cultivators revolted throughout the northern plain. They had learned that Louverture had sent an envoy to Jamaica to purchase African laborers, and that he had reestablished the chain gang as a form of punishment. Holding chains, they cried that his next step would be to restore slavery. "Death to all the white people" was their slogan. In a matter of days, they killed over three hundred planters, a death toll equivalent to that of the great revolt of August 1791, which had also begun in the region of Cap. They seemed intent on launching a colony-wide uprising. The rebels had the sympathy of some black officers, specifically Moïse and Joseph Flaville. The old Bréda attorney Bayon de Libertat was among their victims.[23]

Louverture rushed back from Saint-Marc, where he was attending the wedding of Jean-Jacques Dessalines, to suppress the revolt. The groom followed along. Christophe had already contained the insurgency by the time they reached Cap on November 4, 1801, but Louverture was in a foul mood. He assembled the garrison on the main square and bitterly denounced the soldiers' sympathies for the cultivators' cause. He then called forward the main conspirators.

Joseph Flaville was first in line. He was the commander of the nearby town of Limbé, where Bayon had once owned a plantation, so Louverture had likely known him for decades. He had personally appointed Flaville to his command early in the Revolution and then welcomed him back like a "prodigal son" every time he had rebelled. Not so this time: Louverture had him ripped to shreds by grapeshot in full view of the garrison of Cap. Flaville's men witnessed the scene, arms in hand, but none dared challenge the formidable governor. He appeared trans-fixed, as if possessed by the Vodou spirit of war. "His face breaks down in an extraordinary way" when he gets angry, an observer later remarked: "When he speaks with fire about something that offends him, he looks horrible."[24]

Louverture's natural inclination was to be merciful or to ask his sub-ordinates to do his killing for him, but the Moïse uprising so infuriated him that up to 5,000 cultivators were killed in a matter of weeks. Not even Moïse escaped Louverture's wrath. Moïse was a relative of Suzanne Louverture (he was apparently the son of her brother Gilles), and Louver-ture had known him all his life. He was also a close ally who had assisted Louverture on numerous occasions, most recently during the invasion of Santo Domingo. Yet Louverture insisted that he be court-martialed and shot. Documentation of Suzanne's reaction has not survived.

Louverture, nearing sixty in a colony where few men reached that age, had recently begun to plan for his own death, writing the name of his successor in a sealed envelope to be opened after his passing. No one knew the identity of the heir-to-be, but the three most frequently cited names were those of Moïse, Christophe, and Dessalines, which would explain why Christophe and Dessalines so eagerly contributed to the crushing of the Moïse uprising.[25]

The ultimate goal of the Moïse uprising was to dismantle the plan-tation system in favor of subsistence farming—in other words, to shat-ter Louverture's master plan for the colony's future. This enraged him as much as Moïse's betrayal. After three weeks of repression, he delivered a violent and bitter speech to the population of Cap in which he criticized the followers of Vodou as incessant troublemakers. He also accused par-ents of not properly educating their children, who turned to vagrancy, theft, and prostitution as a result, and he attacked cultivators for not working as hard as they should. A set of punitive measures followed. Those who opposed plantation agriculture would be subjected to the severest of penalties, including death. As for those who merely made comments "that may alter public tranquility," they would be "sent to the fields, with a chain attached to the foot, for six months."[26]

The year ended on a bittersweet note. Louverture was the unchal-lenged master of all of Hispaniola, but he had lost two close partners,

Moïse and Bayon, whom he had known since the prerevolutionary era. The Moïse uprising had also made clear the depth of his unpopularity with the black population. Although Louverture had saved the lives of the whites of the Cap region, he was unsure whether they would repay him the favor in the event of a French invasion. He had effectively excluded France from the management of the colony, but he did not yet know how Napoléon would react to his constitution. Politically, his position was at once formidable and fragile.

Unbeknownst to Louverture, just as he was suppressing the Moïse uprising in a last bid to gain the support of France and the planter class, Napoléon was about to dispatch an expedition to unseat him. Three months later, Louverture would be fighting for his survival.

NINETEEN

RENEGADE
Early 1802

WAVE BY WAVE, the *Enfant Prodigue* plowed her way from the warm waters of the Caribbean to the wintry shores of western France. She was an aviso, a swift and graceful vessel used to transport time-sensitive mail. Initially known as the *Marie-Antoinette* after the queen of France, then renamed *Convention Nationale* during the Revolution, then lost to and recaptured from the British, she had been rechristened one last time in 1797, her name a reference to the biblical parable of the prodigal son. It was now February 1801.[1]

The *Enfant Prodigue* had traveled between France and Saint-Domingue many times during the Revolution, most recently to order Louverture not to proceed with the takeover of Santo Domingo. But Louverture was now sending the boat back with letters informing Napoléon that he had disobeyed him—and deposed the agent Roume—and summoned a constitutional assembly. March came and went until, in the first days of April 1801, the *Enfant Prodigue* cast anchor in Brest, the main military port in France. Brest is four hundred miles from Paris, but during the Revolution the French had built an ingenious network of land semaphores that could display symbols visible from miles away, and it only took an hour before the news reached the capital.[2]

Louverture's letters came as a shock to Napoléon. After years of indecision about what policy to adopt in Saint-Domingue, he had just set his mind on moral suasion. He hoped that by remaining faithful to emancipation he could convince grateful freedmen like Louverture to attack British colonies. "They will produce less sugar, maybe, than they did as slaves," Napoléon reasoned. "But they will produce it for us, and will serve us, if we need them, as soldiers. We will have one less sugar mill, but we will have one more citadel filled with friendly soldiers."[3]

With this reasoning in mind, Napoléon had decided to employ "softness and conciliation" to channel Louverture's ambition. This meant promoting him to the rank of captain general and finally writing him the personal note he had so often requested. "The government could give you no greater sign of its confidence in you," Napoléon explained in a beautifully penned letter that bore his personal seal. In exchange, he hoped that Louverture would "promote agriculture" and "enlarge the glory and possessions of the Republic."[4]

Events in France and Saint-Domingue moved rapidly in opposite directions and timing was essential. Had Napoléon sent his flattering letter in time, it would have gone a long way toward soothing Louverture's bruised feelings and keeping him within the sphere of the French empire. But Napoléon dallied, and Louverture, convinced that Napoléon was actually preparing to overthrow him, invaded Santo Domingo instead. When the *Enfant Prodigue* reached Brest, a furious Napoléon sacked Louverture and abandoned his strategy of moral suasion. The letter that Louverture had so often dreamt of receiving never left France. (In one final twist of fate, it was later stolen from the French naval archives, and then recovered in 2012 just before it could be sold by Sotheby's in New York.)[5]

Napoléon began assembling an expedition in the port of Brest in May 1801. Events in the following months only hardened his resolve. One after the other, the rivals Louverture had expelled during his final rise to power landed in France. André Rigaud reached Paris in April 1801 after losing the War of the South. He was followed by François de Kerversau and Antoine Chanlatte, who had served as French agents in Santo Domingo until the invasion. Kerversau was particularly well informed and was able to provide many details about Louverture's clandestine diplomacy with Britain.[6]

For years, the naval war with Britain and the British blockades had made it virtually impossible for large fleets to embark from French ports, until, in May 1801, Britain sent out the first feelers in nearly a decade. Napoléon responded positively, and five months later treaty preliminaries were signed in London, reopening France's sea-lanes. Napoléon asked that preparations for the expedition be finalized at once. Peace with Britain had come; war in Saint-Domingue could begin.[7]

In August 1801, Charles de Vincent reached Alexandria, Virginia, on the brig *Neptune* after a sixteen-day crossing from Cap. Saint-Domingue's director of fortifications carried with him a copy of Louverture's constitution, which Louverture had asked him to convey to Napoléon. Vincent, a French patriot, was deeply troubled by his mission. After spending his time at sea reading the text at leisure, he concluded that Louverture would be "the most culpable and ungrateful of men" if he persisted with his project. People in the United States had nicknamed him the "king of Saint-Domingue." Vincent wrote a strongly worded letter to urge Louverture to revoke the constitution. Louverture did not comply, but he was sufficiently concerned by Vincent's wavering that he sent a second envoy to Napoléon to "destroy in your mind the calumnies of my enemies."[8]

After a circuitous journey that took him through Philadelphia and San Sebastián in Spain, Vincent finally reached Paris in October 1801. In a series of personal meetings with the first consul, he did his best to dissuade Napoléon from resorting to force, but to no avail: the expedition was almost ready, and the recent cease-fire with Britain had opened a window of opportunity that Napoléon was eager to exploit. Reading the constitution only fueled his ire. "There was no longer room for deliberation," Napoléon later wrote. "The black chiefs were ungrateful and rebellious Africans."[9]

Vincent's briefings helped Napoléon realize the magnitude of what he was trying to accomplish. Louverture was no ordinary man: his army of 20,000 had successively defeated Saint-Domingue's planters, Spain, and Britain. "Saint-Domingue cannot be conquered," Vincent explained. Louverture's soldiers could hide in ambush for long periods of time without resupply, so they were "an enemy one cannot see, who lives off nothing, sleeps where he wants, is full of strength." He also warned of Saint-Domingue's "destructive climate" and difficult conditions, saying, "The army will die of hunger and thirst after landing." More encouragingly, Napoléon learned that Louverture had so angered his black supporters that several of his generals (notably Henry Christophe in Cap) were ready to abandon him.[10]

Napoléon responded to the latest news with more carrot and more stick. The expeditionary army expanded to 21,000 soldiers; Napoléon would end up sending a total of 43,000 soldiers to Saint-Domingue in 1802–1803, not counting sailors. He sent the best regiments in France and put them under the command of his own brother-in-law, a dashing twenty-nine-year-old general named Victoire ("Victory") Leclerc. Napoléon's favorite sister, Pauline (Leclerc's wife), and his brother Jérôme also sailed with the expedition. This was the largest expedition of the Consulate.[11]

Meanwhile, Napoléon devised a strategy that might make the use of force unnecessary. To convince Saint-Domingue's population of color to join the French side, he enrolled black and mixed-race officers in the expedition and reiterated his promise not to restore slavery. "Whatever your origins and your color you are all free and equal before God and the Republic," he explained in a proclamation in French and Kreyòl addressed to black cultivators. "If you are told: these forces have come to ravish our liberty, answer: the Republic gave us our liberty, the Republic will not accept that it be taken away from us." The promise was apparently truthful, since Napoléon privately instructed Leclerc to continue the cultivator system. At the same time, Napoléon planned to keep slavery in French colonies where it had never been abolished, such as Santo Domingo and Martinique, and to restore it wherever it was militarily feasible, such as Guadeloupe and French Guiana. Pragmatism was the order of the day.[12]

Just before the expedition departed, Napoléon summoned Isaac and Placide Louverture to his palace, assured them that he harbored no ill will against their father, and informed them that they would leave with the fleet. He hoped that their long-awaited return would mollify their father. Placide saw through the ruse, but Isaac, who was just seventeen, was so flattered that he composed a poem in the first consul's honor. It showcased a mastery of the French language that would have made his father proud, but a political naïveté that would have horrified him. "Young and valiant hero," Isaac intoned in Napoléon's honor, "your grandeur / Of the shining day, increases the splendor."[13]

Napoléon ordered the expedition to depart just one month after France signed the preliminaries with Britain, before a comprehensive peace treaty was even negotiated. General Leclerc and Louverture's sons made their way to Brest, where the largest squadron of the expeditionary fleet had been gathering strength since May. Awaiting them there were twenty-six warships, including fifteen ships-of-the-line, each of them armed with seventy-four long-range guns and manned by six hundred sailors. The Louvertures embarked on the frigate *La Sirène*.

Contrary winds delayed the fleet's departure for weeks, but in December 1801, three large naval squadrons left the ports of Brest, Lorient, and Rochefort in western France. Others set sail in ensuing weeks from the French ports of Toulon and Le Havre as well as Cádiz in Spain and Flushing (Vlissingen) in the Netherlands.

In the first days of December 1801, a boat crossed the channel separating Jamaica from Saint-Domingue and dropped anchor in Port-Républicain, where Louverture was finishing off the last supporters of the Moïse uprising. It brought a letter from the new governor of Jamaica, George Nugent. Louverture had reason to be optimistic about its contents. His envoy Joseph Bunel had been in Jamaica for months to negotiate a treaty of alliance, and Bunel's last reports had indicated that a formal agreement was imminent. Louverture would then be able to purchase African laborers from British traders and count on the support of the British Navy in case France ever turned against him. For the past year he had also been purchasing massive quantities of gunpowder from US merchants and updating Hispaniola's coastal fortifications. The island would soon be an impregnable fortress.[14]

The boat from Jamaica was actually bringing most unwelcome news: France and Britain had reconciled. Jamaica immediately broke off diplomatic negotiations. Louverture understood what it meant: Napoléon, who had not informed him of the European peace, was free to attack him with Britain's blessing. "He appeared exceedingly depressed," a British envoy reported before departing.[15]

News of the peace left Louverture feeling resentful and betrayed. He had spent years cultivating the goodwill of his British allies, but they were now conspiring with Napoléon to restore white rule in the French Caribbean. He had repulsed Spanish and British invasions in 1794–1798, but Napoléon was now ready to discard him. "All of this was well thought out to lose me, to annihilate me, and to destroy me" he later noted with much bitterness. He was right: "Toussaint's black empire," the British government instructed the governor of Jamaica, "is one amongst many evils that have grown out of the war—and it is by no means our interest to prevent its annihilation."[16]

To avoid unrest, Louverture did not inform the population of Saint-Domingue of the European peace, but word got out nonetheless. In December 1801, he had to publicly deny the "rumors that France will come with thousands of men to destroy the colony and liberty." In an unusual rambling style that was indicative of his fretful state of mind, his proclamation then foretold this very scenario: "A child . . . must show obedience to his father and mother, but if despite his submission and obedience his father and mother are degenerate enough to try to destroy him, then the child can only do one thing, ask God for revenge. I am a soldier, I am not afraid of men, I only fear God."[17]

In this difficult hour, Louverture needed allies, but he could find none. He accused the French of planning to restore slavery, trying to win black freedmen to his side, but because of his record of labor abuse, their response was less than enthusiastic. He recruited civilians to supplement his professional army, but many refused to serve. He attempted to make amends with the "formerly free" population, but they could not forgive him for the massacres of the War of the South, and they planned to side with the French when they arrived. He reminded white planters that he had saved their lives during the Moïse uprising, but they openly rejoiced at the prospect of a restoration of slavery. Louverture sent yet another envoy to France to defend his constitution, but the odds of the envoy reaching his destination in time to make a difference were slim. Only one ally had never failed him: disease. "He trusts not a little to the climate," noted an Englishman.[18]

As rumors of an expedition spread, Louverture increased his arms purchases from US merchants. He brought his regular infantry regiments to their full complement (13 regiments of 1,500 men each, not counting cavalry and honor guards) and called on all adult men to join the national guard, meanwhile keeping close watch on the independent camps of plantation runaways that had challenged his rule for years. He then left for Santo Domingo, which he viewed as the Achilles' heel of Hispaniola, to give personal instructions to his brother Paul, whom he had appointed commander of the province. It was there, on January 22, 1802, that he received confirmation that France was indeed preparing an expedition against him. He assumed the French would not arrive for months, leaving him plenty of time to fortify the island. He was wrong.[19]

One week later, while Louverture was still visiting his brother in Santo Domingo, he learned that French ships had been sighted off Cape Samaná at the northeastern tip of Hispaniola. "Pray God for me," he wrote his godfather with anguish. Crossing Hispaniola, he arrived just in time to witness the arrival of the main squadron from Brest. What he saw took his breath away. Napoléon had not sent a fleet: he had sent an armada. Two-thirds of the French Navy lay before his eyes, starting with the mighty *Océan*, a three-decker with 120 guns and the largest ship in the French Navy. "We shall perish," he allegedly said. "All of France has come to Saint-Domingue."[20]

General Leclerc was informed of Louverture's presence in Santo Domingo, but in violation of his instructions he chose not to send Louverture's sons ashore to negotiate. "Such dispositions were hints that he harbored hostile views," noted Isaac Louverture after vainly demanding to see his father. With so much firepower at his disposal, Leclerc wanted to rush to Saint-Domingue while Louverture was away and take the colony by force. Leclerc, not yet thirty, was ambitious and foolish. He saw the expedition as an easy opportunity to acquire riches and glory, in that order. Lacking any experience in the Caribbean, he expected "all the negroes to lay down their arms when they see an army."[21]

Louverture left for Cap, hoping to warn the city's commander, Henry Christophe—whose loyalty was far from assured—about the invasion. The magnificent horseman flew over backcountry roads. During brief stops along the way, he sent urgent letters to his subordinates to warn them that "the enemy will soon appear. . . . If the enemy is superior, retreat toward my headquarters, but before leaving the town you will torch it. . . . You will be careful above all not to leave anything behind you that has a white skin." Three months after repressing Moïse's uprising, he had, ironically, adopted much of his agenda. After spending his entire life trying to be accepted by white planter society, only to be rejected by it, he had decided to destroy it.[22]

Louverture reached Cap around February 5. Leclerc's fleet was already in the harbor, but Louverture arrived in time to ensure the loyalty of Christophe, who had initially made preparations to welcome the French. On Louverture's orders, Christophe stalled for two days, pretending that his governor was not yet in town. Leclerc finally ran out of patience and landed his troops. Louverture and Christophe had time to burn the city to the ground before retreating into the interior. This was the second time Cap had experienced such a trauma. "A large fleet has reached Cap and has landed troops, but the town is thoroughly burned, as is the plain," Louverture noted. "It seems that we are facing a coalition against liberty, so no half-measures. . . . We must die or live free."[23]

Louverture stopped in Haut-du-Cap to seek some advice from his godfather and to recruit new troops. Although he was native to the area, local cultivators rejected his pleas for assistance. "When we took up arms with Moïse against the whites, didn't the governor exterminate us?" exclaimed a cultivator. "Why doesn't he resuscitate Moïse, if he wants to fight the whites!" Not far from one of the former Bréda plantations, Louverture came upon a French detachment led by General Jean Hardÿ and was almost shot dead in the ensuing skirmish. He had to retreat once again.[24]

Presenting himself as a son of the French Revolution, Leclerc distributed proclamations in which he and Napoléon promised to keep emancipation in place. This came as news to Saint-Domingue's freedmen, since Louverture had led them to believe over the past two years that Napoléon intended to restore slavery. From Louverture's point of view, the key to victory was to convince the black population that Napoléon was lying and that he was the only true defender of abolition. "The whites from France and Saint-Domingue want to take away your liberty," he insisted. "Cultivators must be wary of people who are secretly passing around the proclamations of the whites from France." Louverture secured the colony's printing presses. The written word, which had done so much for him in the past, might save him yet.[25]

The news over the following days was generally bad. In Santo Domingo, Paul Louverture chose to negotiate rather than fight and was eventually tricked into surrendering. The generals commanding Santiago and Cayes capitulated without a shot fired. The commanders of Fort-Liberté, Léogane, and Port-Républicain at least tried to oppose the French landings, but they lost the towns in a matter of hours. The commander of Port-de-Paix, Jacques Maurepas, was the only one who managed to repulse French troops—twice—but even he eventually had to retreat. Port-de-Paix and Léogane were torched, in keeping with Louverture's strategy. All major towns must burn, he instructed his subordinate Jean-Jacques Dessalines. "Don't forget that until the rainy season [yellow fever] rids us of our enemies our only resources are destruction and fire."[26]

Angling for a negotiated settlement, Louverture stopped short of declaring independence. His men fought in the French uniform and under the French tricolor, and they sang French revolutionary songs to publicize that they, not Napoléon's lackeys, were the true heirs to the French Revolution. This tactic confounded their French foes, who half expected to fight naked African savages. Louverture offered to resume negotiations with General Leclerc.

Still awaiting the balance of his troops, Leclerc assented. One week after landing in Cap, he sent Louverture's sons to his plantation in Ennery, where they were to hand-deliver a letter in which Napoléon promised financial rewards if Louverture agreed to step down. After an overnight trek over the mountains of central Saint-Domingue, which they had crossed with their father during the early years of the Revolution, the sons reunited with their mother. She had not embraced them since 1796 and had feared never seeing them again.

A messenger left at once to notify Louverture. The following night, the sound of the trumpet and the rumble of horse and carriage announced his arrival. Isaac and Placide threw themselves into their father's arms. "He held them tightly for a long time and his paternal love manifested itself in the tears that streamed from his eyes," Isaac later wrote. Then, abruptly shifting back to his other lifelong love, politics, he demanded to see Napoléon's letter. He held it tightly for a long time, evidently pleased to finally receive a personal note from the first consul. He did not read it on the spot, probably because his reading was laborious and he did not want to be humiliated in front of his sons, but he immediately saw

Napoléon and Leclerc's friendly overtures for what they were. Leclerc was evidently trying to take his place as captain general of Saint-Domingue.[27]

As the negotiations failed and a broader war became inevitable, Louverture gathered his sons and asked them on which side they would fight: "their fatherland or their father?" His biological son, Isaac, chose France. Placide chose his adopted father. His family, like his colony, was torn in half.[28]

The negotiations over, Leclerc declared Louverture an outlaw, a measure that allowed anyone to kill him with impunity, and annulled all his plantation leases. His all-out campaign began on February 17, 1802. Dividing his forces into five columns, Leclerc instructed each of them to

Isaac and Placide Louverture reunited with their parents in Saint-Domingue (they were actually teenagers at the time). Their teacher, Jean-Baptiste Coisnon, is to the left. [François Grenier?], *Le Gal Toussaint Louverture, à qui le Gal Leclerc* . . . (c. 1821), courtesy Library of Congress, Prints and Photographs Division.

converge on the central part of the colony, where they would surround Louverture's army, pin it down, and destroy it. The main column, led by General Hardÿ, advanced rapidly from Cap. In Ennery, for the second time since the landing, Hardÿ met and defeated Louverture, who again had to move farther into the interior.

Pursued by the division of General Rochambeau (son of the general who headed French forces during the US War of Independence), Louverture made a stand in a steep valley known as Ravine-à-Couleuvres. After dispersing armed cultivators throughout the woods to harass French soldiers as they marched up a single trail, he positioned his professional troops at the valley's exit. For hours, brutal hand-to-hand combat raged as the French division made its way up the ravine. Louverture was almost killed in the engagement and again had to pull back, but he could find some comfort in the knowledge that for the first time he had inflicted significant losses on the French.

Feeling abandoned by the European God he had worshiped all his life, Louverture personally saw to it that the church of Gonaïves, his next stop, was set on fire. For a man who had served and used the Catholic Church all his life, the act was indicative of a crisis of faith; for the rest of his life, he rarely referred to God, and he never again called for the spiritual assistance of priests. With regard to civilians, Louverture gave his subordinates "carte blanche," which implicitly authorized them to kill whites, but did not compromise a future reconciliation with France. Dessalines acted upon the hint with his usual diligence.[29]

Louverture then made his way to Crête-à-Pierrot, a fort located near the Artibonite River in central Saint-Domingue. After inspecting the position, he left Dessalines in command of the fort, where the various French columns eventually converged. The bulk of the French Army laid siege to a mere 1,200 rebels. But these were no longer the inexperienced slaves of 1791, who did not even know how to load a cannon: they were now battle-hardened veterans.

The siege of Crête-à-Pierrot, the signature engagement of the spring campaign, lasted weeks and cost the French 2,000 men. Half the garrison managed to slip through French lines before the fort fell. After celebrating his thirtieth birthday among the dead and the dying strewn at the foot of the fort, Leclerc, who was wounded in the engagement, lost his enthusiasm for Caribbean warfare. "When I am done restoring order here, I will ask to be sent back to France because my health has suffered a lot," he informed Napoléon. This was the first of many gloomy letters he would send to his brother-in-law that year.[30]

War is waged in three dimensions: strategy (the general conduct of a war, including diplomacy and logistics), grand maneuvers (positioning one's forces on a map), and field tactics (leading troops into battle). The last was not Louverture's forte, but he realized that he could make up for his tactical limitations by staying on the move long enough for his long-term strategy to work: let yellow fever ravage Leclerc's army. Louverture asked his nephew Bernard Chancy, a southern native, to incite southerners to revolt, and he sent General Christophe north to threaten Cap. He personally headed to Port-de-Paix to retake that town, but the black commander of Port-de-Paix, General Maurepas, had already defected to the French side. Louverture was almost killed yet again when some of his former troops, now fighting with the French Army, opened fire on him.

Like Maurepas, many of Louverture's men deserted him as the campaign progressed, until he was left with fewer black troops under his command than Leclerc. His son Isaac and his brother Paul had forsaken him. The French took his youngest son, Saint-Jean, into custody. He even lost his favorite horse, Bel Argent, now in the hands of General Hardÿ.

Louverture's abiding goal while in power had been to disarm black laborers and send them back to the fields while concentrating military power in the hands of his professional army. As his regular units deserted him, he reverted back to the guerrilla tactics that had proven so successful during the early months of the Revolution. He hastily armed plantation workers. He appealed to the maroon leaders, who had been a thorn in his side for years, by reminding them that the future of abolition was at stake. It was with this motley group that he headed for the Dondon-Marmelade area in the northern province and decimated a unit led by General Hardÿ in a series of ambushes.

Both camps were thoroughly exhausted by the end of April. In just three months, Leclerc had lost 10,000 dead and wounded to disease and combat. Desertion and combat had also stripped Louverture's army bare. Louverture lost a further 5,500 soldiers and armed cultivators when General Christophe, growing tired of the "nomadic existence of the guerrillas," gave up the fight and joined the French. Abandoned by all but Dessalines, Louverture went to seek his advice. Dessalines insisted on keeping up the fight and even threatened to kill Louverture if he ever surrendered. Louverture concurred—and then immediately opened negotiations with the French. On April 29, he agreed to a ceasefire.[31]

A week later, Louverture traveled to Cap to meet Leclerc in person. Sensing a trap, he arrived unannounced one day ahead of schedule. A heavily armed personal guard rode by his side. White civilians, who could not forgive him for ordering the massacre of planters during the campaign, heckled him along the route. "This is the way men are," Louverture told his former adversary General Hardÿ, who had come to greet him. "I saw them groveling at my feet, these people who are now insulting me; but it will not be long before they long for my return." He was right: in ensuing months, white colonists grew so exasperated by the French officers' covetousness that they began to yearn for the days when Louverture had governed the colony. His ruthless efficiency had often been in their interests.[32]

As he reached the government house of Cap, where he had once reigned supreme, Louverture left his horse in the courtyard and entered the building with his aides-de-camp. French officers thronged inside to catch a glimpse of the famous Toussaint Louverture. One of them snickered that it was impossible "to obtain white flour from a sack of coal." Louverture stopped for a second, glanced at the officers assembled before him, and replied with a bon mot of his own: "Perhaps, but a sack of coal is enough to melt bronze."[33]

After a long and unpleasant conference in which both men accused each other of being responsible for the war, Leclerc and Louverture broke bread. A meal was served, but Louverture was in a sour mood and refused to eat or drink anything. Only at the end of the meal did he accept a piece of Gruyère cheese, the edges of which he cut off for fear that the French had poisoned his food. His brother attended the dinner, too, but Louverture refused to address him, still furious at him for losing Santo Domingo without a fight. The campaign of spring 1802 ended on this acrimonious note.

As part of the cease-fire, Louverture stepped down as governor, but he insisted that his generals be reincorporated into the French Army along with their black regiments. Some of Louverture's own men joined Leclerc's personal guard, which allowed him to keep a close eye on his rival's whereabouts. With time, he hoped to regain the upper hand.

For now, Louverture was allowed to reunite with his sons Saint-Jean and Isaac and return to his plantations in Ennery. Once there, he spent time with his family and resumed a role he had always enjoyed, that of overseer of his estates. It was a return to earlier and simpler times. Though he did not know it, these few quiet weeks were the last happy period of his existence.

Leclerc asked Louverture to help him oversee the return of the cultivators to the fields, but Louverture, in his new incarnation as an enemy of forced labor, refused to collaborate. Leclerc had to draft a new labor code on his own. Carefully balancing the interests of the French planters and the aspirations of the black working class, it was remarkably similar to Louverture's. This was no coincidence. "I will more or less follow Toussaint's labor code, which is very good," Leclerc explained. In fact, Louverture's code was "so strict," he said, "that I would never have dared to propose one like this on my own."[34]

On April 20, 1802, the HMS *Cerberus* left Kingston for Cap to gather intelligence on the massive force that France had sent to Saint-Domingue. The British crew was eager to leave Jamaica, where another long summer of disease and death loomed. They were happy to learn upon reaching Cap that Saint-Domingue was still free of yellow fever. The respite did not last long. The first cases were diagnosed a few days after the crew's arrival, most likely because the crew of the *Cerberus* had brought the disease with them.

The epidemic made rapid progress. That year, it proved particularly deadly. By May 8, General Leclerc wrote of "frightening ravages" in his army and put the death toll at 30 to 50 men a day. In all, of the 35,000 French soldiers and sailors who landed in Saint-Domingue in 1802, 15,000 died of yellow fever, 3,000 died of other diseases, and 6,000 were permanently incapacitated—compared to the 5,000 who died in combat. One of the epidemic's first victims was General Hardÿ.[35]

Louverture learned of the outbreak with evident relief. "Providence is finally coming to rescue me," he joked in reference to the name of a hospital in Cap, La Providence. All he now had to do was wait for the epidemic to take its ghastly toll, and then he could resume the offensive in the fall.[36]

To Leclerc, Louverture insisted that he was done with politics, but the Frenchman had doubts about his long-term intentions. Not far from Ennery, a rebel leader named Sylla refused to lay down his arms, and Louverture made no effort to break him. A French officer assigned to keep an eye on Louverture sent back disturbing reports about his conversations with the deposed governor. Louverture complained about the large number of French troops in rural areas, the officer said, and threatened to "withdraw into the woods and fight again for his liberty." The attempted murder of a French officer was also attributed to his hidden hand.[37]

Leclerc's suspicions were confirmed when General Dessalines, now back in France's employ, accused Louverture of playing a double game. Dessalines's betrayal of Louverture has been largely forgotten in Haiti, where few people want to admit that one revolutionary hero played Judas to another. For Dessalines, it was a logical decision. Louverture had always used him as a "workhorse," he complained. After living his entire life in Louverture's shadow—first as a slave, then as an officer—Dessalines had decided that the time had come to rid himself of his overbearing presence. By playing the role of the brutish African, he was able to deceive every one of his rivals, including Louverture and later Leclerc.[38]

Early in June 1802, Leclerc decided that the time had come to follow Napoléon's orders and arrest Louverture. He delegated the difficult task to the French general Jean-Baptiste Brunet. Brunet stationed many troops on one of Louverture's plantations, which had the intended result of causing a few scuffles. One of Louverture's goddaughters was harassed, as were many cultivators. "My son Isaac was pushing away several soldiers who had come all the way to the door of my house to cut plantains and small bananas," Louverture later complained. With a honeyed tone, Brunet invited him to a tête-à-tête to settle the dispute.[39]

Irritated and physically ill, Louverture arrived at the meeting with a small escort. He informed Brunet that he wanted the meeting to be short. Leaving his men outside, Louverture walked into the main house to iron out the details. Brunet excused himself for a second, time enough for a squad of French soldiers to burst into the house and place Louverture under arrest. Louverture handed over his sword without a word. For the first time in his life, he had let down his guard.

Louverture was taken to the frigate *La Créole* in nearby Gonaïves, where he allegedly told the captain that by capturing him, the French had struck down "the tree of black liberty," but that it would one day spring back from its roots, "which are many and deep." His closest relatives, including his wife, his sons, and his niece, were all arrested in short order and sent to Cap, where the family was transferred to the ship of the line *Le Héros*. Aside from his niece, not one of Louverture's relatives ever set foot in Saint-Domingue again.[40]

And so it was that in June 1802, Louverture found himself aboard a French warship in the middle of the Atlantic. His sons had already made the crossing twice, but for Louverture the experience was new and terrifying. He had studiously avoided ships his entire life; we only know of two cases where he had boarded one prior to this, both times within sight of shore. It is unlikely that he even knew how to swim.[41]

As the *Héros* buckled under him, did Louverture think of his parents, who had once crossed the same ocean on their way from Africa to Saint-Domingue? Anxious about his and his family's fate and most likely seasick, he waited for the weeks to go by while the boat plowed her way from the warm waters of the Caribbean to the windy shores of western France.

TWENTY

PRISONER

1802–1803

WHEN LOUVERTURE AND HIS FAMILY reached the French military port of Brest in July 1802, the weather was likely overcast, cool, and drizzly, as it often is in the maritime climate of Brittany. For one month he had been trapped inside a floating prison as it sailed from Saint-Domingue; for another month he waited in Brest for the boat to clear quarantine.

The trail of letters, which the Atlantic crossing had interrupted, resumed as soon as the *Héros* reached port. Louverture's first concern was for his family. "A fifty-three-year-old housewife deserves the indulgence and goodwill of a liberal and generous nation," he wrote in reference to his wife Suzanne. "I alone must be responsible for my conduct." ("Women, as you know, don't involve themselves in the business of men," she echoed.) She should be allowed to rejoin "the large family we have in Saint-Domingue, most of whom are girls. Left on their own, without guides, what will become of these unfortunate persons?"[1]

Louverture's efforts to shield his loved ones achieved little. His son Placide, who had fought by his side during the spring campaign, was transferred to a brig and then sent on to some unknown destination. "I may never see you again," he wrote his parents. "Please be courageous and think of me every once in a while." Louverture would spend the next months of his life fearing the worst for him. He himself was torn from the rest of his family when he and his servant were peremptorily sent ashore at dawn on August 13, 1802.[2]

Napoléon had initially considered court-martialing Louverture, but he had then concluded that the public trial of such a famous figure would create unneeded controversy. Instead, he chose to jail Louverture without trial, and to do so as far as possible from the Atlantic coast, so as to make escape nearly impossible. Louverture traded one set of wooden walls for another, leaving Brest in an enclosed carriage under heavy guard. He crossed the breadth and length of France from west to east, stopping only briefly in provincial cities, where local notables strained their necks to see the man whose fame extended across Europe. In Tours, where his carriage halted in the dead of night to change horses, Louverture confided to the local military commander that he was eager to finally meet Napoléon in Paris and defend his record. The general preferred not to inform the "poor devil" about his true destination. "Thankfully, you won't suffer long," he thought to himself after noticing that Louverture wore three jackets despite the stifling heat.[3]

Bypassing Paris, Louverture's carriage headed for the Fort de Joux, a medieval castle repurposed as a prison, located deep within the Jura

The Fort de Joux, where Louverture spent his last months. Photo by the author.

Mountains above the town of Pontarlier, at the edge of the Swiss border. It was a forbidding place, bitterly cold in the winter months.

The carriage passed through the first layer of fortifications, a tunnel dug directly into the rock. A moat and a drawbridge followed, after which the carriage halted in the medieval castle's main courtyard. Louverture was led up a flight of stairs, through a gate, another courtyard, another gate, another courtyard, and more gates still. His journey finally ended deep in the fort's innards. His cell was narrow, low, and dark. "I thought I was entering an underground tunnel," his servant noted with horror. They only had two openings to the outside world. The first was the cell's door, whose three bolts only the prison director could unlock. The second was the cell's window, which was obstructed by iron bars, bricks, and storm shutters to prevent an escape. It was almost pitch-dark, even in daytime. Not even as a slave had Louverture's freedom been so restricted. "Isn't it like burying a man alive?" he wondered.[4]

After the initial shock of his incarceration, Louverture quickly regained his spirit. He befriended the prison director, a humane figure named Baille, with whom he had daily conversations about Saint-Domingue politics. He also secured the assistance of a local secretary and began work on a formal petition to Napoléon. His goal was to convince the first consul to award him a public trial where he could defend himself from accusations that he had been plotting a new uprising. There was hope still.

At 16,000 words, the text was by far the longest he had ever authored. This was a monumental task for a man who had never been formally schooled and for whom French was a third language after West African Fon and Haitian Kreyòl. His handwriting was barely legible and his grammar atrocious, but the result was the only full account of the Revolution written by its most important character. Though it is usually described as Louverture's "memoirs," as if it were an autobiography, Louverture used the singular form "memoir" in the title to indicate that the text was a petition. His main objective was to outline and justify his official career for his superiors, not to give a full account of his personal journey. He glossed over his entire pre-revolutionary life in a single sentence, choosing instead to focus on his time as an officer and a colonial official of the French Republic. The forefather of modern-day Haiti, in this document at least, introduced himself as French.[5]

Informed by the prison director of Louverture's eagerness to talk, Napoléon ordered his aide-de-camp, Marie-François Caffarelli, to travel to the Fort de Joux. He was instructed to learn more about Louverture's diplomacy with Britain and the location of the "treasures" he had stashed in Saint-Domingue's mountains. Louverture seemed "calm, tranquil, and resigned," Caffarelli noted when he first entered his cell, though "he suffer[ed] a lot from the cold," even in September. Louverture immediately asked for news of his family, "especially his son Placide." Caffarelli did not respond.[6]

Napoléon's man spent six days in the Fort de Joux. He had thought that Louverture would seize this opportunity to acknowledge his sins and beg for forgiveness, but the prisoner was as combative as ever and deftly refuted every one of Caffarelli's accusations. Only one incident seemed to faze him. One day, the prison director brought civilian clothes while Caffarelli and Louverture were talking in his cell; France's war minister had insisted that Louverture should not wear a uniform now that he had been officially discharged from the French Army. "He was disconcerted when he saw that they were not a uniform, and spent a moment without talking, took them, then placed them on his bed and renewed the conversation. But he only thought of this matter and I could not distract him." Caffarelli had to leave the cell. The following day, Louverture was still troubled by the affront. It insulted his personal honor, the value most cherished by nineteenth-century French officers.

Unable to obtain a full confession, Caffarelli left for Paris with a copy of Louverture's memoir. Louverture was hopeful that the document would earn him a public trial. He was wrong. Nearly a decade after France had welcomed black freedmen into its embrace, Napoléon was in the process of revoking his predecessors' progressive reforms. Slavery was restored in French Guiana and Guadeloupe in incremental steps starting in May 1802; many assumed that Saint-Domingue would be next. France's black officers were being discharged, imprisoned, killed, or even sold as slaves. Napoléon specifically blamed Louverture for the destruction of Leclerc's expedition, calling it "one of his greatest follies." The spring campaign had been a Pyrrhic victory for the French: field hands had renewed the rebellion upon receiving word that slavery was in the process of being restored in Guadeloupe. Dessalines and other plantation-owning black generals at first helped Leclerc fight the rebels—that is to say their employees—only to defect in October after the bulk of the French expeditionary army succumbed to yellow fever, just as Louverture had predicted.[7]

In the end, Napoléon revealed himself to be petty and short-sighted in his treatment of Louverture. There was no historic meeting between the two, no epistolary debate on abolition and colonialism. Napoléon did not bother to read Louverture's memoir because the minister of the navy informed him that "no important confession results from . . . the memoir made by Toussaint to justify himself." He did not even honor Louverture with his hatred; he buried him under his indifference. Only much later, after Napoléon was deposed and deported to the island of St. Helena, did he speak again of Louverture, acknowledging that he "was not a man without merit . . . astute and clever." Perhaps by that time he had finally realized the agony of being exiled, imprisoned, and torn from one's second wife and son.[8]

While waiting anxiously for Napoléon's response, Louverture's thoughts drifted to his family. "You know my love for my family and my attachment to my wife, whom I cherish, why did you not send me any news?" he reproached Suzanne. The family members left behind in Saint-Domingue were suffering. In October 1802, after most of his black generals defected to the rebels, a despondent Leclerc ordered thousands of black troops and civilians summarily drowned. Louverture's sister-in-law and nephew (Paul's family) were among the victims, as were, apparently, Louverture's mixed-race grandson, Toussaint, and his godfather, aged 105, who had played such an important role in his life. Leclerc died of yellow fever in the midst of these mass executions, one day after the Catholic holiday of Toussaint (All Saints' Day), the day of the dead.[9]

"Toussaint, the most unhappy man of men!" William Wordsworth exclaimed in a sonnet written during Louverture's captivity. Louverture's servant could initially provide some moral support, but he was ordered to leave after a few weeks, and Louverture spent the rest of his captivity alone. The magical nights of his boyhood, which he had spent staring at "children of the Moon," were long gone. "He was sad and somber," noted a guard. "He spent the bulk of his days by his small window, his head resting on his hand, against the iron grating, absorbed by a dark melancholy. . . . The poor man thought of his country, his children! He was very chagrined. . . . He was a proud man, but sweet as a lamb."[10]

After his memoir to Napoléon went unanswered, Louverture sent him a plaintive reminder "in the name of God and humanity." The first consul remained silent. Meanwhile, Louverture's life was becoming ever more miserable. In October 1802, a mysterious defrocked priest managed to find his way into Louverture's cell by passing himself off as a doctor. Perhaps he had known Louverture prior to the Revolution, when the Capuchin order of the Franche-Comté region was charged with supplying priests for the Catholic mission in northern Saint-Domingue. Louverture then lost his visitation privileges. The only people allowed inside his cell thereafter were the prison director; his guards, who were forbidden to talk to him; and a dentist, who came by regularly to pull out throbbing teeth.[11]

Initially dictated by security concerns, the rules concerning Louverture's imprisonment became purely punitive with time. His money and his watch were confiscated so that he could not bribe his guards; his cell was searched thoroughly; he was even threatened with an ignominious body search. Such treatment bit deep when he had ached for respect all his life. "When a man is already unhappy, one should not seek to humiliate and vex him," he complained to the prison director, Baille. It finally dawned on him that he might never leave his cell alive. "The day I am executed, send all my belongings to my wife and children," he told Baille sullenly. For two weeks thereafter, he refused to leave his bed.[12]

"Allow me to request again your justice and kindness," he begged Napoléon one last time in late October. The first consul's response was to have Baille confiscate his letters and writing material in an effort to silence him. Louverture never wrote anything else. The end of his life, just like its beginning, must be reconstructed through third-party accounts.[13]

Fall turned into winter and Louverture found himself battling for his life. Wrapped in the light cotton jacket that had been issued to him in lieu of a uniform, he vainly tried to shield himself from the cold. Sorrow was even harder to ward off. Baille, the last friendly figure in his life, was replaced in January 1803 by a younger and more aggressive prison commander named Amiot, who regularly woke Louverture up at all times of day and night to search his cell while the old man stood and shivered.

A native of the tropics, Louverture found himself in the coldest region in France. He always felt bone-cold despite keeping a raging fire going in his cell; then his wood allowance was cut down in the middle of winter to save a few francs. He complained of headaches and stomachaches, and coughed constantly. Worst of all, he did not seem to care anymore. In March 1803, Louverture vomited and felt sharp pains in his left arm for several days, reported Amiot, who also noticed that his voice had changed. But "he never asked me for a doctor."[14]

Louverture's captivity is well documented in the official French records archived in Besançon and Vincennes, but most of these sources merely record petty fights over receipts. There is no way to reconstruct Louverture's last inner battles. Maybe his thoughts wandered back to a comment he had made in his memoir: if he found no justice "in this world," he had written, he would find some "in the next."[15]

"On [Germinal] 17 at 11:30 a.m., while bringing him his food, I found him on his chair by the fire," wrote the prison director on April 7, 1803. Louverture was silent and perfectly still, his head leaning against the mantle. He did not respond when Amiot spoke to him.[16]

TWENTY-ONE

ICON
1803–Present

AT 2 P.M., JUST HOURS after Toussaint Louverture passed away in his cell on April 7, 1803, a justice of the peace, a medical doctor, and a surgeon came to the Fort de Joux from the nearby town of Pontarlier. The prison director, Amiot, unlocked the three deadbolts on the door and let them inside the cell. Louverture was still slumped on his chair by the fireplace. They took his body and lay it on the bed to examine him, then signed the document that officially declared his life to be over. The day was too far gone to do much more, so the four men agreed to reconvene in the morning.[1]

The following day, the group proceeded with the legal and medical business of death. Amiot placed Louverture's personal effects into a box and sealed it while the two doctors opened Louverture's body to conduct the autopsy. After noting some "bloody swelling in the right lung and the corresponding pleura and a mass of purulent matter in this viscus," along with some blood in his nose and mouth, they listed the cause of death as "apoplexy" (stroke) and pneumonia. They also sawed off his skull, which they found to be "extraordinarily thick," in order to examine his brain.[2]

As the doctors removed the madras handkerchief wrapped around Louverture's head, Amiot noticed that Louverture had sewn a stack of papers into the cloth, where they had been hidden from the guards who regularly searched his cell. Among the papers was a copy of his memoir. In one final act of witnessing, he had ensured that it would not be lost to posterity.[3]

Amiot kept detailed records of every step of the process for fear of being accused of foul play or theft, but the mass of notarized documents did little to protect him. Within weeks, wild rumors were circulating that Amiot had deliberately left Louverture alone for days to let him starve, or that he had poisoned him by order of the first consul. "What reason could have pushed me to kill this negro after he arrived in France?" Napoléon erupted when confronted with the accusation. "What could I have gained from such a crime?"[4]

Louverture's life was a matter of controversy from the moment it ended. Napoléon wanted his rival remembered (if at all) as "this negro" who had dared to challenge his will. Louverture countered with a memoir in which he described himself as a French officer who had been denied membership in the colonial elite on racial grounds. The fight over his legacy continues to the present day. Not even splitting open Louverture's head, it seemed, could allow anyone to agree on what he truly believed.

By the time Louverture died in April 1803, the French expedition that Napoléon had sent to overthrow him had become an utter fiasco. General Leclerc had died of yellow fever, as had most of his army. Jean-Jacques Dessalines and other black generals were in open rebellion. When war with Britain resumed in the spring of 1803, Napoléon could no longer send reinforcements. The remnants of the Leclerc expedition spent months starving in Saint-Domingue's coastal cities while being besieged by land and sea by British and rebel forces. In November, Dessalines and the French fought one last climactic battle in Vertières, very close to the plantation of Haut-du-Cap where Louverture had been born. Dessalines prevailed, the French troops evacuated Cap, and the French military presence in Saint-Domingue came to an end.

As ruler of the colony, Dessalines faced the same questions that Louverture, as his mentor, had once faced: Should he maintain ties to France? Should he seek common ground with white planters? Should he dismantle the plantations? Should he export the slave revolt? What form of government should he adopt?

In some regards, Dessalines did what Louverture had never dared to. On January 1, 1804, an event now commemorated each year as Haiti's national holiday, he formally declared the colony independent from France. His incendiary speech offered a sharp contrast with Louverture's equanimity: "Independence, or death . . . let these sacred words unite us. . . . Anathema to the French name, eternal hatred to france [*sic*]: that is our cry." Dessalines abandoned the name of Saint-Domingue, which was too French for his taste, and renamed the country "Haiti" in memory of the Amerindians who had once peopled it—the word means "mountainous island" in the Taino language.[5]

Dessalines did not stop there. In the spring of 1804, he ordered most of the white population still remaining in Haiti put to death. Three to five thousand whites were killed in a matter of weeks. Only a handful of whites with special skills were spared, and they were barred from owning land. Under Dessalines's definition of citizenship, put forth in Article 14 of his 1805 constitution, to be Haitian was to be black. His extreme racial agenda betrayed, in the eyes of many, the egalitarian ideals of the Haitian Revolution. For a century thereafter, abolitionists who wished to emphasize the ability of former slaves to rule themselves pointed to Louverture as a model. Their opponents replied with one word: Dessalines.

Louverture had worked hard in his time to foster good relations with his neighbors; Dessalines's decision to eliminate Haiti's white minority was so controversial that Haiti's former diplomatic partners treated the new black state as a pariah. The British broke off diplomatic negotiations immediately after the 1804 massacre. Not until 1825 did France finally recognize Haiti's independence. The United States did not follow suit until 1862, amid its own civil war. Even today, Haiti remains something of an outlier in the Caribbean due to its unique historical, linguistic, and racial profile. "This is the only Black society in Latin America," a Venezuelan ambassador commented in 1991 to explain his reluctance to become involved in the country's affairs. "Very foreign . . . to our own region."[6]

Haiti went through many constitutions after independence—eight during the period 1805–1849 alone—but all of them echoed the constitution that Louverture had presented in July 1801. Military rule and dictatorship remained frequent features of Haitian political life until the 1990s, when a democratically elected ruler, Jean-Bertrand Aristide, successfully challenged an army coup and then disbanded the military altogether.

Dessalines emphasized how much he "differed from the ex-general Toussaint Louverture," and yet he embraced the latter's economic model. After taking over the plantations of the white planters he had killed, he maintained Louverture's cultivator system and offered to buy African laborers from the British. His successor, Henry Christophe (1807–1820), maintained this course. Domestic popular resistance to plantation work was so strong, however, that subsistence agriculture eventually prevailed. By the 1820s, former slaves finally achieved their dream of individual land ownership. And yet this achievement meant that Louverture's great fear—the breakup of the sugar plantations and the long-term economic decline of the "Pearl of the Antilles"—became reality. Coffee, which could be grown on individual estates, remained an important export crop, but the declining value of commodity prices contributed to long-term underdevelopment in Haiti, not to mention the rest of the Caribbean. The country was also burdened with the other legacies of slavery, including racial tensions and the lack of an industrial base.[7]

Haiti was a beacon of hope for enslaved people of African descent in the Americas, although, in an effort to placate their neighbors, Louverture and his successors generally did not encourage slave resistance overseas. In retrospect, the Haitian Revolution was a one-off event, "both unforgettable and unrepeatable." Slavery actually expanded in other colonies, most notably Cuba, where sugar production surged in the early nineteenth century to make up for Haiti's withdrawal from the international sugar market. Fears of a second Haiti also led to setbacks for the abolitionist movement, particularly in Britain: a 1791 bill to abolish the slave trade did not pass until 1807, largely as a result of the conservative backlash to the French and Haitian revolutions.[8]

As abolition spread from the middle to the end of the nineteenth century, European empires faced a problem familiar to Haitian leaders: how to satisfy their labor needs in a post-emancipation society. They often settled on a solution that Louverture would have recognized. In the British and Spanish Caribbean, formal emancipation was followed by a transition period during which freedmen were forced to remain on their plantations. In the British and French Caribbean, Indian and Chinese indentured servants were imported. Even in the United States and Brazil, where slavery was abolished outright without a transition period, and where massive European immigration alleviated labor shortages, former slaves continued to toil on their masters' land under semi-free systems like sharecropping. The repression of Haiti's Piquet Rebellion (1844–1848) and Jamaica's Morant Bay Rebellion (1865), along with the passage of the Jim Crow laws in the post–Civil War South, showed that "freed" did not necessarily mean "free."

With the passage of time, historians began to think of labor systems in terms of absolutes: on the one hand, slavery, wholly oppressive and universally detested by its hapless victims; on the other, a fully free labor system that was its sole and unadulterated alternative. Louverture's record was smoothed over or even distorted, at least in the public imagination, and he came to be seen as abolition's patron saint. Only recently have we come to better understand the man who tried to solve the central dilemma that slave-owning societies faced in the age of abolition: how to reconcile the ideals of universal freedom with the realities of plantation agriculture.

It was mostly through his offspring that Louverture lived on in the early decades of the nineteenth century. Even then, war and politics thinned out much of his sprawling family tree in Haiti. His brother Pierre had died in 1793 at the hands of Georges Biassou's agents; his other brother, Paul, died fighting a rival rebel group in 1803. Louverture had executed his nephew Moïse in 1801; the French executed another nephew, Charles Bélair, in 1802 at Dessalines's insistence. Yet another nephew, Bernard Chancy, died in 1806 in the prison cell where Dessalines had put him. Louverture's sister Marie-Jeanne was the only member of his immediate family to survive the revolutionary era in Haiti. Because Louverture had illegitimate children, many Haitians today claim him as their ancestor on the basis of family traditions, but these claims are difficult to substantiate: by Louverture's own accounting, only two of his sixteen children were still alive in Saint-Domingue when he was deported to France.[9]

Information about the relatives of Louverture who were exiled is more plentiful because the French government kept them under police surveillance for decades. Shortly after reaching Brest, his son Placide was sent to a prison on Belle-Isle off the southern coast of Brittany, where he shared a cell with Jean-Baptiste Belley, the free black from Cap who had served as the first black deputy in the French National Assembly. The rest of Louverture's family—including his wife Suzanne, her servant, their sons Isaac and Saint-Jean, Louverture's niece Louise Chancy, and Placide's fiancée, Victoire Thusac—was sent to Bayonne, and eventually to Agen in southwestern France, where Placide reunited with them in 1804.[10]

The Louvertures were treated humanely, for the most part. Placed under house arrest rather than imprisoned, they lived on a governmental pension for the rest of their lives, as did their spouses and offspring. But they were not informed of their patriarch's whereabouts, and only learned of his death after several months' delay. The untimely death of the young Saint-Jean in 1804 was another blow. Heartbroken, Suzanne Louverture spent the remainder of her life praying in the church of Agen. Although she was diagnosed with breast cancer in 1806, she did not pass away until 1816.

By that time, Napoléon had abdicated, and a brother of Louis XVI had ascended to the throne. Isaac and Placide, who held Napoléon responsible for their father's death and had inherited his royalist sympathies, welcomed the return of the Bourbon monarchy. Their support for the new king prompted an easing of the conditions of their exile, including their release from house arrest.

The two brothers agreed on little else. Isaac and Placide spent their exile squabbling over the governmental pension, women, even the family servant. Mostly, they argued over Louverture's heritage, both symbolic and financial. They moved into separate houses while in Agen, and in 1817 Isaac moved to Bordeaux with his cousin (and now wife) Louise Chancy. Bordeaux, a cosmopolitan port city, offered them the chance to socialize with other Caribbean exiles. Meanwhile, Placide married a French noblewoman named Joséphine de Lacaze and moved with her to the Dordogne region in central France. The two brothers never saw each other again.

Although the French government was willing to let the Louvertures return to Haiti after Napoléon's fall, Isaac and Placide stayed in France. They had spent most of their lives there, and it was where they felt most at home culturally. Since Dessalines and Christophe had harassed or killed many of their male relatives in Haiti, they also had reason to fear for their safety. Isaac believed he would be "hanged immediately upon his arrival" if he ever went back. Not until the start of Jean-Pierre Boyer's presidency (1818–1843) did a return become truly feasible.[11]

Isaac moved decisively after learning that Placide was planning to visit Haiti and collect his inheritance. Denouncing him as merely the adopted son of Louverture, he sued his brother to deny him the right to a portion of Louverture's estate or even to use his last name. Louverture had always treated Placide as his son; Placide had served his adoptive father loyally in return. Nevertheless, Isaac won the lawsuit, and for the rest of his life Placide could not legally use the last name that Louverture had bequeathed to him. Crippled by rheumatism, Placide canceled his visit to Haiti and spent the rest of his life in France, where he died in 1841.

After disowning Placide, Isaac sent his wife, Louise, to Haiti in 1822, where she spent several years recovering the family inheritance. The couple's acquisitiveness allowed them to fulfill the dream of the nineteenth-century provincial bourgeoisie: they lived off their portfolio for the rest of their lives. In the Bordeaux region of France, they had "three female servants, along with male ones, and . . . regularly host[ed] parties and galas," complained a local official, who noted that they were still collecting their pension from the French government. Isaac also spent years collecting anecdotes about his father. Isaac's papers, which are now kept at the French National Library in Paris, did much to keep the memory of Louverture alive.[12]

Isaac died childless in 1854. His brother Saint-Jean had died as a child, as had two of Placide's sons. Therefore, Louverture's only grandchild from his second family was Placide's lone surviving daughter. Placide had named her Rose after a young girl his father had adopted during the Revolution. Rose and her offspring preserved and cherished the memory of their famous forefather for generations. "I share the blood of my Haitian ancestors," Rose's daughter Gabrielle wrote more than a century after Louverture's death, "and I am proud to say that I resemble them." Gabrielle's son Jérôme (Louverture's great-great-grandson) died wearing a French uniform in the trenches of World War I. Fittingly, the descendants of a character as complex as Louverture are now to be found in both Haiti and France.[13]

In 1843, toward the end of Jean-Pierre Boyer's presidency in Haiti, a group of political opponents drew up a manifesto calling for his overthrow. After lamenting Haiti's political and economic decline, they listed the "illustrious founders of our liberty and independence" who should serve as models for the "regeneration" of the country. Conspicuously missing from the list was the name of the Haitian Revolution's central figure. "And Toussaint Louverture!" his son Isaac angrily scribbled in the margin when he obtained a copy of the manifesto.[14]

The omission was typical of the extent to which early Haitians willfully forgot Louverture, a gifted but stern leader who had made many enemies during his rule. Visiting the country shortly after independence, an American merchant noted with surprise that he was "seldom mentioned, but in terms of reproach." Henry Christophe himself told the merchant that Louverture was "a fool." Christophe's court historian was slightly less severe, but he still faulted Louverture for being "filled with the prejudices of the Old Regime" and unable to conceive that Haitians could be "free and independent."[15]

In the eyes of many early Haitians, Louverture was a transitional figure. The national anthem of Haiti was named after Dessalines. The national flag was based on a design created by Dessalines or the mixed-race officer Alexandre Pétion (accounts vary). The main national holidays of Haiti, from Independence Day on January 1 to Flag Day on May 18 and Vertières Day on November 18, all commemorated events that took place after Louverture's downfall. Black nationalists cherished the memory of Dessalines, while the mixed-race minority celebrated Pétion and Boyer. Accused of being a white man in a black skin, Louverture had few supporters.

Paradoxically, it was outside of Haiti that Louverture first developed a following. He was popular with white abolitionists in France, Britain, and the United States, who viewed him as proof that freedmen possessed the wisdom and the intelligence to rule themselves. Victor Schoelcher, who spearheaded France's second abolition of slavery in 1848, wrote a biography of Louverture that described him as a "man of genius." The British abolitionist William Wilberforce admired his ability to maintain "due subordination on the plantations, *without invading the liberty of individuals*." He was "an African, whose virtues . . . will exhibit him as a Christian and genuine friend of us possessing a different complexion," a

Philadelphian admirer explained. Even proslavery authors in the United States often praised him for his willingness to pardon his former oppressors and for his policies that forced freedmen back to the fields: "The black general Toussaint, (the only truly great man yet known of the negro race), compelled the former slaves to return to the plantations, and to labor, under military coercion," noted one of them. Depending on their stance on race and independence, white authors alternately lauded Louverture for his benevolence or his sternness; with such a conflicted record to pick from, they all found what they were looking for.[16]

By the time of the Civil War, Louverture had become a common reference point in the debates on slavery that were tearing the United States apart. In keeping with earlier abolitionist tropes, the Boston Brahmin Wendell Phillips emphasized Louverture's moderation and intelligence as a means of buttressing his argument "that the Negro race, instead of being that object of pity or contempt which we usually consider it, is entitled . . . to a place close by the side of the Saxon." But an alternate image of Louverture as a man willing to fight for his ideas had begun to take hold among more militant abolitionists. John Brown studied Louverture's military tactics when preparing his raid at Harpers Ferry, and the black abolitionist James Holly urged his countrymen to imitate Louverture and the Haitians, who he said had preferred to be "DEAD FREEDMEN . . . than LIVING SLAVES."[17]

Louverture's political ambivalence, which had so infuriated his contemporaries, continued to contribute to this posthumous revival after the Civil War. Speaking to a white audience in 1893, Frederick Douglass noted Louverture's "humane" treatment of French planters; later that day, to an appreciative black audience, he instead emphasized the "Negro manhood" of Haitian warriors like Louverture. To one group he was a black Washington who had built a functioning state; to the other he was a black Spartacus who had destroyed an unfair system. To W. E. B. Dubois, the "great Negro" had also been directly responsible for several defining moments in US history, starting with the Louisiana Purchase: because the Leclerc expedition was bogged down in Saint-Domingue, Napoléon failed to reoccupy Louisiana and eventually sold it.[18]

Louverture's international acclaim contrasted sharply with his initial unpopularity in his homeland. "We have all heard or read something of Toussaint Louverture, and been taught to think well of him," wrote a British consul. "I was therefore the more surprised, on my arrival at Port-au-Prince, to hear his memory so depreciated." Only after the passing of the first generation of statesmen—those who were veterans of the Revolution and rivals or critics of Louverture—did Haitians begin to warm to him. When Faustin Soulouque became president in 1847, he immediately commissioned a statue to honor the "Precursor." The resulting work, carved from rock and standing eight feet tall, was placed on the grounds of Louverture's favorite plantation, in Ennery. It was the first of many commemorative works over the following decades.[19]

In the twentieth century, as empires broke apart and many colonies across the world declared independence, Louverture was roundly seen as a precursor not only of Haitian independence but of the anticolonial movement more broadly, to the point where one-sided hagiography became the norm both within and outside of Haiti. A copy of the statue carved under Soulouque now stands on the site of the Haut-du-Cap plantation in Haiti, which is also home to a high school named after Louverture. A bust of Louverture has been placed in Bordeaux, where his son Isaac is buried; another one is at the slave-trading port of La Rochelle; and a portrait of Louverture adorns the tramway cars of Besançon, the regional capital near the Fort de Joux. A giant statue of Louverture even looms over Allada in Benin: although he never visited, he is viewed there as a national hero because his parents came from the area. Children's books, banknotes, plays, TV biopics: he has become, both figuratively and literally, an icon.

Few scholars now dare to question some aspects of Louverture's record for fear of appearing critical of the cause for which he fought, an attitude that is seemingly respectful but also simplistic and even patronizing. Turning him into a one-dimensional hero of emancipation obscures the complexities of the Revolution he had to navigate and the skill he displayed in doing so.

For the past two hundred years, as Louverture's memory was parsed, lost, and rediscovered, so was his body. Some accounts claim that he was buried in Saint-Pierre, a hamlet located at the foot of the Fort de Joux; according to the prison director, however, he was interred in the fort's chapel. If the director was correct, that was where the remains lay until a French officer opened the tomb and removed what he thought to be his skull in 1850. The top half was put on display in the library of nearby

Pontarlier; the bottom was placed by the fireplace in his former cell, a conversation piece for tourists. In the 1870s, the fort was modernized and the chapel destroyed; the location of these various remains is unknown today.[20]

Over the years, as Louverture's reputation recovered in Haiti, Haitian presidents made repeated requests for his body—wherever it might be—to be repatriated to his home country. However, Charles de Gaulle replied in the 1960s that Louverture was actually a French general, and that as such he was already buried in his country. Little progress has been made since. In 1983, François Mitterrand had dirt from the Fort de Joux sent to Haiti, so that Louverture could be symbolically reinterred in the National Panthéon of Port-au-Prince. Yet the French government also placed a plaque in Louverture's honor in France's own Panthéon in Paris, claiming him as a French hero as well. Louverture's sons once battled over his inheritance; France and Haiti are now battling over the ownership of his legacy.[21]

Nationalism was born during the revolutionary era, and so the concept of the nation was still vague in Louverture's time. Ultimately, two rival definitions emerged. One relied on fixed criteria, including religion, language, or—in Dessalines's 1805 constitution—race to emphasize that belonging to a nation was a sociological fact rather than a conscious choice. The other, outlined by the French philosopher Ernest Renan in 1882, described nations as social contracts rooted in a shared past and a willingness to live together: "To have done great things together, to want to do more, such are the essential conditions to form a people. . . . Man is not a slave to his race, or his tongue, or his religion."[22]

When Louverture reflected on his own national identity, a shared heritage and shared ideals mattered far more to him than race or birthplace. When trying to convince black field hands that he was their "brother," he reminded them that he had been "a slave, just like you," and that he had been "the first in Cap to fight for liberty." When the racist planter Vincent de Vaublanc questioned his right to be French on account of his African ancestry, Louverture insisted on the "inviolable attachment to France and its Constitution of black and colored generals, who will never betray their oath to live free and French: they will always prefer to bury themselves under the ruins of their country rather than accept the restoration of slavery." As Louverture later wrote, "I am French" because "I love liberty, and French people are free. . . . I will know how to defend the honor of a nation of which I am proud to be the adoptive son." Participating in the epic struggle for emancipation had made him a true son of Saint-Domingue. He had then joined the French nation by a conscious act of will, and he planned to remain a Frenchman as long as France shared his agenda. This conditional patriotism, at once principled and calculated, was the ultimate expression of the pragmatic idealism that defined Louverture's career. He was, in the end, a citizen of both Haiti and France—and of every other nation that has fought and continues to fight for the liberty of man.[23]

ACKNOWLEDGMENTS

I first want to recognize the generous hospitality of the individuals who hosted me while I was conducting research for this book, particularly Nathalie and Emmanuel Blanc, Michelle Berny and Marcel Blanc, Ronald and Elizabeth Cook, Coralie Dedieu, Marie-Thérèse Dessay, Jody Garber, Jacques and Marie-Madeleine Girard, Isabelle and Gildvin Hiélard, Sophie and Guillaume Larnicol, and Nicolas Vercken.

I would also like to thank the many individuals who read and critiqued various segments and drafts of the manuscript, notably my agent Paul Lucas and my editor Dan Gerstle. The participants of a workshop held at the Hutchins Center in November 2014, particularly Kerry Chance, Steven Nelson, and Gregg Hecimovich, helped me refine the Introduction and Chapter 6. Jean-Louis Donnadieu shared some of his research findings with me, especially for Chapter 5, for which I am very grateful.

Research for this book was financed in part by McNeese State University research grants that were made possible through the generosity of David Elks, Juliet Hartdner, Violet Howell, Evelyn Shaddow Murray, the Shearman family, Joe Gray Taylor, and Delores and Tom Tuminello; many thanks to them. I finished writing this book in the fall of 2014 as a Sheila Biddle Ford Fellow at Harvard University's Hutchins Center. I would like to commend the center's staff members for their kind support, starting with Henry Louis Gates Jr., to whom much praise is due for creating such a wonderful research center.

NOTES

Note: Translations from Spanish, French, and Kreyòl in this book are mine. Emphases are in the original documents.

ADD: Archives Départementales du Doubs, Besançon
ADGir: Archives Départementales de la Gironde, Bordeaux
ADLA: Archives Départementales de la Loire-Atlantique, Nantes
AGI: Archivo General de Indias, Seville
AGS: Archivo General de Simancas, Valladolid
AHN: Archivo Histórico Nacional, Madrid
AN: Archives Nationales, Paris
ANOM: Archives Nationales d'Outre-Mer, Aix-en-Provence
APS: American Philosophical Society, Philadelphia
BA: Boston Athenaeum
BFV-FM: Fonds Montbret, Bibliothèque François Villon, Rouen
BNA: British National Archives, Kew
BNF: Bibliothèque Nationale, Paris
BPL: Boston Public Library
CN: Vaillant, Jean-Baptiste, ed. *Correspondance de Napoléon Ier, publiée par ordre de l'empereur Napoléon III*. 32 vols. Paris: Plon, 1858.
CUL: Cornell University Library, Ithaca, New York
DHHAN: Franco, José Luciano, ed. *Documentos para la historia de Haití en el Archivo Nacional*. Havana: Publicaciones del Archivo Nacional de Cuba, 1954.
FBL: François Bayon de Libertat
GC-RTSD: Garran-Coulon, Jean-Philippe. *Rapport sur les troubles de Saint-Domingue*. 4 vols. Paris: Imprimerie Nationale, Ventôse an V [Feb.–March 1797].
HNOC: Historic New Orleans Collection, New Orleans
HSP: Historical Society of Pennsylvania, Philadelphia
HU-HL: Houghton Library, Harvard University, Cambridge, Massachusetts
HU-KFC: Kurt Fisher Collection, Moorland-Springarn Research Center, Howard University, Washington, DC
IL-NH: Louverture, Isaac. "Notes historiques sur Toussaint Louverture, manuscrit d'Isaac Louverture, notes intéressantes sur Banica, etc." (c. 1819). NAF 12409, BNF.

IL-OTL: Louverture, Isaac. "Origine de Toussaint-Louverture racontée par Isaac Louverture" (c. Feb. 15, 1819). NAF 6864, BNF.

JCB: John Carter Brown Library, Providence, Rhode Island

JLD-PHD: Donnadieu, Jean-Louis. *Entre Gascogne et Saint-Domingue: Le comte Louis-Pantaléon de Noé, grand propriétaire créole et aristocrate gascon, 1728–1816*. PhD dissertation, Université de Pau et des Pays de l'Adour, 2006.

LC-MD: Manuscript Division, Library of Congress, Washington, DC

LCP: Library Company, Philadelphia

MHS: Massachusetts Historical Society, Boston

MSM-DPF: Moreau de Saint-Méry, M. L. E. *Description . . . de la partie française de l'isle Saint-Domingue*. 2 vols. Philadelphia: Moreau, 1797–1798.

MSM-LC: Moreau de Saint-Méry, M. L. E. *Loix et constitutions des colonies françoises de l'Amérique sous le vent*. 6 vols. Paris: Moutard, 1784–1790.

NARA-CP: National Archives and Records Administration II, College Park

NARA-DC: National Archives and Records Administration I, Washington, DC

NLS-CM: Crawford Muniments, Acc. 9769, Personal Papers, 23/10/1176–1188, National Library of Scotland

NYPL-SC: Schomburg Center, New York Public Library

PB: Pantaléon de Bréda Jr.

PG-MGTL: Girard, Philippe, ed. *The Memoir of General Toussaint Louverture*. New York: Oxford University Press, 2014.

PMD-PH: Duboys, Pélage-Marie. *Précis historique des Annales de la Révolution à Saint Domingue*. 2 vols. NAF 14878, 14879 (MF 5389, 5384), BNF.

SD: Saint-Domingue

SHD-DAT: Service Historique de la Défense (Département de l'Armée de Terre), Vincennes

SHD-DM: Service Historique de la Défense (Département de la Marine), Vincennes

TL: Toussaint Louverture

UF-RP: Rochambeau Papers, University of Florida, Gainesville

UM-CL: Clements Library, University of Michigan, Ann Arbor

UPR-NC: Nemours Collection, University of Puerto Rico–Río Piedras, San Juan

VR-PR: Vente Rochambeau, Philippe Rouillac auction house

INTRODUCTION

1. "Every body" from David Geggus, "Saint-Domingue and the Rise of Toussaint Louverture," Huggins lecture, Harvard University, February 23–25, 2016. Toussaint Louverture (TL hereafter) was known as "Toussaint" or "Toussaint Bréda" until he coined a last name c. 1793, but I will consistently refer to

him as "Toussaint Louverture" or "Louverture" because he associated his first name with slavery. Napoléon Bonaparte was known as "Général Bonaparte" until his 1804 coronation, but I will consistently refer to him as "Napoléon" because he associated his first name with imperial status.

2. "Jai éte Esclave" from PG-MGTL, 148.

3. "Je suis noir" from Philippe-Albert de Lattre, *Campagne des Français à SD et réfutation des reproches faits au Capitaine-Général Rochambeau* (Paris: Locard, 1805), 46. "Parce que je sui noire" from PG-MGTL, 140. "Ce nègre" from Barry O'Meara, *Napoléon en exil: Relation contenant les opinions et les réflexions de Napoléon sur les événements les plus importants de sa vie, durant trois ans de sa captivité* (Paris: Garnier, 1897), 2:276.

CHAPTER 1: ARISTOCRAT, C. 1740

1. "Roi puissant en Afrique" from IL-OTL. For other accounts by Isaac, see NAF 6864, BNF; NAF 12409, BNF; 6APC/1, ANOM. For family traditions passed through TL's stepson Placide, see [Jérôme Fontan], "Notes biographiques sur la famille de TL" (c. 1927), TLF-3B, UPR-NC. For family traditions passed through his niece Louise Chancy, see Alain Turnier, *Quand la nation demande des comptes* (Port-au-Prince: Le Natal, 1989), 31.

2. "The greatest trading place" from Basil Davidson, *West Africa Before the Colonial Era: A History to 1850* (New York: Longman, 1998), 200. The following account of Allada is based on Robin Law, *The Kingdom of Allada* (Leiden: Research School CNWS, 1997).

3. "Fille d'Affiba" from Turnier, *Quand la nation*, 31. On the royal lineages of Benin, see Jean-Louis Donnadieu, *Un grand seigneur et ses esclaves: Le comte de Noé entre Antilles et Gascogne, 1728–1816* (Toulouse: Presses Universitaires du Mirail, 2009), 96, 310. Gaou Guinou's last name was probably a deformation of the word "Deguenon" ("old man" in the Fon language) or "de Guinée" ("from Africa" in Kreyòl). Hippolyte and Catherine's names were given to them in SD; their original African names are not known to us.

4. The following account of the slave trade from Allada is based on David Geggus, "The French Slave Trade: An Overview," *William and Mary Quarterly* 58, no. 1 (Jan. 2001): 119–138; Robin Law, *Ouidah: The Social History of a West African Slaving "Port," 1727–1892* (Athens: Ohio University Press, 2004). Thanks to both authors for providing clarifications by email.

5. "Fait prisonnier" from IL-OTL. On Hippolyte's family being deported with him, see Turnier, *Quand la nation*, 31.

6. On the Arab trader, see Jean Hoefer, ed., *Nouvelle biographie générale depuis les temps les plus reculés jusqu'à nos jours* (Paris: Firmin Didot Frères, 1860), 32:38. The 1740 date is an estimate based on King Agaja's death (1740) and TL's approximate birth (c. 1743).

7. On the *Hermione*, see Jean Mettas and Serge Daget, *Répertoire des Expéditions négrières françaises au XVIIIe siècle* (Paris: Société Française d'Histoire d'Outre-Mer, 1978), 1:218 (other good candidates include the *Jeune Flore*, 1:222, and the *Reine des Anges*, 1:248). On buying from Le Havre, see FBL to PB (Feb. 3, 1785), d. 12, 18AP/3, AN.

8. On slave revolts, see Franklin Midy, ed., *Mémoire de révolution d'esclaves à SD* (Montréal: Centre International de Documentation et d'Information Haïtienne, Caribéenne et Afro-canadienne, 2006), 48. On TL's fear of sea travel, see Hugh Cathcart to Thomas Maitland (Nov. 26, 1799), WO 1/74, BNA.

9. On the slave population, see the 1790 US census; Charles Frostin, *Les révoltes blanches à SD aux XVIIe et XVIIIe siècles (Haïti avant 1789)* (Paris: L'Ecole, 1975), 28; see also www.slavevoyages.org.

10. On baptizing slaves, see Pierre de Charlevoix, *Histoire de l'isle Espagnole ou de SD* (Paris, 1730–1731), 2:504. "Cher" from FBL to PB (Feb. 4, 1784), d. 12, 18AP/3, AN. "Laborieux" from François Tussac, *Cri des colons contre un ouvrage de M. l'évêque et sénateur Grégoire, ayant pour titre de la littérature des nègres* (Paris: Delaunay, 1810), 65. "Les plus propres à la sucrerie" from PB to FBL (July 30, 1784), d. 12, 18AP/3, AN. "Intelligens" from MSM-DPF, 1:29.

11. "Spectacle déchirant" from MSM-DPF, 1:415.

12. "Chagrin mortel" from Thomas Gragnon-Lacoste, *TL* (Paris: Durand, 1877), 7. Strangely, an African-born Marie-Catherine Affiba died on May 14, 1819, in Port-au-Prince; see Jacques de Cauna, "Les registres d'état civil anciens des Archives Nationales d'Haïti," *Revue de la Société Haïtienne d'Histoire et de Géographie* 162 (1989): 1–34. "Arracher le fils à sa mère" from TL, *Réfutations de quelques assertions d'un discours . . . par Viénot-Vaublanc* (Cap: Roux, [Oct. 29], 1797), 17. On Geneviève and Augustin Affiba, see Pierre Bardin, "Langlois de Chancy-TL," *Généalogie et Histoire de la Caraïbe* 92 (Apr. 1997): 1944.

13. On TL's view of southerners, see TL to Laveaux (Sept. 14, 1795), fr. 12103, BNF. On Pantaléon I, see 18AP/2, AN; E51, ANOM; 73J1, ADGir.

14. For statistics, see Hilliard d'Auberteuil, *Considérations sur l'état présent de la colonie française de SD* (Paris: Grangé, 1776), 1:65, 72, 73; Frostin, *Les révoltes blanches*, 144.

15. On the assets, see "Inventaire" (July 20, 1786), et/LXXXVI/847, AN.

16. "S'abandonne au point" from FBL to PB (Apr. 16, 1785), d. 12, 18AP/3, AN.

17. On Hippolyte, see IL-OTL.

18. "Belle et vertueuse" from IL-OTL. On Pauline as an Aja, see [Valsemey?], "Tableau des Revenus . . ." (Dec. 31, 1785), 261 MIOM, ANOM. TL's adoptive mother was also Aja; see "Etat général des esclaves" (Apr. 4, 1785), d. 12, 18AP/3, AN.

CHAPTER 2: CHILD, C. 1743–1754

1. On the incident, see "Mémoire pour M. Despallieres" (Nov. 1, 1743), F3/143, ANOM.

2. For the family traditions, see chap. 1. For contemporary accounts, see *Moniteur Universel* (Jan. 9, 1799); François de Kerversau, "Rapport sur la partie française de SD" (March 22, 1801), Box 2/66, UF-RP. For the Bréda plantation records, see 73J1, ADGir; E691, ADLA; 18AP3, AN; 261 MIOM, ANOM; JLD-PHD, 353–393. Bréda papers once housed in Amiens did not survive World War I, according to Gabriel Debien, "Un effort nouveau à Haïti," *Annales Historiques de la Révolution Française* 114 (Apr.–June 1949): 141–147.

3. On TL's birth in 1737, see Pamphile de Lacroix, *Mémoires pour servir à l'histoire de la révolution de SD* (Paris: Pillet, 1819), 1:404. On 1740, see Isaac Louverture, "Réfutation . . ." (Aug. 18, 1845), NAF 6864, BNF. On 1743, see Louis Dubroca, *La vie de TL, chef des noirs insurgés de SD* (Paris: Dubroca, 1802), 4. On 1745, see Marcus Rainsford, *An Historical Account of the Black Empire of Hayti* (London: Albion Press, 1805), 240. On 1746, see *Moniteur Universel* (Jan. 9, 1799). On 1750, see Jean de Saint-Anthoine, *Notice sur TL* (Paris: Lacour, 1842), 5. On 1754, see "Etat général des esclaves" (Apr. 4, 1785), d. 12, 18AP/3, AN. On 1756, see [Valsemey?], "Esclaves existant" (Dec. 31, 1785), 261 MIOM, ANOM. The earlier dates are improbable because TL's mother was still fertile in 1774. The later dates are also improbable because TL had a twenty-four-year-old son in 1785. On TL's alleged first names, see David Geggus, "Les débuts de TL," *Généalogie et Histoire de la Caraïbe* 170 (May 2004): 4172. TL's stepson Placide gave TL's full name as "Jean Toussaint Marie Claire Louverture," but he was probably conflating TL's name and that of his biological father to bolster claims that he was TL's biological son; see "Extrait des minutes . . ." (Apr. 15, 1821), TLF-1A3b, UPR-NC.

4. "J'ai éte Esclave" from PG-MGTL, 148.

5. "Gaçon" from Fortuna Guéry, *Témoignages* (Port-au-Prince: Henri Deschamps, 1950), 87. On Allada birthing practices, see Michel-Etienne Descourtilz, *Voyage d'un naturaliste et ses observations* (Paris: Dufart, 1809), 3:119, 198. The following account of slave life is also based on MSM-DPF; Pierre de Charlevoix, *Histoire de l'isle Espagnole ou de SD*, vol. 2 (Paris, 1730–1731); Justin Girod-Chantrans, *Voyage d'un Suisse dans différentes colonies d'Amérique* (Neuchatel: Société typographique, 1785); Francis de Wimpffen, *A Voyage to Saint Domingo in the Years 1788, 1789, and 1790* (London: T. Cadell, 1797).

6. On TL's siblings, see FBL to PB (Apr. 30, 1774), d. 12, 18AP/3, AN; IL-OTL.

7. "Le goût qu'il avait pour l'histoire" from IL-OTL. "Suvi" from Maurice Delafosse, *Manuel dahoméen* (Paris: Ernest Leroux, 1894), 1. On TL's linguistic choices, see Philippe Girard, "Quelle langue parlait TL? Le mémoire du Fort de Joux et les origines du kreyòl haïtien," *Annales* 68, no. 1 (Jan. 2013): 109–132.

8. On TL's preferred dress, see IL-NH, 77; M. A. Matinée, ed., *Anecdotes de la révolution de SD racontées par Guillaume Mauviel* (Saint-Lô: Elie fils, 1885), 36.

9. "Man" from MSM-DPF, 1:42.

10. "Fatras bâton" from Kerversau, "Rapport" (March 22, 1801), Box 2/66, UF-RP. The term "fatras" was defined as "tout ce qui est méprisable" in Pierre du Simitière, "Vocabulaire créole" (c. 1770s), 968.F.9, LCP.

11. "Se vautrant" from Descourtilz, *Voyage d'un naturaliste*, 3:190. "Gloomy" from Wimpffen, *A Voyage to Saint Domingo*, 235.

12. On Agassou, see Jean-Louis Donnadieu, *TL: Le Napoléon noir* (Paris: Belin, 2014), 21. Agassou was still worshiped in Vodou in the 1940s; see Alfred Métraux, *Le vaudou haïtien* (Paris: Gallimard, 1958), 24.

13. "Maisons de débauche" from MSM-LC, 4:156. On soothsayers, see FBL to PB (Sept. 14, 1773), d. 12, 18AP/3, AN.

14. On the number of priests, see Arlette Gautier, *Les sœurs de Solitude: La condition féminine dans l'esclavage aux Antilles du XVIIe au XIXe siècle* (Paris: Editions Caribéennes, 1985), 81; Sue Peabody, "'A Dangerous Zeal': Catholic Missions to Slaves in the French Antilles, 1635–1800," *French Historical Studies* 25, no. 1 (Winter 2002): 73. On public prayers, see FBL to PB (Sept. 14, 1773), d. 12, 18AP/3, AN. The following account of the Catholic Church is also based on F3/90–92 and F5A, ANOM.

15. "Schismatique" (a reference to TL's secretary Nathan) from IL-NH, 74. On the Jews of Cap, see Zvi Loker, "Were There Jewish Communities in SD (Haiti)?" *Jewish Social Studies* 45, no. 2 (Spring 1983): 135–146. On Sasportas, see FBL, "Compte-rendu" (Apr. 4, 1785), d. 12, 18AP/3, AN. On the attempted expulsion, see Elvire Maurouard, *Les Juifs de SD (Haïti)* (Paris: Editions du Cygne, 2008), 40.

16. On the Carib (aka Arawak) in Cap, see *Supplément aux Affiches américaines* (Apr. 4, 1772). For the Taino head, see MSM-DPF, 1:352.

17. On Vodou, see [M. Courtin?], "Mémoire sommaire . . ." (1758), F3/88, ANOM. For alternate takes on TL as a fake Catholic or a *vodouisant*, see Pierre Pluchon, *TL* (Paris: Fayard, 1989), 338; Madison Smartt Bell, *TL: A Biography* (New York: Pantheon Books, 2007), 56, 174, 195, 288. "Bigot" from [Valsemey?], "Esclaves existant" (Dec. 31, 1785), 261 MIOM, ANOM.

18. On the Jesuits, see F5A/22, ANOM; MSM-LC, 4:642. Some historians claim that TL was owned by Jesuits before 1763 (see, for example, Bell, *TL*, 64), but the earliest evidence I have found are two unreliable accounts dated 1800 and 1801; see Pièces 2 and 58, AF/IV/1212, AN.

19. "Curé des nègres" from Peabody, "'A Dangerous Zeal,'" 83. "Accoutumé de catéchiser" from MSM-LC, 4:352. "Faire des prosélytes" from [Valsemey?], "Esclaves existant" (Dec. 31, 1785), 261 MIOM, ANOM.

20. "Les crimes énormes" from MSM-LC, 4:626.

CHAPTER 3: SLAVE, 1754

1. "Partage des nègres" from "Inventaire" (July 20, 1786), et/LXXXVI/847, AN. Slave families could technically not be separated at auction; see art. 47 of the 1685 Code Noir.

2. "I was quite a child" from Frederick Douglass, *Narrative of the Life of Frederick Douglass, An American Slave, Written by Himself* (1845; reprint, New Haven, CT: Yale University Press, 2001), 16.

3. On the population of Quartier-Morin in 1789 (which included 204 whites of all classes and 95 freedmen), see MSM-DPF, 1:245. "Vous autres blancs" from M. J. La Neuville, *Le dernier cri de SD et des colonies* (Philadelphia: Bradford, 1800), 9. The following account of the Bréda family is based on 18AP/2 and /3, AN; E51, ANOM; d. 1, 73J1, ADGir.

4. "Le lait" and "otage" from Charles Frostin, *Les révoltes blanches à SD aux XVIIe et XVIIIe siècles (Haïti avant 1789)* (Paris: L'Ecole, 1975), 116, 369. On punishing a slave who hit a child, see MSM-LC, 4:136.

5. On the split in Manquets, see De Larnage and Maillart to Min. of Navy (Feb. 28, 1744), C9A/64, ANOM.

6. On PB's portrait, see FBL to PB (Nov. 24, 1780), d. 12, 18AP/3, AN.

7. On absentee ownership, see Min. of Navy to M. de Larnage (Oct. 17, 1743), F3/143, ANOM. On Noé (who only inherited a fourth of the Haut-du-Cap estate in 1786, by which point TL no longer was a slave), see Jean-Louis Donnadieu, *Un grand seigneur et ses esclaves: Le comte de Noé entre Antilles et Gascogne, 1728–1816* (Toulouse: Presses Universitaires du Mirail, 2009).

8. For various versions of the Code Noir, see Jean-François Niort, ed., *Code Noir* (Paris: Dalloz, 2012). For later laws, see the royal ordinances of Dec. 30, 1712; March 1724; March 14, 1741; Dec. 3, 1784; and Dec. 23, 1785, in MSM-LC.

9. "VOL" from MSM-LC, 5:342. For the fee schedule and the *droit suppli-cié*, see MSM-LC, 5:378, 284. On the Brédas negotiating a higher *droit supplicié*, see "Nous certifions" (Apr. 12, 1780), E57, ANOM.

10. "The happy slaves" from Peter S. Chazotte, *Historical Sketches of the Revolutions, and the Foreign and Civil Wars in the Island of St. Domingo, With a Narrative of the Entire Massacre of the White Population of the Island* (New York: Applegate, 1840), 8. "Les tourments les plus cruels" from Pierre du Simitière, "De la ville et du quartier de Léogane" (c. 1774), 968.F.28, LCP. "Toutes sortes de tourments" (a comment by the rank and file) from Jean-François and Biassou to Mirbeck, Roume, St. Léger (Dec. 21, 1791), *D/XXV/1, AN.

11. "Ne connut-il guère l'esclavage" from François de Kerversau, "Rapport sur la partie française de SD" (March 22, 1801), Box 2/66, UF-RP. On atrocities near Haut-du-Cap, see Baron de Vastey, *Le système colonial dévoilé* (Oct. 1814), 44, Tract B795 no.2, BA; Malick Ghachem, *The Old Regime and the Haitian Revolution* (Cambridge: Cambridge University Press, 2012), 131–143. "Les insultes, la misère" from TL, *Réfutations de quelques assertions d'un discours . . . par Viénot-Vaublanc* (Cap: Roux, [Oct. 29], 1797), 24.

12. On Faure, see PB to FBL (Apr. 1, 1779), d. 12, 18AP/3, AN. On Béagé (aka Béager), see IL-NH, 60. "Il a eu la faiblesse" from Delribal to M. de la Pom-meraye (Sept. 9, 1773), d. 12, 18AP/3, AN. "Beaucoup de dureté" from Sylvain de Villevaleix to Polastron (July 31, 1790), E691, ADLA.

13. On the average age at death, see David Geggus, "TL and the Slaves of the Bréda Plantations," *Journal of Caribbean History* 20, no. 1 (1985–1986): 36. "Des vrais bourreaux" from TL, *Réfutations*, 26.

14. "Blancs" from Frostin, *Les révoltes blanches*, 320.

15. On hired soldiers, see FBL to PB (June 10, 1773), d. 12, 18AP/3, AN. For the sentence, see "Aujourd'hui" (Sept. 6, 1710), E51, ANOM. Such penalties were outlawed by the 1770s; see D'Ennery to de Sartines (Sept. 3, 1775), C9A/143, ANOM.

CHAPTER 4: REVOLUTIONARY APPRENTICE, 1757–1773

1. For the anecdote, see IL-NH, 60. On TL's horsemanship, see Joseph Peyre-Ferry, *Journal des opérations militaires de l'armée française à SD pendant les années X, XI et XII (1802 et 1803)* (Port-au-Prince: Henri Deschamps, 2005), 186.

2. For examples of three major disturbances in 1775–1777, see MSM-LC, 5:550, 800, 805. For other disturbances in 1772, see M. de Valière and M. de

Montarcher to M. de Boynes (Aug. 25, 1772), C9A/141, ANOM. Blinded by the bright glare of the Revolution, historians tend to forget the early disturbances.

3. "Reconnu depuis bien des années" from Delribal to M. de la Pommeraye (Sept. 9, 1773), d. 12, 18AP/3, AN. "Fainéants" from FBL to PB (Dec. 20, 1775), d. 12, 18AP/3, AN. "Infecté" from [Valsemey?], "Mémoire" (c. Dec. 31, 1785), 261 MIOM, ANOM. "Mauvaise réputation" from Jean Langlois de Laheuse to Count of Noé (June 24, 1789), JLD-PHD, 383.

4. On ties to the Bullet plantation, see [Valsemey?], "Mémoire" (c. Dec. 31, 1785), 261 MIOM, ANOM.

5. On intellectual maroonage, see Marc-Ferl Morquette, *Les nouveaux marrons: Essai sur un aspect de la crise politique, 1989–1998* (Port-au-Prince: L'imprimeur II, 1999).

6. On the surgeon, see Jean-Charles Benzaken, "A propos d'un crime commis sur une esclave à SD en 1736," *Généalogie et Histoire de la Caraïbe* 238 (July–Aug. 2010): 6364.

7. On the lynchings, see MSM-DPF, 1:596.

8. On the two fights, see IL-NH, 60. There is no reason to doubt the veracity of this account because Isaac had a tendency to soften his father's record.

9. On Lavaud, see "Extrait de déclarations" (May 26, 1757), F3/88, ANOM. "Sans rien avouer" from M. de Morigny, "Mémoire sur les poisons" (1763), Box 1/3, UF-RP.

10. On food shortages, see Bart and LaLanne to Min. of Navy (Sept. 20, 1757), C9A/100, ANOM. On spoiled meat and flour, see MSM-LC, 4:187, 262, 287.

11. "Faire le diable" from Fournier de la Chapelle, "Mémoire . . ." (1758), F3/88, ANOM.

12. "Amende honorable" from MSM-LC, 4:217.

13. "Makandal sauvé" from MSM-DPF, 1:653.

14. "Temps de repos" from MSM-LC, 4:717. For runaway notices, see Le Marronnage à Saint-Domingue (Haiti), www.marronnage.info (many runaways, including most of the Brédas', went unreported in the *Affiches américaines* paper).

15. "Je ne sais que faire" from FBL to PB (Feb. 3, 1785), d. 12, 18AP/3, AN. On Sans Souci, see FBL, "Compte Rendu . . ." (July 20, 1787), 261 MIOM, ANOM; Michel Rolph-Trouillot, *Silencing the Past: Power and the Production of History* (Boston: Beacon Press, 1995), 40–69.

16. On the maroon in Port-au-Prince, see *Affiches américaines* (May 14, 1766). On maroons in Santo Domingo (15,000 by 1775), see M. de Valière and M. de Montarcher to M. de Boynes (July 6, 1772), c9a/141, ANOM.

17. "Plusieurs à la fois marrons" from Delribal to PB (Nov. 13, 1773), d. 12, 18AP/3, AN.

18. On private prisons, see Jean-François and Biassou to Mirbeck, Roume, St. Léger (Dec. 21, 1791), *D/XXV/1, AN. On Jean-Baptiste, see chap. 6. TL was perhaps free by 1773, which would explain his absence from the records.

19. For attempts to enforce the Code Noir, see Malick Ghachem, *The Old Regime and the Haitian Revolution* (Cambridge: Cambridge University Press, 2012), 133–143.

20. On the house, see "Vente de maison" (Oct. 15, 1772), ET/LXXXVI/735, AN. On Delribal's firing (effective Nov. 29, 1773), see Delribal to PB (Dec. 22, 1773), d. 12, 18AP/3, AN. Delribal died in 1780; see "Paroisse Notre-Dame" (1780), 1DDPC5339, ANOM (document communicated by Jean-Louis Donnadieu). The following account of FBL's tenure is based on d. 12, 18AP/3, AN; 261 MIOM, ANOM; JLD-PHD.

21. "Comme un Père" from TL to Directoire (July 18, 1797), *F7/7321, AN. "Il avait du talent" and "le reste était à charge" from FBL to PB (March 27, 1775, and Apr. 28, 1778), d. 12, 18AP/3, AN.

CHAPTER 5: FAMILY MAN, 1761–1785

1. "Une foule considérable" from MSM-DPF, 2:708–709. On the funeral, see [Burial record] (Nov. 17, 1785), 1DPPC2324, ANOM.

2. Toussaint Jr. was first mentioned in Jean-Louis Donnadieu, "La famille 'oubliée' de TL," *Bulletin de la Société Archéologique et Historique du Gers* 401 (Summer 2011): 357–365. Cécile was first mentioned in Dominique Rogers, *Les libres de couleur dans les capitales de SD: Fortune, mentalités et intégration à la fin de l'Ancien Régime (1776–1789)* (PhD diss., Université de Bordeaux III, 1999), 160. For an early reference to this marriage missed by scholars, see "Tableau généalogique" (c. 1900), d. 3, EE 1734, ANOM. For a reference to an earlier son, see Isaac Louverture to Jean de Chaudordy (Sept. 1, 1821), 6APC/1, ANOM.

3. On sex ratios, see David Geggus, "TL and the Slaves of the Bréda Plantations," *Journal of Caribbean History* 20, no. 1 (1985–1986): 35. This account of slave marriages is also based on Arlette Gautier, "Les familles esclaves aux Antilles françaises, 1635–1848," *Population* (Nov. 2000): 991; David Barry Gaspar and Darlene Clark Hine, eds., *More Than Chattel: Black Women and Slavery in the Americas* (Bloomington: Indiana University Press, 1996).

4. "Servitude" from Pierre de Charlevoix, *Histoire de l'isle Espagnole ou de SD* (Paris, 1730–1731), 2:505.

5. "Fort adonné à la boisson" from FBL to PB (Nov. 3, 1776), d. 12, 18AP/3, AN.

6. "Vos négresses" from FBL to PB (Nov. 3, 1776), d. 12, 18AP/3, AN. "C'est une pépinière" from [Valsemey?], "Esclaves existant" (Dec. 31, 1785), 261 MIOM, ANOM.

7. On Gabriel and Marie-Marthe, see [Marriage record] (Oct. 4, 1787), 1DPPC2326, ANOM. On the death of eleven children, see *Nouvelle Revue Rétrospective*, no. 94 (Apr. 10, 1902), 13.

8. "Rien de plus commun" from Pierre du Simitière, "De la ville et du quartier de Léogane" (c. 1774), 968.F.28, LCP.

9. On TL's grandchild, see "Liberté" (Jan. 11, 1783), NOT *SDOM 542, ANOM. The grandchild was first mentioned in Philippe Girard and Jean-Louis

Donnadieu, "Toussaint Before Louverture: New Archival Findings on the Early Life of TL," *William and Mary Quarterly* 70, no. 1 (Jan. 2013): 51. A mixed-race Toussaint who had served under TL (his grandson?) was shot in Cap during the war of independence; see Gt. Néraud to Rochambeau (Oct. 8, 1803), 61J17, ADGir.

10. "Ils souillent nos filles" (attributed to Boukman) from Antoine Métral, *Histoire de l'insurrection des esclaves dans le nord de SD* (Paris: Delaunay, 1818), 17.

11. On death rates and growth rates, see, for example, Paul Page, *Traité d'économie politique et de commerce des colonies* (Paris: Brochot, [1801–1802]), 1:14, 212. The following account of the Bréda plantations in the 1770s and 1780s is based on 261 MIOM, ANOM; d. 12, 18AP/3, AN; E691, ADLA.

12. "On en a acheté" from [Valsemey?], "Mémoire" (c. Dec. 31, 1785), 261 MIOM, ANOM. On the *bossale* rate, see Geggus, "Slaves of the Bréda Plantations," 35.

13. "Vous avez perdu" from FBL to PB (Apr. 30, 1774), d. 12, 18AP/3, AN. Hippolyte died Jan. 5, 1774, and Pauline died on Apr. 14, 1774; see [Valsemey?], "Tableau des Revenus . . ." (Dec. 31, 1785), 261 MIOM, ANOM.

14. "Une seconde mère" from IL-NH, 54. "Robuste" from [Valsemey?], "Esclaves existant" (Dec. 31, 1785), 261 MIOM, ANOM. Pélagie was born c. 1738 according to "Etat général des esclaves" (Apr. 4, 1785), d. 12, 18AP/3, AN.

15. On Baptiste's possible professions, see [Valsemey?], "Esclaves existant" (Dec. 31, 1785), 261 MIOM, ANOM. "Il savait le français" from IL-OTL. For literacy rates, see Rogers, *Les libres de couleur*, 516.

16. On Capuchin mores, see Leclerc, "Précis du mémoire" (Oct. 20, 1775), F5A 25/2, ANOM; "Au Roy" (c. 1776), C9B/27, ANOM. On Capuchin services, see Sue Peabody, "'A Dangerous Zeal': Catholic Missions to Slaves in the French Antilles, 1635–1800," *French Historical Studies* 25, no. 1 (Winter 2002): 85. "Vieux Capucin" from Beaubrun Ardouin, *Etudes sur l'histoire d'Haïti, suivies de la vie du général J-M Borgella* (Paris: Dezobry et Magdeleine, 1853–1860), 2:419.

17. "Les dimanches" from *Moniteur Universel* (Jan. 9, 1799). On slaves owned by the Catholic Church, see "Inventaire" (June 22–Aug. 15, 1773), F5A 23, ANOM.

18. For the first register, see "Etat général" (Apr. 4, 1785), d. 12, 18AP/3, AN. The first register was first transcribed in Gabriel Debien, "Sur la sucrerie Bréda du Haut-du-Cap, 1785," *Revue de la Faculté d'Ethnologie*, no. 10 (1965): 18–27. For the second register, see [Valsemey?], "Esclaves existant" (Dec. 31, 1785), 261 MIOM, ANOM. The second register was first transcribed in Jean-Louis Donnadieu and Philippe Girard, "Nouveaux documents sur la vie de TL," *Bulletin de la Société d'Histoire de la Guadeloupe* 166–167 (Sept. 2013–Apr. 2014): 117–139.

19. The 1785 roster was drafted after TL's nominal manumission; he may have been eager to show off his gratitude, because freedmen who failed to do so could be re-enslaved by law.

20. On TL's family network, see Girard and Donnadieu, "Toussaint Before Louverture," 41–78.

21. "Les seuls en lesquels" from TL to Christophe (May 13, 1800), AT-6, UPR-NC.

22. "Band of brothers" from Joseph J. Ellis, *Founding Brothers: The Revolutionary Generation* (New York: Knopf, 2000), 164.

CHAPTER 6: FREEDMAN, C. 1772–1779

1. The Apr. 7, 1776, baptism was first mentioned in Marie-Antoinette Menier, Gabriel Debien, and Jean Fouchard, "TL avant 1789: Légendes et réalités," *Conjonction* 134 (June–July 1977): 65–80. I could not locate the baptismal record in 1DPPC2319, ANOM, as of November 2014 (thanks to Jacques Dion and Jean-Louis Donnadieu for helping me look for the missing record). For evidence that the "Toussaint" in the act was indeed TL (which Menier et al. could not confirm), see [Baptismal record] (Jan. 19, 1784), 1DPPC2324, ANOM; [Valsemey?], "Esclaves existant" (Dec. 31, 1785), 261 MIOM, ANOM. There may have been earlier mentions of TL as a freedman, but French baptismal and notarial records only go back to 1776.

2. On the odds of being freed, see David Barry Gaspar and Darlene Clark Hine, eds., *More Than Chattel: Black Women and Slavery in the Americas* (Bloomington: Indiana University Press, 1996), 268. On Geneviève, see Pierre Bardin, "Langlois de Chancy–TL," *Généalogie et Histoire de la Caraïbe* 92 (Apr. 1997): 1944. Eleven percent figure calculated from Le Brasseur to de Castries (July 26, 1781), c9a/151, ANOM.

3. "Le fardeau pesant" from TL to Directory (July 18, 1797), d. B4/5915, *F7/7321, AN. For rumors about TL's manumission, see François de Kerversau, "Rapport sur la partie française de SD" (March 22, 1801), Box 2/66, UF-RP.

4. "Une punition rigoureuse" from Alfred de Lacaze [probably a relative of Placide Louverture], "Louverture," in Dr. Hoefer, ed., *Nouvelle biographie générale depuis les temps les plus reculés jusqu'à nos jours* (Paris: Firmin Didot Frères, 1860), 32:38. On the maroon Toussaint, see *Affiches américaines* (Sept. 5, 1772). On FBL's coachmen, see FBL to PB (Nov. 3, 1776), d. 12, 18AP/3, AN.

5. "Mon ancien patron" from TL to Directory (July 18, 1797), d. B4/5915, *F7/7321, AN.

6. For the manumission process, see MSM-LC, 2:398; 3:453; 5:190, 807; 6:499. On the tax, see MSM-LC, 5:577. On PB being unaware of TL's manumission, see his letters in d. 12, 18AP3, AN (which never mention TL); and the Dec. 31, 1785, plantation register sent to PB, which erroneously described TL as a slave. If TL's manumission deed is ever to be found, possible locations include the Bréda letters in 18AP/3, AN; the *greffe* (clerk of court) records in 7DPPC, ANOM; the governors' letters in C9, ANOM; the papers of Bréda's Parisian notary in ET/LXXXVI, AN; and the manumission records in NOT SDOM REP 116, ANOM.

7. For the census data, see Charles Frostin, *Les révoltes blanches à SD aux XVIIe et XVIIIe siècles (Haïti avant 1789)* (Paris: L'Ecole, 1975), 28.

8. For the one-third claim, see Julien Raimond's May 13, 1791, speech in Anon., *Réimpression de l'Ancien Moniteur* (Paris: René, 1861), 8:399. For the 10 percent estimate, see John D. Garrigus, *Before Haiti: Race and Citizenship in French SD* (New York: Palgrave, 2006), 255.

9. On Jean-Baptiste, see Abbé Delaporte, [Marriage certificate] (Sept. 3, 1777), 1DPPC2319, ANOM.

10. On Jean-Baptiste, see Delribal to PB (Aug. 18, 1773), d. 12, 18AP/3, AN.

11. On the manumission tax for women of childbearing age (2,000 livres), see MSM-LC, 5:577.

12. "Afin que les enfants" (a reference to either Suzanne or Cécile) from Jean-Louis Clavier, "TL d'après le 'Mémoire abrégé . . . ,'" *Revue Française d'Histoire d'Outre-Mer* 62, no. 228 (1975): 467. For the first mention of Cécile as a freed-woman, see "Testament" (Nov. 14, 1778), NOT *SDOM 524, ANOM. On trying to buy Tony's freedom, see FBL to PB (Nov. 3, 1776), d. 12, 18AP/3, AN. On a slave possibly owned by Cécile, see *Affiches américaines* (Sept. 14, 1779).

13. On Marie-Marthe's first husband, see "Bail" (Aug. 17, 1779), NOT *SDOM 525, ANOM. On Toussaint Jr. being free in 1785 and Gabriel in 1787, see [Burial record] (Nov. 17, 1785), 1DPPC2324, ANOM; [Marriage record] (Oct. 4, 1787), 1DPPC2326, ANOM.

14. For the 1785 registers, see chap. 8. On Marie-Rose (who may have been freed by the white father of her older daughter), see [Baptismal record] (Jan. 19, 1784), 1DPPC2324, ANOM. On Pélagie, see chap. 10.

15. On TL's grandchild, see "Liberté" (Jan. 11, 1783), NOT *SDOM 542, ANOM.

16. On the lot bought by TL, see "Vente d'emplacement" (Aug. 18, 1779), NOT *SDOM 525, ANOM.

17. On FBL's stops, see "Extrait des minutes" (June 26, 1779), COL E21, ANOM. On TL serving food, see Adolphe Cabon, *Notes sur l'histoire religieuse d'Haïti de la révolution au concordat (1789–1860)* (Port-au-Prince: Petit séminaire collège saint-Martial, 1933), 44. Biassou worked on La Charité's plantation in Petite Anse; see "Notes de Mr. Leclerc" (c. 1803), CC9A/5, ANOM.

18. The following description of Cap is based on "Recensement" (June 27, 1776) and "Table du cartulaire" (Nov. 11, 1787), *g/1/495, DPPC, ANOM; R. Phelipeaux, "Plan de la ville du Cap Français" (1785), Caribbean Map Collection, University of Florida, Gainesville; MSM-DPF, 1:293–483.

19. On Christophe, see Alfred de Laujon, *Souvenirs de trente années de voyages à SD, dans plusieurs colonies étrangères, et au continent d'Amérique* (Paris: Schwartz and Gagnot, 1835), 1:355.

20. On untamed horses, see IL-NH, 77. On the ban on galloping, see MSM-LC, 4:498.

21. On the theater of Cap, see MSM-LC, 6:734, 778. "Profession criminelle" from Père Colomban, "Demande . . ." (Dec. 27, 1775), F5A 25/3, ANOM. On *Othello*, see PG-MGTL, 137.

22. On the 1777 execution, see MSM-DPF, 1:332. People of color were executed on Clugny Square by the 1770s.

23. For Bordier's records, see NOT SDOM 168–203, ANOM.

24. "Une jetée prise sur la mer" from Laujon, *Souvenirs de trente années*, 1:353.

25. On Aaron Sasportas, see "Procuration" (Feb. 14, 1780), NOT *SDOM 1627, DPPC, ANOM; FBL, "Compte-rendu" (Apr. 4, 1785), d. 12, 18AP/3, AN. On Corneille, see TL to Laveaux (Nov. 11, 1795), fr. 12103, BNF; Henry Christophe, *The Formation of the New Dynasty of the Kingdom of Hayti* (Philadelphia, 1811), Y*49, HSP.

26. On the Bunels, see Philippe Girard, "Trading Races: Joseph and Marie Bunel. A Diplomat and a Merchant in Revolutionary SD and Philadelphia," *Journal of the Early Republic* 30 (Fall 2010): 351–376. Marie Mouton was officially freed in 1781; see Le Brasseur to de Castries (July 26, 1781), c9a/151, ANOM.

27. On Olivier, see *Affiches américaines* (March 21, 1780); MSM-DPF, 1:224.

28. On Blaise Bréda, see Jean-Louis Donnadieu, *Un grand seigneur et ses esclaves: Le comte de Noé entre Antilles et Gascogne, 1728–1816* (Toulouse: Presses Universitaires du Mirail, 2009), 103.

29. On Provoyeur, see chap. 7.

30. On Jasmin (aka Aloou Kinson), see Cercle des Philadelphes to Intendant (July 30, 1789), 61J5, ADGir; COL E229, ANOM.

CHAPTER 7: SLAVE DRIVER, 1779–1781

1. For the lease (first discovered in 1977), see "Bail" (Aug. 17, 1779), NOT *SDOM 525, ANOM. On Désir's marriage to Marie-Marthe, see Frère Julien, [Burial record] (Nov. 16, 1784), 1DPPC 2384, ANOM.

2. On free people of color, see Dominique Rogers, *Les libres de couleur dans les capitales de SD: Fortune, mentalités et intégration à la fin de l'Ancien Régime (1776–1789)* (PhD diss., Université de Bordeaux III, 1999); Stewart R. King, *Blue Coat or Powdered Wig: Free People of Color in Pre-Revolutionary SD* (Athens: University of Georgia Press, 2001); John D. Garrigus, *Before Haiti: Race and Citizenship in French SD* (New York: Palgrave, 2006).

3. On the appearance of racism, see Pierre H. Boulle, *Race et esclavage dans la France de l'Ancien Régime* (Paris: Perrin, 2007), 63–68. "Persuasion intime" from M. J. La Neuville, *Le dernier cri de SD et des colonies* (Philadelphia: Bradford, 1800), 15. "L'intérêt et la sûreté" from Michel Hilliard d'Auberteuil, *Considérations sur l'état présent de la colonie française de SD* (Paris: Grangé, 1776), 2:73.

4. "Taches" from Huard du Parc to Louis XVI (March 8, 1783), COL E 21, ANOM. On the Chapuizet case, see also MSM-LC, 5:879–882, 895; 6:500.

5. On TL's apparent sympathy toward Chapuizet, see PMD-PH, 2:168. For a 1779 naturalization case involving a Jewish family tied to SD, see COL E210, ANOM.

6. On discriminatory laws, see MSM-LC, 4:412; 5:5, 80, 166, 448, 520, 762, 855; 6:238, 717. "O vous, nos pères!" from Michel Mina, *Adresse à l'Assemblée Nationale par les hommes de couleur libres de SD* (c. July 1790), 10.

7. For the manumission of TL's grandson, see "Liberté" (Jan. 11, 1783), NOT *SDOM 542, ANOM.

8. "Chasse" from "Nous certifions" (Apr. 12, 1780), E57, ANOM.

9. For a lawsuit with Françoise Bonnefoy, see FBL to PB (June 9 and Oct. 21, 1777), d. 12, 18AP/3, AN. With François Bessière, see Jean-Louis Donnadieu, *Un grand seigneur et ses esclaves: Le comte de Noé entre Antilles et Gascogne, 1728–1816* (Toulouse: Presses Universitaires du Mirail, 2009), 179. With Zabeth Port-de-Paix, see PB to FBL (Apr. 20, 1782), d. 12, 18AP/3, AN. With Guillaume Provoyeur, see FBL to Polastron (Feb. 21, 1787), d. 2, 73J1, ADGir. With the Aulnays, see FBL to PB (July 7, 1783), d. 12, 18AP/3, AN. On TL submitting to white harassment, see Thomas Madiou, *Histoire d'Haïti* (Port-au-Prince: Courtois, 1847), 2:125.

10. "Self-evident" from the US Declaration of Independence (July 4, 1776). On rumors of abolition, see d'Ennery and de Vaivres to de Sartine (June 25, 1776), C9A/144, ANOM. The following account of the Bréda plantation in 1776–1783 is drawn from *Affiches américaines* and d. 12, 18AP/3, AN.

11. "Il serait malheureux" from FBL to PB (Feb. 8, 1777), d. 12, 18AP/3, AN. "Tout le monde croit" from FBL to PB (Jan. 2, 1778), d. 12, 18AP/3, AN.

12. On the militia controversy, see MSM-LC, vols. 4 and 5; Charles Frostin, *Les révoltes blanches à SD aux XVIIe et XVIIIe siècles (Haïti avant 1789)* (Paris: L'Ecole, 1975), 297–341. On d'Estaing's losses, see "Liste générale des malades . . ." (Nov. 24, 1779), HOP86, DPPC, ANOM. On creating a volunteer unit, see MSM-LC, 5:860–869.

13. On the motives for enrolling among free men of color, see Laurent de Rouvray, "Extrait d'un mémoire sur la création d'un corps de gens de couleur" (1779), DFC/XXXIII/Mémoires/3/doc. 10, ANOM.

14. On Rigaud in Savannah, see André Rigaud to Napoléon Bonaparte (July 13, 1802), B7/5, SHD-DAT. On Dessalines, see Desaline [*sic*], "Etat des services" (c. 1796), COL E129, ANOM. For other famous Haitians allegedly in Savannah, see King, *Blue Coat or Powdered Wig*, xv.

15. For the lease, see "Bail" (Aug. 17, 1779), NOT *SDOM 525, ANOM.

16. On the land sale, see "Vente d'emplacement" (Aug. 18, 1779), NOT *SDOM 525, ANOM.

17. On Grande-Rivière, see MSM-DPF, 1:220–230.

18. Dessalines's ties to TL were independently revealed in Jacques de Cauna, "Dessalines esclave de Toussaint?" *Outre-Mers: Revue d'Histoire* 374–375 (June 2012): 319–322, and Philippe Girard, "Jean-Jacques Dessalines and the Atlantic System: A Reappraisal," *William and Mary Quarterly* 69, no. 3 (July 2012): 555.

19. On the Savannah expedition, see *Affiches américaines* (Nov. 16, 1779); John Garrigus, "Catalyst or Catastrophe? SD's Free Men of Color and the Savannah Expedition, 1779–1782," *Review / Revista Interamericana* 22 (1992): 109–125.

20. On the hurricane, see Reynaud and Le Brasseur to de Sartine (Dec. 1, 1780), c9a/148, ANOM. "Le pays est dévasté" from FBL to PB (March 10, 1781), d. 12, 18AP/3, AN.

21. On selling part of the lot, see "Vente de terrain" (May 25, 1781), NOT *SDOM 178, ANOM. Désir probably returned with the de Grasse fleet; see Le Brasseur to de Castries (July 26, 1781), c9a/151, ANOM. On the end of the

lease and the death of two slaves (Marie-Marthe and François), see "Résiliation de bail" (July 31, 1781), NOT *SDOM 178, ANOM.

22. On the 648,000 francs claim, see PG-MGTL, 4. On TL allegedly traveling to France and being a Freemason, see Madison Smartt Bell, *TL: A Biography* (New York: Pantheon Books, 2007), 17, 60, 63. "Hob-nobbed" from David Geggus, "TL," *New West Indian Guide* 84, nos. 1–2 (2010): 157. Evidence for the trip to France are two later accounts by Camille Fleuriot de Langle and the Marquis de la Jaille; see Auguste Nemours, *Histoire de la famille et de la descendance de TL* (Port-au-Prince: Imprimerie de l'Etat, 1941), 4; Gabriel Debien and Philip Wright, "Les colons de SD passés à la Jamaïque (1792–1835)," *Notes d'Histoire Coloniale* 168 (1976): 152–157. Evidence hinting at TL's possible membership in a Freemason lodge are dots in his signature and a later lodge register mentioning his brother Paul; see "Tableau des F.F. composant la R. L. la Réunion Désirée . . . ," 1800, Fonds maçonnique 2, BNF.

23. For the register, see [Valsemey?], "Esclaves existant" (Dec. 31, 1785), 261 MIOM, ANOM. The register was first published in Jean-Louis Donnadieu and Philippe Girard, "Nouveaux documents sur la vie de TL," *Bulletin de la Société d'Histoire de la Guadeloupe* 166–167 (Sept. 2013–Apr. 2014): 117–139. TL's name also appears on an earlier register dated April 1785 but without the details found in the December 1785 register.

24. On VD, see FBL to PB (July 7, 1783), d. 12, 18AP/3, AN. On Gálvez, see MSM-DPF, 1:342, 366, 539, 592.

25. On the hospital, see MSM-DPF, 1:596. Most soldiers left in 1782; see FBL to PB (June 18, 1782), d. 12, 18AP/3, AN.

26. On Provoyeur (aka Mirbalizia), see Dominique Rogers, *Les libres de couleur dans les capitales de SD: Fortune, mentalités et intégration à la fin de l'Ancien Régime (1776–1789)* (PhD diss., Université de Bordeaux III, 1999), 106, 623. For the first will, see "Testament" (Nov. 14, 1778), NOT *SDOM 524, ANOM (document communicated by Jean-Louis Donnadieu). On buying lots in Haut-du-Cap, see "Vente d'emplacement" (May 28, 1781) and "Vente de terrain" (July 17, 1781), NOT *SDOM 178, ANOM. For the second will, see Pierre-Guillaume Provoyeur, "Testament" (June 23, 1782), NOT *SDOM 180, ANOM.

27. Cécile was still alive in 1787; see [Marriage record] (Oct. 4, 1787), 1DPPC2326, ANOM.

28. On Jasmin's death, see Frère Julien, [Burial record] (Nov. 16, 1784), 1DPPC 2384, ANOM. On Toussaint Jr.'s death, see [Burial record] (Nov. 17, 1785), 1DPPC2324, ANOM. On the possibility that Gabriel Toussaint survived the Revolution, see Isaac Louverture to Chaudordy (Sept. 1, 1821), 6APC/1, ANOM. On Marie-Marthe's probable return to Haut-du-Cap, see the two Marie-Marthes listed in the Apr. 4 and Dec. 31, 1785, plantation registers, both doing little or no work. On Marie-Marthe's second marriage, see [Marriage record] (Oct. 4, 1787), 1DPPC2326, ANOM.

29. On Dessalines's career, see Desaline [*sic*], "Etat des services" (c. 1796), COL E129, ANOM. On Janvier Dessalines as a slave owner, as well as Marie-Louise Dessalines (a relative?), see "Vente mulâtresse" (Sept. 30, 1782), and

"Vente négritte" (Feb. 24, 1785), NOT *SDOM 1362, ANOM. On ties between Janvier Dessalines and Belley, see [Acte de mariage] (July 10, 1780), 1DPPC 2322, ANOM.

CHAPTER 8: MULETEER, 1781–1789

1. "C'est un des plus beaux points de vue" from Jean-Louis Donnadieu, "Un officier français face à la Révolution outre-mer, les infortunes du lieutenant-colonel Jacques d'Ounous à SD, aux Etats-Unis et en Louisiane (1792–1802)," *Revue Historique des Armées* 265 (Winter 2011): 78.

2. "Maître moulinier" from [Valsemey?], "Esclaves existant" (Dec. 31, 1785), 261 MIOM, ANOM.

3. "Arpents de neige" from Charles Lahure, ed., *Œuvres complètes de Voltaire* (Paris: Hachette, 1860), 15:138.

4. On the number of plantations, see MSM-DPF, 1:100. On exports, see Barré de Saint-Venant, *Des colonies modernes sous la zone torride, et particulièrement de celle de SD* (Paris: Brochot, 1802), 102. The following overview of Haut-du-Cap in the 1780s is based on d.12, 18AP3, AN; JLD-PHD; E691, ADLA; 261 MIOM, ANOM.

5. For salary levels, see Simon Schama, *Citizens: A Chronicle of the French Revolution* (New York: Knopf, 1989), 306. The colonial *livre* was worth one-third less than the French *livre*.

6. On a steam engine, see Anon., "Projet de souscription . . ." (c. July 1778), EB S137 1770 1, JCB.

7. On sugar cultivation, see Saint-Venant, *Des colonies modernes*, 322–418. On singing, see [François Laplace], *Histoire des désastres de SD* (Paris: Garnery, 1795), 88.

8. "Trahison" from "Etat général" (Apr. 4, 1785), d. 12, 18AP/3, AN.

9. On the balloon flight, see MSM-DPF, 1:288. Gallifet had a reputation for being kind to its slaves (see MSM-DPF, 1:277), but the evidence suggests otherwise; see 107 AP/127, AN. On the scientific society (which was in contact with its counterpart in Philadelphia), see Baudry des Lozières, "Discours" (Aug. 22, 1784), 506.7294 C33.1, no. 2, APS.

10. "Chaque Habitant est . . . un Manufacturier" from MSM-LC, 4:644. On slaves as blue-collar workers, see Aimé Césaire, *TL: La révolution française et le problème colonial* (Paris: Présence Africaine, 1981), 37.

11. "Ami" and "fredaines" from Beaubrun Ardouin, *Etudes sur l'histoire d'Haïti, suivies de la vie du général J-M Borgella* (Paris: Dezobry et Magdeleine, 1853–1860), 1:227.

12. "De Libertat" from FBL to PB (Dec. 22, 1772), d. 12, 18AP/3, AN. On falsely claiming noble status, see MSM-LC, 5:184; 6:30, 549.

13. On FBL's in-laws, see E362, ANOM.

14. "Plus nègre que blanc" from FBL to PB (June 9, 1777), d. 12, 18AP/3, AN. "Quel Spectacle" from [Valsemey?], "Mémoire" (c. Dec. 31, 1785), 261 MIOM, ANOM.

15. On Hippolyte / Jean-Jacques, see FBL to Count of Noé (May 19, May 27, and Aug. 2, 1782), JLD-PHD.

16. On domestics in Haut-du-Cap, see "Esclaves existant" (Dec. 31, 1785), 261 MIOM, ANOM. On domestics in Gallifet, see "Recensement des nègres . . ." (Jan. 1783), 107AP/127, AN. "Goût de paresse" from [Valsemey?], "Mémoire" (c. Dec. 31, 1785), 261 MIOM, ANOM.

17. On a union dating back to c. 1778, see *Moniteur Universel* (Jan. 9, 1799). On Isaac's birth on Oct. 19, 1784, see "Etat général" (Apr. 4, 1785), d. 12, 18AP/3, AN. "Married" from [Valsemey?], "Esclaves existant" (Dec. 31, 1785), 261 MIOM, ANOM. On Cécile being alive in 1787, see [Marriage record] (Oct. 4, 1787), 1DPPC2326, ANOM. "Mariage à la créole" from Thomas Gragnon-Lacoste, *TL* (Paris: Durand, 1877), 15. No official marriage between TL and Suzanne Louverture appears in the marriage records of Cap in 1777–1788; see 1DDPC5339, ANOM. Marriages required manumission papers, which could have created a problem if TL lacked them; see MSM-LC, 5:807. Alternatively, perhaps a marriage was celebrated but not recorded due to endemic poor recordkeeping; see Frère Julien to De Castries (Sept. 30, 1785), F5A 25/1, ANOM. Bigamy was frequent in SD; see De Choiseul to [de Sartines?] (May 8, 1777), c9a/145, ANOM.

18. For a possible mulatto daughter of Suzanne, see *Affiches américaines* (July 17, 1781). Placide claimed he was TL's biological son so that he could claim his father's inheritance; see "Extrait des minutes . . ." (Apr. 15, 1821), TLF-1A3b, UPR-NC. Several authors have mistakenly followed his lead, including Auguste Nemours, *Histoire de la famille et de la descendance de TL* (Port-au-Prince: Imprimerie de l'Etat, 1941), 10–21. But Placide was a *griffe*; see "Les enfants de TL" (Oct. 7, 1801), d. 5410, F/7/6266, AN. Placide may have been related to Marie Clere, who served as godmother alongside TL in a Jan. 19, 1784, baptism; see 1DPPC2324, ANOM.

19. "Avalasses" from FBL to PB (Oct. 21, 1777), d. 12, 18AP/3, AN. On soil erosion on the Morne du Cap, see MSM-DPF, 1:596, 598.

20. For PB's will, see "Inventaire" (July 20, 1786), et/LXXXVI/847, AN. "Tout l'ascendant" from FBL to Mr. and Mrs. de Polastron (Feb. 21, 1787), E691, ADLA.

21. On SD's production, see R. Lepelletier de Saint-Rémy, *SD: Etude et solution nouvelle de la question haïtienne* (Paris: Arthus Bertrand, 1846), 60, 66. On production in the British Caribbean (99 million colonial livres in 1788) and the number of workers tied to trade to SD, see Saint-Venant, *Des colonies modernes*, 102, 154. For re-export numbers, see Marcel Dorigny, ed., *The Abolitions of Slavery: From Léger Félicité Sonthonax to Victor Schoelcher, 1793, 1794, 1848* (New York: Berghahn, 2003), 238. On the number of ships, see Paul Butel, "Succès et déclin du commerce colonial français, de la Révolution à la Restauration," *Revue Economique* 40, no. 6 (1989): 1079–1082. On the number of sailors, see "Questions sur la population . . ." (c. 1785), DFC/XXXIII/Mémoires/3/202, ANOM.

22. On Auberteuil, see Michel Hilliard d'Auberteuil, *Considérations sur l'état présent de la colonie française de SD* (Paris: Grangé, 1776), 1:147, 236–244. On profit rates in the 1780s, see Justin Girod-Chantrans, *Voyage d'un Suisse dans différentes colonies d'Amérique* (Neuchatel: Société typographique, 1785), 129; Francis Alexander Stanislaus Wimpffen, *A Voyage to Saint Domingo in the Years*

1788, 1789, and 1790 (London: T. Cadell, 1797), 75, 78. There is no French equivalent to the rich historiography on the profitability of British Caribbean and US plantations; the closest is Caroline Oudin-Bastide and Philippe Steiner, *Calcul et morale: Coûts de l'esclavage et valeur de l'émancipation (XVIIIe–XIXe siècle)* (Paris: Albin Michel, 2015), which mostly repeats contemporary claims.

23. "La sécheresse," "un ouragan pareil," "34 ans" from FBL to PB (June 29, 1776, Nov. 24, 1780, Apr. 18, 1784), d. 12, 18AP/3, AN. "Un temps semblable" from [FBL] to [Count of Polastron] (Feb. 28, 1788), E691, ADLA. On losses at the pottery (23,000 livres in 1784–1785), see "Inventaire" (July 20, 1786), et/LXXXVI/847, AN. On Manquets, see FBL to PB (Aug. 27, 1778), d. 12, 18AP/3, AN.

24. For production figures, see 261 MIOM, ANOM.

25. On FBL's shortcomings, see [Valsemey?], "Mémoire" (c. Dec. 31, 1785), 261 MIOM, ANOM; Count of Butler to Count of Polastron (Oct. 8, 1788), E691, ADLA.

26. On the deal with the merchant, see Lardin to M. de Polastron (Oct. 22, 1786), E691, ADLA.

27. On war costs, see Schama, *Citizens*, 62, 65. On the budget of the secretary of the navy, see P. Fr. Page, *Traité d'économie politique et de commerce des colonies* (Paris: Brochot, 1801), 1:143. On the 5 million livres octroi, see MSM-LC, 5:313. "Soutenu" from MSM-LC, 5:670.

CHAPTER 9: WITNESS, 1788–1791

1. On the Lejeune case, see F3/90, ANOM; Malick Ghachem, *The Old Regime and the Haitian Revolution* (Cambridge: Cambridge University Press, 2012), 167–210.

2. No slave ever prevailed in court according to Joan Dayan, *Haiti, History, and the Gods* (1995; reprint, Berkeley: University of California Press, 1998), 202. But some white owners were sentenced to pay a fine or sell their slave, and a black master was whipped, branded, and sentenced to hard labor; see MSM-LC, 6:622.

3. On the *gouverneur* and *intendant*, see MSM-LC, 4:159, 538; 5:13, 577. The following section on pre-1789 white riots is based on C9A, ANOM; MSM-LC; Charles Frostin, *Les révoltes blanches à SD aux XVIIe et XVIIIe siècles (Haïti avant 1789)* (Paris: L'Ecole, 1975).

4. "Puissances alliées" (Blin de Villeneuve) from GC-RTSD, 1:149.

5. On the 1722–1723 revolt, see Pierre de Charlevoix, *Histoire de l'Isle Espagnole ou de SD* (Amsterdam: François l'Honoré, 1733), 221–312.

6. Chambers of agriculture were created to dilute the power of the Conseils Supérieurs but they proved just as troublesome; see MSM-LC, 4:281, 603, 862.

7. "Les administrateurs actuels" from FBL to [Count of Polastron] (May 4, 1788), E691, ADLA.

8. On balancing the budget, see François Barbé de Marbois, *Etat des Finances de SD . . .* (Paris: Imprimerie Royale, 1790), SA 2151.4.7*, HU-HL. On the capitation tax, see FBL to Count of Noé (June 12, 1787), JLD-PHD. On the labor tax, see PB to FBL (Apr. 22, 1784), d. 12, 18AP/3, AN; de Marbois to La Luzerne (July 20, 1788), E362 ter, ANOM.

9. On transatlantic contacts, see Brissot de Warville to Benjamin Franklin (Jan. 20, 1790), Micr. XR572:11, HSP.

10. On reformist administrators, see Pierre-Victor de Malouet to M. de Barré (Dec. 28, 1777), d. 492, 73J87, ADGir; Michel Hilliard d'Auberteuil, *Considérations sur l'état présent de la colonie française de SD* (Paris: Grangé, 1776), 1:vii, 130–146; Pierre Pluchon, *TL* (Paris: Fayard, 1989), 23. For the ordinance, see MSM-LC, 6:655. "Nous ne serons plus les maîtres" from FBL to PB (Apr. 16, 1785), d. 12, 18AP/3, AN.

11. "Slaves" from Auberteuil, *Considérations*, 2:13.

12. "Le découragement est général" from FBL to [Count of Polastron] (May 4, 1788), E691, ADLA. On Saint-Martin's resignation, see De Marbois to La Luzerne (Oct. 12, 1788), E362 ter, ANOM. On the merger of the superior courts, see also MSM-DPF, 2:343–345. The Conseil Supérieur of Cap was reestablished in January 1790; see Assemblée Provinciale du Nord, "Discours" (Jan. 11, 1790), CC9A/4, ANOM.

13. "Un désordre affreux" from FBL to PB (Apr. 16, 1785), d. 12, 18AP/3, AN. "Il ne manque aux nègres" (passage probably written by Diderot, and which does not feature in all editions) from Guillaume Raynal, *Histoire philosophique et politique des établissements et du commerce des Européens dans les deux Indes* (La Haye: 1774), 4:226. On TL allegedly reading Raynal (a story possibly invented to emphasize his long-standing love of liberty), see *Moniteur Universel* (Jan. 9, 1799).

14. On the rebels' late embrace of independence, see Philippe Girard, "Birth of a Nation: The Creation of the Haitian Flag and Haiti's French Revolutionary Heritage," *Journal of Haitian Studies* 15, nos. 1–2 (Spring–Fall 2009): 135–150.

15. "Le climat en fera raison" FBL to PB (Dec. 13, 1785), d. 12, 18AP/3, AN.

16. On duels, see Honoré le Comte, "Mémoire" (July 1, 1779), c9a/147, ANOM. On the riot, see MSM-DPF, 1:287.

17. "Cela fait horreur" from FBL to Mr. and Mrs. de Polastron (July 28, 1787), E691, ADLA. The following overview of the white revolution in 1789–1791 is based mainly on GC-RTSD; Louis de Blanchelande, "Mémoire . . . sur son administration" (July 1, 1791), 1-SIZE E791.B641m, JCB. On the colonial debate in France, see also Yves Bénot, *La révolution française et la fin des colonies* (Paris: La Découverte, 1988).

18. On Noé as a deputy, see Jean-Louis Donnadieu, *Un grand seigneur et ses esclaves: Le comte de Noé entre Antilles et Gascogne, 1728–1816* (Toulouse: Presses Universitaires du Mirail, 2009), 191, 197. On the Club Massiac, see David Geggus and Norman Fiering, eds., *The World of the Haitian Revolution* (Bloomington: Indiana University Press, 2009), 203.

19. "ON EST IVRE DE LIBERTE" from *Correspondance secrète des colons députés à l'Assemblée Constituante* (Paris: Anjubault, c. Feb. 1794), 7.

20. "Inconcevable révolution" from Count of Polastron to Viscount of Butler (Oct. 17, 1789), E691, ADLA. "Une espèce d'anarchie" from Jean Langlois de Laheuse to Count of Noé (June 24, 1789), JLD-PHD.

21. For the constitution, see "Décret de l'Assemblée Générale" (May 28, 1790), Folder 1A, HU-KFC. For other laws of the assembly, see PMD-PH, 1:22–27.

22. "Licencier les troupes réglées" from M. de Villevaleix to Count of Polastron (July 31, 1790), E691, ADLA. On dissatisfaction with the assembly, see also *Extrait des archives de l'assemblée provinciale du nord de SD* (Cap: Imprimerie Royale, June 30, 1790), *FC7.H1277A.790e, HU-HL. On the exile of the *léopardins*, see Journals and M.S. Papers of Nathaniel Cutting, esq., pp. 400–450, P-275, reel 1, MHS; d'Augy et al. to [Assemblée Nationale?] (Sept. 13, 1790), p. 15, F/3/196, ANOM.

23. On Blanchelande, see Jeremy Popkin, "The French Revolution's Royal Governor: General Blanchelande and Saint Domingue, 1790–92," *William and Mary Quarterly* 71, no. 2 (Apr. 2014): 203–228. On Mauduit's death, see PMD-PH, 1:26–29, 39–40. A powerless interim *intendant* remained in Port-au-Prince; see the Proisy letters in F/3/197, ANOM.

24. "Surrounded by mulattoes" from Francis de Wimpffen, *A Voyage to Saint Domingo in the Years 1788, 1789, and 1790* (London: T. Cadell, 1797), 335.

25. On Raimond, see John D. Garrigus, *Before Haiti: Race and Citizenship in French SD* (New York: Palgrave, 2006), 1, 234–249.

26. On calls for equality among free people of color, see Michel Mina, *Adresse à l'Assemblée Nationale par les hommes de couleur libres de SD* (c. July 1790). "Je fis la rencontre d'un blanc" from Thomas Madiou, *Histoire d'Haïti* (Port-au-Prince: Courtois, 1847), 2:125.

27. "Voilà l'Esclave" in "Copie du Mémoire du Sr Ogé" (Sept. 7, 1789), D/XXV/58, AN (document communicated by John Garrigus). The following overview of the Ogé revolt is based on D/XXV/58, AN; E 325 and E 396, ANOM; F3/196, ANOM. The two best studies of Ogé are Beaubrun Ardouin, *Etudes sur l'histoire d'Haïti, suivies de la vie du général J-M Borgella* (Paris: Dezobry et Magdeleine, 1853–1860), 1:133–163; John Garrigus, "Vincent Ogé Jeune (1757–91): Social Class and Free Colored Mobilization on the Eve of the Haitian Revolution," *Americas* 68, no. 1 (July 2011): 33–62. Drawing from Ogé's interrogation, in which he minimized his role, Garrigus portrays Ogé as a more moderate figure than Ardouin does drawing from Spanish sources (I tend to side with Ardouin).

28. On Veuve Ogé, see Poissac and Dupuy, "Mémoire" (c. 1777), E 396, ANOM. "I begin not to care" (citing Ogé) from Thomas Clarkson to [Joseph Arnould] (Aug. 13, 1828), in Charles Mackenzie, *Notes on Haiti Made During a Residence in That Republic* (1830; reprint, London: Frank Cass, 1971), 2:246–250.

29. "Nous nommerons des électeurs" from Ogé jeune to M. [Alexandre] de Vincent (Oct. 29, 1790), d. 770, D/XXV/78, AN. For other letters sent the same day, see F/3/196, p. 111, ANOM.

30. "Si nous n'avons que ces ennemis" from Mr. de Villevaleix to Count of Polastron (Oct. 31, 1790), E691, ADLA.

31. "Cherchant à être assimilé aux blancs" from "Jacques Ogé dit Jacquot" (March 9–10, 1791), p. 393, F/3/196, ANOM. "Dans le cas où ils auraient du dessous" from "Copie de la Deposition faitte par le nommé Blanc" (Nov. 3, 1790), D/XXV/58, AN. "Brigands" from Ardouin, *Etudes*, 1:133–163. On Ogé's extradition, see Carlos Esteban Deive, *Los Refugiados Franceses en Santo Domingo, 1789–1801* (Santo Domingo: Universidad Nacional Pedro Henríquez Ureña, 1984), 71.

32. TL possibly knew Ogé because (1) TL had managed a coffee estate near Grande-Rivière in 1779–1781; (2) Ogé tried to recruit a coachman of FBL's brother's in-law Guillaume Bullet; see "Extraits de lettres du Cap" (Oct. 30, 1790), F3/196, p. 115, ANOM; (3) Fleury, who signed the Nov. 17, 1785, death certificate of TL's son, may be the same Fleury who was an ally of Ogé and later a mayor of Cap. On Jean-Baptiste Cap, see Attorney of Clément plantation, "Révolution de SD" (c. Oct. 10, 1792), F3/131, ANOM.

33. On Ogé's sentence, see *Arrêt du Conseil Supérieur du Cap contre le nommé Ogé jeune et ses accomplices, du 5 mars 1791* (Cap Français, 1791).

34. "La liberté" from TL, "Frères et amis" (Aug. 29, 1793), d. 1490, aa53/a, AN. On TL's later misgivings when he began to see mixed-race revolutionaries as political rivals, see TL to Laveaux (Apr. 21, 1796), fr. 12104, BNF. "La haine de Toussaint" from Philippe Roume to Pierre Forfait (Dec. 2, 1801), Roume Papers, LC-MD.

35. The famous quote "périssent les colonies plutôt qu'un principe" is an amalgam of two sentences by the deputies Dupont and Robespierre; see *Moniteur Universel* (May 15, 1791) (both men were likely inspired by the entry "Traite des nègres" in the 1766 *Encyclopédie*). "Le spectacle du désordre" from "Instructions du Roi" (Aug. 10, 1791), F/3/197, ANOM. On the 1791 instructions, see also docs. 137–139, B277, ANOM.

36. "Massive resistance" from d'Augy to Habitants de la Province du Nord de SD (June 7, 1791), Box 1, Sc. MG 119, NYPL-SC. "Civil war" from Sylvanus Bourne to [US Secretary of State?] (July 14, 1791), RG 59, Microfilm M446/1, NARA-CP.

CHAPTER 10: REBEL, 1791

1. "La négresse Pélagie" from Maître Grimperel, "Mise en possession" (July 5, 1789), E691, ADLA. Pélagie was first mentioned in Philippe Girard and Jean-Louis Donnadieu, "Toussaint Before Louverture: New Archival Findings on the Early Life of TL," *William and Mary Quarterly* 70, no. 1 (Jan. 2013): 49.

2. "Effrayantes" from Villevaleix to Count of Polastron (Aug. 31, 1790), E691, ADLA.

3. "Chasse" from Alexandre de Vincent, [Untitled] (Dec. 4, 1789), d. 1509, AA54/b, AN. "Parfaitement contents" from Villevaleix to Polastron (July 31, 1790), E691, ADLA.

4. "LES GENS SUSPECTS" from *Correspondance secrète des colons députés à l'Assemblée Constituante* (Paris: Anjubault, c. Feb. 1794), 11. "Les ports" and "plus sages que les blancs" from Villevaleix to Polastron (Oct. 31 and Dec. 31, 1789), E691, ADLA. "Un bien mauvais exemple" from Jean Langlois de Laheuse to Count of Noé (June 24, 1789), JLD-PHD. "Dès les premiers troubles" from Pamphile de Lacroix, *Mémoires pour servir à l'histoire de la révolution de SD* (Paris: Pillet, 1819), 1:404.

5. "Malgré les soins" from TL to Directoire (Aug. 25, 1797), in H. Pauléus Sannon, *Histoire de TL* (Port-au-Prince: Héraux, 1933), 1:8 (Sannon cites AF/ III/210 as the source, but the letter was missing from the box when I went through it in 2010). On TL subscribing to newspapers, see *Moniteur Universel*

(Jan. 9, 1799). "Conversations indiscrètes" from de Peynier and de Proisy to César de la Luzerne (Dec. 1, 1789), C9A/162, ANOM. Dunmore anecdote provided by David Geggus.

6. "Les blancs esclaves" from Marbois to La Luzerne (Oct. 10, 1789), C9A/162, ANOM. "Ils n'entendaient pas que la révolution" from TL to Charles de Talleyrand (Apr. 13, 1799), d. 1, EE1734, ANOM.

7. On other revolts before Aug. 1791, see Marcel Dorigny, ed., *The Abolitions of Slavery: From Léger Félicité Sonthonax to Victor Schoelcher, 1793, 1794, 1848* (New York: Berghahn, 2003), 147–154.

8. For the alleged plot, see Céligni Ardouin, *Essais sur l'Histoire d'Haïti* (Port-au-Prince: T. Bouchereau, 1865), 16; SGU, LEG, 7157, 3, AGS. The following account of the slave revolt is based on DXXV, AN (esp. boxes 1, 12, 78), and F3, ANOM (esp. ledgers 131, 196, 197).

9. On rumors, see Wim Klooster, "Slave Revolts, Royal Justice, and a Ubiquitous Rumor in the Age of Revolutions," *William and Mary Quarterly* 71, no. 3 (July 2014): 401–424.

10. "Il savait lire et écrire" from François de Kerversau, "Rapport sur la partie française de SD" (March 22, 1801), Box 2/66, UF-RP. For mentions of a royalist plot by Biassou, Jean-François, Boukman, and Rouvray, see Biassou to Delahaye (Dec. 18, 1792), CC9A/6, ANOM; Lehoux, "Extrait des pièces" (March 15, 1792), d. 758, *D/XXV/16, AN; "Révolution de SD" (c. Oct. 10, 1792), F3/131, ANOM; Malcolm E. McIntosh and Bernard C. Weber, eds., *Une correspondance familiale au temps des troubles de SD: Lettres du marquis et de la marquise de Rouvray à leur fille* (Paris: Larose, 1959), 64.

11. "Il nous dit que le roi" (account by the mulatto slave François Chapotin, who cited an unnamed quadroon) in "Rapport de la municipalité du Limbé" (c. Aug. 22, 1791), Sc. Micro R-2228, reel 6, NYPL-SC. On documents possibly distributed before the revolt, see David Geggus, "Print Culture and the Haitian Revolution: The Written and the Spoken Word," *Proceedings of the American Antiquarian Society* 116, no. 2 (Oct. 2006): 304, 307. For the forged letter, see SGU, LEG, 7157, 3, AGS.

12. "Fatras bâton" and "caché derrière le rideau" from Kerversau, "Rapport." On Biassou, see Jane Landers, *Atlantic Creoles in the Age of Revolution* (Cambridge, MA: Harvard University Press, 2010), 55–94. On Boukman, see "Notes de Mr. Leclerc" (c. 1803), CC9A/5, ANOM. On Jean-François and Charlotte, see David Geggus, ed., *The Haitian Revolution: A Documentary History* (Indianapolis: Hackett, 2014), 35. Customarily, Jeannot and Jean-François are referred to by their first name and Biassou by his last name.

13. "Este me había propuesto" from Biassou, "Memoria" (July 15, 1793), SGU, LEG, 7157, 7, AGS.

14. "Avez vous oubliés" from TL, "Proclamation" (Apr. 25, 1796), fr. 12104, BNF. For other hints at TL's early role, see chap. 12 and TL to Charles de Talleyrand (Apr. 13, 1799), d. 1, EE1734, ANOM. The possibility remains that TL falsely claimed at a later date to have been the revolt's initiator for political reasons.

15. On Aug. 25 as the target date, see [Moreau?], "Notes de quelques événements . . ." (Jan. 14, 1792), F3/197, ANOM; Bryan Edwards, *An Historical*

Survey of the French Colony in the Island of St. Domingo (London: Stockdale, 1797), 73. "Mettront le feu aux habitations" from "Rapport de la municipalité du Limbé" (c. Aug. 22, 1791), Sc. Micro R-2228, reel 6, NYPL-SC.

16. "Une plus noble vengeance" (speech recorded long after the fact) from Antoine Métral, *Histoire de l'insurrection des esclaves dans le nord de SD* (Paris: Delaunay, 1818), 18. On Bois Caïman being mythologized, see David Geggus, *Haitian Revolutionary Studies* (Blacks in the Diaspora) (Bloomington: Indiana University Press, 2002), 81–92. The exact location of "Bois Caïman" has been a matter of much debate, but the earliest source mentions the Choiseul plantation; see Antoine Dalmas, *Histoire de la révolution de SD* (Paris: Mame frères, 1814), 1:117. There was a "Savane à Cayman" on this plantation; see MSM-DPF, 1:595.

17. On the outbreak in Clément, see "Révolution de SD" (c. Oct. 10, 1792), F3/131, ANOM. "L'habitation Noé roulait" from "Notes de quelques événements . . ." (Jan. 14, 1792), F3/197, ANOM. On the revolt in Manquets, see also Anon., "Considérations pour prendre la régie" (late 1791), JLD-PHD.

18. On burned estates, see Anon., "Mémoire de ce qui est parvenu . . ." (c. Oct. 1, 1791), d. 772, D/XXV/78, AN.

19. On public executions, see Lieuzy Père to Comité colonial de l'Assemblée Nationale (Sept. 30, 1791), d. 1509, aa54/b, AN; Edwards, *An Historical Survey*, 78.

20. On defensive measures, see Philibert de Blanchelande to Antoine de Thévenard (c. Sept. 2, 1791), F3/197, ANOM.

21. "Des femmes jeunes" from P. [Jean Paul Pillet?], "Mon Odyssée" (c. 1798), 85–117-L, Box 1, HNOC. The authenticity of the "flag baby" and other atrocities has been questioned by Laurent Dubois, but they appear in many eyewitness accounts; see David Geggus and Norman Fiering, eds., *The World of the Haitian Revolution* (Bloomington: Indiana University Press, 2009), 111. On black women, see "Révolution de SD" (c. Oct. 10, 1792), F3/131, ANOM. On the death toll, see Acaby to President of the Assemblée Nationale (Sept. 15, 1791), d. 772, D/XXV/78, AN.

22. On Villevaleix (who died in combat later that year), see Lardin to [Count of Polastron?] (Dec. 19, 1791), E691, ADLA. "La perte" from *Moniteur Universel* (Feb. 3, 1799).

23. On Raynal's book, see Leclerc, "Campagne du Limbé" (c. June 20, 1793), CC9A/8, ANOM. "Etre découvert" (by whites or by fellow rebels?) from "Révolution de SD" (c. Oct. 10, 1792), F3/131, ANOM. On TL saving the Bayons, see also FBL's daughter to [Rose Louverture?] (Dec. 19, 1878?), TLF-2A3a, UPR-NC.

24. "Au moment de la Révolution" from *Moniteur Universel* (Jan. 9, 1799). "Des cochers" from "Révolution de SD" (c. Oct. 10, 1792), F3/131, ANOM.

25. "Tantôt ils ont demandé" from Charles Bréard, *Notes sur SD* (Rouen: Espérance Cagniard, 1893), 12. "La mort ou la liberté" from [Jeannot] to citizens of Cap (Sept. 4 [24?], 1791), F3/197, ANOM (Jeannot's address was written by a French captive named Claude Boisbrun, according to Geggus, "Print Culture," 309; the motto echoed Blanchelande's warning that rebels should pick between

"mercy or death" in "Aux nègres en révolte" [Sept. 23, 1791], F3/197, ANOM). On whites in the rebel army, see, for example, Gellie to Chamber of Commerce of St. Malo (Sept. 28, 1791), d. 772, D/XXV/78, AN (the presence of whites led to theories that the revolt was a plot by the Amis des Noirs). On Jeannot's cruelty, see "Notes de Mr. Leclerc" (c. 1803), CC9A/5, ANOM; [Gabriel le] Gros, *Historick Recital of the Different Occurrences in the Camps of Grande Rivière, Dondon, Sainte Suzanne, and Others from 26 October 1791 to 24 December of the Same Year* (Baltimore: Samuel and John Adams, c. 1793).

26. "Liberté générale" from Beaubrun Ardouin, *Etudes sur l'histoire d'Haïti, suivies de la vie du général J-M Borgella* (Paris: Dezobry et Magdeleine, 1853–1860), 1:288–291. "Généraux des armées du Roy" from Jean-Francois and Biassou, "Brevet de Lieutenant Colonel" (Sept. 15, 1791), d. 772, D/XXV/78, AN. On the Vendée, see Geggus and Fiering, *The World of the Haitian Revolution*, 156–176.

27. "Gratification" from Edwards, *An Historical Survey*, xi. "Happiness" from Ada Ferrer, *Freedom's Mirror: Cuba and Haiti in the Age of Revolution* (New York: Cambridge University Press, 2014), 5. Jamaica sent a few guns, the United States sent some money, Santo Domingo sealed the border, and Cuba sent some food.

28. On the South, see Aimé Frère to his brother (Oct. 3, 1791), d. 14, 73J3, ADGir. On the concordats, see "Concordat" (Sept. 11 and Oct. 19, 1791), in FR-5E and FR-5D, UPR-NC. On the burning of Port-au-Prince, see "Précis de la conspiration" (c. Nov. 26, 1791), folder "Paroisse St. Marc," *D/XXV/1, AN. On the West, see Geggus, *Haitian Revolutionary Studies*, 99.

29. "Horrible carnage" from "Bataille livrée par MM de Touzard et de Rouvray" (c. Sept. 20, 1791), F3/197, ANOM. On the attack on Gallifet, see Lieuzy Père to Comité colonial de l'Assemblée Nationale (Sept. 30, 1791), d. 1509, aa54/b, AN.

30. On the size of the rebel army, see Commissaires Nationaux to Antoine de Molleville (Nov. 29, 1791), *D/XXV/1, AN. On rebel tactics, see [Pillet?], "Mon Odyssée"; [François Laplace], *Histoire des désastres de SD* (Paris: Garnery, 1795), 192. "Mettre en avant tous les nègres bossales" from T. Laboissière, "De la révolution à SD" (c. 1793), 3:1113, MS114, SHD-DM. On rebel deaths, see D., "AA-183" (Sept. 27, 1791), d. 772, D/XXV/78, AN.

31. On defections, see Arthaud to [Moreau de Saint-Méry] (Oct. 5, 1791), F/3/197, ANOM.

32. On Jean-François's family, see Journals and M.S. Papers of Nathaniel Cutting, esq., P-275, reel 1, p. 206, MHS.

33. On the first peace overtures, see Louis de Blanchelande, "Aux nègres en revolte" (Sept. 23, 1791), F3/197, ANOM; [Jeannot?] to the citizens of Cap (Sept. 4 [24?], 1791), F/3/197, ANOM. On the November peace initiative, see People of Color of Grande Rivière, "Adresse à l'assemblée générale . . . " (c. Nov. 27, 1791), *D/XXV/1, AN.

34. On the first commission (Ignace de Mirbeck, Philippe Roume, and Edmond de St. Léger), see "Mémoire du Roi" (Oct. 2, 1791), B277, ANOM. On

the first French reinforcements (3,000 men, who arrived in installments and died of disease), see [François Laplace], *Histoire des désastres de SD* (Paris: Garnery, 1795), 214.

35. "Tousaint" from Jean-François, Biassou, et al. to [Mirbeck, St. Léger, Roume] (Dec. 12, 1791), *D/XXV/1, AN. "The negro Toussaint" from Gros, *Historick Recital*, 57.

36. On the December 21, 1791, encounter in Petite Anse, see Mirbeck, "Compte sommaire" (May 26, 1792), CC9A/6, ANOM; Journals and M.S. Papers of Nathaniel Cutting, P-275, reel 1, p. 264, MHS. On TL's alleged presence in the delegation, see Dalmas, *Histoire de la révolution*, 1:226. "Nous n'avons cessé un instant de travailler" from Jean-François and Biassou to Mirbeck, Roume, St. Léger (Dec. 21, 1791), *D/XXV/1, AN (Jean-François's wife was freed, according to Dalmas, *Histoire de la révolution*, 1:227). "L'état général d'effervescence" and "négresses" from Biassou to Mirbeck, Roume, St. Léger (Dec. 23, 1791), *D/XXV/1, AN.

37. On the raid (in which only Biassou's presence is mentioned), see Dalmas, *Histoire de la révolution*, 1:286–292.

38. On the January 1792 negotiations with Spain, see García to Andrés de Heredia (Feb. 3, 1792), in Antonio del Monte y Tejada, *Historia de Santo Domingo* (Santo Domingo: García Hermanos, 1892), 3:vi. On the upheavals in Cap in late March 1792, see "Copie des délibérations des commissaires" (Nov. 1791–Apr. 1792), *D/XXV/1, AN.

39. On Candi, see Candi et al. to Mirbeck, Roume, St. Léger (Jan. 7, 1792), *D/XXV/1, AN. On the Port-de-Paix revolt, see Franklin Midy, ed., *Mémoire de révolution d'esclaves à SD* (Montréal: Centre International de Documentation et d'Information Haïtienne, Caribéenne et Afro-canadienne, 2006), 99–102. On the West and South, see Assemblée provinciale de l'Ouest, *Extrait des Registres* (Sept. 12, 1792); Philippe de Fézensac to Jean-Nicolas Pache (Oct. 28, 1792), B7/1, SHD-DAT.

CHAPTER 11: MONARCHIST, 1792

1. "Messieurs" from Biassou, "En conséquance . . ." (Aug. 24, 1792), CC9A/6, ANOM.

2. "Calumnias" from Biassou and Belair to [Sonthonax?] (Aug. 23, 1793), SGU, LEG, 7157, 8, AGS. "Résistance à l'oppression" from TL to Charles de Talleyrand (Apr. 13, 1799), d. 1, EE1734, ANOM.

3. "Les plus vils animaux" from Jean-François to Laveaux (Nov. 28, 1794), fr. 12102, BNF (it remains customary to refer to Jean-François Papillon by his first name and Georges Biassou by his last). "Chevalier" from Biassou, [Brevet] (Aug. 16, 1791 [1792]), CC9A/6, ANOM. Historians often write that TL bore the title of "médecin général," but the title was actually Jeannot's; see "Adresse à l'assemblée générale . . . " (c. Nov. 1791), *D/XXV/1, AN.

4. On types of rebel groups, see Roume to Min. of Navy (Dec. 18, 1792), CC9A/7, ANOM. "Ainsi que notre religion" from Biassou to Delahaye (Dec. 18, 1792), Dossier 118, D/XXV/12, AN.

5. On TL saying Mass, see Matías de Armona to García (Aug. 30, 1793), SGU, LEG, 6855, 52, AGS; François de Kerversau, "Rapport sur la partie française de SD" (March 22, 1801), Box 2/66, UF-RP. On priests, see Adolphe Cabon, *Notes sur l'histoire religieuse d'Haïti de la révolution au concordat (1789–1860)* (Port-au-Prince: Petit séminaire collège Saint-Martial, 1933).

6. "M. Toussaint" and "faire sa tournée" from Biassou to [Delahaye] (Oct. 28, 1792), d. 118, D/XXV/12, AN.

7. "Toutes ces négresses" from Fayete to Delahaye (Dec. 13, 1792), CC9A/7, ANOM. On selling slaves, see André Vernet, "Déclaration de Pierre . . . " (July 17, 1793), d. 118, D/XXV/12, AN. "Demoiselles" from [Jeannot] to Biassou (Oct. 15, 1791), in *Pièces trouvées dans le camp des révoltés* (Paris: Imprimerie Nationale, Feb. 16, 1792), 209.

8. A July 1792 letter by Jean-François, Biassou, and Gabriel Bélair (Biassou's second in command), and often mistakenly attributed to TL, asked for general emancipation, but it was likely a fake, according to David Geggus; see R. William Weisberger, ed., *Profiles of Revolutionaries in Atlantic History* (New York: Columbia University Press, 2007), 120. On Françoise, see Delahaye, "Codicille" (Dec. 18, 1792), CC9A/7, ANOM.

9. On Biassou as TL's superior (which fits the evidence), see Biassou to [Delahaye] (Oct. 28 and Dec. 18, 1792), d. 118, D/XXV/12, AN. On TL's later denegation, see TL to García (March 20, 1794), in Beaubrun Ardouin, *Etudes sur l'histoire d'Haïti, suivies de la vie du général J-M Borgella* (Paris: Dezobry et Magdeleine, 1853–1860), 2:419.

10. On Dessalines, see Dessalines to TL (Apr. 26, 1802), Sc. Micro R-2228, reel 4, NYPL-SC. "Jai recu une bale" from PG-MGTL, 152.

11. "Comme servantes" from "Notes de Mr. Leclerc procureur syndic" (c. 1803), CC9A/5, ANOM. "Respect" from Jean-Charles Benzaken, "Lettre inédite sur la situation à SD en novembre 1792," *Annales Historiques de la Révolution Française* 363 (2011): 171.

12. "Cette magie" from Barré de Saint-Venant, *Des colonies modernes sous la zone torride, et particulièrement de celle de SD* (Paris: Brochot, 1802), 245. "La moitié de nos ateliers" from Moreau de St. Méry, "Copies de différentes lettres" (c. Aug. 1791), d. 773, D/XXV/78, AN.

13. "Quien no sabe escribir" and "Llevan las riendas" from Antonio del Monte y Tejada, *Historia de Santo Domingo* (Santo Domingo: García Hermanos, 1892), 3:xii, 4:30.

14. On TL learning to read in the 1790s, see IL-NH, 55; Madame J. Michelet, *The Story of My Childhood* (Boston: Little, Brown, 1867), 163.

15. On samples of TL's writing, see Philippe Girard, "Quelle langue parlait TL? Le mémoire du Fort de Joux et les origines du kreyòl haïtien," *Annales* 68, no. 1 (Jan. 2013): 109–132. On TL's library, see Marcus Rainsford, *An Historical Account of the Black Empire of Hayti* (London: Albion Press, 1805), 244. On TL hurting his hand, see IL-NH, 59. On TL possibly being left-handed, see the 1802 portrait by Pierre-Charles Bacquoy and PMD-PH, 2:52.

16. On TL and the Aug. 10 *journée*, see TL to Bonaparte (Oct. 9, 1802), d. 1, AF/IV/1213, AN.

17. On the battle of Tannerie / Camp Pelé, see Antoine Dalmas, *Histoire de la révolution de SD* (Paris: Mame frères, 1814), 2:107–116.

18. "Vice-roi du pays conquis" from [François Laplace], *Histoire des désastres de SD* (Paris: Garnery, 1795), 262.

19. On Maniel, see Charlton W. Yingling, "The Maroons of Santo Domingo in the Age of Revolutions: Adaptation and Evasion, 1783–1800," *History Workshop Journal* 79 (Apr. 2015): 25–51.

CHAPTER 12: SPANISH OFFICER, 1793–1794

1. "Que rendirán los Esclavos" from Andrés de Heredia to [Joaquín García] (Sept. 1792), SGU, LEG, 7157, 18, AGS.

2. On the commissioners' instructions, see "Mémoire du Roi" (June 17, 1792), B277, ANOM.

3. On Sonthonax, see Robert Louis Stein, *Léger-Félicité Sonthonax: The Lost Sentinel of the Republic* (Toronto: Associated University Press, 1985). The third commissioner, Jean-Antoine Ailhaud, was replaced by Delpech, who died in Sept. 1793. The following account of the second commission is based on D XXV/4–44, AN; GC-RTSD. On Blanchelande's departure and trial, see Louis de Blanchelande, *Discours justificatif* (Paris: N. H. Nyon, March 15, 1793), FR-1C, UPR-NC; *Bulletin du tribunal criminel* (Apr. 11, 1793), 61J16, ADGir.

4. On the number of French troops, see García to Pedro Acuña (Nov. 6, 1792), SGU, LEG, 7157, 18, AGS.

5. "Aristocrates" from Sonthonax to Municipality of Paris (c. Dec. 10, 1792), CC9A/6, ANOM. D'Esparbès's successors were Donatien de Rochambeau, Adrien de la Salle, and François Galbaud.

6. For early offers by runaway slaves to enroll in the Spanish Army, see Ignacio Peres Cavo to King of Spain (Nov. 24, 1693), Clairambault 888, BNF. Runaways were welcomed by Spain until a 1776–1777 extradition treaty banned the practice; see MSM-LC, 5:658, 663, 770.

7. "L'Espagnol" from [Jeannot] to [Biassou] (c. Oct. 4 and 15, 1791), in *Pièces trouvées dans le camp des révoltés* (Paris: Imprimerie Nationale, Feb. 16, 1792), 209 (these letters are often mistakenly attributed to TL). "Perfecta neutralidad" from Fernando Carrera Montero, *Las complejas relaciones de España con La Española: El Caribe hispano frente a Santo Domingo y Saint Domingue, 1789–1803* (Santo Domingo: Fundación García Arévalo, 2004), 42. The following account of Santo Domingo in 1792–1794 is also based on SGU, LEG, 6855 and 7157–7160, AGS; Carlos Esteban Deive, *Los Refugiados Franceses en Santo Domingo, 1789–1801* (Santo Domingo: Universidad Nacional Pedro Henríquez Ureña, 1984); Ada Ferrer, *Freedom's Mirror: Cuba and Haiti in the Age of Revolution* (New York: Cambridge University Press, 2014), 83–145.

8. "Infeccion" from García to Andrés de Heredia (Sept. 7, 1791), in Antonio del Monte y Tejada, *Historia de Santo Domingo* (Santo Domingo: García Hermanos, 1892), 3:140.

9. "Comme des bettes feroces" from TL, "Reponse Sentimentale" (Aug. 27, 1793), d. 1511, AA55/A, AN. "Un negro despachado" from Monte y Tejada, *Historia de Santo Domingo*, 4:20.

10. "Los Brigantes" from Acuña to García (Feb. 22, 1793), SGU, LG, 7161, 1, AGS. "Buena disciplina" from Monte y Tejada, *Historia de Santo Domingo*, 4:24.

11. "Mourrir pour mon Roy" from TL, "Reponse Sentimentale" (Aug. 27, 1793), d. 1511, AA55/A, AN. On taking Dondon, see Joaquín Cabrera, "Relacion" (July 11, 1793), SGU, LEG, 7158, 38, AGS. On TL's rank, see IL-OTL.

12. "A vendre ou à louer" from *Moniteur général* (March 12, 1793).

13. "Principes de liberté" from *Révolutions de Paris* 63 (Sept. 25, 1790). On the membership in a Jacobin club, see Léger-Félicité Sonthonax, "A la société des amis de la Convention Nationale" (Oct. 31, 1792), d. 1512, AA55/A, AN.

14. "Les esclaves du nouveau monde" from Sonthonax to Milcent (Feb. 11, 1793), d. 1511, AA55/A, AN. On Sonthonax's calls for reforms, see also Sonthonax to [Min. of Navy?] (Jan. 4, 1793), 61J16, ADGir. On the May 5 regulations, see Etienne de Polverel and Léger-Félicité Sonthonax, "Proclamation" (May 5, 1793), 61J71, ADGir; Polverel and Sonthonax to Min. of Navy (June 18, 1793), CC9A/8, ANOM. "Liberté générale" from Pierrot to [Sonthonax?] (June 4, 1793), d. 1510, aa54/b, AN. On Polverel's abolitionist sympathies, see *Société des amis de la constitution* (Sept. 23, 1790), 61J5, ADGir.

15. On the burning of Cap, see François le Goff, "Manuscrit autographe" (Nov. 8, 1793), 1M591, SHD-DAT; P. [Jean-Paul Pillet?], "Mon Odyssée" (c. 1798), 85–117-L, Box 1, HNOC; Jeremy Popkin, *You Are All Free: The Haitian Revolution and the Abolition of Slavery* (New York: Cambridge University Press, 2010). Popkin argues that the burning of Cap was the turning point that made abolition possible, but Sonthonax and Polverel had taken clear steps toward abolition in previous months.

16. On SD refugees, see Alejandro Enrique Gómez Pernía, *Le syndrome de SD: Perceptions et représentations de la Révolution haïtienne dans le Monde Atlantique, 1790–1886* (PhD diss., École des Hautes Études en Sciences Sociales, Paris, 2010), 86.

17. "Qu'ils voulaient un roy" from Antoine Chanlatte to Laveaux (Aug. 10, 1793), fr. 12102, BNF. "Notre bon roi" from Polverel, Sonthonax, Ailhaud to Min. of Navy (Oct. 26, 1792), CC9A/7, ANOM.

18. "Liberté générale" from Pierrot to [Sonthonax] (July 9, 1793), d. 1512, AA55/A, AN. On freeing spouses, see Léger-Félicité Sonthonax and Etienne de Polverel, "Proclamation" (July 11, 1793), UM-CL. "Vous traîtres republicains" from TL to Antoine Chanlatte (Aug. 27, 1793), CC9A/8, ANOM.

19. On Marie Bleigeat (who was apparently related to the Bréda overseer Villevaleix), see Serge Barcellini, "A la recherche d'une mémoire disparue," *Revue Française d'Histoire d'Outre-Mer* 84, no. 316 (Fall 1997): 124.

20. On Biassou's stories, see Biassou, "Memoria" (July 15, 1793), SGU, LEG, 7157, 7, AGS. On accounts written in 1793 that barely mention TL, see [François Laplace], *Histoire des désastres de SD* (Paris: Garnery, 1795); Antoine Dalmas, *Histoire de la revolution de SD*, 2 vols. (Paris: Mame frères, 1814); Samuel Perkins, *Reminiscences of the Insurrection in St. Domingo* (Cambridge, MA: J. Wilson, 1886).

21. "Etant le premier" from TL, "Proclamation" (Aug. 25, 1793), AE II 1375, AN. On claiming the slave revolt as his own, see also TL, "Frères et amis" (Aug. 29, 1793), d. 1490, AA53/A, AN. For the first appearance of TL's nickname, see Biassou to García (July 6, 1793), SGU, LEG, 7157, 4, AGS (Jesús Ruiz indicated to me in a February 3, 2015, email that he found earlier, as yet unpublished, mentions of TL's last name). "Il fut le premier" (account by Paul Aly) from C. N. Céligni Ardouin, *Essais sur l'Histoire d'Haïti* (Port-au-Prince: T. Bouchereau, 1865), 16.

22. On uses of "Toussaint," see PG-MGTL, 22.

23. "Je suis Toussain louverture" from TL, "Frères et amis" (Aug. 29, 1793), d. 1490, AA53/A, AN.

24. For another letter, see TL, "Reponse Sentimentale" (Aug. 27, 1793), d. 1511, AA55/A, AN.

25. "Toute monde vini" from Léger-Félicité Sonthonax, "DANS NOM LA RÉPUBLIQUE" (Aug. 29, 1793), 61J71, ADGir. For a French version, see Lk12–28, BNF. For a Spanish version, see d. 117, D/XXV/12, AN.

26. "La politique" from Isaac Louverture, "Réfutation des assertions" (Aug. 18, 1845), NAF 6864, BNF.

27. "L'esclavage éternel" from TL, *Extrait du rapport adressé au Directoire* (Cap: Roux, 1797), 6. On countermanding abolition, see Adrien de la Salle, "Proclamation" (Oct. 8, 1793), CC9A/8, ANOM. "Il y a du train en France" from François Tussac, *Cri des colons contre un ouvrage de M. l'évêque et sénateur Grégoire, ayant pour titre de la littérature des nègres* (Paris: Delaunay, 1810), 253.

28. "Engaño" from Biassou, "Proclamación" (Aug. 25, 1793), SGU, LEG, 7157, 9, AGS. "Cette liberté n'est bonne à rien" from Alaou to Sonthonax (March 9, 1794), d. 1512, aa55/a, AN. On Makaya (who later rejoined Spain) and Pierrot (who considered it), see Popkin, *You Are All Free*, 252, 255. Three minor chiefs, named Petit Thomas, Barthélémy, and Louis, joined France in January 1794; see García to Alcudia (Feb. 16, 1794), SGU, LEG, 7157, 20, AGS. Another, Alaou, joined in March; see Poulain to Sonthonax (March 5, 1794), d. 232, D/XXV/23, AN.

29. On TL's conquests, see IL-OTL. This account of TL's service in the Spanish Army is drawn primarily from SGU, LEG, 7157 and 7158, AGS; ESTADO, 11B, AGI.

30. "Las buenas acciones" from García to Alcudia (Jan. 3, 1794), ESTADO, 14, N.89, AGI.

31. "Muchas palabras" from Biassou, "Memoria" (July 15, 1793), SGU, LEG, 7157, 7, AGS. "Generalissimo" from Biassou to García (Aug. 24, 1793), SGU, LEG, 7157, 6, AGS (Jean-François also sent an envoy to Santo Domingo). "No tiene otro oficio" from Cabrera to Gaspar de Casasola (July 17, 1793), in Monte y Tejada, *Historia de Santo Domingo*, 4:66. On imprisoning TL, see IL-OTL.

32. "Fidèles vassaux" from "Au quartier de St. Raphaël" (Nov. 8, 1793), ESTADO, 11B, N.98, AGI.

33. On TL's family, see IL-NH, 55. Freedom papers issued by Santo Domingo would not have been valid in SD; see "Extrait des registres" (Nov. 1, 1792), CC9A/8, ANOM.

34. On the Louvertures' landholdings, see chap. 16. For the 648,000 francs claim (which TL dated to the beginning of the Revolution, i.e., 1792 for him), see PG-MGTL, 4.

35. On gifts, see "Razon de los efectos" (July 10, 1793), in Monte y Tejada, *Historia de Santo Domingo*, 4:59; "Nota de los viveres" (Oct. 14, 1793), SGU, LEG, 7157, 16, AGS.

36. "Mon étonnement" and "homme faible" from TL to García (March 20 and 27, 1794), in Beaubrun Ardouin, *Etudes sur l'histoire d'Haïti, suivies de la vie du général J-M Borgella* (Paris: Dezobry et Magdeleine, 1853–1860), 2:423, 419.

37. On French planters, see Deive, *Los Refugiados Franceses*, 110–119. On Le Borgne, see Laveaux to Sonthonax and Polverel (Feb. 6, 1794), CC9A/8, ANOM. On Petite-Rivière, see "Proclamation du commandant espagnol" (Jan. 1794), F3/199, ANOM. "Protection" from Ferrer, *Freedom's Mirror*, 116.

38. On militarized serfdom, see Belair to García (Sept. 10, 1793), SGU, LEG, 7157, 10, AGS.

39. "Odieux commerce" from TL to García (March 20, 1794), in Ardouin, *Etudes*, 2:419. On Pierre's death, see IL-OTL.

40. "Perfidia" from Juan Lleonart to Conde del Campo de Alange (Feb. 22, 1795), SGU, LEG, 6855, 51, AGS.

41. On plotting against Biassou, see Laplace to García (Apr. 4, 1794), in Ardouin, *Etudes*, 2:429. "Corta cavezas" from Armona to García (Aug. 20, 1793), SGU, LEG, 6855, 52, AGS.

42. On joining France, see Laveaux to Sonthonax and Polverel (May 24, 1794), CC9A/8, ANOM. On Bayon (who survived by disguising himself as a Spanish soldier), see "Demandes de passeport" (1793–1795), 3L-179, ADGir; David Geggus, ed., *The Haitian Revolution: A Documentary History* (Indianapolis: Hackett, 2014), 114.

43. On TL deceiving Spain, see Monte y Tejada, *Historia de Santo Domingo*, 4:280. On deceiving the UK, see *The Times* [London] (Nov. 7, 1794).

44. On the SD delegation, see Louis Dufaÿ to French commissioners (Dec. 4, 1793), d. 758, *D/XXV/16, AN; Popkin, *You Are All Free*, 279, 321–327.

45. On Belley (whose imagined African birth brings to mind that of Olaudah Equiano), see Jean-Louis Donnadieu, "Derrière le portrait, l'homme: Jean-Baptiste Belley, dit 'Timbaze,' dit 'Mars' (1746?–1805)," *Bulletin de la Société d'Histoire de la Guadeloupe* 170 (Jan.–Apr. 2015): 29–54. The white deputy Louis Dufaÿ had also served in Savannah. The mixed-race deputy Mills had once owned slaves; see *Affiches américaines* (Feb. 13, 1773).

46. France had already abolished slavery in France itself on October 16, 1791; see "Loi portant que tout homme est libre . . . " (Oct. 16, 1791), 15 Ms. HD, Sc. Micro R1527, NYPL-SC. On public reaction in France, see Félix Carteau, *Soirées bermudiennes, ou entretiens sur les évènemens qui ont opéré la ruine*

de la partie française de l'isle SD (Bordeaux: Pellier-Lawalle, 1802), xxi–xxxix; Léon-François Hoffmann et al., eds., *Haïti 1804 Lumières et Ténèbres: Impact et résonances d'une révolution* (Madrid: Bibliotheca Ibero-Americana, 2008), 85–98. Because of the British occupation of Martinique and planter opposition in Réunion, the February 1794 law only took effect in French Guiana, and later Guadeloupe and Saint-Lucia.

47. On TL's version of events, see TL to Charles de Talleyrand (Apr. 13, 1799), d. 1, EE1734, ANOM. News of the February 1794 law first reached Jacmel in June; see Chambon to Laveaux (June 25, 1794), CC9A/8, ANOM. On motives for TL's volte-face, see David Geggus, *Haitian Revolutionary Studies* (Blacks in the Diaspora) (Bloomington: University of Indiana Press, 2002), 119–136.

CHAPTER 13: FRENCH PATRIOT, 1794–1796

1. On Laveaux, see Bernard Gainot, "Le général Laveaux, gouverneur de SD, député néo-Jacobin," *Annales Historiques de la Révolution Française* 278 (1989): 433–454.

2. "Dieu merci" from Laveaux to TL (May 5, 1794), CC9A/9, ANOM. The following overview of TL's role in 1794–1796 is drawn from fr. 12102–12104, BNF; CC9A/9–11, ANOM; F3/199, ANOM; AF III/209–210, AN; SGU, LEG, 7160–7161, AGS.

3. On French losses, see "Tableau de l'expédition de SD" (c. Oct. 1, 1792), CC9A/7, ANOM; Laveaux to Jean Dalbarade (March 25, 1795), F3/199, ANOM. On TL's capture of Gonaïves, Gros-Morne, Ennery, Plaisance, Marmelade, Dondon, Acul, and Limbé, see TL to Laveaux (May 18, 1794), fr. 12102, BNF. On TL's capture of San Rafael, San Miguel, and Hinche, see SGU, LEG, 6855, 53, AGS. "Cabale" from TL to Desfourneaux (June 27, 1796), 12104, BNF. "Ruse" from TL to Talleyrand (Apr. 13, 1799), d. 1, EE1734, ANOM. "Goutte de sang" from TL to Laveaux (Aug. 6, 1795), fr. 12103, BNF. Laveaux took Borgne, Port-Margot. Môle Saint-Nicolas remained in British hands and Fort-Dauphin in Spanish hands.

4. "La liberté" from Jean-François, "Mes frères" (June 11, 1795), fr. 12103, BNF. "Libres de droit naturel" from [Officers of TL], "Réponse" (June 13, 1795), fr. 12103, BNF.

5. "Décret de la liberté" from Manlau, Baubert, and Noël Leveillé to Etienne Laveaux (Nov. 13, 1795), fr. 12103, BNF.

6. On Boca Nigua / Oyarzábal and other possible copycat revolts in Hinche and Sámana, see Antonio J. Pinto, "Santo Domingo's Slaves in the Context of the Peace of Basel: Boca Nigua's Black Insurrection, 1796," *Journal of Early American History* 3 (2013): 131–153. "Les habitants espagnols" from TL to Laveaux (Dec. 20, 1795), fr. 12103, BNF.

7. On the auxiliaries' fate, see ESTADO, 43, N.18 and 24, N.53, AGI; Jane Landers, *Atlantic Creoles in the Age of Revolution* (Cambridge, MA: Harvard University Press, 2010), 78–93. TL tried to repatriate Biassou's widow, "to whom he owed his life"; see IL-NH, 73.

8. On members of Jean-François's family who apparently stayed with TL, see TL to Laveaux (Nov. 8, 1795), fr. 12103, BNF.

9. On the Sept. 1794 assault on Saint-Marc (one of several attempts in 1794–1795), see IL-NH, 59. On the July 1796 rout near Mirebalais, see David P. Geggus, *Slavery, War, and Revolution: The British Occupation of SD, 1793–1798* (Oxford: Clarendon Press, 1982), 200.

10. On the loss rate, see Geggus, *Slavery, War, and Revolution*, 355. This account of the British invasion is also based on Roger Norman Buckley, ed., *The Haitian Journal of Lieutenant Howard, York Hussars, 1796–98* (Knoxville: University of Tennessee Press, 1985); Paul Youngquist and Grégory Pierrot, eds., *Marcus Rainsford: An Historical Account of the Black Empire of Hayti* (Durham, NC: Duke University Press, 2013).

11. "Notre climat vengeur" from Dessalines [and Louis Boisrond-Tonnerre], "Proclamation" (Jan. 1, 1804), ESTADO, 68, N.12, AGI.

12. "Il faut espérer" from TL to Laveaux (Dec. 5, 1795), fr. 12103, BNF. On other revolts in the Caribbean, see Michael Craton, *Testing the Chains: Resistance to Slavery in the British West Indies* (1982; reprint, Ithaca, NY: Cornell University Press, 2009); Wim Klooster and Gert Oostindie, eds., *Curaçao in the Age of Revolutions, 1795–1800* (Leiden: KITLV Press, 2011), 23–56.

13. "Doucement allé loing" from TL to Laveaux (March 1, 1796), fr. 12104, BNF.

14. On the Bastille Day fete (which TL did not personally attend), see Laveaux to Rigaud (July 29, 1794), d. 957, AF/III/209, AN.

15. "Etre suprême" from Municipalité du Cap, "Liberté, Egalité, Fraternité, ou la mort" (May 21, 1795), fr. 12103, BNF. On abolishing the revolutionary calendar, see Edward Corbet to Nugent (Sept. 26, 1801), CO 137/106, BNA.

16. "Sans culottes" and "vers de terre" from TL to Laveaux (Jan. 7 and Dec. 5, 1795), fr. 12103, BNF.

17. "Salut en la patrie" from TL to Laveaux (Sept. 14, 1795), fr. 12103, BNF. On the Dokos/Mamzelle, see TL to Laveaux (Sept. 14, 1795), fr. 12103, BNF; IL-OTL.

18. "La protections" from PG-MGTL, 166.

19. On the *ménagère* Marianne, see TL to Laveaux (June 26, 1795), fr. 12103, BNF. "La confiance" and "600 propriétaires" from Laveaux to Jean Dalbarade (Sept. 22, 1794, and March 25, 1795), F3/199, ANOM.

20. "Plein de vertu" from Laveaux to Dalbarade (March 25, 1795), F3/199, ANOM. "Je vous embrasse" and "cher Papa" from TL to Laveaux (March 1 and 18, 1796), fr. 12104, BNF. "Je rêve souvent en vous" from TL to Laveaux (Feb. 6, 1795), fr. 12103, BNF. "L'amant idolâtre" from Castaing to [Sonthonax] (March 7, [1793]), d. 758, *D/XXV/16, AN.

21. On Sonthonax's return to France, see Jeremy Popkin, *You Are All Free: The Haitian Revolution and the Abolition of Slavery* (New York: Cambridge University Press, 2010), 287, 387. Polverel was not tried because he had died; see François Polverel Jr., "A ses concitoyens" (Apr. 15, 1795), Sc. Micro R-2228, reel 15, NYPL-SC.

22. On the 1795 debate, see D/XXV/102, AN; Jean-Charles Benzaken, "Le tour de force du citoyen Guillois," *Annales Historiques de la Révolution Française* 327 (2002): 83–97.

23. On Désageneaux's arrival, see Pierre Pluchon, *TL* (Paris: Fayard, 1989), 117.

24. "Les grands et mémorables services" from Jean-Paul Caze, Etienne Viart, and Philippe Lacroix to TL (Dec. 7, 1795), fr. 12103, BNF.

25. On SD as a *département*, see Truguet, "Instructions" (Feb. 12, 1796), B277, ANOM; Sonthonax to Tonnelier (May 18, 1796), fr. 8986, BNF.

26. "Le sentiment du devoir" from François de Kerversau to Charles de Vincent (Oct. 21, 1797), AF/III, 210, AN.

27. "Notre sûreté" from Francois Reynaud and Joseph Le Brasseur to de Sartine (Aug. 12, 1780), C9A/148, ANOM. On French educational policy, see docs. 212 and 236, B277, ANOM.

28. On TL's children with his first wife, see [Marriage record] (Oct. 4, 1787), 1DPPC 2326, ANOM. On his children with his second wife, see Isaac Louverture, "Notes sur Madame Louverture" (c. 1824), p. 133, NAF 12409, BNF; Mme J. Michelet, *The Story of My Childhood* (1866; reprint, Boston: Little, Brown, 1867).

29. On the laundry, see Suzanne Louverture to TL (July 13, 1794), 61J18, ADGir. For other letters to/from Suzanne, see Sonthonax to Suzanne (July 7, 1796), fr. 8986, BNF; Suzanne to Dupuis (Oct. 23, 1798), in Joseph Elisée Peyre-Ferry, *Journal des opérations militaires de l'armée française à SD pendant les années X XI et XII (1802 et 1803)* (Port-au-Prince: Henri Deschamps, 2005), 398; Suzanne to Decrès (July 11, 1802), d. 1, EE1734, ANOM; Placide to TL and Suzanne (Aug. 12, 1802), d. 1, AF/IV/1213, AN; TL to Suzanne (Sept. 17, 1802), d. 1, EE 1734, ANOM; Mars Plaisir to Suzanne (Sept. 18, 1815), TLF-2A1, UPR-NC. For a rare political comment by Suzanne, see Jean-Louis Clavier, "Toussaint-Louverture d'après le 'Mémoire abrégé des événements de SD depuis l'année 1789 jusquà celle de 1807,'" *Revue Française d'Histoire d'Outre-Mer* 62, no. 228 (1975): 481.

30. "Je fus un jour" from Michel-Etienne Descourtilz, *Voyage d'un naturaliste et ses observations* (Paris: Dufart, 1809), 3:251.

31. On Sansay and Gonaïves, see TL to Laveaux (Aug. 6 and 22, 1795), fr. 12103, BNF. On the Louverture province, see TL, "Arrêté" (July 14, 1801), CC9B/9, ANOM.

32. "Le bonheur de ma vie" from TL to Sonthonax (c. June 16, 1796), fr. 12104, BNF.

33. For concerns about re-enslavement, see Sonthonax to TL (June 12, 1796), fr. 8986, BNF.

34. On Joséphine, see IL-NH, 70.

35. "Ne savaient pas lire" and "dévouement à la patrie" from Michel Roussier, "L'éducation des enfants de TL et l'institution nationale des colonies," *Revue Française d'Histoire d'Outre-Mer* 64, no. 236 (1977): 322, 315. On the school, see also F2C/13, ANOM.

36. "L'instruction qu'il lui a plu" from TL to Truguet (Feb. 1, 1797), d. 1, EE1734, ANOM. "Soyez bien attentif" from TL to Isaac and Placide (June 10, 1798), AF/III, 210, AN. For other letters to and from TL's sons, see TL to Isaac and Placide (Apr. 14, 1799), in Victor Schoelcher, *Vie de TL* (Paris: Ollendorf, 1889), 437; TL to Placide (Aug. 13, 1800), Ms. Hait. 79-3, BPL; TL to Placide and Isaac (Feb. 14, 1801), in Roussier, "L'éducation des enfants," 336; Placide to Suzanne and TL (Aug. 12, 1802), in H. Pauléus Sannon, *Histoire de TL* (Port-au-Prince: Héraux, 1933), 3:156.

37. "Elevés parmi les français" from Isaac Louverture to Decrès (Sept. 16, 1802), d. 4, EE 1734, ANOM. "Sauf la couleur" from Jacques de Norvins, *Souvenirs d'un historien de Napoléon: Memorial de J. de Norvins* (Paris: Plon, 1896), 2:319.

CHAPTER 14: POLITICIAN, 1796–1798

1. "Vous n'êtes pas le peuple" and "mon ami" from Etienne Laveaux to TL (March 26, 1796), fr. 12104, BNF. On the Villatte affair, see also Laveaux, "Compte rendu . . . à ses concitoyens, à l'opinion publique, aux autorités constituées" (Apr. 20, 1797), electronic resources, HU-HL.

2. "Colère bilieuse" from TL to Laveaux (Feb. 6, 1795), fr. 12103, BNF.

3. On Dessalines, see Janvier Dessalines, "Etat des services" (c. 1796), COL E129, ANOM. On Delahaye, see Commissioners to TL (June 1794), d. 232, D/XXV/23, AN. Villatte was apparently related to TL; see Cazemajor to Placide Louverture (Jan. 30, 1825), TLF-2A2i, UPR-NC.

4. "L'Homme prédit" from Laveaux, "Aux corps civils et militaires" (Apr. 5, 1796), ESTADO, 5B, N. 127, AGI.

5. "Après bon Dieu" from Jacques de Norvins, "Louverture (Toussaint)," in Anon., *Dictionnaire de la conversation et de la lecture* (Paris: Belin-Mandar, 1837), 36:14.

6. The other commissioners were Philippe Roume (who headed for Santo Domingo), Georges-Pierre Leblanc and Marc-Antoine-Alexis Giraud (who quickly left), and Julien Raimond. The following account of Sonthonax's second tenure is based on fr. 8986–8988, BNF; CC9A/12–17, ANOM; AF/III, 210, AN.

7. "J'ai fondé la liberté" from Sonthonax to Domergue jeune (June 7, 1796), fr. 8986, BNF. "Je suis blanc" from Philippe-Albert de Lattre, *Campagne des Français à SD et réfutation des reproches faits au Capitaine-Général Rochambeau* (Paris: Locard, 1805), 46.

8. "Le vrai ami des noirs" from TL to Laveaux (Aug. 17, 1796), fr. 12104, BNF.

9. On the dispute with Rigaud, see François de Kerversau, "Récit des événements" (Nov. 23, 1796), 43APC/1, ANOM; Pelletier, "Tableau rapproché . . . " (Feb. 8, 1797), Box 1/40, UF-RP. On the saber, see Sonthonax to Min. of Navy (Feb. 24, 1797), B277, ANOM.

10. On FBL, see Sonthonax to TL (July 4, 1797), fr. 8988, BNF; TL to Directory (July 18, 1797), *F7/7321, AN.

11. "D'un esprit borné" from Sonthonax to Directory (Jan. 30, 1798), AF/III, 210, AN.

12. "Il se répandrait du sang" from TL to Raimond (Aug. 23, 1797), d. 961, AF/III, 210, AN.

13. On Sonthonax being homesick, see Sonthonax to his daughter (May 14, [1797]), ASO-1, UPR-NC.

14. "Gravées dans ma mémoire" from TL, *Extrait du rapport adressé au Directoire Exécutif* (Cap Français: Roux, Sept. 4, 1797), d. 961, AF/III, 210, AN. For a different account of the conversation, see Sonthonax to Bauvais (Aug. 18, 1797), fr. 8988, BNF.

15. "Toussaint ne parle" from Sonthonax to Directory (Jan. 30, 1798), AF/III, 210, AN. On Sonthonax being forgotten, see Serge Barcellini, "A la recherche d'une mémoire disparue," *Revue Française d'Histoire d'Outre-Mer* 84, no. 316 (Fall 1997): 121–158.

16. On Raimond, see TL to Raimond (Apr. 10, 1798), Papers of TL, LC-MD. On Desfourneaux, see TL to Raimond (Aug. 28, 1797), Autograph File, T., HU-HL. On Mentor, see Anon., *Histoire de TL* (Paris: Pillot, 1802), 57–63. On deportations by Sonthonax, see Lecointe-Puyraveau, "Rapport . . . sur les déportés et réfugiés" (March 24, 1797), FR-10V, UPR-NC.

17. "Nègres ignorants" from Viénot de Vaublanc, *Discours sur l'état de SD* (May 29, 1797), 7.

18. "Devint sombre" from Julien Raimond, "Rapport" (Sept. 16, 1798), B277, ANOM. "Affliger les noirs" from TL to Min. of Navy (Oct. 20, 1797), CC9A/14, ANOM.

19. For Laveaux's defense, see Laveaux, *Réponse d'Etienne Laveaux . . .* ([Paris]: J. F. Sobry, June 19, 1797).

20. "Citoyens français" from TL, *Réfutation de quelques assertions d'un discours . . . par Viénot Vaublanc* (Cap-Français: Roux, Oct. 29, 1797), 17.

21. On the deportation of the *fructidoriens*, see Miranda Frances Spieler, *Empire and Underworld: Captivity in French Guyana* (Cambridge, MA: Harvard University Press, 2012), 17, 35.

22. "C'est moi" from *Moniteur Universel* (Jan. 9, 1799). For favorable press, see also *Moniteur Universel* (Feb. 3, 1799) and *Philadelphia Gazette* (March 12, 1799). "L'opinion publique se forme" from Pascal to TL (Apr. 12, 1799), Sc. Micro R-2228, reel 5, NYPL-SC.

23. On Hédouville's arrival, see Dorvo-Soulastre, *Voyage par terre de Santo-Domingo . . . au Cap-Français* (Paris: Chaumerot, 1809). On Hédouville's background, see W/51/3331/31, AN. For his instructions, see B277, ANOM. The following account of Hédouville's 1798 tenure is also based on CC9A/18–19 and CC9B/6–9, ANOM; PMD-PH, vol. 2; Box 1, Sc. MG 119, NYPL-SC; Ms. Hait. 68–72, BPL.

24. "Paraissent de bouche" from TL to Hédouville (Apr. 11, 1798), CC9B/6, ANOM. "Pas assez grand" from Pamphile de Lacroix, *Mémoires pour servir à l'histoire de la révolution de SD* (Paris: Pillet, 1819), 1:340. TL offered to retire in TL to Raimond (May 9, 1798), B277, ANOM.

25. "Si pas gagné soldats" from Pierre Pluchon, *TL* (Paris: Fayard, 1989), 227. "Il s'est récrié" from Hédouville to Directoire (c. 1798), CC9A/19, ANOM.

26. "Ce malheureux vieillard" from TL to Philippe Létombe (June 4, 1798), Ms. Hait. 72–3, BPL.

27. "Vous êtes coupables" from PMD-PH, 2:19.

28. "Tant de déférence" from TL to Hédouville (Sept. 2, 1798), CC9B/6, ANOM.

29. On proposing to resign, see TL to Hédouville (Sept. 5, 1798), Ms. Hait. 71–19 (2), BPL. "Imprécations horribles" from Hédouville, "Rapport" (c. Dec. 1798), AF/III, 210, AN.

30. On the incident of Fort-Liberté, see TL to Dessalines (Oct. 1798), Autograph File, T., HU-HL; Hédouville, "Rapport" (c. Dec. 5, 1798), AF/III, 210, AN; PMD-PH, 2:30.

31. "Croit-il me faire peur?" from François de Kerversau, "Rapport sur la partie française de SD" (March 22, 1801), Box 2/66, UF-RP. For the memoir and the petitions, 1-SIZE E799.T734e and 1-SIZE E799.A774d, JCB.

32. "Surprise" from Eustache Bruix to TL (Feb. 12, 1799), CC9A/22, ANOM.

CHAPTER 15: DIPLOMAT, 1798–1800

1. On the dinner, see Ronald Johnson, *Diplomacy in Black and White: John Adams, TL, and Their Atlantic World Alliance* (Athens: University of Georgia Press, 2014), 19.

2. "La plus grande surprise" from TL to John Adams (Nov. 6, 1798), M9/1, NARA-CP.

3. On Bunel (who is often erroneously described as mixed race), see Philippe Girard, "Trading Races: Joseph and Marie Bunel. A Diplomat and a Merchant in Revolutionary SD and Philadelphia," *Journal of the Early Republic* 30 (Fall 2010): 351–376.

4. "Toussaint clause" from Gordon S. Brown, *Toussaint's Clause: The Founding Fathers and the Haitian Revolution* (Jackson: University Press of Mississippi, 2005), 138.

5. "Commercial intercourse" from Pickering to TL (March 4, 1799), M28/5, NARA-CP. Though TL attributed Adams's snub to racial reasons, Adams may have refused to write in person simply because TL was not a fellow head of state.

6. "A mériter" from Roume, "Extrait de la lettre de l'agent" (Nov. 22, 1798), BN08270 / lot 132, UF-RP. This account of Roume's public record in 1799–1801 is based on Roume Papers, LC-MD; CC9A/21–26 and CC9B/1–2, ANOM.

7. "Ne rien faire" from Roume, "Aux républicains français" (Jan. 23, 1799), CC9B/9, ANOM.

8. On Roume's personal life, see "Contrat de mariage" (Feb. 19, 1799) and "Acte de naissance" (Nov. 19, 1799), ET/XXXI/703, AN.

9. This account of TL's diplomacy with Stevens and Maitland is based on M9/1–2, NARA-CP; CO 137/102–103, ADM 1/249–250, and WO 1/72,

BNA; Philippe Girard, "Black Talleyrand: TL's Secret Diplomacy with England and the United States," *William and Mary Quarterly* 66, no. 1 (Jan. 2009): 87–124.

10. "Dignified prisoner" from Edward Stevens to Timothy Pickering (June 24, 1799), 208 MI/1, AN. "De ma main" from Roume to Min. of Navy (July 3, 1799), Roume Papers, LC-MD.

11. For Hamilton's constitution, see Hamilton to Pickering (Feb. 21, 1799), P-31, reel 24, p. 103, MHS. "Taking his measures" from Stevens to Pickering (Feb. 13, 1800), 208 MI/1, AN.

12. "L'enfant adoptif" from TL to Roume (Oct. 29, 1799), CC9A/26, ANOM. "Il le ferait couper" from François Tussac, *Cri des colons contre un ouvrage de M. l'évêque et sénateur Grégoire, ayant pour titre de la littérature des nègres* (Paris: Delaunay, 1810), 248.

13. "Rebelle" from Hédouville to Roume (Oct. 22, 1798), CC9A/20, ANOM. On Rigaud's background, see "Etat de services d'André Rigaud" (Dec. 1, 1795), 8Yd638, SHD-DAT. This account of the War of the South is based on PMD-PH, vol. 2; CC9A/21–26, ANOM; CO 137/103–104, BNA; M9/1–2, NARA-CP.

14. "Lever le bras gauche" (possibly a Vodou reference) from PMD-PH, 2:52. For estimates of each army, see Thomas Maitland to Earl of Balcarres (June 17, 1799), CO 137/102, BNA; Stevens to Pickering (June 24, 1799), 208 MI/1, AN.

15. On the assassination attempt, see Patrick Fletcher to Stoddert (Aug. 14, 1799), M625/199, NARA-DC. On mass drowning (a tactic reused by the French in 1802), see Hugh Cathcart to Maitland (Oct. 31, 1799), WO 1/74, BNA; Urbain Devaux to Forfait (Dec. 2, 1799), CC9A/23, AN; PMD-PH, 2:107, 120, 127. "L'époux d'une mulâtresse" from Roume, "Discours" (July 18, 1799), CC9B/9, ANOM.

16. "Liberty and the French" from "At a Council Held in Santiago de la Vega" (Dec. 5, 1799), CO 137/103, BNA. On the Sasportas expedition, see Gabriel Debien and Pierre Pluchon, "Un plan d'invasion de la Jamaïque en 1799 et la politique anglo-américaine de TL," *Revue de la Société Haïtienne d'Histoire, de Géographie et de Géologie* 36, no. 119 (July 1978): 3–72.

17. "Toussaint may fairly claim" from Balcarres to Duke of Portland (Oct. 28, 1799), CO 137/103, BNA.

18. "La nature a frémi en moi" from Isaac Sasportas to Balcarres (Dec. 20, 1799), NLS-CM.

19. "Solidarity" from Boaz Anglade, ed., *Jean-Bertrand Aristide in His Own Words: A Collection of the Haitian President's Speeches with Illustrative Notes* (Lulu, 2010), 72.

20. On the refusal to export the slave revolt, see TL to Army of SD (Apr. 26, 1801), CO 137/106, BNA; Julia Gaffield, ed., *The Haitian Declaration of Independence: Creation, Context, and Legacy* (Charlottesville: University of Virginia Press, 2015), 42.

21. "A la mamelle" and other quotes from TL, "Proclamation" (July 19, July 30, Aug. 23, and Sept. 9, 1799) CC9B/9, ANOM.

22. "N'a pas moi Nègre" from PMD-PH, 2:80.

23. "Long ago" from TL to Cathcart (Dec. 19, 1799), WO 1/74, BNA.

24. "The character" from Thomas Maitland to Hyde Parker (May 31, 1799), CO 137/102, BNA. "Cet être à grosses lèvres" (citing approvingly a French planter) from Parker to Earl of Balcarres (June 30, 1800), CO 137/105, BNA.

25. On US naval assistance to TL, see M149/1 and M625/199–200, NARA-DC. On Perry, see MS Am 1815.1, HU-HL; Johnson, *Diplomacy in Black and White*, 124.

26. On mistreating the mission of Charles Vincent, Jean-Baptiste Michel, Julien Raimond, see Vincent to Pierre Forfait (June 17, 1800), CC9A/28, ANOM; Michel to Forfait (Dec. 26, 1800), d. 6, AF/IV/1213, AN.

27. On Geneviève Chancy, see Pierre Bardin, "Langlois de Chancy-TL," *Généalogie et Histoire de la Caraïbe* 92 (Apr. 1997): 1944. On Didine Gustave, see Placide David, *Sur les rives du passé: Choses de SD* (1947; reprint, Ottawa: Leméac, 1972), 99.

28. "Moüe di' yo baliser" from Michel-Etienne Descourtilz, *Voyage d'un naturaliste et ses observations* (Paris: Dufart, 1809), 3:261. For high and low estimates of the massacres, see Thomas Madiou, *Histoire d'Haïti* (Port-au-Prince: Courtois, 1847), 2:68; C. L. R. James, *The Black Jacobins: Toussaint L'Ouverture and the San Domingo Revolution* (1963; reprint, New York: Vintage Books, 1989), 236.

29. "Pardonnez nous nos offenses" from PMD-PH, 2:164. On the ceremony, see also Vincent, "Précis des principaux événements" (c. Nov. 1801), MS. 619, BFV-FM.

CHAPTER 16: PLANTER, 1800–1801

1. "Dieu avait dit" (Matthew 7:7) and other quotes from TL, [Report to Laveaux] (Feb. 14–20, 1796), fr. 12104, BNF.

2. "Conduire comme des aveugles" from TL, "Proclamation" (Apr. 25, 1796), fr. 12104, BNF.

3. On Lafayette's experiment in Guiana, see Box 3:21–25, Lafayette Collection, CUL.

4. On burned estates, see Anon., "Mémoire de ce qui est parvenu . . . " (c. Oct. 1, 1791), d. 772, D/XXV/78, AN.

5. On US abolitionists, see Convention of Abolitionist Societies to Society of the Friends of the Blacks (May 9, 1797), Micr. XR572:29, HSP. "Un désert" from Gabriel Debien, "TL et quelques quartiers de SD vus par des colons (octobre 1799–janvier 1800)," *Revue Française d'Histoire d'Outre-Mer* 142 (1954): 113–124. For production statistics, see Barré de Saint-Venant, *Des colonies modernes sous la zone torride, et particulièrement de celle de SD* (Paris: Brochot, 1802), 51. These figures are consistent with tariff records indicating that the French-occupied part of the colony exported only 1.5 million livres in 1797; see Hédouville to Bruix (June 10, 1798), CC9B/7, ANOM.

6. "Nos mines" from Thomas Gragnon-Lacoste, *TL* (Paris: Durand, 1877), 216.

7. On financial problems, see Edward Stevens to Timothy Pickering (Jan. 29, 1800), 208 MI/1, AN; TL, "Règlement" (May 15, July 3, and Nov. 5, 1800), CC9B/9, ANOM.

8. "Blanc noir" (referring to TL's aide-de-camp Augustin d'Hébécourt) from "Rapport-d'Hébécourt" (Jan.–Feb. 1803), B7/9, SHD-DAT.

9. On TL's assets, see Philippe Girard and Jean-Louis Donnadieu, "Toussaint Before Louverture: New Archival Findings on the Early Life of TL," *William and Mary Quarterly* 70, no. 1 (Jan. 2013): 72; Alain Turnier, *Quand la nation demande des comptes* (Port-au-Prince: Le Natal, 1989), 35.

10. For TL's salary, see art. 41 of the 1801 constitution (the *franc* was the new name of the *livre*). "Je n'ai jamais été riche" from "TL au Fort de Joux," *Nouvelle Revue Rétrospective* 94 (Apr. 10, 1902): 12.

11. On seizing émigré estates, see Etienne de Polverel and Léger-Félicité Sonthonax, "Proclamation" (Apr. 18, 1793), CC9A/8, ANOM. On estates run by the Domaines, see 135AP3, AN; PMD-PH, 2:16.

12. For legal procedures, see "Loi concernant l'organisation constitutionnelle des colonies" (Jan. 1, 1798), CC9B/9, ANOM; Hédouville, "Extrait du registre" (July 14, 1798), Log.1814.F, LCP. For estates leased by TL, see 1 SUPSDOM 1–2 and 5 SUPSDOM 2–4, ANOM (documents communicated by Jean-Louis Donnadieu); PMD-PH, 2:40, 58.

13. "Scheme" from Peter Chazotte, *Historical Sketches of the Revolutions, and the Foreign and Civil Wars in the Island of St. Domingo* (New York: Applegate, 1840), 18, 20.

14. "Ne croyez cependant pas" from Sonthonax, "Proclamation" (Aug. 29, 1793), Lk12–28, BNF.

15. "Le travail" and other quotes from TL to pop. of Verrettes (March 22, 1795), fr. 12103, BNF; TL, [Untitled] (Feb. 14–20, 1796), fr. 12104, BNF; PMD-PH, 2:5; TL, "Discours" (Oct. 5 and Nov. 15, 1798), CC9B/9, AN; Beaubrun Ardouin, *Etudes sur l'histoire d'Haïti, suivies de la vie du général J-M Borgella* (Paris: Dezobry et Magdeleine, 1853–1860), 4:248; *Bulletin Officiel de SD* (July 8, 1801).

16. "Doctrine aussi vicieuse" from TL, "Ordonnance" (Jan. 4, 1800), CC9B/9, ANOM. On the curse, see Thomas Madiou, *Histoire d'Haïti* (Port-au-Prince: Courtois, 1847), 2:91; PG-MGTL, 27. On corn, see Pamphile de Lacroix, *Mémoires pour servir à l'histoire de la révolution de SD* (Paris: Pillet, 1819), 1:409. On wine, see Morin, "Réflexions . . . " (Aug. 13, 1800), Sc. Micro R-2228, reel 15, NYPL-SC.

17. On cultivators in the 1792–1793 rebel army, see Fernando Carrera Montero, *Las complejas relaciones de España con La Española: El Caribe hispano frente a Santo Domingo y Saint Domingue, 1789–1803* (Santo Domingo: Fundación García Arévalo, 2004), 47; Gabriel Belair to Joaquín García (Sept. 10, 1793), SGU, LEG, 7157, 10, AGS. "En France" from Sonthonax, "Proclamation" (Aug. 29, 1793), Lk12–28, BNF. For later labor codes, see H. Pauléus Sannon, *Histoire de TL* (PAP: Héraux, 1920), 1:222; Etienne Laveaux, *Réponse d'Etienne Laveaux . . .* ([Paris]: J. F. Sobry, June 19, 1797), 7; André Rigaud, "La

Loi" (Sept. 25, 1794), F3/199, ANOM; Hédouville, "Arrêté concernant la police des habitations" (July 24, 1798), Box 1/47, UF-RP.

18. "Ne font que courir" from TL, "Proclamation" (Aug. 4, 1800), CC9B/9, ANOM.

19. "*Seront arrêtés et punis*" from TL, "Règlement sur la culture" (Oct. 25, 1800), CC9B/9, ANOM. The earliest version was dated Oct. 12, 1800, according to Ardouin, *Etudes*, 4:247, and PMD-PH, 2:169.

20. "Libertinage" from TL, "Au nom de la colonie" (Nov. 25, 1801), Sc. Micro R1527, NYPL-SC. On keeping women out of barracks, see art. 9 of TL, "Règlement sur la culture" (Oct. 25, 1800), CC9B/9, ANOM. On unequal pay, see Sonthonax, "Proclamation" (Aug. 29, 1793), Lk12–28, BNF.

21. "Je vous mènerai" from TL, "Ordonnance" (Oct. 14, 1800), CC9B/9, ANOM.

22. For TL's decrees, see TL, "Arrêté" (Feb. 7 and Sept. 30, 1801), CC9B/9, ANOM; art. 16 of the July 1801 constitution.

23. "Marche-pied" (quoting cultivators in Dondon) from Roume to Forfait (Sept. 25, 1801), BN08270 / lot 132, UF-RP.

24. "Une balle à la jambe" from TL to Laveaux (June 17, 1795), fr. 12103, BNF. For the penalty for theft (whipping and branding in most instances), see art. 35 and 36 of the 1685 Black Code.

25. On the Nov. 1800 revolt, see Edward Robinson to Balcarres (Nov. 18, 1800), CO 137/105, BNA; PMD-PH, 2:174. On the Moïse uprising, see chap. 18. On labor abuses in 1800–1801, see PMD-PH, 2:71; Madiou, *Histoire d'Haïti*, 2:106.

26. "La révolution en a moissoné" from Philippe Roume, "Moyens proposés . . . " (June 11, 1800), Roume Papers, LC-MD.

27. On slaves in the United States, see *Gazette of the United States* 24 (Oct. 29, 1801). "The importation of negroes" from "Council Minutes" (Nov. 19, 1799), CO 137/107, BNA. "Un projet plus vaste" from IL-NH, 69. Several historians have recycled Isaac's unproven claim, notably C. L. R. James, in *The Black Jacobins: TL and the San Domingo Revolution* (1963; reprint, New York: Vintage Books, 1989), 265.

28. On legalizing the slave trade, see art. 17 of the 1801 constitution. On the Bunel mission, see Nugent to [former] Duke of Portland (Sept. 5, 1801), CO 137/106, BNA; PMD-PH, 2:204. On Dessalines and the slave trade, see Philippe Girard, "Jean-Jacques Dessalines and the Atlantic System: A Reappraisal," *William and Mary Quarterly* 69, no. 3 (July 2012): 575. On the Royal Dahomets of Christophe, see Antoine Coron, "Le 'système de défense' du roi Christophe," *Revue de la BNF* 36 (2010): 74–81.

29. "Le zèle" from TL, *Réfutations de quelques assertions d'un discours . . . par Viénot-Vaublanc* (Cap: Roux, [Oct. 29], 1797), 11. "La cultu et les commerce" from PG-MGTL, 52.

30. For production statistics, see Charles Mackenzie, *Notes on Haiti Made During a Residence in That Republic* (London: Colburn, 1830), 2:159.

31. On TL's finances, see PMD-PH, 2:237. On the war chest, see *Moniteur Universel* (May 28, 1802). On stashes of cash, see Philippe Girard, *The Slaves*

Who Defeated Napoléon: TL and the Haitian War of Independence, 1801–1804 (Tuscaloosa: University of Alabama Press, 2011), 107.

32. On the rebuilding estimates, which varied from a low of 40 million colonial francs (to provide a mere two hundred plantations with a minimal labor force) to a high of 4 billion (to boost production levels to three times the 1791 peak), see Saint-Venant, *Des colonies modernes*, 193, 472.

33. On the Manquets output (500 *milliers* in 1791), see François Guilbaud to Count of Noé (Jan. 31, 1791), JLD-PHD. "Tous jours ame sicaner" from Jean-Baptiste to Dupuis (July 22, 1800), Box 6:11, (Phi)1602, HSP. A piastre-gourde was worth 7.5 French colonial livres.

CHAPTER 17: GOVERNOR GENERAL, EARLY 1801

1. On the run-up to the takeover, see TL, *Procès-verbal de la prise de possession de la partie espagnole* (Jan. 27, 1801), Box L-1801, MHS; Emilio Rodríguez Demorizi, ed., *Cesión de Santo Domingo a Francia* (Ciudad Trujillo: Impresora Dominicana, 1958).

2. "Se réfugie dans la partie espagnole" from TL to Roume (Oct. 19, 1799), CC9A/26, ANOM. On draft-dodging, see Moyse to Roume (Oct. 14, 1799), CC9A/26, ANOM.

3. On Rigaud supporters in Santo Domingo, see Hugh Cathcart to Maitland (Nov. 26, 1799), WO 1/74, BNA.

4. On Roume being locked up for supporting the Sasportas plan, see Roume to TL (Jan. 13, 1800), CC9B/1, ANOM. For a petition sent to Roume, see EB.S146 1800 1, JCB.

5. "Tant de fermeté" from Jean-Louis Clavier, "TL d'après le 'Mémoire abrégé des événements de SD depuis l'année 1789 jusqu'à celle de 1807,'" *Revue Française d'Histoire d'Outre-Mer* 62, no. 228 (1975): 491. On the chicken-coop incident, see also Stevens to Pickering (Apr. 19, 1800), 208 MI/1, AN; DHHAN, 128.

6. "Gouvernée comme par le passé" from Beaubrun Ardouin, *Etudes sur l'histoire d'Haïti, suivies de la vie du général J-M Borgella* (Paris: Dezobry et Magdeleine, 1853–1860), 4:171.

7. On the expedition, see Lazare Carnot, "Projet secret de l'envoi d'une expédition" (Apr. 1800), B7/1, SHD-DAT. "Il paraît évident" from Huin and Augustin d'Hébécourt to TL (Nov. 11, 1800), Folder D8, HU-KFC. Placide actually went to Marseille; see "Rapport au premier consul" (July 8, 1801), d. 6, EE 1734, ANOM.

8. On abductions of black laborers (a claim based on a single disputed case), see TL to Bonaparte (June 25, 1800), d. 1, AF/IV/1213, AN; Demorizi, *Cesión de Santo Domingo*, 557–569.

9. On the invasion, see Ardouin, *Etudes*, 4:288–310. On eluding Bonaparte's orders, see Péries to [Pichon?] (Jan. 28, 1801), Sc. Micro R-2228, reel 1, NYPL-SC.

10. "Yo estaria ahora" from Antonio del Monte y Tejada, *Historia de Santo Domingo* (Santo Domingo: García Hermanos, 1892), 3:211. On the balls, see Alain Yacou, ed., *SD espagnol et la révolution nègre d'Haïti (1790–1822)* (Paris: Karthala, 2007), 256.

11. "No tiene necesidad de vtros bienes" from Fernando Carrera Montero, *Las complejas relaciones de España con La Española: El Caribe hispano frente a Santo Domingo y Saint Domingue, 1789–1803* (Santo Domingo: Fundación García Arévalo, 2004), 460. "Quiero que travajen" from TL, "Proclamación" (Feb. 8, 1801), ESTADO, 60, N.3, AGI.

12. "N'avait point proclamé" from François Desrivières Chanlatte, *Considérations diverses sur Haïti* (Port-au-Prince, [n.s.], 1822), 14. On manumission documents, see Graham Nessler, "'They Always Knew Her to Be Free': Emancipation and Re-Enslavement in French Santo Domingo, 1804–1809," *Slavery and Abolition* 33, no. 1 (2012): 89.

13. "Papá Boyé" from Sara E. Johnson, *The Fear of French Negroes: Transcolonial Collaboration in the Revolutionary Americas* (Berkeley: University of California Press, 2012), 71.

14. On Dominican emigration, see ESTADO, 60, N.3, AGI; Darién J. Davis, ed., *Beyond Slavery: The Multilayered Legacy of Africans in Latin America and the Caribbean* (Lanham, MD: Rowman and Littlefield, 2007), 27 (Dominicans claim that Columbus's body is still in a mausoleum near Santo Domingo). On TL's economic reforms, see PMD-PH, 2:184; Gilbert Guillermin, *Journal historique de la révolution de la partie de l'Est de Saint-Domingue, commencée le 10 août 1808* (Philadelphia: Lafourcade, 1810), v.

15. "Dieu nous l'a donné" from Thomas Madiou, *Histoire d'Haïti* (Port-au-Prince: Courtois, 1847), 2:90.

16. "Mannequin" (citing Roume) from [Genêt to Pierre Forfait?] (May 26, 1800), CC9B/27, ANOM. On sending Roume to Dondon, see TL to Roume (Nov. 26, 1800), BN08270 / lot 132, UF-RP.

17. "Pas rendu assez de justice" from TL to Min. of Navy (Feb. 12, 1801), 61J18, ADGir. On Roume's departure, see Roume to Forfait (Sept. 25, 1801), BN08270 / lot 132, UF-RP.

18. "Mieux disciplinés" from TL to Napoléon Bonaparte (Feb. 12, 1801), d. 1, EE1734, ANOM.

19. "Ne divulguez" from "Extrait des registres de l'Assemblée Centrale" (Apr. 7, 1801), CO 137/106, BNA. On the constitutional assembly, see also TL, "Proclamation" (Feb. 5, 1801), ESTADO, 60, N.3, AGI.

20. "Conquérant de son Pays" and "O vous mes concitoyens" (next paragraph) from Administration Municipale du Cap, *Extrait des Registres* (July 6, 1801), electronic resources, HU-HL.

21. On the constitutional delegates, see PMD-PH, 2:186.

22. "Il ne paraît plus douteux" from Louis-André Pichon to Pierre Forfait (June 3, 1801), CC9A/28, ANOM. "En révolte ouverte" from Pichon to Charles de Talleyrand (Aug. 6, 1801), CC9B/21, ANOM.

23. "A black independent government" from Edward Corbet to Balcarres (March 31, 1801), CO 137/105, BNA. On tensions with Anglo-Americans, see TL to Edward Corbet (Apr. 1, 1801), CO 137/105, BNA; Lear to Madison (July 17, 1801), 208 MI/2, AN.

24. "Pendant que vous secondez" from Chef du bureau du contentieux to TL (June 12, 1799), MS7, p. 100, SHD-DM.

25. "Dictée" from TL to Coisnon (June 3, 1798), d. 963, AF/III, 210, AN.

26. "Mon intention" from TL to Napoléon (June 25, 1800), d. 1, AF/IV/1213, AN. "Toussaint est fort attaché" in "Les enfants de TL" (Oct. 7, 1801), d. 5410, F7/6266, AN.

27. "Dégager entièrement ce général" from Philippe Joseph Letombe, "Extrait pour le Premier Consul" (Aug. 6, 1800), d. 6, AF/IV/1213, AN. For the plots (possibly masterminded by Thomas Maitland), see d. 5410, F7/6266, AN.

28. "Votre mère" from Michel Roussier, "L'éducation des enfants de TL et l'institution nationale des colonies," *Revue Française d'Histoire d'Outre-Mer* 64, no. 236 (1977): 336.

29. "La plus dangereuse ambition" from Vincent to TL (Aug. 7, 1801), Box 2:1, MG 140, NYPL-SC. "Force occulte" (paraphrasing TL) from Pamphile de Lacroix, *Mémoires pour servir à l'histoire de la révolution de SD* (Paris: Pillet, 1819), 2:24.

30. For a manuscript copy of the constitution (probably Vincent's), see Pièce 48, AF/IV/1212, AN. On the Vincent mission, see TL to Bonaparte (July 16, 1801), d. 1, AF/IV/1213, AN.

CHAPTER 18: GOD? LATE 1801

1. On the Oct. 6, 1801, ceremony in Port-au-Prince, see PMD-PH, 2:212. On TL as Jesus, see, for example, TL to Roume (Sept. 8, 1799), CC9A/26, ANOM. "L'homme propose" from PG-MGTL, 140.

2. "Il n'appartient qu'à Dieu" from Thomas Madiou, *Histoire d'Haïti* (Port-au-Prince: Courtois, 1847), 1:307. "J'ai pris mon vol" from Pamphile de Lacroix, *Mémoires pour servir à l'histoire de la révolution de SD* (Paris: Pillet, 1819), 2:23.

3. "His movements are very rapid" from Tobias Lear to James Madison (July 20, 1801), 208 MI/2, AN. "On s'est grossièrement trompé" from Pascal to Louis-André Pichon (July 21, 1801), CC9/B21, ANOM.

4. For the laws passed from July 18 to August 12, 1801, see "Lois de la colonie fr. de SD" (c. Aug. 1801), CO 137/106, BNA. On the Catholic Church, see M. A. Matinée, ed., *Anecdotes de la révolution de SD racontées par Guillaume Mauviel* (Saint-Lô: Elie fils, 1885), 35.

5. "Le travail de cabinet" from [Pascal], "Mémoire secret" (c. 1801), Sc. Micro R-2228, reel 8, NYPL-SC.

6. "Gens de l'art" (an apparent reference to abortion) from PMD-PH, 2:173. For the penal code, see "Lois de la colonie fr. de SD" (c. Aug. 1801), CO 137/106, BNA.

7. "Partout" from Jean-Baptiste Lemonnier-Delafosse, *Seconde campagne de Saint-Domingue du 1 décembre 1803 au 15 juillet 1809, précédée de souvenirs historiques et succints de la première campagne* (Le Havre, France: Brindeau, 1846), 34.

8. On reading official mail, see TL to Laveaux (Apr. 14, 1796), fr. 12104, BNF; [Hédouville] to Rigaud (June 18, 1798), Box 1, Sc. MG 119, NYPL-SC. On intercepting couriers, see Kerversau to Bruix (Jan. 4, 1799) and Kerversau to Roume (Feb. 14, 1799), CC9B/23, ANOM.

9. "Vous ne doutez pas du sort" and "plusieurs domiciliés" from [Pierre] Collette to [Médéric Moreau de Saint-Méry?] (Aug. 14, 1800), F3/202, ANOM.

10. "Si le général" from Urbain Devaux to Pierre Forfait (Dec. 2, 1799), CC9A/23, ANOM. "Une petite guerre" from Captain Baptiste, "Notes sur la colonie" (c. 1801), CC9C/1, ANOM.

11. "Pas assez de connaissance" from TL, *Réfutations de quelques assertions d'un discours . . . par Viénot-Vaublanc* (Cap: Roux, [Oct. 29], 1797), 20. On white employees of TL, see Faine Scharon, *TL et la révolution de SD* (Port-au-Prince: Imprimerie de l'Etat, 1957), 2:128.

12. "Fat negro" from Marcus Rainsford, *An Historical Account of the Black Empire of Hayti* (London: Albion Press, 1805), 216. "On riait quelquefois" from Charles Bréard, *Notes sur SD* (Rouen: Espérance Cagniard, 1893), 21. "Les blancs sont obligés" from Captain Dulac to Commandant Labarthe (Feb. 19, 1800), F3/202, ANOM.

13. "Doucement, M. le gérant" from Lacroix, *Mémoires*, 1:399. "Ceux auxquels vous avez été attaché" ("attaché" can mean "close to" or "tied to") from Noé to TL (Apr. 6, 1799), CO 137/50, BNA (document first uncovered by David Geggus). It is not clear whether TL, who had leased Noé's estate in his absence, sent him the cash he requested. On TL sending money, see Jean de Saint-Anthoine, *Notice sur TL* (Paris: Lacour, 1842), 23. For contradictory evidence, see Earl of Balcarres to S. King (July 27, 1800), CO 137/104, BNA.

14. "Les pommettes" from *Nouvelle Revue Rétrospective* 94 (Apr. 10, 1902): 1. On the cane (now in a museum in Mirande), see IL-NH, 77.

15. For grocery bills, see Box 6:6, (Phi)1602, HSP.

16. On the town of Louverture, see "Arrêtés des différentes communes" (Oct. 23, 1798), 1-SIZE E799.A774d, JCB. On the street and the province, see "Arrêté" (Apr. 5, 1800, and July 14, 1801), CC9B/9, ANOM. "Vous autres nègres" from Lacroix, *Mémoires*, 1:400.

17. "Les ennemis des noirs" (citing TL) from Colonel Malenfant, *Des colonies, et particulièrement de celle de SD: Mémoire historique et politique* (Paris: Audibert: 1814), 95.

18. "Tresses de cheveux" from Lacroix, *Mémoires*, 2:105. On mistresses, see also PMD-PH, 2:133, 159, 173, 180, 216; Michel-Etienne Descourtilz, *Voyage d'un naturaliste et ses observations* (Paris: Dufart, 1809), 30, 153.

19. "Premier des noirs" from Joseph Saint-Rémy, *Vie de TL* (Paris: Moquet, 1850), 309. "Salut et respect" from TL to Bonaparte (Sept. 16, 1802), d. 1, EE1734, ANOM. "Un petit mot d'écrit" from TL to Bonaparte (June 25, 1800), d. 1, AF/IV/1213, AN. "Vous écrire plusieurs lettres" from TL to Bonaparte (July 16, 1801), d. 1, AF/IV/1213, AN.

20. "Being neglected" from Tobias Lear to James Madison (July 17, 1801), M9/3, NARA-CP. "Si j'étais blanc" (citing TL) from [Vincent], "Réflexions sur l'état actuel de la colonie . . . " (Oct. 13, 1801), F3/283, ANOM.

21. "D'une méfiance excessive" from [Pascal], "Mémoire secret" (c. 1801), Sc. Micro R-2228, reel 8, NYPL-SC. "Vous" from Paul Louverture to TL (March 26, 1801), CO 137/105, BNA. On TL's godfather, see Alphonse de Lamartine, *TL* (Paris: Lévy, 1850), xviii.

22. "Un furieux orage" from Roume to Forfait (Sept. 25, 1801), BN08270 / lot 132, UF-RP.

23. "Death to all the white people" from Edward Corbet to [Anon.] (Nov. 16, 1801), CO 137/106, BNA. On the Moïse uprising, see also Silas Talbot to James Madison (Oct. 30, 1801), 208 MI/2, AN; TL, *Récit des événements* (Nov. 7, 1801), CO 137/106, BNA; *Aurora* (Nov. 30, 1801); [Painty?] to Moreau de Saint-Méry (Feb. 27, 1802), F3/202, ANOM; PMD-PH, 2:214–221.

24. "Enfant prodigue" from TL to Laveaux (Sept. 16, 1795), fr. 12103, BNF. "Lorsqu'il parle" from "TL au Fort de Joux," *Nouvelle Revue Rétrospective* 94 (Apr. 10, 1902): 17.

25. On TL's political inheritance, see art. 30 of the 1801 constitution; Charles Bréard, *Notes sur SD,* 16.

26. "La tranquillité publique" from TL, "Au nom de la colonie" (Nov. 25, 1801), Sc. Micro R1527, NYPL-SC.

CHAPTER 19: RENEGADE, EARLY 1802

1. On the recapture of the *Enfant Prodigue*, see Sonthonax to TL (July 15, 1797), fr. 8988, BNF.

2. On the *Enfant Prodigue*'s recent arrival in SD, see Péries to [Pichon?] (Jan. 28, 1801), Sc. Micro R-2228, reel 1, NYPL-SC.

3. "Ils feront moins de sucre" from P. L. Roederer, *Mémoires sur la Révolution, le Consulat, et l'Empire* (1840; reprint, Paris: Plon, 1942), 131. On Napoléon's colonial policies, see Philippe Girard, "Napoléon voulait-il rétablir l'esclavage en Haïti?," *Bulletin de la Société d'Histoire de la Guadeloupe* 159 (May–Aug. 2011): 3–28.

4. "Voies de la douceur" from "Instructions . . . au citoyen Mongiraud" (c. March 1801), AF/IV/1212, AN. "Marque de confiance" in Napoléon to TL (March 4, 1801), HU-KFC (picture of the original).

5. On TL's firing, see Ministère de la Guerre, "Relevé de services" (c. 1803), 7Yd284, SHD-DAT. On the letter's fate, see Embassy of the United States of America, Press and Information Office, 75382 Paris Cedex 08, "Le Bureau des Enquêtes en Matière de Sécurité collabore à la restitution d'un manuscrit portant la signature de Napoléon," http://photos.state.gov/libraries/france/5/pressreleases/pr20140819fr.pdf.

6. On the first preparations for the expedition, see Napoléon, "Extrait des registres" (May 3, 1801), BB4 151, SHD-DM.

7. On the first peace feelers with the United Kingdom, see CN, 7:202. The Quasi-War with the United States ended with the Peace of Mortefontaine in 1800.

8. "Le plus coupable" from Vincent to TL (Aug. 7, 1801), Box 2:1, MG 140, NYPL-SC. "Détruire dans votre esprit" from TL to Napoléon (Aug. 24, 1801), d. 1, AF/IV/1213, AN. Gaston Nogerée reached France after the Leclerc expedition had left; see "Rapport au premier consul" (Jan. 5, 1802), d. 5410, F/7/6266, AN.

9. "Africains ingrats" from Napoléon Bonaparte, *Mémoires pour servir à l'histoire de France sous Napoléon* (London: Martin Bossange, 1823), 1:193.

10. "Ne peut être soumis" from Vincent, "Précis des principaux événements de SD" (c. Nov. 1801), MS. 619, BFV-FM. On Christophe's doubts, see Roume to Forfait (Sept. 25, 1801), BN08270 / lot 132, UF-RP.

11. On the size of the expedition, see "Etat des troupes . . . " (Nov. 2, 1801), BB4 162, SHD-DM.

12. "Quelles que soient vos origines" from Napoléon, "Proclamation du Consul" (Nov. 8, 1801), F3/202, ANOM. For Napoléon's secret instructions, see Paul Roussier, ed., *Lettres du général Leclerc* (Paris: Société de l'histoire des colonies françaises, 1937), 263–274.

13. For the letter to TL, see CN, 7:410. "Jeune et vaillant héros" from Joseph Boromé, "Louanges de Napoléon Bonaparte par un fils de TL," *Revue de l'Institut Napoléon* 133 (1977): 169.

14. On the Bunel mission, see CO 137/106, BNA. On buying US weapons, see TL to Moïse (Nov. 26, 1800), AT-4, UPR-NC. On fortifications, see TL, "Instructions . . . " (May 14, 1801), CC9A/28, ANOM.

15. "Exceedingly depressed" from W. L. Whitfield to Nugent (Dec. 9, 1801), CO 137/106, BNA.

16. "Tous cela a été bien conbiné" from PG-MGTL, 140. "Black empire" from [Robert Hobart?] to George Nugent (Nov. 18, 1801), CO 137/106, BNA.

17. "Le bruit que la France" from TL, "Proclamation" (Dec. 20, 1801), CO 137/106, BNA. This printed proclamation was first transcribed (based on a handwritten third-party account) in Pierre Pluchon, "TL défie Bonaparte: L'adresse inédite du 20 décembre 1801," *Revue Française d'Histoire d'Outre-Mer* 79, no. 296 (Fall 1992): 383–389.

18. On courting supporters, see Peter S. Chazotte, *Historical Sketches of the Revolutions, and the Foreign and Civil Wars in the Island of St. Domingo, with a Narrative of the Entire Massacre of the White Population of the Island* (New York: Applegate, 1840), 24. On imprisoning planters, see Tobias Lear to James Madison (Jan. 17, 1802), 208 MI/2, AN. "The climate" from Edward Corbet to William Molleson (Dec. 5, 1801), CO 137/106, BNA.

19. On defensive preparations, see M. A. Matinée, ed., *Anecdotes de la révolution de SD racontées par Guillaume Mauviel* (Saint-Lô: Elie fils, 1885), 44. On learning of the expedition, see TL to Colonial Assembly (Jan. 22, 1802), Sc. Micro R-2228, reel 5, NYPL-SC.

20. "Prier Dieu pour moi" from TL to Simon Baptiste (Jan. 27, 1802), BB4 162, SHD-DM. "Il faut périr" from Pamphile de Lacroix, *Mémoires pour servir à l'histoire de la révolution de SD* (Paris: Pillet, 1819), 2:63. The following account of the spring 1802 campaign is based on Philippe Girard, *The Slaves Who Defeated Napoléon: TL and the Haitian War of Independence, 1801–1804* (Tuscaloosa: University of Alabama Press, 2011).

21. "Ces dispositions" from Antoine Métral, *Histoire de l'expédition des Français à SD* (Paris: Fanjat, 1825), 232 (some sources claim that TL went directly from Santo Domingo to Cap). "Tous les nègres" from Charles Malenfant, *Des colonies, et particulièrement de celle de SD* (Paris: Audibert, 1814), 299.

22. "L'ennemi ne tardera pas" from TL to Clerveaux (c. Jan. 30, 1802), in Matinée, *Anecdotes*, 45.

23. "Une escadre nombreuse" from TL to Augustin Clerveaux (Feb. 6, 1802), 61J24, ADGir.

24. "Quand nous avons pris les armes" from Thomas Madiou, *Histoire d'Haïti* (Port-au-Prince: Courtois, 1847), 2:222.

25. On hiding Bonaparte's pro-emancipation leanings, see Roume to TL (July 8, 1800), Box 1:5, MG 140, NYPL-SC. "Les blancs de France" from TL to Jean-Baptiste Domage (Feb. 9, 1802), CC9B/19, ANOM. On confiscating presses, see TL to Bartalie (Feb. 15, 1802), Sc. Micro R-2228, reel 5, NYPL-SC.

26. "La saison des pluies" from Joseph Elisée Peyre-Ferry, *Journal des opérations militaires de l'armée française à SD pendant les années X XI et XII (1802 et 1803)* (Port-au-Prince: Henri Deschamps, 2005), 402.

27. "Il les tint pendant longtemps" from Métral, *Histoire de l'expédition*, 239.

28. "Leur patrie et leur père" from Lacroix, *Mémoires*, 2:125.

29. "Carte blanche" from TL to Domage (Feb. 9, 1802), CC9B/19, ANOM.

30. "Rentrer en France" from Roussier, *Lettres du général Leclerc*, 116.

31. "Existence nomade" from Madiou, *Histoire d'Haïti*, 2:243.

32. "Voilà ce que sont les hommes" from Alphonse de Lamartine, *TL* (Paris: Lévy, 1850), xx.

33. "D'un sac de charbon" from Jean de Saint-Anthoine, *Notice sur TL* (Paris: Lacour, 1842), 25.

34. "Le règlement de culture" from Leclerc to Decrès (May 4, 1802), B7/26, SHD-DAT.

35. "Ravages effrayants" from Leclerc to Denis Decrès (May 8, 1802), CC9B/19, ANOM. On French losses, see Girard, *The Slaves Who Defeated Napoléon*, 179.

36. "La Providence" from Lacroix, *Mémoires*, 2:199.

37. "Il se retirait dans les bois" from Brunet to Rochambeau (May 26, 1802), lot 224, VR-PR.

38. "Bête de somme" from Brunet to Rochambeau (May 20, 1802), lot 224, VR-PR. On TL's arrest, see Philippe Girard, "Jean-Jacques Dessalines et l'arrestation de TL," *Journal of Haitian Studies* 17, no. 1 (Spring 2011): 123–138.

39. "Mon fist Isaac" from PG-MGTL, 122.

40. "L'arbre de la liberté des noirs" from Lacroix, *Mémoires*, 2:204. The quote echoes TL, "Proclamation à ses concitoyens" (Sept. 9, 1799), CC9B/9, ANOM. TL actually said "the suffering of our Savior would teach him to bear his situation patiently," according to George Nugent to John Sullivan (Aug. 12, 1802), CO 137/108, BNA; or "Heaven is just. I shall be avenged" according to Baron de Vastey, *Revolution and Civil Wars in Haiti* (1823; reprint, New York: Negro University Press, 1969), 35.

41. On TL visiting La Tortue in 1796 and a US frigate in 1800, see Sonthonax to Vaillant (Dec. 23, 1796), fr. 8986, BNF; Ronald Johnson, *Diplomacy in Black and White: John Adams, TL, and Their Atlantic World Alliance* (Athens: University of Georgia Press, 2014), 124.

CHAPTER 20: PRISONER, 1802–1803

1. "Une mère de famille" from TL to Bonaparte (July 20, 1802), d. 1, AF/IV/1213, AN. "Les femmes" from Suzanne Louverture to Denis Decrès (July 11, 1802), d. 1, EE1734, ANOM. "Elle aurait pu secourir" from TL to Victoire Leclerc (July 18, 1802), Folder 3C, HU-KFC. The following account of TL's captivity is based on AF/IV/1213 and 135AP/6, AN; CC9B/18 and EE1734,

ANOM; Sc. Micro R1527, NYPL-SC; 7Yd284 and B7/6 to B7/9, SHD-DAT; M696, ADD; UPR-NC.

2. "Je ne vous verrai jamais" from Placide to Toussaint and Suzanne Louverture (Aug. 12, 1802), d. 1, AF/IV/1213, AN.

3. "Pauvre diable" from Fernand Clamettes, ed., *Mémoires du général Baron Thiébault* (Paris: Plon, 1893–1895), 3:303.

4. "Un souterrain" from Mars Plaisir to Isaac Louverture (Oct. 3, 1815), NAF 6864, BNF. "En teré un homme vivant" from PG-MGTL, 141.

5. Versions 1, 2, and 4 are in d. 1, AF/IV/1213, AN. Version 3 is in d. 2, EE1734, ANOM. A fifth version in West Mss. 6, Northwestern University Library, is likely posthumous. For an English translation, see Philippe Girard, *The Memoir of General TL* (New York: Oxford University Press, 2014).

6. "Ses trésors" from CN, 8:39. "Calme" and other quotes from *Nouvelle Revue Rétrospective* no. 94 (Apr. 10, 1902): 1–18.

7. "Folies" from Barry Edward O'Meara, *Napoléon en exil: Relation contenant les opinions et les réflexions de Napoléon sur les événements les plus importants de sa vie, durant trois ans de sa captivité* (Paris: Garnier, 1897), 2:276.

8. "Il ne résulte du rapport" from Decrès to Leclerc (Oct. 16, 1802), d. 1, EE 1734, ANOM. "Pas un homme" from Emmanuel de las Cases, *Le Mémorial de Sainte-Hélène* (Paris: Gallimard, 1956), 1:770.

9. "Vous savé mon namitier" from TL to Suzanne Louverture (Sept. 17, 1802), d. 1, EE 1734, ANOM (TL was eventually informed that his family was well treated; see Baille to Decrès (Nov. 1, 1802), CC9B/18, ANOM. On Paul's family, see IL-NH,. 122. On a mixed-race Toussaint who had served under TL and was shot in Cap, see Gt. Néraud to Rochambeau (Oct. 8, 1803), 61J17, ADGir.

10. "Toussaint" from Stephen Gill, ed., *The Major Works: Including The Prelude* (Oxford: Oxford University Press, 1984), 282. "Il était triste" from J. F. Dubois to [Henri?] Grégoire (May 25, 1823), NAF 6864, BNF.

11. "Au nom de dieu" from TL to Bonaparte (Oct. 9, 1802), d. 1, AF/IV/1213, AN. On Dormoy, see Jean de Bry to Baille (Oct. 15, 1802), TL-2B4a, UPR-NC. On the Capuchin mission, see Frère Julien to De Castries (Sept. 30, 1785), F5A 25/1, ANOM.

12. "Quand un homme" from TL to Baille (c. Oct. 18, 1802), CC9B/18, ANOM.

13. "Per mete moi" from TL to Bonaparte (Oct. 26, 1802), d. 1, AF/IV/1213, AN.

14. "Il ne m'a jamais demandé" from Amiot to Denis Decrès (March 19, 1803), TL-2B7g, UPR-NC.

15. "Dant ce mondre" from PG-MGTL, 140.

16. "Le 17" from Amiot to Decrès (Apr. 9, 1803), CC9B/18, ANOM.

CHAPTER 21: ICON, 1803–PRESENT

1. "Réellement mort" and other quotes from Gresset, "Procès-Verbal . . . " (Apr. 8, 1803), TL-3A2, UPR-NC.

2. "D'une épaisseur extraordinaire" from TL-3B2, UPR-NC. The skull may have been sawed at a later date; see Edouard Girod, "Documents inédits sur TL" [1867?], NAF 6864, BNF.

3. On hidden papers, see Berthier to Bonaparte (June 2, 1803), d. 1, AF/IV/1213, AN; Amiot to Count of Poul (Aug. 24, 1814), 7Yd284, SHD-DAT.

4. "Quelle raison" from Barry Edward O'Meara, *Napoléon en exil: Relation contenant les opinions et les réflexions de Napoléon sur les événements les plus importants de sa vie, durant trois ans de sa captivité* (Paris: Garnier, 1897), 2:276. On starvation, see Antoine Métral, *Histoire de l'expédition des Français à SD* (Paris: Fanjat, 1825), 202.

5. The following account of Dessalines's record is based on Philippe Girard, "Jean-Jacques Dessalines and the Atlantic System: A Reappraisal," *William and Mary Quarterly* 69, no. 3 (July 2012): 549–582; "Indépendance, ou la mort" from Julia Gaffield, ed., *The Haitian Declaration of Independence: Creation, Context, and Legacy* (Charlottesville: University of Virginia Press, 2016), 241. No original manuscript of the Jan. 1, 1804, declaration of independence has been found yet. Gaffield's transcript is based on printed copies transmitted to the governor of Jamaica in Jan. 1804; see Edward Corbet to George Nugent (Jan. 25, 1804), CO 137/111, BNA. For early manuscript copies, see also d. 15, AB XIX/3302, AN; d. 1, EE1734, ANOM; ESTADO, 68, N.12, AGI.

6. "Very foreign" from "Showdown in Haiti," *PBS Frontline* (June 14, 1994).

7. "Peu semblable" from Dessalines, "Proclamation" (Apr. 28, 1804), d. 15, AB XIX/3302, AN.

8. "Unforgettable" from David P. Geggus, ed., *The Impact of the Haitian Revolution in the Atlantic World* (Columbia: University of South Carolina Press, 2001), 13.

9. On Chancy, see Francis Arzalier, "Déportés haïtiens et guadeloupéens en Corse (1802–1814)," *Annales Historiques de la Révolution Française* 293–294 (1993): 469–490. On Marie-Jeanne, see Joseph Saint-Rémy to Isaac Louverture (June 19, 1848), NAF 6864, BNF. On TL's sixteen children (two of them illegitimate and alive in 1802), see *Nouvelle Revue Rétrospective* 94 (Apr. 10, 1902): 13. Haitian traditions mention at least three illegitimate children in Haiti (Jean-Pierre, Didine-Gustave, and Zizine); see IL-NH, 124; Placide David, *Sur les rives du passé: Choses de SD* (1947; reprint, Ottawa: Leméac, 1972), 99.

10. On Placide's captivity, see Henri Roulland to Alexandre Berthier (Aug. 15, 1802), B7/6, SHD-DAT. On Belley (who died in captivity), see Belley to Jullien (July 7, 1805), HM-2B, UPR-NC. This account of the second family's exile is based on EE1734, ANOM; d. 5410, F/7/6266, AN; 6APC/1, ANOM; TLF, UPR-NC; Sc. Micro R1527, NYPL-SC; Auguste Nemours, *Histoire de la famille et de la descendance de TL* (Port-au-Prince: Imprimerie de l'Etat, 1941). Victoire Thusac (aka Victorine Tussac) absconded and then later returned to Agen.

11. "Pendu à son arrivée" (quoting Isaac) from Auguste Bergevin to Min. of Navy (March 20, 1817), d. 7, EE 1734, ANOM.

12. "Ils ont trois domestiques" from Duval to Min. of Navy (1823?), d. 7, EE 1734, ANOM. For early French works that borrowed heavily from Isaac, see Métral, *Histoire de l'expédition*; Jean de Saint-Anthoine, *Notice sur TL* (Paris: Lacour, 1842); Thomas Gragnon-Lacoste, *TL* (Paris: Durand, 1877). Isaac was also in contact with the French-Haitian historian Joseph Saint-Rémy.

13. On Rose, see IL-NH, 71. "J'ai le sang" from Gabrielle Fontan to [Auguste Nemours] (Oct. 25, 1929), Sc. Micro R1527, NYPL-SC. Placide's daughter was also in contact with the Bayons; see TLF-2A2d and TLF-2A3a, UPR-NC.

14. "Illustres fondateurs" from Charles Hérard aîné et al., "Manifeste," *Feuille du commerce [de Port-au-Prince]* (Apr. 2, 1843), NAF 6864, BNF.

15. "Seldom mentioned" from R., "Memoirs of Hayti" (c. Feb. 14, 1804), *The Port Folio* 2, no. 2 (Aug. 1809): 110. "Imbus des préjugés" from "Relation de la fête de S. M. la Reine d'Hayiti" (c. Aug. 1816), p. 60, Tract B795 no.2, BA.

16. "Homme de genie" from Victor Schoelcher, *Vie de Toussaint Louverture* (Paris: Ollendorf, 1889), 381. "Due subordination" from William Wilberforce, "Thoughts, etc.," in *An Appeal to the Religion, Justice, and Humanity of the Inhabitants of the British Empire* (London: J. Hatchard, 1823), 27. "An African" from Anon., *The Life and Military Achievements of Tousant Loverture* (Philadelphia: self-published, 1804). "The black general" from Alfred Hunt, *Haiti's Influence on Antebellum America: Slumbering Volcano in the Caribbean* (Baton Rouge: Louisiana State University Press, 1988), 89.

17. "The Negro race" from Thomas Reed, ed., *Great Orations by Clay, Fox, Gladstone, Lincoln, O'Connell, Phillips, Pitt, Webster, and Others* (New York: Appleton, 1901), 301. On Brown, see Select Committee of the Senate on the Harper's Ferry Invasion, *Report* (June 15, 1860), 96. "DEAD FREEDMEN" from Matthew Clavin, *Toussaint Louverture and the American Civil War: The Promise and Peril of a Second Haitian Revolution* (Philadelphia: University of Pennsylvania Press, 2010), 44.

18. "Humane" and "manhood" from Maurice Jackson and Jacqueline Bacon, eds., *African Americans and the Haitian Revolution* (New York: Routledge, 2010), 127, 135. "The great Negro" from Clavin, *Toussaint Louverture*, 182.

19. "We have all heard" from Spenser St. John, *Hayti or the Black Republic* (1884; reprint, London: Frank Cass, 1971), 70. "Précurseur" from *L'illustration* (Oct. 27, 1849), HN1B, UPR-NC. A series of drawings by François Grenier in 1821–1822 also gave pride of place to TL; see David Geggus and Norman Fiering, eds., *The World of the Haitian Revolution* (Bloomington: Indiana University Press, 2009), 371–378.

20. On St. Pierre, see Beaubrun Ardouin, *Etudes sur l'histoire d'Haïti, suivies de la vie du général J-M Borgella* (Paris: Dezobry et Magdeleine, 1853–1860), 5:225. On the chapel, see TL-3A3, UPR-NC. On the head, see Edouard Girod, "Documents inédits sur TL" [1867?], NAF 6864, BNF. On Bordeaux, see TL-3B6c, UPR-NC.

21. On the Haitian Panthéon, see Musée du Panthéon National, *TL* (Port-au-Prince: Henri Deschamps, [1983]), 9.

22. "Avoir fait des grandes choses" from Ernest Renan, *Qu'est-ce qu'une nation?* (Paris: Calmann Lévy, 1882), 26.

23. "Frères" from PMD-PH, 2:80. "Attachement" from TL, *Réfutations de quelques assertions d'un discours prononcé au Corps Législatif le 10 Prairial, an 5, par Viénot-Vaublanc* (Cap: Roux, Oct. 29, 1797), 30. "Je suis français" from TL to Roume (Oct. 29, 1799), CC/9A/26, ANOM.

BIBLIOGRAPHIC ESSAY

To make this biography accessible to a wide public, I chose not to discuss sources and historiography in the main text. This bibliographic essay is meant to clarify the archival basis for this book and to list some of the historical works that informed my analysis of the primary sources.

ARCHIVAL SOURCES

Archival sources on the Haitian Revolution and Toussaint Louverture are plentiful, but they are widely dispersed and not well cataloged. For a description of the main holdings, see David Geggus, "Unexploited Sources for the History of the Haitian Revolution," *Latin American Research Review* 18, no. 1 (1983): 95–103; David P. Geggus, "L'histoire d'Haïti dans les archives nord-américaines," *Annales des Antilles: Bulletin de la Société d'Histoire de la Martinique*, no. 32 (1998); Philippe Girard, "The Haitian Revolution, History's New Frontier: State of the Scholarship and Archival Sources," *Slavery and Abolition* 34, no. 3 (Sept. 2013): 485–507.

The most thorough catalog of Louverture's papers (which have yet to be systematically published) is Joseph A. Boromé, "Toussaint Louverture: A Finding List of His Letters and Documents," Box 1, Sc. MG 714, NYPL-SC. A selection of key documents is available in David Geggus, ed., *The Haitian Revolution: A Documentary History* (Indianapolis: Hackett, 2014).

Some documents relating to Louverture's early life are available in print. One can read his son's memoirs in Antoine Métral, *Histoire de l'expédition des Français à Saint-Domingue* . . . (Paris: Fanjat, 1825), an interview of Louverture in the *Moniteur Universel* (Jan. 9, 1799), and the plantation letters that were transcribed in Jean-Louis Donnadieu, *Entre Gascogne et Saint-Domingue: Le comte Louis-Pantaléon de Noé, grand propriétaire créole et aristocrate gascon, 1728–1816* (PhD diss., Université de Pau et des Pays de l'Adour, 2006), 353–393.

The University of Florida in Gainesville has made available a nearly complete run of the *Affiches américaines* at http://ufdc.ufl.edu/AA00000449. Maroonage notices in that paper are searchable through www.marronnage.info. For major laws and legal decisions, see M. L. E. Moreau de Saint-Méry, *Loix et constitutions des colonies françoises de l'Amérique sous le vent*, 6 vols. (Paris: Moutard, 1784–1790). Malick Ghachem has indicated to me that a seventh unpublished volume is at the *Bibliothèque haïtienne des frères de l'instruction chrétienne* in Port-au-Prince.

Archives that complement print and online material include the papers of Isaac Louverture, which have to be read carefully because Isaac was eager to aggrandize his father and marginalize his brother Placide (NAF 6864, BNF; NAF 12409, BNF; 6APC/1, ANOM). The papers of Placide's family are in UPR-NC. Many Bréda plantation records, most of them from after 1772, have survived in 18AP3, AN; E691, ADLA; 73J, ADGir; and 261 MIOM, ANOM. For church and notarial records related to Louverture's post-manumission years, see 1DPPC and NOT SDOM, ANOM. Many church records are available on the ANOM website www.archivesnationales.culture.gouv.fr/anom/fr/index .html, as are personal files of the E series.

Three massive collections contain extensive background information on colonial politics before and during the Haitian Revolution. The C9 series at the ANOM includes most of the official documents for Saint-Domingue and consists of the C9A series (168 boxes, mostly prior to 1792) and the CC9A series (mostly 1789–1825, 50 boxes), along with the supplemental series C9B (41 boxes), C9C (7), CC9B (29), and CC9C (25). The F3 series in the ANOM (297 boxes and registers) was amassed by the legist Moreau de Saint-Méry and consists of various prerevolutionary documents organized topically, as well as copies and originals of official documents for the revolutionary period. The *DXXV series in the AN (188 boxes) was assembled by a French legislative committee to investigate the 1791 slave revolt. These documents were the basis for Jean-Philippe Garran-Coulon, *Rapport sur les troubles de Saint-Domingue*, 4 vols. (Paris: Imprimerie Nationale, Ventôse an V [Feb.–March 1797]).

Some letters dating from Louverture's service in the Spanish Army in 1793–1794 have been published in Gérard M. Laurent, *Trois mois aux archives d'Espagne* (Port-au-Prince: Les Presses Libres, 1956). Other documents pertaining to this period and the 1801 invasion of Santo Domingo are available in José Luciano Franco, ed., *Documentos para la historia de Haití en el Archivo Nacional* (Havana: Publicaciones del Archivo Nacional de Cuba, 1954), and Emilio Rodríguez Demorizi, ed., *Cesión de Santo Domingo a Francia* (Ciudad Trujillo: Impresora Dominicana, 1958). Most of the archival collections for that period are in Spain, most notably ESTADO 1–17 and SANTO DOMINGO 954–1110, AGI; and LEG 7157–7164, SGU, AGS. Many of these documents are available online through http://pares.mcu.es.

Gérard Laurent published Louverture's letters to Etienne Laveaux in *Toussaint l'Ouverture à travers sa correspondance, 1794–1798* ([Madrid?], 1953). The originals of Louverture's letters to Laveaux and Sonthonax are in fr. 12102–12104 and fr. 8986–8988, BNF. Most are available online at http://gallica.bnf.fr.

Pamphlets published by Louverture in the late 1790s are available in a variety of archives, including Harvard University's Houghton Library, the Boston Athenaeum, and the John Carter Brown Library. The latter has made many of its resources available online (http://josiah.brown.edu/search).

Louverture's correspondence with the US consul Edward Stevens was first reproduced in "Letters of Toussaint Louverture and of Edward Stevens, 1798–1800," *American Historical Review* 16, no. 1 (Oct. 1910): 61–101. The originals are in M9/1–4, NARA-CP. Documents pertaining to his diplomacy with Britain are at the British National Archives in Kew (CO 137, ADM 1, and WO 1 series).

Leclerc's letters have been published in Paul Roussier, ed., *Lettres du général Leclerc* (Paris: Société de l'histoire des colonies françaises, 1937). Aside from the aforementioned CC9 series, the richest archival collections on the Leclerc expedition are B7, SHD-DAT (27 boxes); the Rochambeau collection and BN08268–BN08272 at the University of Florida (24 boxes and 5 reels); 61J, ADGir; BB4, SHD-DM; and a private collection auctioned off in 2008 that is accessible through http://rouillac.com/Calendrier/da-FR-9-0-0-grid-1-2008-resultats.

Many primary sources retracing Louverture's captivity and his family's fate were reproduced in M. Morpeau, *Documents inédits pour l'histoire: Correspondance concernant l'emprisonnement et la mort de Toussaint Louverture* (Port-au-Prince: Sacré Cœur, 1920), and Auguste Nemours, *Histoire de la famille et de la descendance de Toussaint Louverture* (Port-au-Prince: Imprimerie de l'Etat, 1941). A transcript of Louverture's interrogation appeared in *Nouvelle Revue Rétrospective*, no. 94 (Apr. 10, 1902). There are several editions of his 1802 memoir, including Philippe Girard, ed., *The Memoir of General Toussaint Louverture* (New York: Oxford University Press, 2014). The richest archival collections on that period are AF/IV/1213, AN and EE1734, ANOM (which contain various drafts of Louverture's memoir); and UPR-NC.

SECONDARY LITERATURE

Although the literature on Louverture and the Haitian Revolution is uneven, the field is making great strides. For general overviews, see the Toussaint Louverture entry at Oxford Bibliographies (www.oxfordbibliographies.com) and David Geggus's piece at Brown University's John Carter Brown Library (www.brown.edu/Facilities/John_Carter_Brown_Library/toussaint).

Early works on the Haitian Revolution remain useful, particularly Thomas Madiou's *Histoire d'Haïti*, 3 vols. (Port-au-Prince: Courtois, 1847), and Beaubrun Ardouin's *Etudes sur l'histoire d'Haïti, suivies de la vie du général J-M Borgella*, 11 vols. (Paris: Dezobry et Magdeleine, 1853–1860). In recent years, the most widely used overview of the Haitian Revolution in English has been Laurent Dubois's *Avengers of the New World: The Story of the Haitian Revolution* (Cambridge, MA: Harvard University Press, 2004).

Many biographies of Louverture have appeared in the past two centuries, although most of them recycled oral traditions or previous secondary works. The first full-length biography, which attacked Louverture as a pro-independence traitor to France, was Louis Dubroca, *La vie de Toussaint Louverture, chef des noirs insurgés de Saint-Domingue* (Paris: Dubroca, 1802). Even early Haitian authors were ambivalent owing to Louverture's harshness toward black cultivators and mixed-race rivals; see Joseph Saint-Rémy, *Vie de Toussaint Louverture* (Paris: Moquet, 1850).

Subsequent nineteenth-century works rehabilitated his name, often to serve an abolitionist agenda (Beard, Schoelcher) or to celebrate the family traditions preserved by Isaac Louverture (Gragnon-Lacoste): see John R. Beard, *The Life of Toussaint L'Ouverture: The Negro Patriot of Hayti* (London: Ingram Cooke, 1853); Thomas Prosper Gragnon-Lacoste, *Toussaint Louverture* (Paris: Durand, 1877); Victor Schoelcher, *Vie de Toussaint Louverture* (Paris: Ollendorf, 1889).

Subsequent Haitian and French scholarship verged on hagiography. The best works in this school were H. Pauléus Sannon's *Histoire de Toussaint Louverture*, 3 vols. (Port-au-Prince: Héraux, 1920–1933), and Aimé Césaire, *Toussaint Louverture: La révolution française et le problème colonial* (Paris: Présence Africaine, 1981). At the other extreme stood Pierre Pluchon's *Toussaint Louverture* (Paris: Fayard, 1989), which depicted Louverture as a petty and self-interested planter wannabe. More recently, Jean-Louis Donnadieu, *Toussaint Louverture: Le Napoléon noir* (Paris: Belin, 2014), presented important new documents on the pre-revolutionary era.

In English, the most seminal work, though factually outdated today, was Cyril Lionel Robert James's *The Black Jacobins: Toussaint L'Ouverture and the San Domingo Revolution* (1938; reprint, New York: Vintage Books, 1989), a Marxist analysis that introduced Louverture as a tragically flawed leader to an English-speaking audience. The most widely used English-language biography today, written engagingly but based on limited primary research, is Madison Smartt Bell's *Toussaint Louverture: A Biography* (New York: Pantheon Books, 2007).

For general background on the French slave trade and the kingdom of Allada (chap. 1), see Robin Law, *The Slave Coast of West Africa, 1550–1750: The Impact of the Atlantic Slave Trade on an African Society* (Oxford: Clarendon Press, 1991), and David Geggus, "The French Slave Trade: An Overview," *William and Mary Quarterly* 58, no. 1 (Jan. 2001): 119–138. On Louverture's family background (chaps. 2 and 5), see Philippe Girard and Jean-Louis Donnadieu, "Toussaint Before Louverture: New Archival Findings on the Early Life of Toussaint Louverture," *William and Mary Quarterly* 70, no. 1 (Jan. 2013): 41–78.

On the Haut-du-Cap plantation (chaps. 3 and 8), see David Geggus, "Toussaint Louverture and the Slaves of the Bréda Plantation," *Journal of Caribbean History*, no. 20 (1986): 30–48; Jean-Louis Donnadieu, *Un grand seigneur et ses esclaves: Le comte de Noé entre Antilles et Gascogne, 1728–1816* (Toulouse: Presses Universitaires du Mirail, 2009); Jean-Louis Donnadieu and Philippe Girard, "Nouveaux documents sur la vie de Toussaint Louverture," *Bulletin de la Société d'Histoire de la Guadeloupe* 166–167 (Sept. 2013–Apr. 2014): 117–139.

The first article to document Louverture's emancipation and slave ownership (chaps. 6 and 7) was Gabriel Debien, Jean Fouchard, and Marie-Antoinette Menier, "Toussaint Louverture avant 1789: Légendes et réalités," *Conjonction*, no. 134 (1977). The two best published works on free people of color and race on the eve of the Revolution are Stewart King's *Blue Coat or Powdered Wig: Free People of Color in Pre-Revolutionary Saint-Domingue* (Athens: University of Georgia Press, 2001), and John D. Garrigus's *Before Haiti: Race and Citizenship in French Saint-Domingue* (New York: Palgrave, 2006). On white political infighting before the Haitian Revolution (chap. 9), see Charles Frostin's *Les révoltes blanches à Saint-Domingue aux XVIIe et XVIIIe siècles (Haïti avant 1789)* (Paris: L'Ecole, 1975), and Malick Ghachem's *The Old Regime and the Haitian Revolution* (Cambridge: Cambridge University Press, 2012).

On Louverture's role during the 1791 uprising (chap. 10), see David Geggus, "Toussaint Louverture and the Haitian Revolution," in R. William Weisberger, ed., *Profiles of Revolutionaries in Atlantic History* (New York: Columbia

University Press, 2007), 115–135. The best book on the 1793–1794 abolition of slavery (chap. 12) is Jeremy Popkin's *You Are All Free: The Haitian Revolution and the Abolition of Slavery* (New York: Cambridge University Press, 2010). On Louverture's 1794 switch from the Spanish to the French Army, see David Geggus, "The 'Volte-face' of Toussaint Louverture," in Geggus, *Haitian Revolutionary Studies* (Blacks in the Diaspora) (Bloomington: Indiana University Press, 2002), 119–136.

Geggus is also the author of the definitive work on the British invasion of Saint-Domingue (chaps. 13–14), *Slavery, War, and Revolution: The British Occupation of Saint-Domingue, 1793–1798* (Oxford: Clarendon Press, 1982). On the Spanish invasion, see Fernando Carrera Montero, *Las complejas relaciones de España con La Española: El Caribe hispano frente a Santo Domingo y Saint Domingue, 1789–1803* (Santo Domingo: Fundación García Arévalo, 2004).

The best overview on US diplomacy with Louverture (chap. 15) is Gordon S. Brown, *Toussaint's Clause: The Founding Fathers and the Haitian Revolution* (Jackson: University Press of Mississippi, 2005). On Louverture and the British, see also Philippe Girard, "Black Talleyrand: Toussaint Louverture's Secret Diplomacy with England and the United States," *William and Mary Quarterly* 66, no. 1 (Jan. 2009): 87–124.

To put Louverture's labor policies (chap. 16) in their context, see Robert K. Lacerte, "The Evolution of Land and Labor in the Haitian Revolution, 1791–1820," *Americas* 34, no. 4 (Apr. 1978): 449–459. Also notable for their emphasis on the divide between Creole leaders like Louverture and the black rank and file are Carolyn E. Fick, *The Making of Haiti: The Saint Domingue Revolution from Below* (Knoxville: University of Tennessee Press, 1990), and Michel Rolph-Trouillot, *Silencing the Past: Power and the Production of History* (Boston: Beacon Press, 1995).

On Louverture's apex and downfall (chaps. 17–19), see Philippe Girard, *The Slaves Who Defeated Napoléon: Toussaint Louverture and the Haitian War of Independence* (Tuscaloosa: University of Alabama Press, 2011). On his captivity and legacy (chaps. 19 and 20), see Alfred Nemours, *Histoire de la captivité et de la mort de Toussaint Louverture: Notre pélerinage au Fort de Joux* (Paris: Berger Levrault, 1929). On Louverture as an author, see Deborah Jenson, *Beyond the Slave Narrative: Politics, Sex, and Manuscripts in the Haitian Revolution* (Liverpool: Liverpool University Press, 2011); Philippe Girard, "Quelle langue parlait Toussaint Louverture? Le mémoire du Fort de Joux et les origines du kreyòl haïtien," *Annales* 68, no. 1 (Jan. 2013): 109–132.

INDEX

Philippe Girard is professor of history at McNeese State University in Louisiana and spent 2014 as a fellow at the Du Bois Institute at Harvard. Girard is the author of *Haiti: The Tumultuous History—from Pearl of the Caribbean to Broken Nation*, among other books, and also translated and edited *The Memoir of Toussaint Louverture*. He lives in Lake Charles, Louisiana.